Israeli Holocaust Drama

ISRAELI holocaust drama

Edited and with an Introduction by

michael taub

Syracuse University Press

The paper used in this publication meets the minimum requirements of American National Standard for Information Sciences—Permanence of Paper for Printed Library Materials, ANSI Z39.48-1984. ∞™

Library of Congress Cataloging-in-Publication Data
Israeli Holocaust drama / edited and with an introduction by Michael
Taub. — 1st ed.
p. cm.
Includes bibliographical references.
Contents: Lady of the castle / Leah Goldberg — Hanna Senesh /
Aharon Megged — Children of the shadows / Ben-Zion Tomer — Kastner
/ Motti Lerner — Adam / Joshua Sobol.
ISBN 0-8156-2673-8   ISBN 0-8156-2674-6 (pbk.:
1. Israeli drama—Translations into English.   2. Holocaust, Jewish
(1939–1945)—Drama.   I. Taub, Michael.
PJ5043.I87   1995
892.4'26080358—dc20   95-10506

In loving memory of my father, Huna Leyb Taub z'l,
survivor of Hungary's labor camps,
and to my mother, Sara Dub Taub,
survivor of Auschwitz, A-11269.

Michael Taub is a visiting professor at Vassar College, where he teaches Hebrew. He is the author of *Modern Israeli Drama in Translation* and is coeditor of the forthcoming *Contemporary Jewish-American Writers: A Biocritical Source Book.*

Contents

Editor's Note: The language of the original translations of *Lady of the Castle, Children of the Shadows,* and *Kastner* has been edited to reflect American idiom.

Acknowledgments

The idea for this book emerged in large part from my previous anthology, *Modern Israeli Drama*. In completing *Israeli Holocaust Drama*, I benefited from the keen insight of my friends and colleagues Steven Katz, George Wellwarth, Glenda Abramson, and Ellen Schiff. Sarah Blacher Cohen was a major force behind the publication of this collection, and for that and other reasons, I am forever grateful. A debt of a different kind is owed to Shimon Lev-Ari of the Israeli Theater Archives and Nilly Cohen of The Institute for Translation of Hebrew Literature. I wish to thank the authors and translators for granting permission to print the plays. Once again, Leonard Rogoff's editorial assistance made my English readable. I salute Dr. Robert A. Mandel, director of Syracuse University Press, for his faith in the project.

Yet, all of this would not have been possible without the support and understanding of my wife, Pat Hecht, and of my brother, Martin Taub.

Part One: Introduction

1

The Problematic of Holocaust Drama

The debate continues on whether it is possible to write about the Holocaust, and if so, what kind of writing is appropriate. We agree that art can only create an illusion of reality, so how can it depict an event as overwhelming as this? Frustrated about the possibility of writing about the Holocaust, George Steiner and T. W. Adorno went so far as to try deterring anyone contemplating such activity.[1] Despite their admonition, hundreds of writers—survivors and others—have broken their silence creating a variety of artistic works out of their Holocaust experiences. In fact, the writing only increases as the number of survivors decreases. Regardless of one's background, intentions, and circumstances, the moment words are recorded for posterity, artistic considerations of language and style inevitably come into play. And, as readers, whether it is Chaim Kaplan's *Warsaw Diary*, Elie Wiesel's *Night*, or Paul Celan's "Todesfuge," we cannot, whatever other emotions might be present, escape an aesthetic reaction as well, possibly even a strange feeling of "pleasure." Holocaust scholar Lawrence Langer feels such reactions to be inappropriate and counterproductive, which is why he praises the more "unrealistic" works that, he believes, have the power to subvert "pleasure." These are works that, in Langer's words, use "disfiguration, the conscious and deliberate alienation of the reader's sensibilities from the world of the usual and familiar . . . the grotesque, the senseless, the unimaginable.[2]

Firstly, gauging reader response to Holocaust literature is problematic. Secondly, contemporary realism, as Ilan Avisar convincingly argues in his study of Holocaust films, can be as "compelling, can coax the reader into credulity and complicity" as those surrealistic or grotesque works that Langer feels are more desirable.[3] By its very nature, art is schematic and subjective and stands at some distance

3

from the reality it depicts. The gap is wider or narrower depending on the medium, the literary genre, and the style employed. A diary is generally closer to the events than a poem, a starkly realistic narrative by Primo Levi strikes us as being more faithful than the dreamlike writings of Jerzy Kosinski or Arnošt Lustig. By closeness and faithfulness I mean the physical reality, not, of course, the inner, emotional one, which may be better captured in poetry, as for example, the war poems of A. Sutzkever, a survivor of Vilna's ghetto.[4]

The reader may even respond with aesthetic pleasure to Holocaust literature, and achieving an "alienating effect" may not be more appropriate than aiming for "normal" emotional involvement. I agree with Robert Skloot, who argues (referring to Holocaust drama but applicable to all Holocaust literature) that in the final analysis what counts is that the works pay homage to the victims, educate about history, produce an emotional response, raise moral questions, and draw important lessons.[5]

In evaluating Holocaust literature, we should not use the same criteria as with other artistic expressions because what are most important are the criteria mentioned above, not so much literary quality. This does not mean that we should not, separately, discuss and evaluate Holocaust works on artistic merit as well. It is therefore possible to criticize Elie Wiesel's narrative style in *Night*, which has some detractors to be sure, and at the same time praise its enormous value as a testimonial by a survivor who comments on the events with unmatched power and conviction.[6]

From Adorno to Langer, we see scholars struggling with questions pertaining to aesthetics and the Holocaust: which subject matter is appropriate and which is not, what reaction can be elicited and what cannot, what can be described and what cannot. Is realism or surrealism the proper mode? Drama and film present unique problems because events unfold right before our eyes with flesh and blood actors pretending to be the "real" people of the action. The distance created by the written text is removed in drama; we are not allowed to "imagine" the characters, we cannot properly reflect, pause, go back and forth, as we normally do with a novel or a poem. The question of realism is particularly critical in the theater; for, if authors/directors choose to show history as "real" as possible, they expose themselves to criticism from survivors and experts who will invariably find fault with this or that aspect of the production. Such was the case with the NBC television movie *Holocaust* and Joshua Sobol's play *Ghetto*.[7] On the other hand, stripping the stage (or text) of realism may run the risk of elevating events to metaphorical, symbolic levels, something we often find in poetry, most notably in the work of Paul Celan. But this approach is viewed by some as dangerous, as for instance preeminent Holocaust historian Yehuda Bauer, who fears that "symbolic descriptions . . . become just another escape route for the superficial."[8]

Drama critic Ellen Schiff sums up this apparent artistic dilemma by saying that "the subject eclipses theatrical illusion . . . the difficulties inherent in representing the events of the Holocaust on stage offer a most convincing argument for dealing with it on the oblique, focusing on those who live—stunned and stunted—in the Aftermath."[9]

Although it is true that some Holocaust plays, most recently Barbara Lebow's *Shayne Meydl*, do focus on survivors, a host of works are set in the ghettos and camps, featuring fictional and historical characters we know did not survive: Joshua Sobol's Vilna trilogy—*Ghetto, Underground, Adam;* Edith Lieberman's *Throne of Straw;* Peter Barnes's *Auschwitz;* and no doubt, the most famous of all, Rolf Hochhuth's *Deputy*.[10]

Finally, Irving Howe offers this opinion to the debate surrounding Holocaust drama: "The Holocaust is not, essentially, a dramatic subject. Much before, much after, and much surrounding the mass exterminations may be open to dramatic rendering . . . of those conflicts between wills, those inner clashes of belief and wrenchings of desire . . . there can be little in the course of a fiction focused mainly on the mass exterminations."[11]

Howe's criticism recalls Hegel's concept of tragedy, which is based on a conflict of forces ruling man's will and actions—that is, his "ethical substance"—and featuring heroes who represent equally high moral values (*Gleichwertig*) with equally justified claims (*Gleichberechtigt*).[12] This kind of drama is impossible in the context of the Holocaust proper, particularly if we are imagining conflicts between Jews and Nazis; however, other types of drama, even some types of tragedies, can be envisioned. In fact, the works mentioned earlier (those depicting the war years) span a full range of dramatic approaches and with varying degrees of success inspire us, move us, and teach us something about the events presented.

A discussion of the Holocaust and aesthetic issues raises a host of problems involving personal taste, choice of subject matter, dramatic styles, and historical fidelity. Naturally, on a topic of this nature consensus cannot be reached. Still, when dealing with Holocaust drama, we should ask two basic questions: is it good literature, but more importantly, is it successful in fulfilling the nonartistic criteria mentioned earlier. Undoubtedly, the first question is more problematic because evaluative criteria may vary, with results varying accordingly. In regard to the second question, if a play met one or more of Skloot's criteria—pays homage to victims, educates, produces emotional response, raises moral questions, draws lessons—then that particular play would have achieved its goal.)

The Holocaust is a unique event; but at the same time, I think it is wrong to suggest that it is incomprehensible, unfathomable, incredible, thus relegating it to the realm of mysticism, a tendency I feel is present in Langer's writings on the subject. If we really believe that it is too mystical, too incomprehensible, then we could not write about it at all. Also, as already suggested, it is inappropriate for critics to prescribe artistic choices: which style is proper and which is not, which subject matter can be dealt with and which not. Artists will feel free to do whatever they want with our history, even with this horrible piece of history. They should even be free to change facts to suit their particular vision, imagine situations missing or absent from historical documents, or reconstruct reality for artistic aims. True, we have witnessed instances, especially in the movies, where exploitation through sensationalism takes place for commercial purposes. As survivors and scholars familiar with the events, we should point out the truth; but beyond that we must rely on the public to make its own judgment on the matter. The Holocaust, with Auschwitz as its main symbol, is not only etched in Jewish memory and consciousness, it is now part of Western culture as well. We need to recognize that, once something is in the public domain, we cannot control the way it is going to be handled. If a particular treatment of the Holocaust offends us, either because it is in poor taste or it violates historical facts, we should state our position without trying to censure it.

Notes

1. George Steiner's comments are found in *Language and Silence: Essays on Language, Literature, and the Inhuman* (Harmondsworth: Penguin, 1969), and in *In Bluebeard's Castle: Some Notes Towards the Redefinition of Culture* (New Haven: Yale Univ. Press, 1975). T. W. Adorno's statement that it is impossible, even perhaps immoral, to write about the Holocaust appears in "Engagement," in *Noten zur Literatur III* (Frankfurt am Main: Suhrkamp Verlag, 1965), 109–35. Major scholars of Holocaust Literature—Langer, Ezrachi, Young, and Rosenfeld—have all reacted strongly to these extreme positions by Adorno and Steiner.

2. Lawrence Langer, *The Holocaust and the Literary Imagination* (New Haven: Yale Univ. Press, 1977), 3.

3. Ilan Avisar, *Screening the Holocaust* (Bloomington: Indiana Univ. Press, 1988), 2–3.

4. These poems are collected in Abraham Sutzkever, *Lider Fun Yam Hamoves: Poems from the Sea of Death* (Tel Aviv: Farlag Bergen-Belzen, 1968). In fact, in *By Words Alone* (Chicago: Univ. of Chicago Press, 1982), Sidra Ezrahi tries to arrange Holocaust literature by how close a given text is to the actual events. By this criteria, Ida Fink's memoirs would naturally fall into a different category from Bart's highly imaginative novel, *The Last of the Just.*

5. Robert Skloot, *The Theater of the Holocaust* (Madison: Univ. of Wisconsin Press, 1982), 14. Also in Skloot's critical study of the plays included in his anthology, *The Darkness We Carry* (Madison: Univ. of Wisconsin Press, 1988).

6. An early critic of Wiesel's style is Frederick Garber, "The Art of Elie Wiesel," *Judaism* 3 (1973). An excellent discussion of the problem of literary evaluation and Holocaust literature is found in *A Double Dying—Reflections on Holocaust Literature* (Bloomington: Indiana Univ. Press, 1980), 12–37.

7. The NBC TV production of *Holocaust* a decade ago, had sparked debates in newspapers and elsewhere for showing sanitized camps and "normal looking" people, which, critics contended, was a "false" picture of the events. Elie Wiesel criticized Sobol's play *Ghetto* for daring to present some of the victims as immoral Jews while some Nazis possessed redeeming qualities. Wiesel claimed that it is indecent and improper to do so: *New York Times,* May 2, 1989. In Wiesel's view, there should be no ambiguities on the matter—Jews should be depicted as good and Germans as evil.

8. Yehuda Bauer, *The Holocaust in Historical Perspective* (Seattle: Univ. of Washington Press, 1978), 46; quoted by James Young in *Writing and Rewriting the Holocaust* (Bloomington: Indiana Univ. Press, 1988), 7.

9. Ellen Schiff, "Plays about the Holocaust," *New York Times,* Dec. 2, 1979.

10. There are two international Holocaust drama anthologies in English: Elinor Fuchs, ed., *Plays of the Holocaust* (New York: Theater Communications Group, 1987). (This collection contains: Joshua Sobol, *Ghetto;* Nelly Sachs, *Ely;* Josef Szayna, *Replika;* James Schevill, *Cathedral of Ice;* Peter Barnes, *Auschwitz*). Robert Skloot, ed., *The Theater of the Holocaust* (Madison: Univ. of Wisconsin Press, 1982). (This one features: Harold and Edith Lieberman, *Throne of Straw;* Shimon Wincelberg, *Resort 76;* George Tabori, *The Cannibals;* Charlotte Delbo, *Who will Carry the Word?*)

11. Howe's essay is found in Berl Lang, ed., *Writing and the Holocaust* (New York: Holmes & Meier, 1988), 189.

12. Anne and Henry Paolucci, eds., *Hegel—On Tragedy* (New York: Harper and Row, 1975).

2

Israeli Theater and the Holocaust

The plays featured in this collection represent two distinct trends in Israeli drama. In the fifties and sixties, stage depictions of the Holocaust centered primarily on Jewish resistance and survivor problems in Palestine/Israel. Typical works of that period glorified Jewish heroism and condemned Nazi brutality and Jewish "collaboration." Basically, two groups were considered "collaborators": the majority of Jews in Palestine who stood by passively and Jews who participated (mostly involuntarily) in carrying out the horror—officials of the Judenrats (the Jewish Councils in the ghettos), and kapos (barrack supervisors in the death camps). Survivor plays drew attention to the psychological problems of dealing with freedom and with life in an independent Jewish country. Though protecting the survivors from persecution and danger, Palestine/Israel—a new and forward-looking society—tried for decades to suppress the Holocaust with all its diasporic, negative symbols. The radically different life style of this basically Mediterranean country presented another major obstacle in the absorption of these Eastern- and Central European Jews.

From this group of dramas, I chose Leah Goldberg's *Lady of the Castle* (1955), Aharon Megged's *Hanna Senesh* (1958), and Ben-Zion Tomer's *Children of the Shadows* (1962).[1] Popularity, subject matter, and translation status played a major role in my choice. Three plays not included here but certainly worth mentioning are Nathan Shacham's *New Reckoning* (1954), Moshe Shamir's *The Heir* (1963), and Aharon Megged's *The Burning Season* (1967).[2]

In the mid-eighties, after a hiatus of roughly fifteen years, Holocaust drama began reappearing on the Israeli stage. Even when dealing with similar topics, the younger playwrights view the Holocaust very differently from their predecessors. Essentially, these later works take a more critical, even controversial, view of the events. We should keep in mind that, in the intervening years, Israel had undergone radical changes, in great part owing to three major military conflicts: the Six-Day War (1967), the Yom Kippur War (1973), and the Lebanon War (1982). The occupation of the West Bank and Gaza, however, has probably made more of an impact than the actual military conflicts because, for the first time in modern history, Jews found themselves in the problematic role of masters over another people. Consciously or not, this unique situation has, to some extent, led to a reexamination of the Shoah where the victims were, of course, Jews.

Joshua Sobol and Motti Lerner are the leading figures of this new trend in Holocaust drama. Not surprisingly, their plays are documentary dramas: Lerner's *Kastner* (1985) deals with the Budapest ghetto; and Sobol's *Ghetto* (1984), *Adam* (1989), and *Underground* (1990) focus on the Vilna ghetto.[3] Any of the three plays in the Vilna triptych would have been appropriate for this collection; but *Ghetto* and *Underground* have already appeared in English, hence the choice of *Adam*.

As mentioned, the main difference between these two groups of plays is the authors' treatment of the subject matter. The theme of armed resistance versus passive compliance is at the center of two plays in this volume, *Hanna Senesh* and *Adam*. Clearly, the choices made by Megged's protagonist are unambiguously admirable and morally correct. Thus, when anti-Semitism takes hold in Hungary, Hanna leaves a relatively comfortable life in Budapest for an uncertain future and a harsher existence on a kibbutz in Palestine. When news of Nazi atrocities reach her, she unhesitatingly joins the Jewish Brigade—a unit in the British Army—and volunteers to parachute into her native land to help organize the underground and save Jewish lives. Finally, when caught by the enemy, she heroically accepts torture and death over promises of a lesser sentence if she reveals her radio code and the names of her contacts in Hungary. Megged's play is clearly a tribute to pure heroism, and in Glenda Abramsom's words, "It calls for courage in the face of oppression, it is an indictment of those who were taken by the Nazis without any show of opposition."[4]

Adam Rolnick, nom de guerre of Itzik Wittenberg, leader of Vilna's Jewish underground, on the other hand, is a controversial figure. The failed revolt he was supposed to lead following the Warsaw ghetto example is equally controversial. Based on a close reading of historical documents, Sobol concentrates on a critical moment in the life of the Vilna ghetto in *Adam*. Upon confirming suspicions that an underground force led by Adam is active there, the Germans, on July 16, 1943, issue an ultimatum: hand over the leader or we liquidate the ghetto. What follows is a day of tense hours. In the end, the Gestapo get their prey, who dies shortly after his capture. Unfortunately, witness testimony of those tense hours presents a contradictory picture of the dramatic events. Confusion abounds concerning the methods employed to uncover Adam's identity as well as the reception of the ultimatum by Adam and the top command of the underground forces.[5]

In his play, Sobol interprets the events surrounding what came to be known as "Wittenberg Day" differently from conventional, albeit conflicting, historical accounts. In Sobol's stage version, Gens, head of the Jewish Council, believes that mobilizing a general revolt would have been possible had the military command not publicly announced its decision to hand over their leader and had Adam not accepted their verdict. In this version, the military command votes to sacrifice Adam for the hope of preserving the lives of thousands still living in the ghetto, thousands who, unlike their Warsaw brothers, were generally against an armed struggle that would have meant certain death, albeit death with honor. Although this representation of the events could be justified in the historical context, Sobol's portrayal of Adam is unique and controversial. Clearly, in Sobol's play, the entire operation, the success or failure of the revolt, hinges on the leader's resolve, on his willingness to risk lives for an honorable exit from history. In the end, Sobol's leader equivocates because he is a liberal man, a humanist who places people over ideas, individuals over lofty ideals. To emphasize this point, Sobol creates a totally fictional scene; while in captivity, an anonymous woman is tortured in a room next to Adam's as long as he refuses to cooperate. Unable to justify her pain, meaning individual sacrifice for the common, noble cause, Adam commits suicide. Naturally, this example extends to a larger context and another time. Those familiar with Sobol's work know that history serves as a lesson for current political situations in Israel. Here, through the character of Adam, the author is no doubt arguing with leaders who are too quick to sacrifice lives in the name of some "noble cause," or for "the good of the country."[6]

Ultimately, *Adam* is a plea for humanity and respect for the sacredness of human life. Clearly, no one can tell with any degree of certainty what would have happened had the revolt materialized. Adam, however, had no doubts that an armed conflict under existing circumstances would have been militarily futile; it would only have filled some with a sense of revenge and Jewish pride.

A comparison of Megged's *Hanna Senesh* and Sobol's *Adam* illuminates the differing attitudes to the Holocaust between these two generations of dramatists. The earlier play asks us to applaud and admire Hanna's heroic stand and ultimate sacrifice; for like a modern day Joan of Arc she would rather die than compromise her principles. Like the hero of old, here too the cause becomes more important than personal desire, even life itself. Adam, on the other hand, is more pragmatic, more rational. He does not see much value in maintaining a struggle if it means little in terms of saving lives, regardless of the means employed. For Adam, a cause is only good as it serves a practical purpose; once stripped of that purpose, it loses its worth.

The question of Jewish collaboration, a recurring theme in both early and late Holocaust plays is debated in Ben-Zion Tomer's *Children of the Shadows* and Motti Lerner's *Kastner*. Interestingly, Tomer brings together two "collaborators," survivors who, though of radically different backgrounds, experience similar psychological problems. Yoram (formerly Yossele), is a twenty-eight-year-old bachelor who in 1941, at the age of fourteen, arrived in Palestine from Goray, near Lwów, Poland. He escaped the Nazis because his parents, who could not feed a large family, had placed him in an orphanage; when the Germans came, these children were smuggled to Palestine via Tehran; later they were known as "the Tehran children." His family—parents, two sisters, and a brother—had remained in Poland and had been sent to various concentration camps. With the exception of his sister Esther, they miraculously survive the war and arrive in Israel as the action of the play unfolds. The play is set in 1955.

Yoram had been struggling to "fit in" ever since arriving in Palestine fourteen years earlier. First, it was the encounter with the brash, self-confident, aggressive sabras like Dooby, whom he had met on the kibbutz. In an effort to be like them he changed his name and tried to speak only Hebrew. In effect, he tried desperately to suppress Poland and the diasporic experience of the humiliated, downtrodden Jew. When news of Nazi atrocities reached Palestine, he began to feel guilty for not sharing in his family's suffering, worse yet, of having enjoyed himself while they were living in Hell. The fact that he fought in the War of Independence in 1948 cannot atone for the guilt he feels for not being "there," for not suffering or fighting like his brother, a veteran of the Warsaw ghetto uprising.

Having stood on the sidelines while Hitler was destroying Europe's Jews, Yoram feels that he is indeed a "collaborator"; he is so ambivalent and guilty toward his family that he cannot even write to them, and their arrival causes him extreme anxiety. His desperate efforts at repressing the past and fleeing its ghosts ill prepare him for the crucial meeting with them. As Gideon Ofrat correctly states, "The constant running from the past, from memories, from certain values does not mean that one can run away from the guilt of running away."[7] Within the larger context of the reaction to the Holocaust by the *Yishuv* (prestate Jewish community in Palestine), Yoram represents the genuinely penitent Palestinian/Israeli Jew who has problems reconciling the tragic fate of his European brethren with his relatively good life, excluding, of course, the war of 1948. Consumed by the efforts to build a new country in an ancient land, the *Yishuv* Jews, as Ben-Ami Feingold observes, were "passive and neglectful of events taking place in Europe."[8] Although the *Yishuv*'s stance vis-à-vis the Holocaust is still a matter of heated debate, no one denies the fact that to cover up their feelings of guilt, many Israeli Jews, mainly during the first post-Holocaust decade, "began blaming the victims for marching to their death like sheep to slaughter."[9]

Yoram's wounded conscience, however, seems to be gradually healing following a painful but constructive reunion with his family, and later on, with Sigmund, his brother-in-law, and former member of Lwów's Jewish Council, the Judenrat. Listening to their stories, Yoram can feel their pain; somehow he is finally able to identify with their plight, which to some degree becomes his, eventually easing his guilty feelings toward them. The meeting with Sigmund, the mysterious vagabond on the Tel Aviv beaches, turns out to be more problematic. Before the war, Sigmund was a professor of Renaissance art at the University of Lwów. Needless to say, this Heidelberg-educated intellectual, like many European Jews at the time, was most shocked when the Nazis began rounding up people, among them devoted fans of German culture. He survives the war by apparently being appointed to the Judenrat, no doubt, in part because of his German background.

We may surmise that he was, among other things, involved in the gruesome and highly controversial selection process—assisting the Germans in deciding who was to go and who stayed, who died and who lived. In coping with the ghosts of his past, he withdraws into himself, opting for anonymity by living on the beaches of Tel Aviv, a homeless man wearing multiple disguises and going by a variety of assumed names. He feels low esteem, self-pity, and deep remorse. In explaining his actions during the war before Yoram in the final scene of the play, Sigmund essentially inculpates all humanity, including Yoram. (His replies are typical of the humanist whose firm beliefs in enlightened ideas, in goodness, were so shaken by evil that he holds very little hope for the future of humanity.) After all, if even someone like him, Professor Sigmund Rabinowitz, "erstwhile doctor of philosophy, authority on Renaissance art, fervid believer in humanism," can be corrupted, then why be surprised that the world has gone insane?[10] Although he personally feels that he had sunk too deep in the moral mire of "collaborator" ever to emerge clean, he refuses to believe that the Germans succeeded in eradicating all ideals. He wants to believe that something is still alive, that the Nazi camp commander and former Heidelberg colleague, who told him that "there won't be a rag of an ideal to cover our nakedness with," was wrong.[11]

When Yoram and Sigmund eventually confront each other, Yoram realizes the depth of Sigmund's remorsefulness and the need to expiate his sins. This crucial encounter, as Glenda Abramson points out, "allows Yoram insight into his own apparent need to atone . . . he could not deliver Sigmund to the authorities partly because he felt that in a way he shared Sigmund's guilt and partly through his belief that by forgiving the tormented old man a much deadlier crime than his own he was to a certain extent forgiving himself."[12]

In essence, *Children of the Shadows* shows the tormented world of guilty consciences in two survivors who live because of sheer luck in Yoram's case, and a combination of luck and resourcefulness in Sigmund's. In this post-Holocaust context of 1955 Israel, we are only allowed brief, somewhat foggy glimpses into Sigmund's activities in the Lwów ghetto a decade or so earlier. Motti Lerner's *Kastner*, on the other hand, directly confronts these activities, examines the moral character of Judenrat members, and most importantly, tackles the difficult question of heroism.

Set in Budapest, July 1944, *Kastner* re-creates dramatic events in the life of Hungary's Jews, of which half a million were murdered only in a matter of months by Adolf Eichmann's efficient killing machine, as advancing Russian and Western Allied troops were tightening the noose around Hitler's neck. During these fateful months, Budapest's Jewish Council is debating the manner of dealing with the Germans. The more militant members, mainly Zionists, maintain that it is their duty publicly to denounce deportations and to tell the truth about their destination. Some moderates, including Rezsö Kast-ner, a respected jurist and a German-educated liberal, argue to the end that their only chance of saving lives is through negotiations in the hope of delaying or slowing down the killing process.

Kastner opposes armed resistance, believing that telling the truth about Auschwitz will only create panic and incite the Germans to speedier and crueler actions. He has good reasons to believe that the Germans are negotiating in good faith: late summer 1944, as the *Wehrmacht* is retreating from Russia, military equipment and money are in short supply, and no one doubts that Germany is destined for a major defeat; it is only a matter of time. It makes perfect sense to Kastner that, given the gravity of the situation, the Germans will be more than eager to trade Jewish lives for military material. He also thinks that, with defeat staring them in the face, some Germans will want to curry favor with the Jews and perhaps thereby save their skins when the Allies put them on trial for their crimes. In fact, Kastner is aware of Himmler's desire to keep some Jews alive as a gesture of goodwill for when the Allies do actually arrive.

Of course, in hindsight, Kastner appears naïve to have believed Eichmann and his henchmen in Budapest. But at the time, this ap-proach seemed logical. Though not mentioned in the play, Raoul Wallenberg, the now legendary Swedish diplomat was saving Jews by issuing them citizenship and visas to Sweden. In any event, it is a fact that Kastner did manage to save many Hungarian Jews—in one dra-matic coup he wrested a whole train from the claws of death with 1,684 passengers on it. In regard to accusations of his using his posi-tion for personal gain, the facts, as told by his close associates, are that Kastner was a courageous man, constantly risking his life. He insisted on staying in Budapest as long as he could be effective. In fact, he left only when the Germans offered him an exit visa—an unsolicited gesture of goodwill—contrary to testimony given after the war by his detractors who tried to paint him as an opportunist, a morally corrupt, power-hungry man. In the words of Malkiel Grün-wald, his main accuser, Kastner had "sold his soul to the Devil," deal-ing with the likes of Eichmann; he withheld information on Auschwitz, Grünwald claimed, which made possible the deportations of Jews like "sheep to slaughter."[13] Although Lerner's play tries to exonerate Kastner from charges of collaborating with the Nazis, by no means is Kastner's figure romanticized. On the contrary, Lerner is very careful to highlight both his humanitarian attributes and his failings as a husband and son, his vanity, and his forays into Bud-apest's shady night life. Lerner's Kastner is reminiscent of Oskar

Schindler, another savior of Jews, whose drinking and womanizing resist any attempts of elevation to sainthood or mythological stature. Kastner and Schindler become more remarkable precisely because they were not at all the heroic type; in fact, they were very far from perfection.

In the final analysis, *Kastner* is an attempt to shake conventional notions of collaboration and heroism. As we see in *Children of the Shadows,* Sigmund Rabinowitz is consumed by remorse for what he has done. His reference to the authorities implies a legal basis for charging him with crimes against the Jewish people. Though in many regards Kastner's case is different, he was actually put on trial in Jerusalem in 1954 for collaborating with the Nazis, using his position to help his family and friends, and preventing the truth about Auschwitz to be known, thus facilitating the deportation of hundreds of thousands of Hungarian Jews. The verdict was a mixed one—he was found innocent on the collaboration charge but was reprimanded for having associated with mass murderers like Eichmann. On the issue of heroism, Kastner himself answers in the Epilogue to the play: "But how many lives did these heroes (the Warsaw ghetto fighters) save? What was the purpose of their heroism? And the man (i.e., Kastner) who managed to wrest a whole train from the claws of the Nazis, with 1,684 lives on it, that man is a collaborator?"[14] We should note that in Sobol's *Ghetto,* Gens, the head of Vilna's ghetto, is accused of collaboration by an idealist who finds his dealings with the Germans reprehensible. Gens's defense is essentially based on the belief that saving lives takes precedence over principles and ideals. He justifies collaboration because, as in his case, it leads to fewer killed. He selected the very old and sick rather than let the Germans conduct random roundups. This concession would never have occurred if the job were carried out by crueler guards, perhaps Lithuanians or Ukrainians. Even though Gens and Kastner do admire the bravery of Warsaw's fighters, they are convinced that, in the end, what really counts is survival at all costs.

In effect, both Lerner and Sobol are trying to revise our thinking about collaboration and heroism against a forty-year-old history of Israel celebrating and glorifying the deeds of such national figures as Hanna Senesh and Mordecai Anielewicz, leader of the Warsaw uprising. Naturally, it is always easier and simpler to make national heroes out of brave soldiers than morally ambiguous ghetto leaders like Gens and Kastner. No doubt the reputation of these Jewish leaders has been forever tarnished by the well-publicized actions of the most famous ghetto chief of all—Haim Rumkowsky of

Lodź, who abused his position in ways that can best be described as grotesque and outrageous. But even Rumkovsky has his defenders. Survivor/author Primo Levi, in a collection of essays, *Moments of Reprieve*, asks for leniency because Rumkovsky was subject to a system that "exercises a dreadful power of seduction, which it is difficult to guard against . . . it makes them [the victims] similar to them (the Nazis), surrounds itself with great and small complicities."[15]

Whether we accept Levi's notion that applying conventional norms to the Holocaust experience would be unfair, or Gens's and Kastner's position that moral principles are impractical in such extreme circumstances, we are compelled to reexamine our view of collaboration and heroism. After reading these authors' interpretations of the events, we might consider any savior of lives a hero, even if the methods employed were suspect. Heroism is difficult to define; through Gens, Adam, and Kastner, Sobol and Lerner seem to suggest that daring military actions are not the sole criteria for judgment.

As we have seen, the action of these four plays is either set in Eastern Europe during the war or in Palestine, where many survivors migrated after the liberation. Leah Goldberg's *Lady of the Castle*, however, is dealt with separately because of the author's unique treatment of the Holocaust. This particular play is neither set in Eastern Europe during the war nor does it focus on survivor problems in Palestine. Instead, it takes place in a castle somewhere in Central Europe, and Lena, the "survivor" in this mysterious gothic drama, is fortunate to escape the horrors of ghettos and concentration camps. True, Yoram, Tomer's protagonist, also escaped the war, but he lived in Palestine/Israel half his life, while in Lena's case, we can merely speculate on her problems adjusting in the new land.

The focus of Goldberg's play lies elsewhere. The text, in Rachel Brenner's words, "explores the encounter of Israeli rescuer with the Holocaust survivor."[16] This encounter is fraught with tensions and anxieties. Though it only lasts a few hours, it serves as a microcosm for a phenomenon that has shaped Israeli society for decades. On Lena's side, the prospects of leaving the "old world" with its familiar and safe surroundings (illusory, to be sure), is frightening. As someone who has frequently been mistreated and abused, she is hesitant, even distrustful, of Dora's promises of a better and freer life in a Jewish state. Like the typical survivor, she becomes cynical and paranoid. In an unstable, dangerous world, it is no wonder that at first she prefers the constancy and steadiness of the Count—with all the mystical, apocalyptical implications—over the uncertainties awaiting her in Dora and Michael's "promised land."

For the rescuers, the meeting with Lena, and with survivors in general, forces them to confront a world they left behind for a new life in Palestine. For Michael and Dora, Europe means persecution, humiliation, and ultimately, the Holocaust. It is true that for Michael these memories and associations are ambiguous at times, for, unlike Dora, he is able to transcend Europe's anti-Semitism and elitism and appreciate its rich cultural traditions. But on the whole, and for Dora in particular, Europe signifies a bleak past, the Diaspora, while Palestine symbolizes a much brighter future, freedom, and hope. And although the Europe of the immediate postwar period held little hope for these Jews, Dora's cliché-ridden, almost propagandistic statements about Palestine lessens our admiration for her and what she represents in the play and add credence to the Count's defense of old values and old Europe, a world the Nazis and the war have managed to destroy.

As a Zionist most of her life, Lithuanian-born Leah Goldberg actually went to Palestine from Germany in 1935 after completing her doctoral studies at Bonn. Furthermore, although she composed some of the most beautiful Hebrew poetry ever written, she taught comparative literature at the Hebrew University until her death in 1970. Her German background and dedication to teaching the masterpieces of European literature could explain the positive, even perhaps, tragic portrayal of the Count, whose intellectualism, conservatism, nobility, and high aesthetic sense, are what, after all, produced the Goethes and Schillers of European culture. Between Dora's extreme views and the Count we find Michael, a practicing Zionist committed to building a Jewish homeland in the Asian desert, who seems to be capable of integrating his European past, both good and bad, into his new life. He is perhaps, the example of the hard-working farmer, who after plowing his fields somewhere in the Galileean hills relaxes to Beethoven and Tolstoy.

Notes

1. The original texts are: Leah Goldberg, *Baalat Haarmon* (Tel Aviv: Sifriat Poalim, 1955). Aharon Megged, *Hanna Senesh* (Tel Aviv: Hakibutz Hameuhad, 1958). Ben-Zion Tomer, *Yaldei Hatzel* (Tel Aviv: Amikam, 1963).

2. Original texts are: Nathan Shacham, *Heshbon Hadash* (Tel Aviv: Masach A, 1954). Moshe Shamir, *Hayoresh, Teatron* 9 (1963), and Or Am, 1989. Aharon Megged, *Haona Haboeret* (Tel Aviv: Amikam, 1967).

3. Original texts are: Joshua Sobol, *Ghetto* (Tel Aviv: Or Am, 1984), and second version, Or Am, 1992. (There are three English translations of this play.) Joshua Sobol, *Adam* (Tel Aviv: Or Am, 1989). Joshua Sobol, *Bemartef* (Tel Aviv: Or Am, 1990). Motti Lerner, *Kastner* (Tel Aviv: Or Am, 1985).

4. Glenda Abramson, *Modern Hebrew Drama* (New York: St. Martin's, 1979), 137.

5. For historical background to the events surrounding Wittenberg's arrest and death, I read Abraham Foxman, "The Resistance Movement in the Vilna Ghetto," in Yuri Suhl, ed., *They Fought Back* (New York: Schocken, 1975), 148–59.

6. Most critics have identified parallels between Sobol's Holocaust plays and current-day Israeli politics. In English, the best study of this feature in Sobol's drama is Yael Feldman's "Identification with the Aggressor or the Victim Complex," *Modern Judaism* (May 1989). Feldman's "Notes" provide a good bibliography on the subject.

7. Gidon Ofrat, *Hadrama Haisraelit* (Israeli Drama) (Jerusalem: Tcherikover, 1975), 100. The translation is mine.

8. Ben-Ami Feingold, *Hashoa Badrama Haisraelit* (The Holocaust in Israeli Drama) (Tel Aviv: Hakibutz Hameuhad, 1989), 37. The translation is mine.

9. Ibid.

10. Ben-Zion Tomer, *Children of the Shadows*, trans. Hillel Halkin (Tel Aviv: The Institute for Translation of Hebrew Literature, 1982), 87.

11. Ibid., 88.

12. Glenda Abramsom, 131.

13. Motti Lerner, *Kastner*, trans. Imre Goldstein, ed. Michael Taub *Modern International Drama* (Special Israeli Issue, 1993), 40.

14. Ibid., 91–92.

15. Primo Levi, *Moments of Reprieve*, trans. Ruth Feldman (New York: Summit, 1986), 167.

16. In an article on Goldberg's play, Rachel Brenner points out: "Whereas the Israeli-born characters are capable of empathizing with the survivors' desire to assert their freedom, the common origins of the European-born rescuers and survivors seem to preclude such empathy. In addition to bringing home the well-known discourse of suffering that the 'reborn' Jew in Israel would rather forget, the survivors' experience exacerbates the sense of guilt and fear in that it confronts the European-born Israelis with the arbitrariness of their own survival." Rachel Brenner, "Discourses of Mourning and Rebirth in Post-Holocaust Israeli Literature: Leah Goldberg's *Lady of the Castle* and Shulamith Hareven's "The Witness," *Hebrew Studies* 31 (1990):76.

Part Two: The Plays

Leah Goldberg

Leah Goldberg was born in Kovno, Lithuania, in 1911. She received a doctorate in Semitic languages at the University of Bonn, and went to Palestine in 1935. A poet, theater critic, translator, and newspaper editor at various times, she also founded and chaired the Comparative Literature Department at the Hebrew University from 1952 until her death in 1970. She received the Israel Prize (posthumously).

Among her major works is *Collected Works* in nine volumes, eight of which are poetry. After writing *The Lady of the Castle*, she also wrote the play *Hahar Hailem* (The Mute Mountain), which she apparently completed in 1957.

Translations of her poetry and drama have appeared in English, French, Polish, and Russian.

Lady of the Castle

1955

(Translated by T. Carmi)

Characters

MICHAEL SAND, a librarian from Palestine, about forty years old.
DR. DORA RINGEL, social worker, about forty years old.
ZABRODSKY, caretaker of the castle, about fifty-seven years old.
LENA, nineteen years old.

Scene

An old castle in Central Europe. The same set is used throughout the play.

Time

About two years after the Second World War (September 1947).
Act I. Between 9:00 and 10:00 P.M.
Act II. Between 10:00 and 11:00 P.M.
Act III. Between 11:00 P.M. and midnight.

ACT I

The library. Bookcases along the walls. Paintings by old masters and tapestries. One window with heavy curtains (which are now open). Two medium-sized tables and deep-set armchairs. A sofa. On one of the tables, an electric kettle and tea service for two. On the second (by the sofa), a telephone. A librarian's ladder by the right bookcase. Above the wall tapestry, between the bookcases, center, an old cuckoo clock. Doors to the right and left.

A rainy, stormy evening with occasional lightning and thunder. Sand, Zabrodsky, and Dora are standing in the room. Dora carries a raincoat on her arm and a briefcase in her hand.

SAND. I'm very sorry, Mr. Zabrodsky, but we have no choice. We must impose on your hospitality tonight.

ZABRODSKY. (*Unrelenting.*) I'm only the caretaker here. I have no authority to lodge strangers for the night.

SAND. But what shall we do?

ZABRODSKY. I would advise you to call the city; perhaps those who sent you will be kind enough to propose some solution . . .

DORA. At this hour?!

SAND. I've already tried to call. The line is cut. Probably because of the storm. I'd be very grateful if you . . .

ZABRODSKY. I have no authority.

SAND. (*Forcefully.*) The government's instructions, which I handed over to you, explicitly say that you are to place the library at my disposal and render all possible assistance. I think that also covers the possibility of lodging here in case of emergency. Look what's going on outside! And there's plenty of room here!

ZABRODSKY. This castle is now a museum. It is not customary to sleep in a museum. And . . . you have brought a guest, of whom no mention is made in the instructions . . .

DORA. (*A bit hurt; hesitantly.*) Really, Sand, maybe we should try to go!

SAND. You're out of your mind! Look! It's sixty kilometers to the nearest town. And you know what condition the car is in . . . (*A thunder clap cuts him short.*)

ZABRODSKY. (*Seeing he has no choice in the matter.*) I quite understand, sir, that it's difficult to travel now. But the castle is a museum. . . . There are no sleeping accommodations . . . and when one is only an employee responsible to the authorities, a mere caretaker . . . one hesitates to violate the law. . . . (*Thunder.*)

SAND. But on such a night the law wouldn't force even a dog out of doors!

ZABRODSKY. Not so, my dear sir, nowadays the law dispatches men to perdition—without the slightest qualm.

SAND. And are you the representative of the law here?

ZABRODSKY. Hardly. I'm its victim.

SAND. Ah, it's not such a terrible offense. Nobody will jail you for not throwing people out on a stormy night. If you wish, I'll go over to the ministry tomorrow, as soon as I get to town, and explain the whole matter to them . . . at any rate, we're not leaving this place tonight! Well?

ZABRODSKY. (*Cornered.*) Well, then, you have no need of my consent—but please do not think it's a question of ill will on my part—after all, there are no accommodations at all in the castle, no beds, no linens or anything of that sort . . . and I . . . rather thought that some hotel along the highway would be more to the lady's taste.

DORA. I would really prefer some country inn . . .

ZABRODSKY. For that very reason I suggested . . .

DORA. Old castles are quite beautiful, but not to live in . . .

ZABRODSKY. (*Staring at her.*) I see! (*Listens to the thunder.*) Please sit down! (*Dora sits down, Sand stands.*)

SAND. (*To Dora.*) Really, Dora, I'm terribly sorry. . . . I only meant to show you the castle. . . . And now I'm afraid it's all been a bother to you. And what's more—we're a burden on Mr. Zabrodsky . . .

ZABRODSKY. No, not at all. I will arrange everything for you immediately. . . . Would you like to lie down and rest?

DORA. Now! At nine o'clock?!

ZABRODSKY. Yes, yes . . . it is still quite early. If you would prefer to sit here awhile, please do so. (*To Sand.*) Why are you standing, sir? Please sit down. You are my guests now. (*Sand sits down.*)

DORA. Unexpected guests are a nuisance, I know.

ZABRODSKY. I shall see to the arrangements. When you wish to retire, please call me. I shall be in my room, below. (*To Sand.*) You know where that is, sir.

SAND. Thank you very much. And forgive us for having forced ourselves on you, Mr. Zabrodsky, but we really had no choice.

ZABRODSKY. No matter, no matter. . . . (*Turns to go, hesitates by the doorway.*) But, nonetheless, perhaps you are tired?

SAND. No, no! And if you're not tired, Mr. Zabrodsky, and if you don't mind spending an evening with strangers, we'd be very happy if you'd stay on with us.

ZABRODSKY. That's very kind of you. (*Approaches them, but does not sit down.*)

SAND. (*To Dora.*) That's how life knocks one about! Wars, storms, upheavals . . . and one is always a burden on somebody, unintentionally, against one's will. (*To Zabrodsky.*) Won't you sit down, sir? (*Zabrodsky continues to stand.*)

SAND. (*To Dora.*) By force of accident you break into a different world and then find yourself captive. (*Looks around the room.*) But what a wonderful captivity! I'd be willing to stay in this library for many months . . . with these books and these paintings . . .

DORA. (*To Zabrodsky.*) Please don't be frightened. Whenever he sees books, he can't tear himself away. But we won't impose on you more than it's absolutely necessary. I'll see to that. We'll leave tomorrow morning at dawn. I must get back to the city early.

ZABRODSKY. (*Courteously.*) Why no, on the contrary . . . I hope you will enjoy your stay here. . . . Please do not blame me for my rudeness. It is many years since I have had the pleasure of entertaining guests. Living alone in a forest, one becomes uncivilized and uncourteous.

SAND. Why, not at all. We're the ones who should apologize, not you. . . . But won't you sit down, please?

ZABRODSKY. (*Standing.*) And you're most probably hungry and thirsty—would you like some tea?

SAND. It's very kind of you, but . . .

ZABRODSKY. No, no, it is no trouble at all . . .

DORA. Tea, now, in this storm and cold . . . that would be wonderful. (*Bends over the kettle.*) Well, this is a woman's job. . . . (*Raises the cover of the kettle.*) Yes, but water . . .

ZABRODSKY. I will bring some immediately . . .

DORA. Please, sir, if you'd like us to feel at home, then let me fetch the water. At the end of the corridor, behind the small room (*points at the door*). I noticed a tap . . .

ZABRODSKY. (*Trying to suppress his indignation.*) I see that madam has already made a thorough survey of the castle . . .

DORA. (*Sensing his anger.*) While Mr. Sand was busy in the library, I looked over the rooms a bit. I didn't know it was forbidden . . .

ZABRODSKY. Why, not at all.

DORA. Then, with your permission . . . (*Takes the kettle and starts for the door.*)

ZABRODSKY. But nevertheless, madam, perhaps I . . . (*Dora exits.*)

SAND. (*After Dora leaves the room.*) Don't worry about her, sir, she'll find her way. Her work has taught her to get along in strange places. Do sit down. Please! (*Short pause. Zabrodsky sits. Sand, at a loss to open the conversation, surveys the books.*) What a wonderful collection.

ZABRODSKY. I am pleased, sir, that you have found books of interest to you. . . . Have you had time to examine all of them?

SAND. No, there are still two shelves (*rises*)—these two—ah, when I come to places like these and see such a library—such fine libraries where the Nazis did as they pleased, vandalizing books collected here over generations . . .

ZABRODSKY. You're quite right, they did as they pleased . . .

SAND. (*Goes over to the shelf.*) Here is a first edition of Voltaire—and they ripped off the covers. . . . What for?

ZABRODSKY. They turned the leather covers into pocketbooks for their mistresses.

SAND. I can't look at such things calmly. . . . It makes my blood boil . . .

ZABRODSKY. I quite understand your feeling. After all, you are a librarian!

SAND. As a matter of fact, I'm *not* a librarian . . .

ZABRODSKY. I beg your pardon?

SAND. I *was* a librarian, many years ago . . .

ZABRODSKY. But the official instructions describe you as . . .

SAND. Yes, I now have to deal with books again. (*Laughs.*) Oh, I didn't come here under false pretenses! (*Sees Zabrodsky's anxiety.*) You see, sir, in our country you will hardly find anyone who has stuck to the same profession during all these years. I've changed mine quite often . . . . I used to be a librarian—and then our country needed farmers, so I went to a collective settlement; the children grew up and had to be educated—so I became a teacher; then, back to the land again; when the war came—I turned soldier; when the war was over—back to farming. (*Shows his hands.*) Here, look at my hands . . .

ZABRODSKY. (*Smiles.*) "The hands are the hands of Esau." . . . (*Sand looks at him.*) Isn't that how the Bible puts it?

SAND. Yes, indeed.

ZABRODSKY. And now you have again turned librarian?

SAND. For a short while. I was slightly wounded during the war, and afterward I went back home, to the fields . . .

ZABRODSKY. Perhaps I'd better go and show the lady where the water is!

SAND. No. Why bother? She'll find it!

ZABRODSKY. Are you sure?

SAND. Of course. I told you she's accustomed to strange houses. That's part of her job.

ZABRODSKY. I see . . . ah, please excuse the interruption . . . you said you were wounded during the war and then went home.

SAND. Yes, and then the wound acted up again. I've been disqualified for physical labor, and I don't have the patience to sit around in a convalescent home. Recently, we learned that many of the books stolen from Jewish libraries in Germany were scattered about by the Nazis in this country. I've been sent here to track them down and ship them to our National Library in Jerusalem . . . it's a wonderful vacation for me, without being a complete waste of time.

ZABRODSKY. And so you travel from castle to castle.

SAND. From library to library and from castle to castle, and the more remote the place, the greater the surprises. And that intrigues me. I'm a hunter by nature, you know, a book hunter.

ZABRODSKY. (*Looking at the door through which Dora left the room.*) And the lady?

SAND. She's searching for Jewish children who survived the war . . .

ZABRODSKY. Fascinating. And where does she look for them?

SAND. Everywhere, in the homes of peasants who sheltered them from the Nazis, in remote villages, in convents.

ZABRODSKY. Most interesting . . . and you, sir, help her in this search?

SAND. I? No, I just happened to meet her in the capital. We're childhood friends. Her work had exhausted her, and I offered to entertain her by bringing her here to see this beautiful castle.

ZABRODSKY. (*Smiling.*) You make it sound as if only she worked while you rested!

SAND. My work is much easier. The books follow me very willingly.

ZABRODSKY. Ah. Then the children do not follow her as willingly?

SAND. That's not what I said. But there are all kinds of cases, there are children who have become accustomed over the years to a life the war had forced on them . . .

ZABRODSKY. And they refuse to follow her to your country?

SAND. There *are* such cases . . . . But ultimately I believe they all go with her. She has one invincible ally.

ZABRODSKY. Indeed? And who is that?

SAND. The healthy instincts of the children themselves, their feeling for life, their will to live, even after the war has destroyed half their lives . . .

ZABRODSKY. Most interesting. . . . (*Looks at the door.*)

SAND. I found her almost completely exhausted. A most unfortunate thing happened to her last week. Ah, it's terrible work! I myself worked with children like these during the war . . . (*notices that Zabrodsky is not paying any attention to him*) . . . but I'm afraid you're tired of listening . . .

ZABRODSKY. (*Absently, his eyes glued to the doo*r.) Why, no, on the contrary, on the contrary . . . (*Enter Dora.*)

DORA. Here's the water . . . please excuse me . . . I lost my way at first. I couldn't find the light.

ZABRODSKY. (*Rises.*) Yes, yes, it is entirely my fault, madam. I should have gone instead. I know my way about this house even in the dark.

DORA. (*Plugging in the kettle.*) But the table is only set for two . . . (*Sits down.*)

ZABRODSKY. And you are two, madam. (*Sits down.*)

SAND. No. No, Mr. Zabrodsky, we won't have tea without you . . .

ZABRODSKY. As a matter of fact, I . . .

SAND. Really, it's out of the question. I beg of you.

ZABRODSKY. If you insist. . . . It is a long time since I have had the pleasure of entertaining guests. A solitary old man, practically a recluse, in this manor, buried in a virgin forest so to speak . . . yes . . . the table is always set for two here . . . that is, when they notify me that one person is coming. Madam's arrival (*with exaggerated courtesy*) was a pleasant surprise. With your permission, I shall fetch another cup.

SAND. We're sorry to trouble you. (*Zabrodsky goes to the right door, bows and is about to exit. Thunder.*)

ZABRODSKY. (*Murmurs to the thunder, with his face to the window.*) "And the stars of heaven fell unto earth, even as a fig tree casteth figs, when she is shaken of a mighty wind." (*Exits.*)

DORA. What did he say?

SAND. Nothing . . . a verse from the New Testament . . .

DORA. Awful! Till I found the light in this labyrinth. . . . Oh, damn it, Sand, all this makes me nervous. . . . I want to go home . . .

SAND. You know that's impossible now, Dora. I'm sorry. Dora, you must stop thinking about it. It's not your fault the boy committed suicide. (*Begins climbing the ladder.*)

DORA. Yes, yes . . . it wasn't my fault, wasn't my fault . . . I know . . . but . . . where are you climbing to?

SAND. Excuse me a moment, Dora. I haven't gone over these books yet, up here . . . (*Climbs up.*)

DORA. You and your books! In such a storm . . . and you don't give up. I can't stand it! And this old man, with his verses from the New Testament.

SAND. (*On top of the ladder. Pulls out a book and mumbles to himself.*) Interesting. These books hardly have any dust on them. Somebody's been reading them.

DORA. Leave the books alone for a moment! I tell you that here . . . maybe we can still get out of here!

SAND. (*On the ladder.*) If I could do anything for you . . .

DORA. Really, I don't know what's come over me. This old man! I'm afraid of him. It's as if he—rose from the grave!

SAND. No, it's nothing at all. All caretakers of castles and museums are queer birds . . . . I rather like him, seems to be well educated. Who knows what he used to be.

DORA. Yes, who knows! And have you noticed how he tried to get us out of here! And there are no accommodations at all here (*imitating him*), "no linens or anything of that sort!" And now, all of a sudden he has everything! An electric kettle, hot water, cups, everything!

SAND. (*Leafing through a book.*) What's the trouble, Dora?

DORA. And what high falutin' talk! "I haven't had the pleasure of entertaining guests" —as if the castle were his! If only we could get out of here!

SAND. I'm rather pleased that the storm has held us up here. Two more shelves to go—I'll work a bit tonight, and that'll save me an extra trip.

DORA. But what will I do here?

SAND. You go to sleep and rest. It'll do you good.

DORA. Sleep! In this place?! (*Thunder.*) You don't understand anything!

SAND. (*Goes down to her. Worried.*) What's come over you, Dora? What's happened to you all of a sudden?

DORA. (*Laughs nervously.*) I don't know. I want to go home.

SAND. But how can we get home now?

DORA. I told you you don't understand. I don't mean the hotel in town. I want to go home, really home. To *my* house! To the heat and the hot winds! This castle is only one stop along the way . . . . I was born here, I grew up here, I spent my childhood here. And suddenly it's all so unreal, so strange and alien! The cities, the villages, the monasteries, they're no longer real to me! My home is in Palestine!

SAND. So is mine, Dora. There are such moments of nostalgia on every trip, I know. (*Turns back to the books.*)

DORA. No, you don't! Because this country is really strange for you! But for me—this was once home! And then these children— day in, day out, I have to talk them into leaving this country . . . while I stay on here—in this world . . . . I want to go home so badly!

SAND. (*On the ladder.*) And do you think that I don't want to go back?!

DORA. But you'll go back!

SAND. So will you.

DORA. Yes, yes. But with you it's different! (*Calms down a bit.*) With you everything is always under control. You always know your way, you always find your place. You'll leave at the right time and go back at the right time. (*Flaring up again.*) And you'll always be calm and wise and sure of yourself . . . . I used to think of myself as a practical person, I used to think I'd always be prepared for reality! But this weariness! This storm! This old man! No, I can't bear it! I've known you for twenty years already and I've never seen you lose your head! It can drive one mad! I don't understand how your wife stands it!

SAND. (*Laughs.*) Well, as a matter of fact, it does upset her. It upsets all women . . .

ZABRODSKY. (*Enters with cup, plates, and biscuits.*) We are in for a fine night! (*Dora rises and goes toward him to help him.*)

ZABRODSKY. (*Sees Sand at the top of the ladder.*) I see, sir, that you are still searching for hidden treasures up there!

DORA. (*To Sand.*) Really, Sand, it's time you came down! Let's have some tea!

SAND. (*Descending.*) Yes, yes . . . (*Takes plates from Zabrodsky and carries them to the table. Sand sits down. Dora begins to set the table.*)

ZABRODSKY. With your permission, madam. (*Sits down.*) I'm afraid there is one difficulty I cannot overcome. The adjoining room, here (*points at the left door*) is completely furnished . . . that will be for you, madam. But the rest of the rooms are kept as a museum. However, I'd be glad to place my room at your disposal, sir. I hope you will be comfortable.

SAND. No, thank you very much. I'll stay here, in the library. There's a sofa here and I don't need any sheets.

ZABRODSKY. That's out of the question. This is no place to sleep, and I'm really accustomed to anything and everything.

SAND. So am I, Mr. Zabrodsky. In my travels during the war, and before that as well, I slept on benches, crates, tables, floors . . .

ZABRODSKY. All the more reason you should sleep in a bed to-night; we're at peace now, you know. People say the war is over.

SAND. No, Mr. Zabrodsky, I'll remain here . . .

ZABRODSKY. My room is narrow and most modest, nonetheless, it's a bedroom . . .

SAND. No, we've been enough of a bother as it is!

ZABRODSKY. Bother! After all, you've worked all day long!

SAND. And that's precisely why I'll be happy to spend the night here. I haven't finished my work and there are still two shelves over there to be examined.

ZABRODSKY. (*The issue is obviously important to him.*) I don't think you'll find anything of interest there: only the family archives which the owner of the castle left behind.

SAND. I'm familiar with this sort of thing! Just where you don't expect to find anything, you discover the most amazing treasures. No, don't insist . . .

ZABRODSKY. But . . .

DORA. The water is boiling! (*Begins to pour tea into Zabrodsky's cup.*)

ZABRODSKY. Thank you very much, madam! (*To Sand.*) But you really should not work all night!

SAND. I'll work a bit and then I'll lie down to rest! (*To Dora, who has served his tea.*) Thank you!

ZABRODSKY. How can you possibly rest here in this storm, and where will you lie down?

DORA. (*Pours out her tea; to herself.*) Now for a cup of hot tea, it's wonderful! I can't get used to the weather here, and they say this is a hot summer!

ZABRODSKY. This sofa is short! (*To Dora, who serves him biscuits.*) Thank you very much. (*To Sand.*) Much too short!

DORA. (*Offering biscuits to Sand.*) Please have some . . . (*To Zabrodsky.*) Back home, September is one continuous heat wave. It's unbearably hot even at night!

ZABRODSKY. Really?

DORA. When I think that I once loved the frost . . . (*Drinks her tea.*)

ZABRODSKY. Well then, sir?

DORA. And now my teeth chatter at the very thought of it . . . brrr!

SAND. (*To Zabrodsky.*) It's very kind of you, Mr. Zabrodsky. But, really, I'm doing this for myself, not for you. I've become attached to this library room here, in the shadow of these wonderful books, all these treasures I would be quite willing to sleep even on the floor! (*Dora surveys the room again as Sand speaks; it is obvious that she does not share his opinion. Zabrodsky sighs.*)

DORA. (*Sipping her tea.*) But you're not drinking! (*They begin to drink.*) Incidentally, we never used to drink tea. We always drank coffee. Only "fashionable society" drank tea . . . (*Listens to the wind.*) And this is how you live here, Mr. Zabrodsky?

ZABRODSKY. This is how I live.

DORA. And you're not afraid?

ZABRODSKY. What should I be afraid of?

DORA. It's far from town, and the loneliness, and all these old things . . .

ZABRODSKY. Old things?!

DORA. Yes, yes, I know, fashionable people like to think that the older the object, the more beautiful it is.

SAND. But they really are beautiful!

DORA. (*Looking around.*) These enormous rooms . . . it's beautiful, but not to live in!

ZABRODSKY. Yes, madam, you have already said that, if I'm not mistaken.

DORA. Really?

ZABRODSKY. But people lived here, spent all their lives here, and lived well! And their lives were immeasurably fuller and more beautiful than the lives of those who inhabit these modern boxes . . .

SAND. As for beauty, I quite agree. As for fullness, we should ask the people themselves, those who used to live here; or rather, we should have asked them then, not now. After all, what do we know about them?!

DORA. And as for those modern boxes, they, at least, have the virtue of not collecting centuries of dust, and a great many people can live in them.

ZABRODSKY. Certainly, everything is polished there, smooth and electrical! Above all, electrical!

DORA. Well, right here, you now seem to have an electric kettle as well as a telephone.

ZABRODSKY. But there is also something else here.

DORA. For instance?

ZABRODSKY. (*Explaining to her as if to a child.*) You see, madam, I can introduce an electric kettle and a telephone into this ancient castle—it will bear it. But try introducing this tapestry or this old bookcase into one of your modern, low-roofed boxes—it simply can't be done! It would be ludicrous! Your boxes would fall to pieces! . . . These modern lives, all cast in one mould, cannot tolerate beauty.

SAND. Yes, perhaps we no longer have any feeling for that sort of thing. Perhaps we've forgotten something in our haste. These old books, look how beautiful they are! Even the type face . . .

DORA. I've heard this tune before. Everything was better in the good old days! And these lovely books of yours, these wonderful manuscripts—who saw them? How many people read them?

ZABRODSKY. (*Ironically.*) Yes, so many people now read books!

DORA. You mean that the covers are dirty and sticky and the pages are soiled, and the writing is cheap! Of course!

ZABRODSKY. And all of them standardized products, the literature as well as the houses!

DORA. Yes, it's all very nice to visit the old city of Jerusalem or the ghetto of Prague and then rave about the beauty of the antiquities! But let me see the same aesthetes try living in those picturesque ruins! Let them try it for one week. You know, people live their entire lives there! I've seen it with my own eyes! I've been to those places!

SAND. But we weren't speaking of ruins, Dora! We were speaking of a castle.

DORA. (*In full swing, not to be restrained.*) Castles and ruins are always found side by side! Perhaps I have no aesthetic sense. Perhaps I've witnessed too much sorrow and anguish and poverty during these years, tracking down these poor children, homeless, delinquent, infected with vermin and T.B. I hate all this old stuff, all this useless ash!

SAND. What's hate got to do with it?

DORA. I love sunshine and cleanliness, and I want people to be able to live a healthy, simple life! Yes! People! As for all the rest, I don't care if . . .

SAND. Dora!

DORA. (*Suddenly notices that Zabrodsky is listening.*) Here . . . I mean, there are really beautiful things here. I beg your pardon. I must be overtired . . . I've exaggerated, of course. . . . I once loved these things, too. Perhaps I still love them.

SAND. (*To Zabrodsky.*) As far as I'm concerned, this is one of the most beautiful castles I've seen, and I've been through quite a number lately. . . . I can't take my eyes off that clock. It's French, right?

ZABRODSKY. I see you are quite a connoisseur.

SAND. Hardly.

ZABRODSKY. Very few identify it correctly by sight: there are similar clocks in Saxony.

SAND. (*Laughs.*) I have a weakness for old clocks. My father was a watchmaker, and cuckoo clocks are a childhood love. Does it work?

ZABRODSKY. No, it's out of order. (*Changing the subject.*) Tomorrow morning I will gladly show you a very fine Saxonian clock. It is kept in that chest, there, below . . . when you get up tomorrow morning . . .

DORA. No, no! Please, Mr. Zabrodsky, don't show him anything tomorrow. If he starts looking at clocks and books we'll never get out of here. And I think you've had quite enough, with us spending the entire night here.

ZABRODSKY. I hope you will sleep well here tonight, madam.

DORA. I'm not so sure. The castle isn't haunted, is it?

ZABRODSKY. (*Seriously.*) Of course. All old castles are haunted!

DORA. Then I'll really sleep well! I'll dream about all the English novels I read as a child. Sand, I'm sure you never read ghost stories!

SAND. No, I read travel books and Indian stories!

DORA. Then you haven't the faintest idea!

SAND. I can very well imagine: "And at night, when the clock in the tower struck twelve times, and all the inhabitants of the castle were deep in sleep, there appeared the ghost of the beautiful Lady of the Castle." . . . Is that it?

DORA. Exactly! When I was thirteen, those ghosts wouldn't let me shut my eyes at night!

ZABRODSKY. There is nothing fearful about ghosts. (*Zabrodsky rises, goes over to the window, lowers the heavy curtain. Mumbles to himself.*) "And there followed hail and fire mingled with blood, and they were cast upon the earth."

DORA. (*To Sand.*) I'll always remember the chill that used to grip me when I read those novels. Ghosts walking through the night, and secret doors opening, and choked voices howling from the cellar . . .

SAND. Naturally! If the castle is haunted by ghosts, it stands to reason that there should be hidden cellars and labyrinths and secret doors in the walls. I'm sure you'll find all these here as well.

ZABRODSKY. (*Still standing by the window, his back turned.*) No, there are no hidden cellars and secret doors here. (*Turns and goes back to his place.*)

SAND. Don't be so sure. Why in Wallenstein Manor, just a few months ago, they discovered two secret trapdoors under the carpet in the mistress's room.

DORA. (*Laughing.*) Two!

SAND. She probably had to hide her lover from her husband, as well as one lover from another! That's what I call living! (*To Zabrodsky.*) So you see, Mr. Zabrodsky, never say no until you've checked and double checked.

ZABRODSKY. I am thoroughly familiar with this house.

SAND. You never know, you never know! How long have you been serving as caretaker of this castle?

ZABRODSKY. (*Ironically.*) I have been serving as caretaker of this castle ever since private property was nationalized in this country.

SAND. Well, that's not so long: a year or a year and a half at most. You can't get to know a castle like this in such a short time.

ZABRODSKY. Quite correct, sir.

SAND. (*Joking.*) Well, then, perhaps we'll all spend the night together examining all the entrances, all the wings, who knows . . . (*Rises. Zabrodsky makes an imperative gesture, which forces him down again.*)

ZABRODSKY. I have no need to examine this castle. I know it— and I knew it before I became its caretaker. I knew it from the day I came into this world. I knew it from my mother's womb. I know every corner in it, every crack. This castle, sir, belonged to me. To my father's fathers and to their ancestors. This was my home. (*Silence. Zabrodsky rises. Collects the dishes and places then on the tray.*)

ZABRODSKY. (*Quietly and dryly.*) With your permission, I will prepare the bed for the lady. (*Exits.*)

SAND. (*As Zabrodsky leaves.*) Mr. Zabrod . . . (*But Zabrodsky has closed the door behind him. A prolonged silence between Sand and Dora.*)

DORA. Really embarrassing. . . . who could have guessed? . . .

SAND. Terrible!

DORA. From the very beginning, I didn't want to stay here . . .

SAND. Nonsense! That has nothing to do with it.

DORA. I told you we should try to leave . . .

SAND. There you go again!

DORA. If we had left, all this wouldn't have happened . . .

SAND. I'll go find him . . .

DORA. You will not. . . . I don't want to stay here alone! And after all, what did we really do?

SAND. Don't you see what we did?

DORA. What if he is the owner of the castle, can't I say what I think?!

SAND. Ah, what you said doesn't matter!

DORA. Then what are you so excited about? It's slightly embarrassing, I agree, but why get all worked up?

SAND. Because of what I said!

DORA. You didn't say anything out of the ordinary . . .

SAND. Ah, Dora, don't you understand? First, I ask him: "How long have you been serving here as caretaker?"—and then I begin explaining to him, you understand, I explain to *him*, that in such a short time it's impossible to know the castle.

DORA. But you couldn't have known who he was!

SAND. I should have sensed how much he loves this place—and all these things. I don't care at all if he's the owner of the castle . . . that's not the question! You just don't talk this way to a man about the things that are dearest to him.

DORA. My God, Sand, what do you know about the things that are dear to him? What do you know about him at all?

SAND. What I know is enough for me . . .

DORA. But not for me. First of all, I want to know what this man did during the war, when the Nazis were here . . .

SAND. (*With assurance.*) This man, no! Not him!

DORA. Don't be naïve, Sand. I've seen lots of people these past months.

SAND. So have I. And I tell you, not this man!

DORA. And I tell you: look at this library, that you've been fussing about all day long. Were the Nazis here or not?!

SAND. They were . . .

DORA. And where was he?

ZABRODSKY. (*Enters as she completes her question. He is completely calm.*) I have placed the linens in madam's room. The adjoining room is the washroom. The towels are there. (*Dora and Sand rise as he enters. He advances to the center of the stage, as if to turn out the lights. To Sand.*) Shall I light the upper shelves for you, sir?

DORA. Mr. Zabrodsky, please forgive me . . .

SAND. Do forgive us, that idiotic joke about secret doors . . .

DORA. Really, everything we said, we didn't mean to . . . it wasn't meant personally . . .

ZABRODSKY. Please do not apologize, madam, how could it possibly have been personal?

SAND. But if we have offended you, you must understand that we had no such intention, we couldn't possibly . . .

ZABRODSKY. Far from it, sir, I am no longer vulnerable to offense . . . . Why do you not sit down? Won't you sit down, please . . . and if I am in the way . . .

DORA. No, no, of course not . . .

ZABRODSKY. Please sit down, madam . . . (*Dora goes over hesitantly to her place. Sand continues to stand.*)

SAND. I fell into a manner of speech . . .

ZABRODSKY. (*Looks at him, begins to smile.*) You amaze me, sir! Why, that is the accepted manner of speech nowadays. No one has spoken to me otherwise—for many years . . .

SAND. But I beg your forgiveness. . . . I didn't want to talk that way!

ZABRODSKY. Yes, yes . . . I am quite aware of that. Generally, when people come here—they talk and I do not listen. I stopped listening to what people say long ago, long ago! And if I deviated from my custom tonight, sir, it was only because, at first, you spoke a different language. I began to listen . . . that is the essential . . . and as for the rest, let it be forgotten, do sit down, please!

SAND. (*Hesitates.*) Only if I am certain that you've forgiven me!

ZABRODSKY. But what is it that troubles you?! Nothing has come between us. (*In order to prove that, he sits down. Sand follows suit. Once again—a moment of uneasy silence.*)

DORA. And what I said about this house . . .

ZABRODSKY. (*Brushing it away.*) Ah, could it be otherwise? Who still understands nowadays what it means to stay, to live (*with a wide gesture, encompassing the castle*) in such a house?!

SAND. Yes, we've led a different kind of life, Mr. Zabrodsky, our past is different. . . . (*Zabrodsky is silent.*) But one thing I can imagine: what it means to live always with these books. Was the library always here?

ZABRODSKY. Yes, always.

DORA. (*Also looking at the library.*) It must be very old?

ZABRODSKY. Very.

SAND. Today, while I worked here, I kept thinking with what devotion these books were collected! Even after the vandalism of the Germans, you still feel how generation after generation played its part here . . . such a sure instinct, such fine taste . . .

ZABRODSKY. Yes, that is true.

SAND. And there are more precious old books here than in any library I've seen.

ZABRODSKY. The uncle of my father's grandfather—the Bishop—was a distinguished scholar; most of the old books are his.

SAND. Ah, is that his portrait below, in the drawing room?

ZABRODSKY. No, that is Cardinal Morelli. My mother's cousin. His father was Italian.

SAND. Cardinal Morelli? The one who wrote the new commentary on St. John's Revelation? That was published in Rome, in 1882, if I'm not mistaken? I believe he also had some connection with the royal house.

ZABRODSKY. Ah, you are most learned, sir! Yes, he was Her Majesty's father confessor. *Him* I still remember. (*Smiling to a distant memory.*) When I was eight years old he presented me to the Empress . . . she was a charming woman, the Empress, and she did not fancy me at all. "This child," she said, "this child has stubborn eyes." Yes, that is what she said . . . that was Cardinal Morelli. And this is the Bishop. (*Rises, picks up a miniature and shows it to Sand.*) He lived in the eighteenth century.

SAND. (*Looks from the miniature to Zabrodsky.*) He resembles you.

ZABRODSKY. Yes, so they say. The bishop was an ardent Voltairian, extremely free-minded, a philosopher and naturalist . . .

DORA. (*Who has not looked at the picture.*) That's something that has always puzzled me, how could these priests and monks possibly reconcile religion with science?!

SAND. (*Fearing that Dora will give the conversation a wrong twist.*) And the old books, then, are his?

ZABRODSKY. Yes, this entire section of the library. Fortunately, the Nazis did not touch it . . .

SAND. Ah, those books, the first editions . . .

ZABRODSKY. Yes, he collected them.

SAND. The parchment bindings, and the faded letters . . .

ZABRODSKY. The faded letters . . .

DORA. (*Caught up in the mood of the conversation.*) The faded letters! We had such books in our house. My father said they belonged to the Maharal, the famous Rabbi of Prague. . . . I never read them.

Neither did my father. But my grandfather. . . . I was very small. . . .
I remember grandfather's white beard. . . . He was always poring
over some book. . . . I don't know what he was reading. I used to be
afraid to go up to him—not always, only when he was reading. . . . It
seemed as if there were such a silence in the house when he bent
over these books. . . . Once, I remember it so clearly, a mouse came
out and started to roam around the room—and I was terribly frightened. But I was afraid to scream out because grandfather was reading and it was so quiet. . . . I didn't know how to read, but I still
remember the faded letters and the heavy bindings . . .

ZABRODSKY. Yes, faded letters and heavy bindings . . . so! This
grandfather of yours, madam, whom you described so well, knew
the significance of such books. If he were to come here, he would
perhaps understand more than all the professors of history and art.
. . . Did you also have such a grandfather, sir?

SAND. My grandfather was a poor Jew. A watchmaker, like my
father. But he too had books, which he inherited from his father.

ZABRODSKY. Yes, I once knew such old Jews. . . . (*Pauses, surveys
the books and the room.*) Not fit to live in! Why, look here, sir, one may
also come to you, to the Holy Land, to your city of Jerusalem, and
say: "All this is very nice, but not fit to live in! This is history, arche-
ology, antiquity . . . but not fit to live in!" But you Jews, don't you
claim that no country is as fit for living in as yours? Precisely because
it is part of an old tradition. Yes, perhaps that is why I broke my
silence tonight and spoke to you. I think the Jews are the only people in the world today who are still capable of understanding the
meaning of tradition.

SAND. This is the second time tonight, sir, that you astound me
with your knowledge of my people.

ZABRODSKY. I know very little. But I have always admired the
Jewish people for not succumbing to the vanities and fashions of this
world, for persisting in their own way. I saw these people in their
agony during these years.

DORA. You were not the only one who saw, sir. The whole world
saw. They saw and kept quiet and didn't raise a finger!

ZABRODSKY. The world? But what could you expect from such a
world? Deaf and dumb and dull hearted. And the dead walking
amongst the living. And I was at first among the dead. It is written
in St. John's Revelation: "The last, which was dead, and is alive"—I
am that man.

DORA. (*Looks at Sand with a questioning silence.*)

ZABRODSKY. This is not mysticism. These are hard facts, to which we can all attest. I ask you: What is the sign of life? That a man eats and drinks and moves? Not at all! How many dead walk amongst us on earth—sleep at night and rise in the morning—without knowing that they are dead. I, at least knew. To live, you see, is to take part in the deeds of this world, whether one is moved by love or hate or heart's desire. But if this is lacking, then it is death. Is this not the truth?

SAND. Yes, it is.

ZABRODSKY. Well, then. In 1918, the life I loved came to an end. The empire was gone; and what are we with all our titles and castles, without the empire which was the crown of our existence from the very first? Nothing but ghosts, yes, ghosts! (*Looks piercingly at Dora, who shrinks under his gaze as if chilled to the marrow.*) Of course, there were also those who, without much ado, instantly found the way to that other world, the one in which we now have the good fortune of living. I remember, one fine day, a friend of mine and of my father's, came to me and said: "What a pity you didn't manage to sell that tapestry a month ago to America. Now the price has gone down considerably!" This tapestry, to America! I thought he had lost his mind; but as it turned out, he and his like thought I was the stupid one! Why, after the war, I came back to my castle, penniless. Conclusive proof that I should have sold all these things to America! Or better yet, to the war profiteers who had grown rich!! And I, yes, what did I have left to do in such a world? It no longer had any meaning. And without meaning there can be no life. So I died. It was an easy death, comparatively speaking. In this part of the world, they did not persecute people like myself; we were respected, even venerated. . . . Yes, and I continued to eat, drink, sleep, move, but as a matter of fact I was dead, buried in this castle like an Egyptian king embalmed in his pyramid . . . but even death is not eternal in this world! (*Sinks into silence.*)

SAND. (*To break the silence.*) Because in the final analysis, people who eat and drink, especially those who have not forfeited their spiritual world, are alive.

ZABRODSKY. Sometimes! (*To Dora.*) You've asked me before, madam, whether ghosts haunt this castle. Well, now you see such a one before your very eyes. But I am no longer dangerous. I am not dangerous!

DORA. (*Somehow uneasy.*) I don't know . . . I'm not sure.

ZABRODSKY. That I am alive?

DORA. No . . . not that . . .

ZABRODSKY. (*Dora keeps quiet.*) That I'm not dangerous?

DORA. (*Gathering courage.*) Yes!

ZABRODSKY. But how can a weak, old man possibly endanger anyone?

DORA. (*At first still somewhat confused, but she pulls herself together and says angrily.*) I don't know. I'm not at all sure of it. But I wanted to ask . . . (*Cuts herself short*).

ZABRODSKY. You wanted to ask a question, madam?

DORA. And where were you all these years? During the war?

ZABRODSKY. (*Quietly and dryly.*) Here.

DORA. In your pyramid?

ZABRODSKY. If you wish. . . . I was here. In the castle.

SAND: But . . . but, why . . . (*points at the books*) the Nazis were here.

ZABRODSKY. Yes, they were here.

SAND. But, how is that? If you were here?

ZABRODSKY. I asked them over. The Nazi headquarters was located here throughout the last year of the war. Until the liberation.

DORA. (*Gets up emphatically.*) What?!

ZABRODSKY. (*Ironically.*) Why, you understood at once, madam, that I am one of them. Isn't that so?

DORA. (*His intonation puts her on her guard.*) Nowadays, everybody is suspect.

ZABRODSKY. Quite.

SAND. (*Sensing that there is something more to this, but still groping in the dark.*) But you just now said, sir, that you sat here with the Nazis during the war!

ZABRODSKY. I sat with them. I ate with them at one table, I heard their obscenities, I saw them carving their names in my furniture . . . (*As he speaks, his anger flares up. Dora does not yet grasp its meaning—but the light begins to dawn on Sand.*)

DORA. And after all this you . . .

ZABRODSKY. And after all this . . .

SAND. Ah, Dora. Stop this, really! (*To Zabrodsky.*) The German headquarters? In this castle? The headquarters, you said! But, sir, then you must be. . . . What a fool I am! You must excuse me, how could I possibly have missed the connection?! . . . Your name and the name of the castle . . .

ZABRODSKY. Ah, my good sir, that is all in the past. It's not worth recalling!

SAND. Then . . . then you're the man? You're the one they called the Count? But how could I have missed the connection? (*Dora sits, looking with surprise from one to the other.*)

ZABRODSKY. How could you possibly have guessed? I am surprised you know the story at all.

SAND. But it's a famous story. I heard it in Holland, when I was in the Jewish Brigade. . . . So you're the Count? And it was from here that you contacted the underground?

ZABRODSKY. Yes. It was quite simple. Hate brought me to life. When the war broke out, I thought I could continue living apart from all those matters, I thought it had nothing to do with me . . .

DORA. Many thought so at first.

ZABRODSKY. Yes. I closed myself up here, to withdraw from the world, to live out the rest of my days in peace, far from all of them, from everything. But when I saw them here in the land of my fathers, when I set eyes on those officers, close-cropped, vulgar, ignorant, arrogant, prophesying the new life, setting up a new religion—a new religion of cannibals, a new life of savages, a new culture of swineherds! Always, it is always the scum of humanity, those who cannot grasp the ancient tradition and the true culture, who prophesize a new life, build another culture, and meanwhile they riot, murder, rape, and spit on the carpets . . .

SAND. Yes, I understand. But how did it actually happen?

ZABRODSKY. The castle was abandoned, hidden in the forest. An ideal site for the General Headquarters. They took me into their confidence, and I passed on their secrets to the underground, which operated from the forest, not far from here. The idiots! Just because I looked on complacently while they drank the wines from my father's cellar, pillaged my library, and wallowed in their vomit on these carpets. . . . I detained them here until the very last moment. I handed them over, all of them, one by one, arms, plans, and all . . .

SAND. Sir, it's a wonderful thing you did. Really, a most heroic act.

ZABRODSKY. (*Bitterly.*) And in recognition of this act they offered me a bonus after the victory: they did not evict me like a stray dog to die in an alley. They did me a favor: they let me guard this castle, this "museum," as they call it. To guard it for them!

DORA. (*His bitterness has offended her.*) What can you expect, Mr. Zabrodsky? The government changed after the war.

ZABRODSKY. (*More bitterly.*) Changed, madam? Changed, very much so! For this we fought! We saved man's culture so that it could be turned not into ruins, as the others had planned but, according to the new dispensation, into bathrooms!

DORA. Why are you so bitter? After all, you live in your castle, in your pyramid; what do you care if officially you're the owner or only the caretaker? Of course, maybe you can no longer have soirées here! But, let's say children were to come here, organized excursions from schools, and they would also have the chance of enjoying the beautiful things that were collected here for generations . . .

ZABRODSKY. Yes, the schools come. And quite often at that. And the teacher stands and shows them the "beautiful things," as you were kind enough to say, madam, and delivers a talk about the cruelty and *ignorance* of those "feudal lords," who once lived here, until *they* came and rescued the people from oppression. *Feudal Lords!* I, madam, as you see, am a specimen of this genus; I am nothing but a remnant of the Middle Ages, the "dark" ages, that is to say . . . and the whole of life, the culture we painstakingly built generation after generation was done so the young people would be told that it was nothing but licentiousness and exploitation of down-trodden peasants. Yes, that's how it was, madam! No?

DORA. Yes, it was that, too . . .

SAND. Dora!

DORA. And those who lived here, who built this wonderful "culture," did they have any inkling of what was going on beyond the walls of their estates? Built a culture! And didn't take the trouble to move this culture one step out of their castles! And now they turn up their noses because the visitors are not as refined as they are!

SAND. It's not a question of refinement, Dora!

DORA. As if I didn't know that! It's a question of everything, everything, everything that went on outside this castle for hundreds of years! At first people couldn't set foot here! They used dogs to guard places like these, to keep out intruders! And now that they're finally permitted to come in here, not only the children, but their teachers, and you and I, they're suddenly expected to behave as if they had lived *here,* and not in their tenements, all their lives! As if they were brought up by French governesses! And it's very good that they've finally come here! Very good! Now they'll begin to understand what was done to them and how they were forced to live, they'll begin to understand that now! And the "culture" will come in due time. I don't care if it takes even a hundred years. I've got plenty of time to wait, as long as people now have something to eat! Yes! And if you stay here, sir, as caretaker or owner, you're still living far better than all the others! And if the things they say are spoken to your face, as they are today or behind your back, as they were before, it doesn't make any difference at all! I don't see how it changes the facts!

ZABRODSKY. (*Dryly.*) There are many things you don't see,

madam. (*Rises.*) But I believe I must go. (*Thunder. All listen.*) You should rest now. What time is it? (*Sand looks at his watch, Dora at the wall clock.*)

SAND. Twenty to ten. } (*Together*)
DORA. Ten.

ZABRODSKY. Ten o'clock?!

SAND. No. My watch is accurate. It's twenty to ten.

DORA. Ah, I looked at that wall clock which is out of order.

ZABRODSKY. So. (*Slight pause.*) I will make your bed, madam, in the adjacent room. Here. (*Sighs.*)

DORA. Thank you. If the linens are there, I'll make it myself.

ZABRODSKY. As you wish. (*Gathers up the tea dishes, places them on the tray. To Sand.*) Nevertheless, I do insist that you go down to my room.

SAND. No, really. Thank you very much.

ZABRODSKY. But you'll be far more comfortable there. The storm is less audible there . . .

SAND. I like the sound of thunder, I'm an old storm lover . . .

ZABRODSKY. But . . .

SAND. No, no. . . . I won't take your bed! Under no circumstances!

ZABRODSKY. (*Shrugs his shoulders.*) Then I will at least remove the ladder to make the room look more livable.

SAND. No, please don't bother. I still want to look over the two shelves up there, to the right.

ZABRODSKY. Perhaps it would be wisest to put that off until morning.

DORA. Tomorrow we leave at sunrise!

ZABRODSKY. (*Ignores her outburst. Controls himself. Dryly and politely.*) Well, then. The linens are already in madam's room. (*Bows.*) Have a good rest, as good as possible in such a storm.

SAND. Good night. (*Zabrodsky exits. Short pause.*)

DORA. Are you angry?

SAND. (*Silent.*)

DORA. Why don't you answer me? Why are you keeping quiet? Oh, really! Didn't I feel it, you were embarrassed for me! I'm very sorry! You brought a guest with you and she doesn't know how to behave properly in the presence of princes and counts.

SAND. (*Sighs.*)

DORA. As a matter of fact, why do you care at all? Tomorrow morning we'll leave the place and never see him again. Finished and done with.

SAND. Yes. Finished. We'll go, leaving behind an old, solitary man, who'll remember to his dying day, that one night he broke his silence, perhaps for the first time in many years, to speak humanely to people, and they insulted him!

DORA. Humanely! And all this talk of "bathrooms" sounds terribly "humane" to you!

SAND. I'm not obliged to prove that I'm right to everybody.

DORA. What do you mean right? And when he says: "It's always the scum of the earth that prophesize a new life!"

SAND. Why, he was talking about the Nazis!

DORA. Not only the Nazis, you know that very well.

SAND. Yes.

DORA. And to answer that, in your opinion, that is insisting on being right!

SAND. Yes. Because the whole argument is superfluous. No good can come of it to anyone. His voice is from the past. His past. He lives in it. He loves it. Then leave him be. We're already of a different time and different place. That's all.

DORA. And that's why you say *kaddish* and mourn at the grave of this splendid past, praying to God that He resurrect it! Well?

SAND. Only the son says *kaddish*. I'm no count's son. I, as you know, am the son of a Jewish watchmaker.

DORA. Such wit!

SAND. I'm not joking. I'm speaking quite seriously. I'm the son of a watchmaker and I'm personally interested, very much so, that the future be in the hands of watchmakers and their children.

DORA. But you're completely captivated by this past.

SAND. The past, my dear, has many things which watchmakers' sons should also know, and even love. Even Zabrodsky's past. What to take from this past, that we'll decide for ourselves. But to argue with him about it? I don't want to. Why should I? *He* has the right to love what he loves and hate what he hates. Don't you understand, Dora, that he's now obliged to speak the loftiest and most bitter words? This is his end. His tombstone. And we . . . there are many of us, that's why we can afford to be mediocre and fulfill our obligations silently.

DORA. Ah, I don't understand all this philosophy! I'm scared, simply scared of being sentimental about this whole vanishing world. I was closer to it than you. And I know that its dangers aren't yet past.

SAND. Dangers!

DORA. Yes! If you had to deal with children hiding in strange families, in monasteries, you'd see how this "beauty" still grips them!

Can you imagine what I go through every day? A constant war. The dead, with skeletal hands, are clinging to living children and are pulling them down to the grave.

SAND. But the living don't want to go down to the grave!

DORA. Ah! It's easy for you to talk! With your dead books! You pack them up and they follow you. But the children . . . I would gladly send you to do the terrible work I'm doing, then maybe you'd talk differently.

SAND. Dora, what *are* we fighting about?

DORA. Yes. I'm tired. I'll go to sleep. Good night. (*Turns to the door.*)

SAND. Good night, Dora.

DORA. (*Standing by the left door.*) And if Hamlet's father comes tonight, or Zabrodsky's great, great grandfather, General Zabrodsky, just call for help. I'm here, in the next room.

SAND. (*Laughs.*) Ah, I'll manage on my own. Go to sleep, Dora, and have a good rest.

DORA. Yes, I need a rest. Good night. (*Exits.*)

SAND. (*Puts out the center chandelier so that the side lamp lights up only the right bookcase against which the ladder is leaning and throws a weak light on the center stage and the cuckoo clock. Sand whistles a quiet tune to himself and begins to mount the ladder to the books. But he changes his mind, goes down, and moves the ladder to the center, below the clock.*) Now let's have a look at this old clock! (*Climbs the ladder, opens the clock and pulls out a key.*) Ah, the key! (*He winds up the clock, which begins to play. Then the cuckoo pops out and calls the hours. At the last call—suddenly and indiscernible—a secret door opens up in the wall. Lena comes out. Lena is a very beautiful young girl, dressed in a long white dress. She takes several steps into the room, suddenly sees Sand, emits a cry and collapses to the floor. A tremendous thunder clap.*)

CURTAIN

ACT II

The curtain rises on the same scene: Lena kneeling on the floor, Sand bent over her.

LENA. Don't kill me, don't kill me! Please don't kill me!

SAND. What are you talking about? Who are you? Please get up! (*Tries to help her up, but she pulls away.*)

LENA. Don't touch me! Don't kill me! Don't pull me! I'll go myself! My God! My God! (*Thunder.*) It's an air raid! They're bombing us! They'll come and liberate me. If they come, when they come, I'll tell them you didn't touch me. They won't do anything to you, I'll ask them . . . don't kill me!

SAND. But what are you talking about, child?! Who wants to kill you? (*Thunder.*)

LENA. They're bombing!

SAND. Who's bombing? It's only thunder. A storm. Listen! Nobody's bombing. It's thunder! (*Lena listens a moment to distant thunder and is silent.*)

LENA; I'm not Jewish. I . . . I'm the Lady of the Castle. I'm not Jewish. You can ask the Count . . .

SAND. But I am Jewish.

LENA. (*Raises her head and looks at him.*) Maybe you're really Jewish. Do you want to hide? Come, I'll hide you . . . I'll show you the place. The Count will agree. He's hidden Jews here before. They won't find you.

SAND. Hide from whom? I didn't come here to hide. (*Pause.*) I'll go call Zabrodsky. Wait, I'll be right back.

LENA. Don't call him. He's not to blame. He saved me. And now *they're* sitting in his room downstairs. They'll murder you both, they'll murder the three of us . . .

SAND. Who will?

LENA. The officers, the generals, the Nazis . . .

SAND. Listen, child, I'm a librarian . . . I'm from Palestine. . . . Nobody will hurt you. Listen carefully to what I'm saying: There are no Nazis now, no German generals. I came here to look for Jewish books . . . I . . . nobody wants to harm you. . . . The war is over.

LENA. You were sent to me, they sent you. You're their accomplice; I know, there are Jews who work for them. . . . Why did you wind up the clock? Why did you call me? You know the secret!

SAND. Good heavens! I've already told you, the war's over. It ended a long, long time ago. There's no more war. We defeated the Nazis. Do you understand what I'm saying to you? (*She doesn't answer.*) Is there a doctor who looks after you?

LENA. You think I'm crazy? My God! Ah! I'm not crazy! But he says . . . I've been living here three years . . . and all the time, war. And if they find me, they'll kill me. They exterminate all the Jews. I've seen them do it! . . .

SAND. But there are no Nazis here. . . . (*Completely at a loss, Sand stands over her, looking at her; suddenly, he remembers, he pulls out a newspaper from his pocket.*) Here! (*Offers her the paper.*) Read it, it's today's paper. Take it.

LENA. (*Makes no move to take the paper.*) I don't want to. Don't touch me! (*Grasps the black ribbon around her neck.*) You'll never get a chance to abuse me. No, never!

SAND. (*Handing her the paper.*) Do you know how to read? Do you know what a newspaper is? Can you read?

LENA. What do you want from me? . . . I know how . . .

SAND. But if you read the papers, you must know the war's over . . .

LENA. I don't read newspapers. I haven't read any, for three years . . . (*Cautiously extends her hand to the newspaper as if afraid it will scorch her.*)

SAND. Here, take it. What are you afraid of? Take it, it's today's paper. (*Sees that she's eyeing the paper.*) Here! Look, here's the date.

LENA. (*Finally takes the paper.*) The date's correct. I wrote the date on the wall. Everyday, for three years . . .

SAND. On the wall?

LENA. (*Doesn't answer. Sitting on the floor, she begins reading, frightened yet transfixed. Sand stands above her, watching her. Finally, she looks up at him.*) I don't understand. . . . I don't understand it.

SAND. But this is no way to read! Get up, sit over here, and read this through! (*She goes over to the sofa.*)

SAND. There's not enough light here. Wait a moment, I'll put on the light, it'll be easier for you to read.

LENA. (*By the sofa.*) Don't put on the light! Don't put it on. They'll see. They never go very far. They might see the light through a crack.

SAND. But there's nobody around here. No Nazis, don't you understand? You can put on the lights and open all the windows . . .

LENA. Don't put on the light! Don't open the windows.

SAND. All right, I won't. Can you read in this light?

LENA. Yes . . . (*Sits down on the sofa, begins reading.*)

SAND. (*Stands and observes her.*)

LENA. This is a real newspaper?

SAND. Here, have a good look at me, do I look like someone who means to harm you?

LENA. (*Continues looking at the headlines. Turns the paper over, reads a bit, then drops it to the floor.*) Tell me, tell me, is this a real paper?

SAND. This newspaper I bought this morning in the capital, and yesterday I bought a newspaper just like this one and the day before yesterday, and a week ago. Everybody in this country reads this paper, except you, maybe . . .

LENA. (*Looking at him with bewildered eyes.*) Yes! Yes! Ah, this. . . . But he didn't tell me! Good God, he didn't tell me! He never said anything! (*Buries her face in her hands, sits rigidly.*)

SAND. (*Goes over to left door, opens it slightly and calls out quietly.*) Dora! Dora!

DORA. (*Comes in. She had begun undressing and now she buttons up her blouse again.*) What happened? I thought I heard a scream?

SAND. Come here!

DORA. I thought I was imagining things. There was thunder . . . and my nerves tonight . . . but what . . .

SAND. (*Points to Lena.*) Here. You must help me, you must do something.

DORA. Who is she? Where did she come from?

SAND. A secret door opened, in the wall, I think, I don't know who she is.

DORA. (*Puts on all the lights to have a good look at Lena.*)

LENA. Ah! . . . Now they'll see! Now they'll come! You . . .

SAND. Calm down, child. . . . You needn't be afraid of light any more. (*Lena buries her face in her hands again. Sand whispers something to Dora, of which only the last words are heard.*) And maybe . . .

DORA. She's not sane?

LENA. I am sane! But not—I don't know . . .

SAND. She claims Zabrodsky saved her . . .

LENA. He did! Yes, he saved me . . .

SAND. (*Making a gesture of despair.*) You talk to her. In the meantime I'll call Zabrodsky. I didn't want to leave her alone, now I'll call him, maybe he can explain the whole thing.

LENA. No! No! Don't call him! Don't go to him! No, no!

SAND. All right, I won't call him. (*Steps aside.*)

DORA. (*Goes over to the sofa; to Lena.*) May I sit down next to you? (*Lena doesn't answer, Dora sits down.*) You're so pale! (*Silence.*) I can see you haven't been out in the sun for a long time! Don't you ever go out?

LENA. (*Shakes her head no.*)

DORA. What a pity! The days have been so lovely! The sun was out even this morning. I didn't think there'd be a storm!

LENA. A storm?

DORA. Didn't you hear the thunder? (*Lena doesn't answer.*)

SAND. She thought it was an air raid.

DORA. Air raid? But there haven't been any air raids for over two years. You thought the war was still going on?

LENA. The war . . .

DORA. (*Picks up the newspaper from the floor.*) But there's no war! The war's over. Have you read the paper?

LENA. Yes.

DORA. Well, then you know there's no war! I understand, you were closed up here and didn't go out . . . maybe you didn't meet people and they didn't tell you? Is that so?

LENA. Yes . . .

DORA. Now, then, as soon as the storm is over we'll go outside . . . don't you be afraid, we'll go out with you. Tomorrow morning will be a beautiful day and you'll see for yourself. Yes? (*Lena doesn't answer.*)

DORA. We came from Palestine, and I've met lots of young people here who are still afraid of the war. But now they're not afraid any more. They go out, wherever they please, for walks, to the theater, to the movies . . . do you understand what I'm saying?

LENA. Yes.

DORA. (*Shows her the newspaper.*) Here, you see: It says here . . . but you read it yourself. Well, then, let's get acquainted: my name's Dora, what's yours?

LENA. It's a real paper? There's really no war now? No Nazis? It's a real paper? Tell me! Is that true?

DORA. It's true, dear. The war's been over for a long time. Hitler was killed, the Nazis were defeated. That's why we're here, he and I. We're both Jews. Don't you see: We're free and we're not afraid.

LENA. And this newspaper was. . . . There are newspapers like this now?

DORA. Yes, but who are you?

LENA. And who are you? Why did the Count let you into the castle? Why did you wind up the clock? Why did you call me? Why did you bring me out? Why did you wind up the clock?

DORA. What clock?

SAND. When you left, I climbed up this ladder to have a good look at the clock.

LENA. Yes, the clock . . . this clock.

SAND. I opened it and found a key inside. I wound it up and it rang . . .

LENA. Ten times. That's the signal.

SAND. What signal?

LENA. For me to come out. It means there are no Nazis here, that I can come out.

SAND. (*To Dora.*) And then she appeared. It was all so quick and unexpected, I didn't even see how it happened. But there she was, all of a sudden.

LENA. Because that's the signal between us.

DORA. Between whom?

LENA. Between me and the Count.

SAND. I didn't know anything about this signal. I'm a watchmaker's son and I like clocks. . . . I was just tinkering with it, and the cuckoo . . .

LENA. But where did you come from?

DORA. We're from Palestine, both of us. You know where that is?

LENA. Yes.

DORA. (*To Sand.*) She's Jewish?

SAND. Yes, of course . . .

DORA. Are you from here? From these parts or from the city?

LENA. From the city. It's far. . . . I think it's very far away.

DORA. Yes, it's far. And you came here on foot?

LENA. Yes.

DORA. During the war? You ran away?

LENA. Yes.

DORA. And you found shelter here?

LENA. Yes . . . here, shelter . . .

DORA. And do you have anyone? Are any of your family still alive?

LENA. Why are you questioning me? Questions, questions, questions! I have no one, no one!

DORA. If you don't want to answer, you don't have to. Nobody will force you. But I thought you wanted us to help you.

LENA. But who are you? Yes, who are you? That's what you don't want to tell me!

DORA. I do, very much. Look here, this man, his name is Michael Sand. He's a librarian and he was sent here to look for books, after the war . . . (*Sees that Lena is not convinced by this. To Sand.*) Show her your papers, Sand! (*Sand hesitates.*) Yes, yes, show her. Also the Palestinian passport! (*Sand gives the documents to Dora, who hands them over to Lena.*) You can sit down and examine them, take your time and read them through. (*Lena takes the papers, looks at them and at Sand by turns.*)

DORA. (*To Sand.*) She came out of a secret door, you said?

SAND. Yes, I think so . . . from there. (*Points at the tapestry. Dora is about to go over there, but at that very moment Lena hands back the papers. Dora goes over to her and takes them.*) Well, did you have a look?

LENA. Yes.

DORA. And my name is Dr. Ringel, Dora Ringel. I work for an organization called Youth Aliya. Of course, you don't know what that is.

LENA. I do. . . . Before . . . when I was a child . . . people from Palestine used to come to our house. . . . my father was . . . my father knew those people . . .

DORA. Excellent! Then I don't have to explain to you. . . . You know, it's quite possible that I knew your father. And even you, too, when you were a child. What's your last name?

LENA. (*Doesn't answer.*)

DORA. (*Doesn't repeat the question, sensing that it is premature.*) And you've been here a long time?

LENA. Yes, a long time . . . but how did *you* come here?

DORA. I've shown you the papers. He's looking for books here . . . and I came along to see the castle. And because of the storm, we stayed on for the night. Now, is that clear?

LENA. Storm? (*Listens.*) It's quiet now. They're not bombing any more. Why did they stop bombing the moment you came here?

DORA. But listen . . .

LENA. You put on the light and that was the signal and they stopped the bombing . . .

SAND. But can't you understand, child, there was no bombing. You know yourself that there are no more bombings . . .

LENA. Yes, but what was it? I heard explosions.

SAND. There was a storm, thunder and lightning . . .

LENA. (*As if to herself.*) A storm . . . thunder and lightning . . . and behold a pale horse and his name that sat on him was death . . . yes . . . (*As if awakening.*) A storm? There was just a storm outside?

DORA. Yes.

LENA. (*Listening.*) And now the storm is over. And the rain has stopped. There's no more rain.

SAND. (*Listening.*) Yes.

LENA. And where's the Count?

SAND. Probably in his room, below. Do you want to see him?

DORA. Sand!

LENA. I don't know. I don't think so. There was a storm. . . You can't hear the cuckoo downstairs . . . unless you listen very carefully, very carefully. He told me.

DORA. But who are you? How did you get here?

LENA. You came here to interrogate me . . . yes, yes, now I know. You won't get a single word out of me! You want to find out about me and the Count! But I won't tell you. I won't talk, you can kill me. I won't talk!

DORA. You don't have to. Nobody will force you to say anything, if you don't feel like it. But now you know all about us. And you know, you know just as well as we do, there's no war any more.

LENA. I don't know anything. Newspapers and documents can be forged. Everything is possible, the Nazis know everything, they're evil . . .

SAND. There are no Nazis any more.

DORA. Look, the storm is over, go and open the window, look out and see how quiet everything is, there's no war.

LENA. Don't touch the windows! It's forbidden! It's forbidden, they'll see . . .

DORA. My God, what have they done to this girl, who did this to her?! Don't you believe us? I'll tell you what: we'll turn out the light and shut our eyes, and then you can disappear just the way you came. We won't even know where you've gone to.

SAND. Or else you can leave, you can go to Count Zabrodsky and tell him we're here. You're free to do as you please, absolutely free. Well, tell us what we're supposed to do, order us out of here and we'll go.

LENA. No! No! Don't go, I'm afraid now! I'm afraid to stay by myself, without you. . . . I'm even afraid of the Count now.

SAND. All right, if you want us to, we'll stay and help you. But we don't even know who you are.

LENA. My name's Lena.

DORA. And how did you get here?

LENA. How did I get here? Ah, I didn't know anything . . . I thought . . .

DORA. Did they torture you here?

LENA. Torture? Me?—They didn't even know I was here. And he was good to me, he was so good to me! He did everything. . . . He took good care of me . . . there, below, in my secret room . . . I had everything I needed. He brought me everything . . . himself . . . good food . . . at first, when I was hungry and couldn't eat like everybody, he used to come down and feed me with a spoon, like a baby. . . . I was sick then, too. . . . And afterwards, he brought me beautiful dresses, and I also had books down there, I still have them—now. Only it's forbidden to open the windows. . . . Yes, they might see. And at night, I am the Lady of the Castle, and everything, everything is mine . . . when the Nazis aren't here.

DORA. But there have been no Nazis for a long time, for over two years.

LENA. Ah, yes, yes . . .

DORA. But how did you get here?

LENA. When the Nazis came . . . that is, they'd been in the country a long time before that—but when they came to our house . . . I ran away. At first, I hid in the house, and then I ran away, I don't know how. They took father and mother, and little Zoska and Paul, and I ran away. I hid in a forest for a few days, and at night, I walked, I walked and walked and sometimes I sang . . .

SAND. You sang?!

LENA. Yes . . . yes . . . quietly. . . . They didn't hear . . . it doesn't matter . . . and one night I didn't have any strength left and came here, I collapsed here. . . . He came out with the Nazis who lived here, he hates them . . . he really hates them! And I was hungry and exhausted. . . . He brought me in, he risked his life for my sake, but he took me in, he hid me here, in this secret room, he saved my life and gave me everything . . . everything . . . and he . . . (*Silence.*)

DORA. (*Softly.*) And afterwards—when victory came—and the Nazis were taken captive—he didn't tell you? (*Silence. To Sand.*) What a low trick!

LENA. (*Rises. With sudden fury.*) I'll go! I don't want to talk to you! How can you speak that way about the Count? How do you dare? He saved me! *He* did!

SAND. (*Stopping her.*) Please, sit down.

LENA. (*Goes back and sits down, exhausted.*) Ah, what do I care now?!

DORA. But don't you understand: he deceived you.

LENA. He loves me.

DORA. And you, him?

LENA. (*Doesn't answer.*)

DORA. If you loved him, there would be no need to hold you here in constant fear of a war that's over, you could remain of your own free will, because of your love, nobody would force you to leave him. Do you understand? (*Silence.*)

DORA. How old are you?

LENA. Nineteen . . . and a half . . .

DORA. And a half? (*Dora and Sand exchange glances.*)

LENA. It's not his fault . . . I told him the truth. Yes, yes! I said that when the war was over, I'd go away. Maybe I shouldn't have told him that, but I dreamed, oh I dreamed all the time, that I would be able to walk outside, free as a bird, in the sun, in the open air . . . to go and walk, when the war was over . . .

DORA. Well, the war *is* over. You're free. You can go anywhere and do whatever you like.

LENA. No.

DORA. Why?

LENA. When you dream it's different. He used to say that the war would never come to an end. That one day they'd discover us and kill us. He wanted us both to die on the same day, together. And I wanted to live. He said, that the Fourth Kingdom would come after death—the Fourth Kingdom! Do you know what that is?

SAND. Have you become a Christian?

LENA. No. The Count says, there's no difference between Jew and Christian. He says it's not important. He believes only in the Fourth Kingdom.

SAND. What is that?

LENA. The Fourth Kingdom? (*Sand nods.*) There will be no living and dead there, no young and old. There will be great love there and eternal glory, and he that overcometh shall not be hurt of the second death . . . and everything will be as it once was, only different! Oh, I don't know. . . . In my heart I wanted a simple life, like the one I once had. Yes, just an ordinary life. But now . . . everything was a lie. I don't want anything.

DORA. Now you can leave this place.

LENA. Where will I go? To whom? They murdered father and mother and the children. He's the only one in the whole world who loves me. (*Passionately.*) His love made him deceive me! He really loves me! I knew it, I knew it even before he told me. I pitied him so much. I told him first that I loved him . . . sitting there by myself in the secret room—and the windows shut all the time, and you can't even peek outside. He was so wonderful to me and so unhappy . . . and everything together. . . . I never saw people like that before. . . . Ah, it's not that, I don't know, maybe I deceived him. Yes, of course, I deceived him even more, I didn't tell him the truth, not about loving him, I don't know about that, but the other thing . . . yes, yes, I never told him that if we'd have to die I wouldn't die like him, I wouldn't let them torture me, I never told him that I have . . . (*Suddenly, her hand grips the black ribbon around her throat; she stops short.*) Ah, what am I saying! What do you want from me? It doesn't matter.

DORA. But how did you live here all the time?

LENA. At night, when there was no danger, he used to wind up the clock, always at ten, and I would come out to him. I would be the Lady of the Castle. He looked after me as if I were a small daughter. He read lovely books with me, and taught me things I never learned in school. Much more beautiful than what they teach in school. Sometimes he would read about the Revelation, about the end of the world and the Resurrection. . . . And he used to sit with me in the music room. . . . Have you been there?

SAND. Yes.

LENA. . . . and play for me. He plays like an angel. He plays Chopin for me.

DORA. (*Mockingly.*) Chopin! Just what I thought!

LENA. No, no. You mustn't talk that way about him. He plays like an angel . . . ah, you don't know. Sometimes, when I wasn't afraid . . . when the Nazis would go for a long time . . . that is . . . well, yes, when he said that the Nazis were gone, we would even dance a little. (*To Dora.*) Do you waltz?

DORA. Then you want to stay on here. To waltz, to be the Lady of the Castle at night, and during the day, during the day he isn't even the owner any more. They confiscated it and nationalized it, and now he, your Count, is only the caretaker of the castle, you should know that. And you want to listen to Chopin, read books about the end of the world, be bound to a man who deceived you . . . to live with him until he dies and rots, then what?

LENA. I don't know. I don't want to live that way. I don't want to live at all any more. . . . I want to die. Why did you come here? Who asked you to come?

DORA. We're here, and we're going to help you leave this place. You'll come with us to Palestine. You'll join a group your own age. You'll live, work, you'll be healthy, free, and happy, like other young people.

LENA. No.

SAND. You still don't believe us?

LENA. I believe you. But . . . what's the good of it? I'm already . . . what will I do there with young people? I'm impure!

DORA. (*Looks at Sand. To Lena.*) You know, in this war, lots of young girls had much more horrible experiences.

LENA. I don't know anything about other girls. I'm impure!

DORA. (*To Sand.*) Well, what do you say to that?

SAND. (*Begins laughing, good naturedly, but both women look at him almost in fright.*) Well, what can you do about it? All young girls like to use such pretty words. My little niece, on her fifth birthday, announced to me, with great jubilation, just like Lena did now: "Uncle Mike, you know, I'm now a woman with a past!"

LENA. (*Laughs.*)

SAND. So, you see, you'll find there another woman with a past. And believe me . . . (*Lena's laughter turns into crying.*)

SAND. You're crying? Good, cry it out. It'll do you good. (*She calms down slowly.*) That's enough. You've cried, and that's that. Give me your hand, lady with a past. You're not mad at me? (*He extends his hand and she touches it hesitantly.*) No. Not this way. A good squeeze. That's right! That's good, isn't it?

LENA. (*Smiling through her tears.*) Yes.

DORA. (*Patting her head.*) Here . . . you're smiling. That's nice. And now, calm down, dear, calm down . . . (*As she talks and pats Lena's head, Dora notices an amulet hanging from the black velvet ribbon around her neck.*)

DORA. (*Panicky, holding on to the amulet.*) And what is this?

LENA. This . . . nothing at all. It's an amulet my mother gave me.

DORA. (*Without letting go.*) No. You tell me what this is.

LENA. Leave me alone! I told you: an amulet. Against the evil eye. My mother gave it to me when I was a child.

DORA. You give that to me right now, do you hear?! (*To Sand.*) Do you know what she has there? Poison! They used to keep it in amulets like this: Jews who succeeded in getting poison. Much good it did them: The Nazis usually found it right away when they searched for valuables. But there were those who managed to swallow it when they had no choice . . . in those days it was . . . yes! but now you don't need it. Do you hear?

LENA. (*Doesn't answer.*)

DORA. You give that to me right now! But right this very minute without another word! Do you hear?

LENA. My God! What do you want from me? I won't give it to you! I won't. . . . It was the only thing I had left. Mother gave it to me, mother said that maybe I'd need it. . . . This was my secret . . . even the Count didn't know. I deceived him! Yes. Yes. Yes!!! I deceived him. I've already told you that. He didn't know that if the Nazis came to kill us, I wouldn't die at their hands, like him. I . . . I didn't want them to abuse me . . . I didn't want them to torture me. And I had a way out . . . only for me and not for him. . . . I didn't tell him. . . . Ah, I didn't tell him, not only because of the Nazis. Sometimes I thought I wouldn't be able to bear this life any longer and then . . . ah, what am I telling you? . . . Now you come . . .

DORA. But understand, Lena, try to understand. Now it's all over. Now you don't need it any more, you don't need it at all.

LENA. (*Doesn't answer.*)

DORA. (*To Sand.*) Maybe you'll . . .

SAND. (*Who has walked away a bit, comes closer to Lena.*)

LENA. (*Kneeling.*) Don't take it from me! No! Please! Don't take it.

DORA. Hush . . . he'll hear you . . .

LENA. (*In a lower voice; she's used to controlling her voice under stress.*) No! Don't take it! Don't take it!

SAND. (*Closing in.*) Lena!

LENA. I won't give it up! It's mine. Mother gave this to me. It's the last thing. The last way out . . .

SAND. But Lena . . .

LENA. No, no, no! I won't give it to you. . . . You're strong . . . you can take it by force . . . but you'd better kill me! . . .

SAND. I won't take anything from you by force. But you'll give it to me yourself. Of your own free will. Right now!

LENA. I won't give it. No!! You come and take everything. You take my life and the Count and everything I had. . . . You take away my freedom, to live or to die . . . you . . .

SAND. But understand . . . (*Suddenly changes his mind.*) You're right, Lena. (*To Dora, who motions to him that he should trick Lena and take away the poison.*) No, leave her alone . . . (*To Lena.*) We meant to help you, Lena. But . . . calm down, come sit here. . . . From now on nobody will take anything from you by force. You're absolutely free. You're free even to die, if you choose death. To live or to die, any time *you* make the choice. (*Tries to help her up, but she avoids him.*) Don't you believe me? There are no tricks here, Lena. I swear to you by everything that's holy to me. We won't take anything away from you, we won't force you to do anything against your will. I swear to you! Now, get up! (*Lifts her up carefully; completely spent, she lets him seat her.*)

DORA. In the end, Lena, you'll see that you, yourself, will give us the poison. Now, you want to live, to live and not to die. You still have no idea how much you want to live. . . . But you want to, don't you?

LENA. I don't know.

DORA. You must want *life*, you must want it very badly, and then . . .

LENA. What then? What good is it? I don't have anybody in the world. No one at all. There was the Count, but now . . . I don't have a living soul in the whole world.

DORA. How can you be so sure?

LENA. I know. I know they took father and mother and the children . . .

DORA. That was your entire family?

LENA. There were others . . . but what's the use, they're probably all dead. I have no one.

DORA. What's your last name, Lena? (*Lena is silent.*)

DORA. I asked you what your last name was?

LENA. (*Bursting out.*) Oh, what a fool I am, what a fool! You sit there and get all the information out of me! You want to know everything, all their names, and how it happened, and everything! Why did I open my mouth! Why did I trust you? Why did I believe all your lies? Now I know that the Nazis sent you. I've told you everything about me and the Count . . . and now only this last detail is missing, maybe somebody is still alive, that's what you want to know!

SAND. But you know very well that now you're talking nonsense. You've gone through the newspaper!

LENA. Newspaper! How do I know your newspaper isn't forged?! Why is all this going on without the Count? Why should I believe you more than him? I've known him for three years, he's been good to me, he saved me! He hates the Nazis! And you . . . who are you?! Where's the Count? Where is he right now? Tell me, why don't you answer?

SAND. I've already told you, he's downstairs, in his room.

LENA. Yes, you told me! And fool that I am, I believed you! But you've already taken him! You've handed him over to the Nazis! They're torturing him. Maybe they've murdered him? . . .

SAND. You can go down and see for yourself if he's there.

LENA. (*As if threatening them.*) I will. I'll go down and call him.

DORA. Go right ahead, you're free to do whatever you please.

Lena. That's what you say!

DORA. Well, find out. Go and call him. Why aren't you going? (*A taut silence. After great hesitation, Lena rises and goes to right door. She exits. Pause.*)

DORA. There you are. She's really gone!

SAND. Very good.

DORA. What's so "very good"?

SAND. Very good that she's decided to do something. You know yourself that it was necessary!

DORA. Oh, please! She's gone down these steps, with the poison! What will become of her?! Go, call her!

SAND. I will not. Let her do what she pleases.

DORA. But she . . . with the poison . . .

SAND. Nothing's going to happen. She really wants to live now more than she knows.

DORA. Oh, you're so sure of yourself! And now she'll really call him! That criminal!

SAND. Oh, now he's a criminal!

DORA. Well, isn't he? Or is this part of that refined culture that charms you out of your wits? Huh? That wonderful tradition! That noble class of delicate souls! Now you see how harmless they are, there's no need to argue with them any more! Ah!

SAND. There's no need to argue about abstractions, and in general, my dear, you exaggerate!

DORA. How am I exaggerating? Tell me how! Didn't you see what he did to her, to this poor girl? Ah! Last week I had a similar case with a Father Superior and a boy! But I could still understand that. . . . When people want to continue educating a child in their religion . . . or when a family that adopted children becomes attached to them . . . but this!

SAND. This you can't understand?

DORA. I can't and I don't want to!

SAND. The main thing is you don't want to. A man whose world has fallen to pieces! A man who fought with courage and devotion for a world that isn't his. And then he found something in this world, one human being that he could love. . . . All right, I'm not justifying what he did, just as I don't justify your Father Superior. But I can understand, and I *want* to understand, his weakness. Don't you see, it's not just an ordinary erotic relationship, the love of an old man for a young girl; this is the straw he's clinging to in an imaginary world, which is dearer to him than anything else! Why she, she's not an ordinary girl for him, she's the Lady of the Castle!

DORA. Lady of the Castle! The devil take all your philosophy! I'm only capable of seeing things the way they are, and that's how I want to see them . . . and that's the way they really are, yes! Ah, I'm getting all mixed up myself, this, this is such a, it's not real . . .

SAND. It is real, Dora. Reality has many faces, some of which are very strange . . .

DORA. But she'll call him! She'll call him now. That horrible man . . . and the whole thing will start all over again. You don't . . . but I . . . I'm afraid of him!

SAND. In any event, we can't avoid meeting him. We all have to leave this place and he has the keys.

DORA. We'll have to find another way out.

SAND. There is no other way.

DORA. Maybe there's an exit from her room?

SAND. I don't imagine he left her a way out of here!

DORA. There you are! And after all this you say he's not a criminal!

SAND. After all this, I think he's the most unfortunate man I've met in all these years!

DORA. Ah, I don't care about that! I want to save Lena. And I don't want to see him. . . . She won't dare leave if he's here.

SAND. Then we may have to leave her here for a while until she decides to go of her own free will.

DORA. Leave her here?! In this house? With that old man? And the poison? Ah, what . . . (*Listens attentively.*) There, there, there! Do you hear?

SAND. I don't hear anything. What's come over you?

DORA. Quiet! He's coming!

SAND. But she just went to call him . . .

DORA. (*Without paying attention to him.*) I can't stand it . . . I hear steps!

SAND. (*Listening.*) There are no steps, Dora. You're imagining things.

DORA. Imagining? Yes, maybe . . . maybe you're right. You're probably right. I think this whole business was inconceivable from the very beginning. . . . How can it be? . . . A girl suddenly steps out of a wall at night! And this castle! And this man . . . I'm almost prepared to swear that I'm imagining things. That all this is a dream . . . that there's been nobody here besides us. . . . What a silence. Why, it's all impossible. Things like this happen only in dreams . . . in bad dreams. . . . Look . . . listen! Do you really hear my voice? Was she really here?

SAND. Take it easy, Dora. What a sad business . . .

DORA. No. Was she really here?

SAND. But I saw her, too . . .

DORA. Yes, yes, I know. I'm tired . . . and it's all so strange. Was she really here? (*The door opens and Lena comes in.*)

SAND. Here she is.

DORA. (*Stares blankly, as if shaking off a dream.*)

SAND. (*To Lena.*) Did you call him?

LENA. No.

DORA. Isn't he there?

LENA. I don't know . . . I . . . I went out of here . . . and then I started going down the steps. I've never been below . . . because there . . . I've never been there at all . . . only the first night, when he brought me in. I'm afraid to go down there. I can't.

DORA. (*Strengthened, making an effort.*) Maybe you want me to go down with you? You'll see, there's nothing to be afraid of.

LENA. No . . . no. I don't want to call him. I stood on the steps. I stood there and thought. Now I know: I'm not afraid of being with you. It was silly, what I said to you. I believe you.

DORA. That's wonderful, Lena. Is there anything you want?

LENA. I don't know. I don't want anything. Only talk to me some more. I haven't talked to anybody for so many years . . . except for the Count. You asked me something before, didn't you? What was it?

DORA. I asked for your last name. But if you don't want to, you don't have to answer.

LENA. My last name is Brabant.

SAND. What a strange name!

DORA. It's a name that sticks in your memory.

LENA. Memory! Now we have to remember everything. There's nothing left in the world except our memory. And we're just tombstones. That's what the Count says . . . but don't call him!

DORA. (*As if she hadn't heard her.*) Tell me, Lena Brabant, I remember this name very well. Your parents had a jewelry shop near the museum.

LENA. Yes! You know that?

DORA. I grew up here. Most of the Jews here more or less knew each other.

LENA. And then you went to Palestine.

DORA. Yes.

LENA. (*Bitterly.*) You had an easy time of it, you were safe! You weren't persecuted, killed, tortured, what do you know about us! (*Sand wants to reply, but Dora silences him with a gesture.*)

DORA. Was there a woman in your family by the name of Lisa Brabant?

LENA. Yes. My aunt. My father's younger sister.

DORA. We went to school together. Many years ago. Then she married a doctor. Sherman was his name, wasn't it?

LENA. Yes. Why are you talking about them? They're probably all dead.

DORA. No, Lisa is alive. Back home. In Palestine. Her husband and my husband work in the same hospital. Even Sand knows her. Sand you know Lisa Sherman, right?

SAND. Yes.

LENA. (*As if figuring out something.*) You might see her sometime?

SAND. Yes. I'll surely see her when we get back.

LENA. Then, please, please tell her, that I sang the song. I sang and that helped me.

SAND. What song?

LENA. She'll know . . . (*To Dora.*) You went to school with her? Maybe you know the song, too?

DORA. What song?

LENA. Ah, I keep on talking this way and you . . . you don't understand what I mean. But I can explain everything. I'm completely sane. It's this way. When I was little I used to be afraid of the dark. And then Aunt Lisa taught me a song. Just a children's song. She said, that when you sing it in the dark, the fear goes away. And best of all, is to sing the song while walking. It's a simple children's song, you know, you probably heard it, too. It goes like this: (*Begins to walk the room and sing, as children do.*)

> Rooster, rooster,
> Your comb so fine,
> Cry out, cry out,
> The sun will shine
> Cry out, cry out
> And that Lord of mine
> Will chase away the dark
> And the sun will shine.

You know this song?

DORA. Yes, we sang it when we were children.

LENA. Lisa taught me to sing it. And I, that night, when I ran away to the forest, I was no longer a child, but it was such a horror! I don't know how to pray . . . I ran by myself in the night, in the dark, it's a good thing it was dark, because in the light it's easier to find those who run away. . . . But I was afraid not only of the Nazis but also of the dark; and so I ran all by myself in the forest and sang in a low voice: rooster, rooster, with your comb so fine . . . and that helped me a bit . . . (*To Sand.*) When you see Aunt Lisa, tell her I'm thankful for the song.

SAND. I will.

DORA. You'll tell her this whole story yourself.

LENA. How do you mean?

DORA. Well, I've told you that Lisa is in Palestine. You'll come there with me. You'll go over to Lisa and tell her everything yourself.

LENA. Me?

DORA. Of course! I told you . . .

LENA. (*To Sand.*) You'll tell her. And if you don't feel like it, don't tell her. I don't care. They got away, they're alive there! And I was here, I could have died, I could have been murdered, what do they care? . . .

DORA. But how do you know? Maybe they looked for you? Who could have guessed that you're still alive? After looking in vain for a long time, she was probably sure that you'd been killed with your family.

LENA. (*To Sand.*) She looked for me? She asked about me? She did something? You tell me. You. You always tell the truth. I know!

SAND. I don't know. I don't know her very well. We always spoke very little, and about other things.

LENA. Other things! They didn't even try to find me. But they're right, they're right. . . . Why look for me! The Count, he knows, he said we're already dead anyhow, that no one dies twice. And to come to life in the world of those who haven't even died once, that we can't do!

DORA. What has this man done to you! He's dead, he's a corpse. That's the truth. He belongs to the world of the dead. But you, a young, healthy, lovely girl—life is still ahead of you. How many times have I seen people who went through worse horrors, who were sick, broken, wounded, dehumanized. And you should come with me if only to see them now. With what happiness, with what lust for happiness they've begun to live again like human beings. And they really had no one in the world, not a living soul, but at your age it's not so difficult to start again. If you only saw them . . .

LENA. Maybe the others can, I can't. No. Maybe the others don't know what I know.

DORA. What do you know?

LENA. (*Suddenly as if in a dream.*) I know, that I was really dead. I know that I have no way back to the living. Only he who was faithful unto death was given the crown of life. I know that physical death is only a stage, a gateway to the Fourth Kingdom!

SAND. Again the Fourth Kingdom!

LENA. "In the Fourth Kingdom there are no dead and no living. No young and no old. He who has overcome death while alive, shall enter the Fourth Kingdom. And he that overcometh shall not be hurt of the second death" . . .

DORA. Do you really believe this?

LENA. (*Pensive, as if coming out of a dream, trying to answer honestly.*) Sometimes yes, sometimes no. When I dreamed of life by myself, secretly, without knowing then I dreamed otherwise. Then I didn't believe. But when there was no more hope, when I knew I would die, when I knew that one way or the other, it was sure death, then the Count gave me this dream. And this was my own dream. I dreamed it when hope was gone . . . and I believed. . . . Why did you come here? This was the last dream!

SAND. But that was a dream of hopelessness, Lena. Now you have more than hope. You have life itself.

LENA. But I love my dreams.

DORA. And do you think that people who are alive and free have no dreams? Do you think that in our world, his and mine, people don't dream? Before you came here, didn't you have dreams you loved?

LENA. Then . . . yes . . . but everything was different then . . .

DORA. Right, and now everything will be different again. . . . It may not be so easy in the beginning, Lena, it may not be so simple, but . . . . Do you still remember something of your life before you came here? Didn't you yourself say that you wanted to walk freely outside? Do you remember what that is, how it felt?

LENA. I think . . . I do . . . to walk outside . . .

DORA. But to walk outside you've got to leave this place. First of all, you've got to get out of here.

LENA. Yes . . . to get out of here . . .

DORA. And to do some other very simple things, that everybody does, but you've already forgotten how they're done.

LENA. What?

DORA. Well, for instance, to work, to meet people, or . . . here, you can't walk in town in these shoes. You're used to having everything brought to you, done for you. But tomorrow, when we leave this place, you'll have to go into a shop and buy shoes.

LENA. But I have no money!

DORA. Here, you see! That will also be one of the problems later on. But in the meantime we'll give you . . . and then, we'll have to take care of that, too.

LENA. (*Looks at Dora's shoes.*) That's what they wear now?

DORA. Yes . . .

LENA. You bought them?

DORA (*Laughing.*) Naturally!

LENA. You simply stepped into a store and said, "Give me a pair of shoes" and picked them out?

DORA. One night last week, I was taking a walk and I passed a shop window . . .

LENA. At night?! In a shop window?!

DORA. Yes . . .

LENA. At night, in the street?!

DORA. Yes. What's so surprising?

LENA. The windows are lit up? There's light in the streets at night? And lamps? You're allowed to switch them on?

DORA. Yes, yes, of course!

LENA. In a lighted street . . . I've forgotten. It's been so long. . . . And during the day?

DORA. What, during the day?

LENA. I haven't seen the sun . . . nor the moon. Not even the moon all these years . . . only a bit, in this window . . . here . . . but it was closed.

DORA. You see! Such simple things! That everybody takes for granted! And you'll see them; the sun, the shop windows, and the moon. You can even see the moon right now, is the moon out tonight, Sand?

SAND. Yes.

DORA. All we have to do is open the window . . .

LENA. No . . . and in the daytime—lots of people walk in the streets?

DORA. Yes, Lena, the streets are packed with people. They leave their homes, go to restaurants, just walk around. . . . Do you want to walk in the street, in the sun?

LENA. Yes, and when the rain comes down. . . . (*Suddenly.*) But I don't want to see them always! No, I don't want to see them. Always the same . . .

DORA. See who?

LENA. Those who were here before. . . . They knew father and mother. They let them be killed. I know, they walk the streets, all of them, even our neighbors, I don't want to!

DORA. But you won't see them. We'll go far away from here. We won't stay in this country.

LENA. Ah, yes, yes . . . I forgot. (*To Sand.*) Far away, yes, and never—you'll take me away from here? Won't you?

SAND. Yes, Lena.

LENA. And the Count?

DORA. What about the Count?

LENA. He'll stay on here? Always by himself? Always closed up?

DORA. But understand, Lena! He wasn't closed up here all these years! *He* went outside, breathed the fresh air, walked the streets. He only told *you* that it's forbidden to go out and see the sun.

LENA. There, I know, there's lots of light and sun. I want to go out. I want so much to go out!

DORA. Well, then . . .

LENA. But the Count, he'll stay here.

DORA. Again the Count!

LENA. Again, again, again! Don't look at me that way! You don't know. (*Points at Sand.*) He knows . . . I don't know why, but he knows!! Ah, when we were locked up here, and death surrounded us. Death! No. I don't love him, don't look at me that way!! Maybe I . . . he was the only living soul! I want to go, but I can't, I can't.

SAND. Lena, listen, I'll tell you something, something that can't be put into words. I know it's hard for you. I know you're sorry for the Count. And you're right, I do understand. I'm also sorry for him. Very sorry. But you've got to go. You understand, you mustn't stay here! I can't explain it. But you know that you've got to go. You must live. You must live free, without him. What went on here is finished. You understand, Lena?

LENA. Yes, yes, I understand. I, I want to go somewhere else, to another country, far away . . . and not come back . . . ever . . .

DORA. Then you're coming with us! And the best thing would be to leave right away. (*In a practical tone.*) But you can't go like this. Do you have any clothes down in your room?

LENA. (*Mechanically; her thoughts are elsewhere.*) Yes.

DORA. Could you go down quickly and get dressed?

LENA. (*Doesn't answer.*)

DORA. Hurry up, Lena, hurry up and get dressed!

LENA. (*Unhesitatingly.*) I'm staying here.

(*Silence. After a long pause, the cuckoo pops out of the clock. Eleven. Immediately after this Zabrodsky bursts into the room.*)

CURTAIN

ACT III

The curtain rises on the same scene: Zabrodsky standing at some distance from Lena.

ZABRODSKY. (*To Lena.*) Well, the war is over, Lena.

DORA. It was over two years ago.

ZABRODSKY. The war is over, Lena. You are free, you can leave.

DORA. The war has been over for more than two years. Two years of lost freedom! If you hadn't . . .

ZABRODSKY. Do you hear, Lena, you could have been free two years ago, even more than two years ago. You could have been living in this earthly paradise of theirs. You could have wandered with refugee convoys, looked for work, struggled with hunger, filth, ugliness until you dropped. . . . And instead, you were held captive here, you wasted the best years of your life on an old man . . .

DORA. Who deceived you for two years.

ZABRODSKY. (*Now almost out of his mind.*) Who deceived you for two years. The others do it much more quickly. They are known as honest people. They come to your house under false pretenses, tell you a story about a search for books, spy on you, wind up the clock and deceive two people . . .

SAND. We didn't spy on you, we knew nothing about your secrets. I just happened to wind up the clock . . .

DORA. He'll soon say we also engineered the storm . . .

SAND. Mr. Zabrodsky, I don't know what you've been through, don't know what made you do such a thing, I'm trying to understand . . .

ZABRODSKY. (*Disdainfully.*) My good sir! Don't bother! We shall never understand each other. (*To Lena.*) Well, Lena, you are free to do as you wish. You may even help them hand me over to the police, you may testify against me. . . . After all, if it was not for me . . .

LENA. (*Keeps quiet.*)

SAND. (*With sudden understanding.*) You know very well, Count, that she won't do that. You saved her life. . . . Only let her leave in peace.

ZABRODSKY. Do you hear that, Lena? Such exemplary generosity! You may leave in peace, Lena.

DORA. What's all this talking about, all these fine phrases and plots? She has eyes to see!

LENA. (*Keeps quiet.*)

ZABRODSKY. She has eyes to see. . . . Surely, you see what I have done to you! Why are you silent? Tell them, *you* tell them everything you have against me . . . (*burying his face in his hands*) . . . for if I should tell them, who would believe me? If I should tell the true story of my life, if I should say that I have never deceived anyone (*now, without sensing it, he turns to Sand*) that I have never violated the honor of a woman, that it has never even occurred to me to seduce a girl, that I have never done a dishonest deed. . . . Yes! Who would believe me? Who would believe me that when I saw this poor creature running and stumbling in the forest, I did not for one moment think of myself? When I brought her in, carrying her in my arms, the castle was full of armed Nazis? Who would believe that in those days I did not even take a good look at her face because I was afraid to put on the light even in the secret room?! And all those days, guarding her here like a precious stone, I had no idea what she looked like, I neither had the time nor the inclination to wonder whether she was beautiful or not? And who, who would believe me, an old man, already half-dead, that this began, and it was not only my doing . . . I was not alone in this? . . .

LENA. (*Nods her head yes. Silence.*)

ZABRODSKY. And this began while they were still here in the house, and this meant everything to me, everything, everything . . . and afterwards. . . . If I have wronged you, Lena, I must answer to God, only He shall judge me. . . . (*To Sand.*) Do you know what that is, an old man's fear of losing everything? . . .

SAND. I understand, Count, . . . but still . . .

ZABRODSKY. (*Suddenly grasps that he's been talking to Sand.*) Ah! (*Dryly.*) I am very sorry. . . . All this is not to the point. It never occurred to me that I might—(*Cuts himself short.*)

SAND. That you might lower yourself to talking to people like me about yourself?

ZABRODSKY. You have said it, sir. Yes.

DORA. (*Rises.*) Mr. Zabrodsky, right now we're not at all interested in your life history, in analyzing your intimate world. And we don't care what you feel toward us, whether you think talking to us is beneath you or not. We don't care whether or not you excuse yourself. We're not a court of justice. We only care about one thing: that this girl should begin living again the normal life of girls her age, that she should forget all the terrible things that happened to her. You saved her life, now she *knows* . . . and she's got to decide whether she'll choose a free, decent life, without fear and deceit or— She'll decide. And that's the only reason we're still talking to you.

LENA. (*Is silent.*)

ZABRODSKY. (*Who hasn't even glanced at Dora as she spoke.*) I know you have already made your decision, Lena. You always told me you would leave the day the war came to an end. Well, for you it has come to an end tonight.

LENA. (*Still silent.*)

ZABRODSKY. Would you like me to beg your forgiveness? I will not. I shall beg pardon and forgiveness in another court. And as for you, I know very well. Either you will curse me for the rest of your life, and then—of what use is forgiveness?! Or else you will curse *them,* after you see what they offer you there, in their free, beautiful world, in their decent, proper world, with their liberty, the liberty of ruling slaves. But now you must go to this world.

LENA. (*Still silent.*)

SAND. We'll give you time to consider everything, Lena, and decide for yourself.

DORA. Nobody can hold you here . . . (*Pause.*)

LENA. I'm staying here. (*To Zabrodsky.*) With you . . .

ZABRODSKY. (*Elated, but immediately rises and speaks as if harboring a great pain.*) No. It is all over. It is finished. You will not remain here with me.

LENA. I want to stay.

DORA. Lena, listen . . .

ZABRODSKY. What will you do here now? Will you be the wife or mistress of the caretaker? Will you sell tickets to tourists who come here, to this *museum?* They, these two, have destroyed everything. It cannot be undone. You are not the Lady of the Castle because I am not the Lord. This is the end.

LENA. Why are you torturing me? All of you! (*Makes a gesture of desperation.*)

ZABRODSKY. Lena, understand, I want you to understand . . .

DORA. Mr. Zabrodsky, we all want her to understand . . .

SAND. Lena, you . . .

ZABRODSKY. Lena, I wanted to tell you . . .

SAND. Mr. Zabrodsky, wouldn't it be better to leave her alone just now and let her think and decide? After all, she's got to know what she's doing. Isn't that right, Lena?

LENA. (*Doesn't answer. It is obvious that she is engrossed in some private thoughts; she is undergoing a complex spiritual experience which none of the others can share.*)

DORA. (*To Zabrodsky.*) Why, when you say to her "Go," it's clear to her and to us, too, that you're trying to hold on to her with all your might . . .

LENA. (*Suddenly.*) And with this telephone you can reach the city? (*Short pause.*)

ZABRODSKY. Yes . . .

LENA. You can talk with people?

ZABRODSKY. Yes . . .

LENA. You can talk to—let's say—the capital?

ZABRODSKY. Yes, Lena, but . . .

DORA. You want to call somebody up? Come . . .

LENA. No. (*Shrugs her shoulders.*) No. Why?

DORA. Then why did you ask? Maybe you want me to call for you?

LENA. No. (*To Sand.*) I only wanted to know, if it's possible. Really . . . (*Lena sinks back into her thoughts, as if she were not the crux of the conflict.*)

ZABRODSKY. I did not want to hold you by force, Lena. I did not want to deceive you. But I did deceive you. . . . I held you by force. . . . I knew, that one day it would all be destroyed. . . . But what there was, Lena . . . I wanted to guard for you, for us, this world which only the two of us knew . . . and then I . . .

DORA. Sir, why don't you let her think and decide?! You're still preoccupied with yourself! Even now you're not thinking about her . . .

ZABRODSKY. There was a world, Lena, in which the two of us, only the two of us lived . . .

LENA. (*As if coming out of a dream, yet still dreaming.*) And you used to open the windows?

ZABRODSKY. Which windows?

LENA. This window—here!

ZABRODSKY. This one?

LENA. Yes . . . here. This one!

ZABRODSKY. I, sometimes, during the day, yes . . .

LENA. And at night?

ZABRODSKY. No, at night I didn't open it, all these years . . .

LENA. But are you allowed to, are you allowed to open the window at night, are you?

ZABRODSKY. Yes.

LENA. (*Rises and advances to the window as if pulled by an unseen force. Draws the heavy curtain aside and looks outside. Then she turns out the lights. Moonlight.*)

DORA AND SAND. What are you doing?

LENA. (*Ignores them. Returns to the window and opens it wide. The room is inundated by moonlight. Lena raises herself up to the window sill. All move toward her, fearing she might throw herself out the window. But she only leans out and utters a cry, as if calling someone in the garden or in the big forest. They look at her, amazed. Bathed in moonlight—she seems to be a vision. She settles herself on the window sill and speaks to them and to herself.*) Such a moonlit night . . . there, the moon's outside. And there's no war! You're allowed to shout, listen! (*Shouts again to the garden.*) How many years! How many years have I dreamed of being allowed to . . . please, come, you shout too, talk out loud! It's permitted now, there are no Nazis, nobody will come to kill us. . . . (*For an instant, she looks at her hand in the moonlight, examines it, shakes the fingers.*) How lovely! No . . . maybe the dead have hands like these . . . (*Looks out again.*) This air! The garden is wet from the rain. Do you know what that is? It's the smell of the earth after rain! I haven't forgotten it . . . maybe it's the only thing I haven't forgotten . . . but that's it, now! It's a smell of . . . rotten leaves, yes! And mushrooms . . . the smell of mushrooms, yes! To run in the garden—barefoot. . . . I always dreamed that this moment would come and I would open the window and touch the leaves and the branches, and the drops would fall on my head from the roof and wet my hair. Just like now. (*Smooths her hair with her hand and laughs.*) That's it. And there's the garden and . . . (*Sings a short tune to the night.*) Once in the spring, you remember, Count, do you remember? I begged you so much, I so much wanted to smell the spring outside, I begged you. (*Suddenly to Dora and Sand, as if their presence was a matter of course.*) In my room, down there, there's no window at all. . . . I longed so much, for fresh air! I was very frightened . . . but I wanted so much to breathe this air! And you opened a small crack in the window, you put out the lights and opened a small crack. I thought I would go mad! That was happiness. . . . It was wonderful, Count, that you allowed me to open the window then . . . (*Suddenly jerked back to reality.*) But that was only a few months ago! The Nazis had gone by then, there was no . . . and if I had only known. I could have run in this garden. . . . I could have opened the window then, talked out loud, shouted, shouted, like tonight. . . . I could have done everything, anything . . . but, my God! Four months! Two years! Two and a half years! I want air, I want to run, to walk and walk . . . I want to. My God! (*Pauses, listens.*) It's quiet. There are no birds in the garden—after the storm, ah, why it's night . . . (*She slips down from the window sill. Passes them very quickly, very lightly. Goes over to the wall tapestry, presses something, and disappears behind the wall in silence. Only something like the creaking of a bolt is heard.*)

ZABRODSKY. (*The first to understand what happened, jumps to the secret door and beats on it with his fists.*) Lena!

DORA AND SAND. (*Screaming.*) Lena! Lena! (*No answer.*)

DORA. Lena! (*No answer.*) She locked the door from the inside.

SAND. And can't you open it?

ZABRODSKY. (*Suddenly calm.*) No.

SAND. Don't you have a key?

ZABRODSKY. No.

SAND. I'm sure the door can be opened, I'm sure.

ZABRODSKY. No . . .

SAND. Go and bring the key, if you don't have it here; why she's got poison, she has poison hidden in the amulet . . .

ZABRODSKY. Poison? Yes . . .

SAND. Poison, I tell you, don't you understand?!

ZABRODSKY. Poison . . . I know . . . God will judge us . . .

SAND. Maybe you'll stop thinking of yourself! Give me the key!

ZABRODSKY. I have no key, I've told you.

SAND. (*Grabs him tightly.*) Give me the key, give it to me right now. (*Applying pressure.*) Right now, I tell you!

ZABRODSKY. (*Twisting in pain.*) I don't have one . . . it won't open. Let go!

SAND. (*Releases him.*) But she'll die . . . there, now she'll kill herself.

ZABRODSKY. The dead do not die twice, you have heard . . .

SAND. Nonsense! Who knows what she's doing there now?!

ZABRODSKY. (*Sitting down in the armchair.*) Who?

SAND. Don't play the idiot. I tell you she's got poison, it's dangerous.

ZABRODSKY. Who are you talking about?

SAND. (*To Dora.*) Look, now he's going mad . . .

ZABRODSKY. I am not mad, sir. I ask you, whom are you talking about?

SAND. About Lena, for God's sake!

ZABRODSKY. Who?

SAND. The girl who was just here, half a minute ago.

ZABRODSKY. (*Calmly.*) There was no one here outside the three of us.

DORA. (*The tension and fatigue have overcome her and now she begins to lose her sense of reality.*) How is that, there was no one?

ZABRODSKY. No one was here. It's a dream you've dreamed, madam. Or are still dreaming? Only we were in this room. You, madam, Mr. Sand, and myself. The three of us. No one else.

DORA. But I saw her, I talked to her, I touched her. She was here, just a moment ago. (*Stares at him blankly.*) I touched her . . .

ZABRODSKY. (*Laughs.*) When you dream—the dream is tangible. She was not here. No one was here. You dreamed it.

SAND. But I didn't dream! (*Goes over to the wall tapestry; looks threateningly at Zabrodsky.*)

ZABRODSKY. Go ahead!

SAND. (*Raises the tapestry, exposing a white, smooth wall, which reveals nothing. He runs his hand over it again and again. There is not the slightest sign of a secret door.*) Strange!

ZABRODSKY. Strange, indeed. Very strange. You attack me. You speak of some key. You are both suffering from delusions. You can see for yourselves, no one was here. No one is here, it is inconceivable.

DORA. But . . . a moment ago that girl was here. Lena. She appeared when the clock struck. The clock with the cuckoo. She told us that she's been here in a secret room . . . for three years. She was . . . of course she was . . . here, the window's still open . . .

ZABRODSKY. Naturally. The moment I came in I saw you opening the window, madam!

DORA. Me?

ZABRODSKY. (*To Sand.*) You saw how madam went over to the window and opened it? And then she called out something into the garden.

DORA. Me?

SAND. I saw how Lena went over to the window and opened it, and shouted and sang and talked to the night. I saw it and heard it.

DORA. So did I.

ZABRODSKY. Yes, yes. This is a curious phenomenon. Two people sharing the same hallucination. It is strange, indeed. When I rushed in here, after hearing madam's scream, you were still talking about something. And then Mr. Sand attacked me and demanded some key. . . . Perhaps the castle is really haunted by ghosts.

SAND. Don't expect me to believe such fairy tales.

ZABRODSKY. You do not believe in such fairy tales, sir, but that a girl can step out of a wall without sign of a door, at the sound of a cuckoo, this you believe! That a girl can sit here captive for three years in peace time, this you believe! And you don't find this strange at all?

DORA. It's . . . Sand, what's going on here?

ZABRODSKY. Ah, what's going on here! Madam, I observed how tired you were tonight before we parted, and what a fright this castle gave you. You were overwrought earlier in the evening, and I can well imagine how the misery you have seen in your work, the pain you have witnessed, the twisted lives of all those children. . . . Yes, it's no simple matter, all this could easily give rise to delusions on a stormy night, in a house like this, which, moreover, has an owner who proclaims himself dead . . . perhaps my joke was not well taken, madam. . . . Please forgive me . . .

SAND. But I . . .

ZABRODSKY. And you, sir, have probably been certain until this very day that you see nothing but reality. . . . May I remind you of what you told me earlier in the evening: you were wounded during the war, and you are not yet fully recovered. Have you never seen such fantasies when you were delirious with fever?

SAND. Please, Mr. Zabrodsky, this is not the time to discuss our psychology.

ZABRODSKY. But what shall I discuss when before me stand two people who see ghosts where none are to be found? . . . This is the source of your delusion, in our conversations at the tea table, we spoke of this, madam. You asked me if the castle was haunted. And I said that it was. Then you informed me, madam, for you are very brave, that you are not afraid of them . . .

DORA. Yes . . .

ZABRODSKY. (*Emphatically.*) So you see, all this was a dream. I am not too well versed in psychology, but I remember having heard that sometimes two people share the very same delusion when subjected to the same stimuli, and not only two people, even much larger groups. . . . The Hindus, for example, know very well how such things happen. But calm yourselves, after all I am here now . . . I have dispelled the evil spirits. . . . Still, it is most interesting. How did it happen, actually?

DORA. (*Submitting completely.*) Sand wound the clock. The clock struck ten times. And then, Lena came out of the wall . . .

ZABRODSKY. Yes, that is exactly how you told it before. Out of the wall!

SAND. Not out of the wall. How you can twist words around. You know very well. She came out of a secret door that is under this tapestry.

ZABRODSKY. Secret doors exist only in novels for young ladies. . . . There is no secret door there. You have seen for yourself.

SAND. But it was there.

ZABRODSKY. Would you like to check again? (*Rises, goes up to the tapestry, raises it.*) Well! (*No door can be seen. Sand feels the surface again.*) There you have it! Such things are found only in novels in dreams. Lena was her name, you said?

DORA. Yes.

ZABRODSKY. (*Seats himself again in his place.*) Lena—a beautiful name. Yes. . . . I also dreamed a dream. (*Unwittingly he falls into a reverie.*) Lena was her name. One day she came to me, and with her my youth came back . . . the old days had returned . . . the nights were, it was as if the moon rose here, in the castle . . . the prophecy had come true: there were neither living nor dead, neither young nor old . . . the truth was in memories . . . and if one were to die suddenly, that would be the gateway to another reality, a fiercer reality . . . for reality was a dream. We all dreamed.

SAND. (*Harshly.*) We'll find out right away! (*Turns on the light. In the electric glare, everything becomes more real. Sand goes over to the table.*)

SAND. (*Very soberly.*) And now I'll tell you something, Count, this is where your real crime begins, beyond that secret door which can't be found . . . maybe we're already too late. But maybe you will hand over the key right now!

ZABRODSKY. I have no key . . .

DORA. (*Now completely alert; goes over to the telephone.*)

ZABRODSKY. (*As Dora tries, unsuccessfully, to put her call through.*) And do you think there is anything more terrible than what you have done to me? Do you think you will frighten me with the police? Do you think I wish her harm? She means a thousand times more to me than to you!

DORA. (*To the telephone.*) Hello! Hello! No answer, damn it! (*To Zabrodsky.*) We'll see! Hello!

ZABRODSKY. (*To Sand.*) The truth of the matter is, I have no key. . . . What could I have done? It closes in such a way that only the person inside can open it . . .

SAND. Why didn't you say that right away?

ZABRODSKY. I said it but you didn't listen . . .

SAND. But she has poison . . .

ZABRODSKY. (*Doesn't answer. Sinks back into his own thoughts, mumbles.*) "And he that overcometh shall not be hurt of the second death" . . .

DORA. (*By the telephone.*) That won't help you! Hello! Hello! (*At that very moment the secret door opens; as it opens slowly, we see that part of the bookcase serves as a door. Lena's dressed in clothes she wore the day she ran away from home. In this simple dress she looks even more childish than before, but the dreamlike quality is gone. She is simply a frightened young girl.*)

LENA. I changed my clothes. . . . I couldn't have gone that way . . . (*To Dora and Sand.*) Will you take me with you?

DORA. (*Hangs up.*) Well! (*Regaining her confident, professional manner.*) What sort of question is that?!

LENA. I can't stand it any more. . . . I want fresh air, outside.

DORA. Do you have any more belongings?

LENA. No. This is the way I came here.

DORA. (*To Sand.*) Do you have a blanket in the car? Now that the storm is over, we can go?

SAND. (*Silently looks at Zabrodsky, at Lena, it is obvious that he finds it difficult to adjust to this practical tone.*) Yes . . . we can . . . if we have enough . . .

DORA. We'll fill up at the nearest open gas station. (*To Lena.*) I'll just collect my things in the room. (*To Sand.*) You . . . your books are already packed up downstairs. . . . (*To Lena.*) We'll leave right away. I'll explain everything to you on the way. (*Goes to her room.*)

LENA. (*Goes over to Sand. Stands by him as if seeking shelter and protection. Says apologetically.*) I opened the window . . . and then . . . I want to breathe fresh air outside . . .

SAND. You'll soon breathe fresh air, Lena, and now . . . Would you like me to step out for a moment?

LENA. (*In a fright.*) No, no!

ZABRODSKY. (*Looks at her.*) I won't stop you. (*To Sand, who makes a motion as if to leave.*) Please stay, sir! The two of us, she and I, have nothing more to say to each other. It is over for us! All dreams come to an end with the awakening. (*Lena, without looking at him, moves almost imperceptibly toward him.*) You need not give me your hand, I am not even sure I could feel it. You were, and you are no longer. I was and I no longer am.

LENA. (*Looks questioningly at Sand. He makes an encouraging gesture. To Zabrodsky, with great effort.*) Count . . .

ZABRODSKY. No. There is no need, Lena. You must go this way. You must forget everything if you wish to live there . . . in their world.

SAND. (*Takes Lena's hand.*) She'll live there.

ZABRODSKY. Evidently, that is the only world that is now real. A reality of the wide-awake, the open-eyed. You have chosen it, and you must accept your choice. Dreams must be banished from the heart.

LENA. (*Again looks imploringly to Sand.*)

SAND. Dreams that have ended, vanish of themselves. . . . But not all dreams end with the awakening. In the world of the wide-awake there are dreams, many dreams. Only they're dreamed differently . . . (*Sees her looking at the window.*) Yes, there, in the garden. There are trees. There are more gardens and trees. You know, maybe you still remember, you can lie under a tree, watch the sky through the branches . . . yes . . . and perhaps there's wind . . . it doesn't matter. You're very tired. You lie stretched out, with your hands under your head . . . and daydream . . . open-eyed . . . the wide-awake dream in the light . . .

ZABRODSKY. So they think! They believe in all honesty that they really are dreaming! I am a great sinner, Lena, I have sinned against you out of weakness. But *I* gave you a true dream! The dream was true, and if there was something false in it . . . who was the one who lied, Lena?

LENA. (*Holds the amulet lace around her throat.*)

ZABRODSKY. Ah, you thought you were deceiving me? I knew. You carried your death with you always without telling me. But I knew. . . . I said nothing, Lena, because each of us is entitled to a refuge from his fellow man . . .

SAND. But this refuge was death!

ZABRODSKY. Death. Both of us, you and I, Lena, knew so much about death, that this bit of poison faded to insignificance in all the real death that surrounded us. This you learned here. And now . . .

SAND. And now she'll learn something about life. Not everything, not all at once. In these years all of us learned something about death. We learned . . . yes . . . that death can sometimes be known in an instant. But to know life, you must learn a great deal, little by little, not without difficulty, that takes a man's entire life, and only then, well, maybe he'll know something . . . but (*smiles*), it's worthwhile.

ZABRODSKY. (*Looking at her, as if for the first time.*) Yes, Lena, all of life. You . . . you are . . . so young, Lena.

DORA. (*Enters dressed, with raincoat and briefcase.*) Well, then . . . we're ready. Let's go, Sand. Come, Lena. Good-bye, Mr. Zabrodsky . . .

SAND. (*Looks at Zabrodsky, wants to extend his hand. Hesitates. Zabrodsky doesn't notice him. Sand bows slightly, shrugs his shoulders and goes. They leave. Lena does not look back at what she is leaving behind. She clings to Sand as if seeking protection from her past. They go out.* After *they've gone, Zabrodsky goes over to the window, lowers the curtains, puts out the side light, so that only the small lamp, which was on at the beginning of Act II, lights the room. He sits motionless in an armchair, as if he were one of the museum pieces. The cuckoo pops out and calls twelve times.*)

ZABRODSKY. (*Raises his head slowly to the clock.*) Midnight.

CURTAIN

Aharon Megged

Aharon Megged was born in Poland in 1920. He went to Palestine in 1926. He lived in Kibbutz Sdot-Yam from 1939 to 1950, where he met Hanna Senesh. Megged was cultural attaché at the Israeli embassy in London, and writer-in-residence at Oxford University and at the University of Haifa. He is the winner of the Bialik Prize for literature.

Megged is the author of nearly twenty novels and short stories. Among the better known are: *The Living on the Dead* (1965), *Of Trees and Stones* (1974), *Asahel* (1978), and *Foigelman* (1988). His plays include *Hedva and I* (1954), *I like Mike* (1956), *Hanna Senesh* (1957), *Genesis* (1962), and *The Burning Season* (1967).

His novels are available in English, German, Romanian, and Russian.

Hanna Senesh

1958

(Translated by Michael Taub)

Characters

ROZSA, Hungarian investigating officer
The OFFICER
HANNA SENESH
PIERRE TARANDIER, French Resistance fighter
The MOTHER
PROFESSOR MOLNAR, Hungarian teacher

The DETECTIVE
ELIAHU, Haggana fighter
GERI, paratrooper
STEPHAN, Yugoslav partisan
FRUMA, Polish Jewish refugee
HILDA, prison guard
CLARY BENEDEK, Hungarian prisoner
YANOS, Hungarian prison guard
DEVCSERY, Hungarian lawyer
The JUDGE
SIMON, Hungarian military judge
POLICEMEN, JUDGES, SOLDIERS

Time

June–November 1944

Place

Budapest: investigation cell and the prison

ACT I

Investigator Rozsa's room. He sits at a table covered with maps, documents, small transmitter radio. Near him, a Hungarian Police Officer.

OFFICER. (*Bends over a map, points to spots on it.*) Here, in Szombothy. They crossed the border near the Yugoslav village of Apatovac.

ROZSA. No border guards there?

OFFICER. I haven't noticed any. They crossed the Drava River at night; and at 10:00 A.M., one of the smugglers handed them over to us. The two Jews, Kardosh and Feldman, were caught walking in the village.

ROZSA. Where are they?

OFFICER. Feldman is in prison, on Conti Street; Kardosh shot himself the moment we caught him.

ROZSA. So that's how you guarded him!

OFFICER. It happened in a flash. He grabbed his gun the moment he saw us. We thought he was aiming it at us, but he was pointing it to his head. We took Feldman to the guard post; and after a few hours, he admitted that there were two more besides them.

ROZSA. (*Looks at the documents.*) The Frenchman and the girl . . .

Maria Ardy. (*Laughs.*) Nice name she picked for herself. And she was the one who revealed the location of the transmitter radio.

OFFICER. Oh, no. We couldn't get a thing out of her. She was silent as the grave. Torture was useless on her. But, since we found the headset on Kardosh, she had to admit that they had a transmitter radio somewhere. Its location, however, she would not reveal. That we had to find out by ourselves.

ROZSA. How?

OFFICER. (*Points to the map.*) Here, in the field. She buried it in the ground. We had to clear the whole area to find it. Then, we started asking her about the code, but she said it was in a book, near where the radio was found. That, of course, is a lie.

ROZSA. Did you look?

OFFICER. We combed all the fields in the village. We found nothing.

ROZSA. The book is just a story. She has memorized the code, and if we can make her talk, it'll be the greatest coup since the Germans got here. Its use can go both ways, if you get my drift.

OFFICER. Oh, yes!

ROZSA. A card against the Allies if necessary, and a card against the Germans (*laughs*) if necessary . . .

OFFICER. Oh, yes! Yes!

ROZSA. So what is she saying?

OFFICER. Not a word. They've worked on her for three days and three nights. Still no results.

ROZSA. And you think she's Jewish.

OFFICER. Probably. The whole thing smells Jewish to me. She knows Hungary well, and Budapest like the back of her hand.

ROZSA. And still claims her name is Maria Ardy.

OFFICER. Yes, sir. (*Enter Policeman, salutes.*)

POLICEMAN. (*To Officer.*) She passed out again.

OFFICER. Pour water on her and resume the whipping.

POLICEMAN. Yes, sir. (*About to leave.*)

ROZSA. Just a minute. What is she saying?

POLICEMAN. She's quiet. But as soon as we leave her alone, she starts talking as if we were the prisoners and she the guard. You slap her and she responds with insults. . . . What a mess. . . . I swear.

ROZSA. That's enough for now. Give her a break.

POLICEMAN. Yes, sir. (*Exit.*)

ROZSA. Did you check if she has any relatives here?

OFFICER. First she denied it. She said she had none. Then, when she couldn't take the beating anymore, she made up some addresses. We checked it out. Lies. There is no Ardy. In any case, we deduced from this that she knows Budapest very well.

ROZSA. And, no doubt, she has connections in the city. At least one address, and if we find out, we may know everything. And what did you get out of the Frenchman, what's his name?

OFFICER. Pierre Tarandier.

ROZSA. You couldn't get her real name out of him?

OFFICER. Nothing helped, no torture. Maybe he doesn't know. The only thing we got out of him was that he had met her at General Mtatich's Headquarters, and that she was a British officer.

ROZSA. Is there something between them? I mean besides their mission?

OFFICER. Can't tell, sir. When they saw us—from their hiding place—they posed as lovers having fun outdoors. Of course, this was only camouflage. And they're two hard nuts to crack. They beat her to death in Szombothy, but all she kept saying was that the book was near where the radio was found. They put her in a cell, and she almost jumped out of the window. In the train coming here, she tried to kill herself. And here (*points to adjacent room*), they whipped her feet for three hours, and still nothing. The dead would have talked after such torture. I myself felt bad looking at her. She's good looking, you know . . .

ROZSA. And a Jew, you said.

OFFICER. Probably. Although it's hard to believe they'd be so brave. The more you beat her, the tougher she gets.

ROZSA. Still, she must have a vulnerable spot.

OFFICER. Not physically. Strip her, whip her, and you think you're hitting a dummy. She passes out, when she recovers—repeats the same story, or else, she's quiet. One time, a guard collapsed before she did. He couldn't take it. And, you know, our boys are not exactly wimps.

ROZSA. Still, as I said, she must have a weak point. Creatures like her don't break under physical torture. Their courage is their strength. But, it's their weakness as well. Got it?

OFFICER. Not exactly.

ROZSA. Bring her in. (*Officer goes into adjacent room. A minute later returns with Hanna and two Guards. Her face and body bear signs of torture.*)

ROZSA. (*to the Guards.*): You, leave. (*They do. To Hanna.*) You may sit . . . (*sarcasm*) Maria Ardy. (*She falls into the chair; fixes her eyes on him.*)

ROZSA. (*Looks her over, smiling.*) Nice girl. . . . So young. . . . How old are you, Maria Ardy? (*No answer. To Officer.*) What's your guess, how old is she?

OFFICER. Twenty, twenty two, no more.

ROZSA. Yes, therabouts. (*To Hanna.*) And probably from an educated family, as far as I can see. Right? (*To Officer.*) Isn't it a crime to send a girl like this on such a dangerous mission, when the chances of getting caught are a hundred times higher than of escaping?

OFFICER. A crime, sir.

ROZSA. Of course. What brought you to undertake such a dangerous mission? It can't be the sense of adventure! You don't strike me as the type! A holy mission? Such as directing bombers over our towns and villages with your transmitter? (*Points to it.*) Or, was there no one else ready to sacrifice himself for this? (*To the Officer.*) You shouldn't have beaten her. Such beauty, it's a shame to ruin it. (*To Hanna.*) The officer told me the book you spoke about is nowhere to be found. I'm sure if you searched your memory, you'd be able to tell us one sentence to close this case. This will end the investigation, which has not caused you much pleasure. Neither us, I can assure you.

HANNA. I said all I know.

ROZSA. (*Softly.*) You know what's in store for you.

HANNA. I know. But some things are more important than life.

ROZSA. That includes the lives of the people close to you as well?

HANNA. Luckily, they are far away from here.

ROZSA. We'll see about that. True, so far we haven't found any Ardy, and the addresses you gave us were all made up. People like you generally stick to the truth.

HANNA. You are not the one to preach to me on that. Neither are those who tortured me to death.

ROZSA. I told them to stop it. I know that brutality has no effect on sensitive souls like you.

HANNA. I never asked for mercy.

ROZSA. Not out of mercy. You don't deserve it. This instrument (*points to it*) might have caused serious bloodshed in this country. Your relatives included.

HANNA. I have none.

ROZSA. But you know Budapest very well. (*Looks at the papers.*) Terez-Korot 32, Andrasi Road 48, Saint-Istvan Square 23 . . .

HANNA. I made it all up, as I said.

ROZSA. The name too, of course. What's your real name? Well?

HANNA. Maria Ardy.

ROZSA. You're forcing me to accuse you of lying. There is no such Jewish name.

HANNA. I'm a British officer, as I've already stated.

ROZSA. Born in Hungary, which makes you doubly guilty. In legal terms this is called treason.

HANNA. And what do you call the tortures you have subjected me to for four days now?

ROZSA. This will stop, as I've told you. And I hope you'll know how to appreciate it properly.

HANNA. Oh, yes, a lot! After behaving like wild animals!

ROZSA. You could have prevented it, young lady, if you had told us the truth.

HANNA. I asked to be treated according to the law.

ROZSA. That will come, but first you must reveal a few details, the first being your true name.

HANNA. I won't tell you anything more.

ROZSA. You'll force me to use a different language.

HANNA. You already did.

ROZSA. You show courage, miss. More than your French friend. He did reveal things you refused to utter a word about. You want him to reveal more?

HANNA. I trust him as much as I trust myself.

ROZSA. You put too much trust in man's ability to suffer, young lady, and you're testing my patience too much! (*To Officer.*) Bring him in. (*He leaves.*)

ROZSA. I'm sorry for you. Beauty like yours was not created to be destroyed with iron sticks, definitely not with bullets. So, why did you do this?

HANNA. You'll know everything in due time.

HANNA. It might be too late, I'm afraid. (*Officer returns, Pierre behind him, handcuffed. Two Guards.*)

HANNA. (*Scared.*) Pierre! (*Buries her face in her hands. The two Guards leave.*)

ROZSA. Mr. Pierre Tarandier, your friend here trusts you very much, as she has just told us. Please tell her what you told us so we won't have to subject her to unnecessary questioning. (*Waits. Pierre is quiet.*) Tell her that she is Jewish, that she was born in Hungary—this city, that she was sent by the British to spy and carry out sabotage missions here. (*As before.*) Tell her the transmitter was supposed to relay instructions to the British Air Force Headquarters in Cairo, to direct bombers over Hungary, and sow death and destruction upon our people. (*Stops. Pierre's head drops, remains silent.*) Tell her that we have the means to make even the Egyptian Sphinx talk, and that there is a limit to how much pain one can bear! (*Stops, looks at them. Hanna hides her face in her hands. Pierre's head drops.*) Tell her if she doesn't tell us her name, you will, and it's not fair that you should suffer because of her! (*Stops. A Guard gets up.*) We don't really care who tells us; in fact, I'll leave it up to the two of you to decide. I'll leave you alone. Sensitive creatures like you don't like to bare their souls in public. (*To the Officer.*) Let's leave. (*Rozsa and Officer leave. First. Pierre, then Hanna, lift their gaze.*)

PIERRE. (*Whispers.*) Forgive me.

HANNA. (*Her face lights up.*) For what, Pierre?! I'm sure you didn't reveal more than was already known.

PIERRE. They tortured you, the bastards.

HANNA. The worst is over. I don't feel a thing anymore. Only our failure to carry out the mission depresses me.

PIERRE. This is not the end. It's not the end yet.

HANNA. I feel an eternity has gone by since we got caught. The first hours are the worst. When you don't trust yourself. When you don't know if you'll be able to stand it all. Afterwards, it's as if the soul parted from the body. The body suffers the torture, but the soul is outside it, as if free. It's such a relief, Pierre.

PIERRE. You're a strong girl, even stronger than I thought.

HANNA. Remember our talks about God, Pierre? There, on the other side of the border?

PIERRE. I remember how you used wonders and miracles to prove that God doesn't exist. Nobody could stand up to your strong logic.

HANNA. I'm ashamed about the things I said, Pierre. There are greater things than logic. When they tied up my feet and whipped me until I bled, and no longer had any feeling in them, and I knew I was stronger than my torturers . . .

PIERRE. You always believed, I know that. Even your atheism had more faith in it than our proof. Otherwise you wouldn't be here.

HANNA. Now I carry only one prayer in my heart—that I shouldn't cause others pain. They're asking my name. I would tell them if my mother's fate did not depend on it. I cannot cause her more grief after what she has already suffered for me. She shouldn't suffer for my actions.

PIERRE. You can trust me.

HANNA. Pierre, you don't need to mention it. My trust in you and those who sent me is in my heart these terrible days.

PIERRE. I never felt stronger friendship than when I was near you, and near your compatriots. If only for this, the suffering was worth it.

HANNA. Pierre, do you believe we'll ever meet again . . . free?

PIERRE. I believe their end is near, very near.

HANNA. Pierre, you have no idea how I don't want to die! So many things I want to do in my life. Even now, there are moments when I see myself over there, the lovely landscape all around me. (*Enter Rozsa and Officer.*)

ROZSA. I hope you had sufficient time to arrive at the crucial decision. (*Looks at them, sees no reaction.*) Or would you rather let me decide for you? (*Stops. As before.*) So, you're leaving it up to me. Mr. Tarandier, you know the name of this Jewish woman. What is it? (*Waits.*) You've already seen the means by which we get anything out of you, isn't that right? (*Waits. To Officer.*) Take him out. (*Officer and Pierre leave.*)

ROZSA. (*Speaks much more aggressively, still standing.*) I see you've decided to take total control of your fate and spare unpleasantness from your friend. It is both right and brave of you.

HANNA. I demand to be treated according to the law.

ROZSA. We don't like to hear demands from spies, young lady. So far, I've treated you fairly, but that's over now. You should thank us we didn't hand you over to the Gestapo. The Germans would have closed your file in one hour. By pulling the trigger. (*Short pause.*) That's all. Or, by calling on the Judenkommando. . . . I hope you're familiar with their tactics these days . . .

HANNA. You really think I discriminate between one murderer and the other. I've learned from experience how little humanity is left in all of you.

ROZSA. You are ungrateful, young lady. Your Jewish friends do know how to appreciate our generosity. They've lived here peacefully until March 19. Now they're trapped in enclosures like sheep waiting for death to save them. I hope your relatives are not among them yet. . . . (*Hanna's shaken up. Rozsa notices.*) Or perhaps they are. I couldn't tell, since you haven't told me your name . . . (*Stops.*) If they're there, I'm sorry for them, because their fate is only one—Auschwitz, if the word means anything to you. . . . (*Stops. As before.*) Maybe something could be done for them—if you gave us the information. . . . (*Stops. Waits.*) So, what's your name? (*Long silence. Her face takes on a cold, bitter look. Rozsa sits down.*) So be it. Your French friend will tell us then. We had pity on you, miss. But we don't intend to treat him the same way. They say women are stronger under torture than men. I think so, too. Do you want him to suffer for your stubborness? On top of what he has already suffered? (*Silence. More forcefully.*) Do you want to hear his screams through the walls? (*Waits.*) I'll call the officer right away and give the order. (*Waits. Puts his finger on a button on the table.*) One push is enough. Should I?

HANNA. (*Shouting.*) Stop!

ROZSA. I'll wait for you to decide. (*Intense silence.*)

HANNA. (*Crying, choking.*) Your day will come too, Officer Rozsa! It's not that far! Someone else will ask your name and I'll know it!

ROZSA. (*Totally collected.*) Have you decided? (*Puts his finger on the button.*)

HANNA. Stop, I said! (*Head erect, proudly.*) My name is Hanna Senesh.

ROZSA. (*Stunned, after a pause.*) Senesh? Relative of the writer Bela Senesh?

HANNA. (*Proudly.*) Yes. His daughter.

ROZSA. Sooo. The apple fell far from the tree. . . . (*Silence.*) And your mother is still alive, if I'm not mistaken . . . she's here, in Budapest . . . (*Expects her answer. Hanna, head up, does not answer. Silence. He gets up.*) I thank you. Enough for today. (*Walks to the door.*)

HANNA. (*Shouts after him as he's at the door.*) Officer! (*Rozsa stops. Returns to the table.*)

ROZSA. Yes?

HANNA. (*Inner struggle shows, then.*) I have a favor to ask.

ROZSA. Which is?

HANNA. (*Inner struggle shows, then.*) My mother doesn't know I'm here. I left her five years ago. My brother, too. She lives here all by herself.

ROZSA. (*Pause.*) Knows nothing?

HANNA. No. She could never imagine a thing like this.

ROZSA. I see. You don't want us to tell her?

HANNA. That is my only wish.

ROZSA. So you don't want her to know about your shameful act?

HANNA. (*Mocking.*) Shameful?! I don't want her to witness this misfortune. She couldn't bear it after what she has gone through.

ROZSA. (*Pause.*) This depends on you, Anna* Senesh. We won't

Anna is the Hungarian equivalent of *Hanna*.

tell her if you give us the information we need. The code for the transmitter radio.

HANNA. (*Harshly.*) I've told you already. I left it by the transmitter.

ROZSA. (*Furious.*) That's a lie. The soldiers turned the place upside down and found nothing where you sent them. You know where it is! It's in your head!

HANNA. (*Pause.*) If there is one spark of humanity left in you, don't tell her! She won't be able to bear it! She's not responsible for my deeds!

ROZSA. What is the code?

HANNA. Punish me anyway you like! I can bear anything in the world! Don't tell her!

ROZSA. Are you ready to tell us, Anna Senesh?

HANNA. She's not guilty! She's not guilty! (*Bursts out crying, buries her head in her hands.*)

ROZSA. (*Gets up.*) If you choose to make your mother suffer for your crimes—that's fine with me. (*At the door.*) Great suffering is in store for her—Anna Senesh!

HANNA. (*Shouts after him, scared.*) Officer . . . (*Rozsa does not turn to her, leaves the room. Hanna buries her face in her hands. Lights dim. Piano plays a Chopin prelude in the distance. Her Mother appears. Approaches Hanna slowly, touches her head lightly.*)

MOTHER. What are you thinking about my child?

HANNA. I'm so happy you came, mother! I have news to tell you!

MOTHER. What news?

HANNA. Guess!

MOTHER. You're head of your class again?

HANNA. Oh, no, no! Don't you know a Jew cannot receive that honor anymore?

MOTHER. OK, so you are the ping-pong champion of the girls team!

HANNA. (*Laughs.*) No! No, again! I got only nineteen points and took third place!

MOTHER. (*Ironic tone.*) How sad! So, a nice boy from a good family asked you to go with him to the opera!

HANNA. (*Laughs.*) Nonsense! There were four, and I refused them all. I have not accepted one invitation yet!

MOTHER. So, what's the news?

HANNA. (*Short pause.*) I got first prize in literature.

MOTHER. (*No enthusiasm.*) Very nice.

HANNA. Aren't you happy for me?

MOTHER. It doesn't surprise me at all. For what?

HANNA. For a poem I wrote. Want to hear it?

MOTHER. Of course! (*Sits down.*)

HANNA. (*Kneels next to her.*) Now listen:

> Night falls slowly, silently,
> I know—it's the eternal order.
> And evening by evening it will be so.
> Oh, how great, how limitless,
> Wonderful, miraculous, mysterious,
> And sweet and lovely—

MOTHER. (*Continues.*)

> That spirit and soul,
> Will enlighten my life
> On my way to eternity.

HANNA. (*Stunned*). How did you know?

MOTHER. (*Laughs.*) I must confess my sins. I looked at the paper you left on the table. It's a very nice poem, Aniko. Dad would have loved it. He used to say to me: Remember, Kate, our little Aniko will one day write better than I. One day she'll be somebody!

HANNA. Yes. Dear Dad. . . . (*Whispers.*) Remember, when I was small—you didn't tell me he died. You said, Dad went away, far away.

MOTHER. Yes, Dad went away, far away.

HANNA. Then I didn't understand, but now I do. Only those die whose lives were insignificant. The true great ones live forever. . . . You think I deserve to carry his name? (*Enter Professor Molnar.*)

MOLNAR. (*Declaims.*) Good evening to Mrs. Senesh and her daughter!

MOTHER. (*Gets up.*) Oh, Professor Molnar! At such an hour . . .

MOLNAR. (*Shakes her hand.*) A blessed hour! I came to congratulate you, Mrs. Senesh. On your daughter's prize . . .

MOTHER. I'm grateful to you from the bottom of my heart. It was you who gave her the prize . . .

MOLNAR. It was a great honor to give it to her. I'm just sorry her father, Mr. Senesh, may he rest in peace, did not live to share our pride in her today.

MOTHER. He predicted great things for her even when she was a child, Professor Molnar.

MOLNAR. (*Favors Hanna with his attention.*) It's not proper to shower praise on people in their presence, but I'm sure this won't inflate your ego too much. (*To Mother.*) Mrs. Senesh, I'm old enough to predict that if your daughter continues to excel the way she does in poetry—she'll be the pride and joy of her country, Hungary.

HANNA. I'm afraid I must disappoint you, Professor Molnar. If, as you so generously predict, I am to become the pride and joy of anyone, it won't be Hungary . . .

MOLNAR. (*Stunned.*) Why?

MOTHER. (*Sad tone.*) She has decided to leave us. Right after her graduation.

MOLNAR. (*Stunned.*) Where to?

MOTHER. To Palestine. She believes in the Zionist ideal.

MOLNAR. (*Shaken up, to Hanna.*) You?

HANNA. Yes, Professor. I have found my true homeland, and I want to live there.

MOLNAR. (*Pause, looks at both, to Mother.*) And you agree with this, Mrs. Senesh?

MOTHER. I did my best, but she prevailed.

MOLNAR. (*Pause, shakes his head.*) The cursed disease of politics! Cancer! Cancer for our youth! Socialism, Fascism, Communism, Zionism! All this leads to only one thing, Miss Senesh, the enslavement of the spirit, the loss of personal freedom! To actions that lead to disaster! . . . God, I would have never imagined that someone who wrote these beautiful lines: "The spirit and soul . . . Will enlighten my life . . . On my way to eternity," will end up this way. (*Goes to the Mother, shakes her hand.*) Sorry, Mrs. Senesh. I must go. Good night. (*Leaves. Silence.*)

MOTHER. Didn't I tell you the same things exactly? Over and over, that you are ruining your future with your own hands! Why? Why? Everyone admires your talents, everyone is so proud of you, sees greatness in your future, and you . . .

HANNA. I won't live in a place where I must constantly walk with my head bent down.

MOTHER. With your head bent down? Why don't I feel that way? Why didn't your father feel this way? Did anyone make you bend your head?

HANNA. Have you already forgotten the humiliation you felt when you tried so hard to enroll me into a special high school, and they rejected me, even though I was the best in my class. And why was that? All because I was born Jewish.

MOTHER. We're all fighting against that, Aniko. We're fighting, not running away! Professor Molnar, who is not Jewish, is also fighting against persecution, prejudice, and racial bigotry! Just because we haven't won yet is no reason to run away from everything—your home, social life, literary successes, high hopes. You'll leave all this for a God-forsaken place, a place where you don't even know what's awaiting you?

HANNA. I know what's awaiting me there, Mom. I know that there I'll be free and proud of myself, that I'll be able to fulfill all my dreams, that no one will insult me there, no one will block my way.

MOTHER. Oh, yes! Some ambition—to work in the fields like a peasant! Is this why you studied so much and excelled in everything?

HANNA. Mom, some things are more important than studies.

MOTHER. Yes. You've told me: work, sharing, equality. . . . Are you ready to sacrifice your happiness for a dream you're not sure of?

HANNA. Sacrifice my happiness? I'm not sacrificing a thing, Mother! I'm sure I'll be happiest there! My life here seems so empty compared with my life there! Didn't you and Dad teach me that we should live by great ideas?

MOTHER. (*Silence, broken spirit.*) All my life I have dreamed that you'll grow up to be what your father wanted. I was so happy when you brought me the first five pengös you earned with your writing. . . . Today, too, when you told me about the prize . . . I thought . . . the house is bright again. . . . For, what makes a mother happy, if not the joys of her children?

HANNA. I know, Mom, I know how hard it'll be without me, especially since Giora is gone, too . . .

MOTHER. No, not that. I don't ask for any sacrifice, you know that! But, after all these years. . . . . Oh, Aniko, Aniko, you're giving up a home, and I'm not sure you'll find another! You're giving up a country where you loved every rock and flower—and I'm not sure you'll find another in its place. . . . After all, it was you who wrote about these beautiful things! The hills, the rivers, the lakes, the sky, and the stars! How is it that suddenly all this became so strange to you?

HANNA. Yes, Mother, strange. Not mine. And that distant land looks so bright to me that I think my life will only start there anew.

MOTHER. Aniko, are you sure you'll never regret this?

HANNA. How could I, Mom, when I know that this is the right thing! (*Pause.*) Unless you tell me you won't be able to live all by yourself . . .

MOTHER. (*Scared.*) No, no, no! I can! Don't think of me! I . . .

what do I want, Aniko? Only your happiness! (*Stands up.*) Go to sleep my child. . . . Pray to God, like when you were small.

HANNA. Yes, I will. (*Places her hands on her knees, lifts her head.*) Please God, make me worthy of the life You gave me. That I should never be ashamed of myself and my deeds. Give me strength to serve goodness and beauty. Open my eyes to see the small lights near me and the faraway light of the stars. And please support me should I fail in carrying out your mission . . . (*Hanna tiptoes out. It gets brighter. The Mother sits at the interrogation table. Enter Rozsa and a detective carrying folders. They sit at the table opposite her.*)

DETECTIVE. When did your husband die, Catherine Senesh?

MOTHER. 1927.

DETECTIVE. (*Makes notes.*) How many children do you have?

MOTHER. Two, Giora and Hanna.

DETECTIVE. What is their birth date?

MOTHER. My son, Giora, was born in 1920. My daughter, Hanna, in 1921.

DETECTIVE. Where are they?

MOTHER. Fortunately far from here . . . in Palestine.

ROZSA. Both?

MOTHER. Yes, my son Giora arrived there only four months ago.

DETECTIVE. How did he get there?

MOTHER. He left Hungary some years ago. He studied in France, and from there went to Spain. My daughter obtained an entrance visa for him.

DETECTIVE. When did your daughter arrive in Palestine?

MOTHER. Five years ago. September 1939.

ROZSA. You agreed that she leave?

MOTHER. At first I was against it because it was difficult parting with her, but eventually I understood her reasons for doing so.

ROZSA. What did she do while she lived here?

MOTHER. She was a student. She graduated from a special parochial high school.

ROZSA. If I'm not mistaken, Jews were not allowed there.

MOTHER. True, it was difficult, but she got accepted because she was an exceptional student. She was the best in her class; I think she was the best in the entire school.

ROZSA. So why did she leave her country for Palestine?

MOTHER (*Bitter smile.*) Because she was smarter than I, she saw what was in store for Jews in this country.

ROZSA. Was she that concerned with her safety?

MOTHER. I don't understand your question.

ROZSA. I asked if she left Hungary to save herself.

MOTHER. Not really. She believed that the only place youngsters like her have any future is in their own homeland.

ROZSA. And she was ready to abandon you for this?

MOTHER. Oh, no, no, no. She is very attached to me. She believed I would get there, too.

ROZSA. How?

MOTHER. She tried very hard to get me a visa. But after the occupation, nothing came of it . . .

ROZSA. Do you think she would have done anything to get you there?

MOTHER. (*Bitter smile.*) What could she do now that the borders are sealed? These days Jews are taken somewhere else . . .

ROZSA. What connections did she have while she was here?

MOTHER. I don't understand.

ROZSA. I mean social connections. Was she involved with any party, organization? . . .

MOTHER. Oh, no. Her only contacts were with friends, teachers, friends of the family . . .

DETECTIVE. Do you know where she is now?

MOTHER. I told you already! I don't know why you keep asking me this . . .

DETECTIVE. Where in Palestine is she now?

MOTHER. In a fishing village, it's called Sdot-Yam.

DETECTIVE. She fishes?

MOTHER. No, she works in the fields.

ROZSA. After excelling so in her studies, as you've told us?

MOTHER. Yes, that's what she wanted. But why is it your business? . . .

ROZSA. Was it her ambition to work the fields when she lived here, too?

MOTHER. No. She wanted to be a teacher, writer, poet. . . . She was destined for greatness, sir!

ROZSA. (*Bursts out laughing.*) Oh, yes!

MOTHER. You don't think so. . . . Yes, but you don't know her. . . . No wonder . . .

ROZSA. Have you received any letters from her lately?

MOTHER. Last one was four months ago. But then the Germans came and all contacts ended . . .

DETECTIVE. Do you have her last letter?

MOTHER. Yes, I have them all.

DETECTIVE. Could you show it to us?

MOTHER. (*To Rozsa.*) Officer, could you explain the meaning of this interrogation? If you intend to transfer me to the Jewish ghetto, I'll pack my bags and go. My whole family is there already.

ROZSA. Did your daughter write about other activities besides . . . agriculture?

MOTHER. She is very satisfied with her work.

ROZSA. And you're certain she's still doing that now?

MOTHER. I don't know. . . . But why are you asking?

ROZSA. And she hasn't left Palestine?

MOTHER. (*First scared, then smiling.*) Where could she go anyway? She is happy there.

ROZSA. Are you sure about that?

MOTHER. (*Excited.*) Sir, my daughter possesses unique talents and exceptional traits. If you're interested in more specifics, you should ask her former teachers, Dr. Borishka Ravas and Dr. Elis—they'll confirm my statements.

ROZSA. (*Gets up. Detective also.*) And she didn't excel in anything except her studies, Mrs. Senesh?

MOTHER. I don't get the meaning of your words. . . . You are not accusing me of something, are you? And I don't see how my daughter's character is the business of the Hungarian Police!

DETECTIVE. Are you willing to swear that everything you told us is true?

MOTHER. (*Scared.*) My God. . . . Tell me what you want from me. At least you should tell me what I am accused of.

ROZSA. You mean to tell me, Mrs. Senesh, that you don't know where your daughter is? (*She looks at him scared.*) If so, I'll show you in a minute . . . (*Pushes a button on the table. The door opens. Hanna is brought in by two Guards; disheveled, signs of torture on her face. Her Mother turns around, sees her.*)

MOTHER. (*Screams.*) Aniko!

HANNA. (*Frees herself from Guards, runs to her Mother.*) Mother! (*Overcome by emotion, she hugs her a few moments while the other four look on.*)

ROZSA. (*To the Mother.*) My advice to you, Mrs. Senesh, is to make your daughter tell us all we need to know, if her life is dear to her. If not, this is the last time you'll see each other. (*Indicates for all to leave except Hanna and the Mother.*)

MOTHER. Aniko—why?

HANNA. Forgive me, Mother, forgive me.

MOTHER. Because of me? . . .

HANNA. No, Mom. I can't tell you. Someday you'll understand everything.

MOTHER. So terrible seeing you here now.

HANNA. I meant no harm, Mom, believe me.

MOTHER. They've tortured you, Aniko.

HANNA. No, they did nothing. You suffered a lot . . .

MOTHER. I was happy knowing you were there, far away from this. (*They look at each other, deep pain in their eyes.*) They keep sending people away from here everyday, Aniko. . . . I knew nothing when they came for me.

HANNA. (*After a pain-filled pause.*) I couldn't do otherwise. I had to . . .

MOTHER. (*Hugs her, holds her tight.*) You're so young, my child, so young. . . . Why did you do this? Why?

HANNA. I couldn't, Mom, I couldn't just sit still and watch . . .

MOTHER. Oh, what a disaster you brought upon yourself, what a disaster . . . (*Enter Rozsa and Detective. Hanna and Mother separate.*)

ROZSA. (*To the Mother.*) So, Mrs. Senesh, have you convinced her to reveal the secrets? (*She looks into Hanna's eyes. To Hanna.*) Will you? (*Hanna, looking scared, is silent.*) Would you like us to execute your mother, Hanna Senesh? (*Stops, waits.*) In that case, this is your last meeting. (*Loudly.*) Take her out.

MOTHER. (*Shouts.*) What do you want from my daughter? What do you want from her? (*The Guards take the Mother out.*)

HANNA. (*Agonizes.*) Mother . . . (*The Detective leaves. Rozsa paces. He looks frustrated, helpless.*)

ROZSA. So, you're risking your mother's life, too . . . (*Stops.*) Or, perhaps you think we'll have mercy on you—or her. . . . (*Angry.*) We have no mercy on traitors and spies! We'll get it out of your mouth even if we have to use iron pincers! You'll talk, like all the other spies we caught! Jewish blood is not more precious to us than the blood of others, as you know! It flows these days like water—and yours will flow with it! (*Comes near her, shouts.*) Speak! Damn Jew! (*Recoils from her frozen look, retreats, paces, returns to the table. Softly.*) Sit. (*She collapses into the chair. Rozsa, shaking his head.*) The daughter of the writer Bela Senesh. . . . I saw some of your father's plays, in my youth, I even admired him, *Tchibi*, right? A beautiful story. . . . Your father, he was a good Hungarian, even though a Jew. . . . Do you think he would approve of this act of treason against your nation? (*Stops, awaits an answer. Hanna still wears a frozen look on her face.*) I saw a few of your notebooks in your mother's house. I must admit, you wrote fine compositions when you were younger. I found one interesting sentence in one of them: "A curse on the enemies of Hungary—*Nem Nem Soha*—We'll never accept the Trianon Treaty!" Wonderful! You were a great patriot! Would you repeat those words today—"A curse on the enemies of Hungary"? (*Stops, waits. Lifts a page off the table.*) A touching poem—"On the Margarete Bridge": "A breeze from the Danube blows in my face / The scent of Buda too is mingled here / I know the Spring has passed there." . . . On this very Margarete Bridge you were going to direct enemy bombers, to destroy Budapest. . . . The same bombs could have killed your mother too, right? (*Stops, waits.*) Fortunately, we caught you before you carried out this shameful act. This, however, does not change the fact that you are a daughter capable of killing her mother. . . . Don't you think this is one of the most despicable crimes? We're leaving a crack for you to save yourself. We feel sorry for your young life. We're sorry for your mother. You saw her eyes begging you—do not abandon me, my child! A stone heart would have melted at that look! This is your last chance to save her life! Tell me the code, and I guarantee no harm will come to her. It is in our power to spare her the fate awaiting all of Budapest's Jews. We'll do it, if you talk. Will you? (*She's silent. He gets up, shouts furiously.*) Open your mouth! Speak! (*Walks to the door, at the doorstep.*) You'll speak on the gallows, in the throes of death, you damn Jew! (*Leaves. Lights slowly dim. In Rozsa's place at the table now sits Eliahu, a veteran, gray-haired Haggana fighter. One candle lights the room.*)

ELIAHU. Certainly! Certainly someone must go there! To save what's left! But not you! Not you!

HANNA. Why not me? Why?

ELIAHU. Because you're inexperienced in this! Because you're only five years in Palestine! Because you're too young!

HANNA. Is age important here? I want this! I must do it, and when a person feels this way he is very strong! Eliahu, please understand me . . .

ELIAHU. How can I? Do you know that thousands of lives depend on one word from you, one word, besides your own life? Have you ever been on a secret mission?

HANNA. No, but . . .

ELIAHU. Can you shoot?

HANNA. Yes.

ELIAHU. Have you ever faced a situation where the choice was between your life and your duty to the mission?

HANNA. Eliahu . . .

ELIAHU. So, how can you come to me and ask that I entrust you with such an important and dangerous mission, when the chances of failing are far greater than succeeding?! I'm risking the entire plan! (*Waits for an answer. She's silent. Softly.*) You just told me your mother is there. Let's say you're caught. Let's say they threaten you . . .

HANNA. (*Softly.*) I can stand up to it.

ELIAHU. How do you know? Let's assume they torture you! They whip you to death! That you're faced with a death sentence!

HANNA. Believe me, Eliahu, I can stand up to it. I knew that when I decided to do it. I cannot sit and wait anymore, I can't. . . . Isn't this enough, that I believe in myself so strongly?

ELIAHU. No! No! Commitment and enthusiasm are not enough! Impatience sometimes is worse than fear!

HANNA. I'm not reckless, Eliahu, if need be I know how to control myself when necessary. I came to you because I felt strength within me . . .

ELIAHU. But what if you're caught! You don't know what the threat of death means!

HANNA. Nothing is dearer to me than this mission.

ELIAHU. For God's sake, Hanna! You are an obstinate young girl! What self-confidence at your age!

HANNA. (*Cups her face, cries.*) I'll go. I'll go even if you don't consent . . . I'll go.

ELIAHU. (*Suddenly softens up, as if finding in her something he hasn't noticed before.*) Well, you're still a child, really. . . . Imagine they catch you. . . . And if they do. . . . You have a mother there. . . . Do you know what a mother's life means? . . .

HANNA. I know, I know . . .

ELIAHU. Imagine. . . . If, God forbid, you don't return. . . . How can I look my friends in the eye, your friends? . . . What will I say when they ask me: "Why did you send such a tender young girl, a recent arrival in the country, on a terrible mission like this?"! It's on my head! On my conscience!

HANNA. I'll go. I'll go. . . . You don't know me, Eliahu. Ask my friends from Nahalal, ask kibbutz members, Geri . . . (*Enter Geri in military uniform, sits down.*)

HANNA. (*Lifts her head, excited.*) Geri, tell him how I came to you two weeks ago and told you that we must go there, that we cannot sit here quietly, when over there they're waiting for help, and there's no one to save them. . . . Tell him I'm going even if he won't let me go. I'll find a way . . . (*Silence.*)

ELIAHU. (*Rests his hand on her shoulder.*) What are you doing tomorrow?

HANNA. Going back to Sdot-Yam.

ELIAHU. To work in the chicken coop?

HANNA. No, the kitchen.

ELIAHU. Can you stay here another day?

HANNA. Yes.

ELIAHU. (*First hesitates, then.*) Ever been in a plane?

HANNA. No.

ELIAHU. Ever seen people parachuting? . . . Jumping from planes?

HANNA. Yes! A wonderful sight!

ELIAHU. If they'll tell you to try, will you?

HANNA. (*Deeply grateful.*) Yes, Eliahu.

ELIAHU. (*After short pause.*) Stay until tomorrow. . . . And this evening, I order you to go to the movies. They're showing a good British comedy at one of the movie houses, very funny . . .

HANNA. (*Glowing with joy.*) I'll do anything you say.

ELIAHU. (*Feigns anger.*) And do not think of what we talked earlier! Not for a moment!

HANNA. I won't!

ELIAHU. (*Feigns anger again.*) Your self-confidence really scares me . . .

HANNA. (*To Geri.*) Tell him, Geri, that I can go with you, and that he can fully trust me. That I'm strong, strong . . .

ELIAHU. (*Pain in his voice.*) It's all on my head! All on my conscience! Don't you understand that? Don't you? (*Eliahu leaves. A Yugoslav partisan song is heard in the distance, sung by many men. The song is heard on and off from close up and from a distance. Geri and Hanna listen until the singing ends.*)

HANNA. Who are they?

GERI. The partisans of General Mtatich. Probably returning from a battle.

HANNA. Will we again wander with them, far from the border?

GERI. Probably. These days, there are Germans roaming around at the border.

HANNA. What are we waiting for, Geri, what?

GERI. We're waiting for the word. When the word comes, we'll be on our way.

HANNA. I've been waiting for it three months, and still nothing. Why were we sent here to fight with the partisans? We're late for our mission.

GERI. So, you want to rush straight into the fire? And end your mission before it even started? We cannot cross the border now!

HANNA. You want me to wait until there is no risk left? I should wait here weeks and months?

GERI. Learn from Pierre. A veteran of the French underground. His mission is not easier than ours: to free French fighters from Hungarian jails. He waits, and waits . . .

HANNA. But Geri, understand, his job is not as urgent as ours!

GERI. Impatience is killing you, Hanna. (*Firm.*) Don't you understand, if you fail, it's the end of this operation.

HANNA. Don't you know that if we sit here there won't be any need for action? I'm going, Geri. Avoiding risk, that's a crime I don't want to be accused of.

GERI. (*Shouts.*) Hanna, you'll wait until the order is given! You won't go on your own!

HANNA. (*Softly.*) I'm going. I have one favor to ask you. Give me a pill for the road. Cyanide. If I'm caught. (*Steps are heard outside. Enter Stephan, a Yugoslav partisan.*)

STEPHAN. (*Stands in the door, smiles.*) So, we'll have to part, right?

GERI. Are you leaving for the mountains again?

STEPHAN. We're staying here, you're going . . .

HANNA. Where, Stephan?

STEPHAN. I think the hour you've waited for, comrade, is here. The road is clear.

HANNA. (*Shouts of joy.*) Stephan! (*Runs to him, hugs him.*) You are wonderful, Stephan! (*Rests her head on his shoulders, overcome by emotions.*)

STEPHAN. (*To Geri.*) I've watched her face dangers with us for three months and she never cried, and now . . .

GERI. She has defeated me, Stephan.

STEPHAN. Another victory! So why are you crying? He's a man worthy of a fight!

HANNA. What a man! (*To Stephan.*) See how serious he is! (*To Geri.*) People want to cry when they see you!

GERI. You've cried already.

HANNA. From joy, Geri! Want to dance with me, do you?

GERI. When you get back!

HANNA. (*Gesture of disappointment.*) Oh, always thinking about fate, or God! (*To Geri.*) Don't you see, one shouldn't waste one moment of joy. (*To Stephan.*) Shake hands, Stephan.

STEPHAN (*Shakes.*) Good luck!

HANNA. Shake hard! Harder! (*Shouting from pain.*) Oh, God.

STEPHAN. It's difficult saying good-bye, comrade, you were like one of us.

HANNA. I was? And what am I now? Not one of you? I can compete with any of you in target shooting—and I'll win.

STEPHAN. Proud as a peacock, this girl! How many Germans did you kill in the mountains with us?

HANNA. I didn't count, Stephan. I only counted those I left alive! You remember, Geri?

GERI. (*To Stephan.*) I'm alive thanks to her. We were hiding in the forest, and suddenly four Germans appear. I was ready to pull the trigger, but she stopped me with a knock on my hand. Had I shot, we would be somewhere else today.

STEPHAN. She never told us, the warrior! After a battle she would sit by the bonfire, rest her head on Geri's shoulder . . .

HANNA. Sometimes on yours too, Stephan . . .

STEPHAN. Mine? (*Touches his shoulder.*) Oh, yes, twice!

HANNA. Three!

STEPHAN. Such a memory! (*Laughs.*) And sing songs as if there was no war at all. . . . What a beautiful voice, comrade.

HANNA. Who, me? (*Laughs.*) The owls would fly away from the forest if I sang.

STEPHAN. But not us. Comrade, they love you, these partisans. I swear, when they hear that you left, they'll be very upset. (*To Geri.*) At a partisans' party once, she spoke—there was such applause after every sentence that the walls were shaking! "Mankind will be victorious!" she said—and "hail to those who chase away the forces of darkness!" . . . I do remember, comrade.

HANNA. You have a wonderful memory, Stephan.

STEPHAN. She sure excited us. After a speech like that, one runs into the fire against an entire army! And afterwards, she danced the kolo like one of the natives!

HANNA. Oh, don't remind me of that! (*To Geri.*) He picked me up—I twisted around, and grenades fell out of my belt all over the place! Tell me, Stephan, you still remember the dance I taught you?

STEPHAN. And how I remember! The hora! We were drenched to the bone from dancing! When will we dance again, comrade?

HANNA. We'll meet again, Stephan, in better times than these!

STEPHAN. Will you send us regards?

HANNA. On the waves of the Drava, Stephan. I'll send people in boats, and you'll get my messages. If all goes well, of course.

STEPHAN. It will. Everywhere you go, luck goes with you. You came to us, and we haven't lost one battle! How did you get so lucky? Were you born with it?

HANNA. (*Laughs.*) Oh, no! It comes from my village. People there are of the sign of Aquarius. That's a good sign!

STEPHAN. Oh! The commune! They call it kibbutz in your language. I'd love to see it once! Very interesting!

HANNA. We'll welcome you with open arms, Stephan. We could really use a driver who knows horses like you do!

STEPHAN. Oh, yes. (*A whistle, gesture of whipping horses.*) Yippie, brrrr! To the Holy Land! (*Enter Pierre.*)

HANNA. Pierre! We're leaving tonight.

PIERRE. (*Calm.*) Oh, yes?

HANNA. Look at him! He's not happy at all!

PIERRE. Is the road clear?

STEPHAN. Clear! You'll have to cross the Drava, over the border, swimming.

PIERRE. (*To Hanna.*) And you—you thought this day would never come. Right?

HANNA. Don't remind me of my sins, Pierre. You're a veteran fighter, you have more patience . . .

PIERRE. Know how to swim?

HANNA. You forgot I'm from a kibbutz on the seaside?

PIERRE. Oh, yes, Caesaria! (*Hugs her neck.*) Oh, my girl, *ma petite fille,* a little girl in the forest with wolves. (*Pretends he's going to devour her.*)

HANNA. You can't frighten me!

STEPHAN. (*To Pierre.*) You can trust her, comrade. She has a warm heart and cool head like the Drava in the winter—two of the most important things for being a good partisan! Ready to leave, friends? I'll walk with you to the river.

GERI. Let's go. I, too, will walk with you to the border.

HANNA. Geri, you stay. (*Shakes hands.*) No need to risk your life. Sorry, if I hurt you, Geri. I didn't mean it.

GERI. I must admit, even when you hurt me—you were always right. I remember how you encouraged me. (*Points a finger upwards.*) Remember? The moment before jumping?

HANNA. You were pale as chalk!

GERI. (*Laughs.*) If not for your funny faces, I would have never jumped . . .

HANNA (*Laughs.*) I would have pushed you out! . . . I'm not as brave as you think. . . . And remember the code!

GERI. Sdot-Yam, Caesaria. How can I forget?!

HANNA. Stephan, let's go.

GERI. When will we see each other, Hanna?

HANNA. Soon! In Palestine! We'll travel by plane, and when we get there we'll jump out like doves from a cage, each to his kibbutz.

And the first Friday evening, we'll meet at my house. We'll sit by the sea, listen to the waves . . .

STEPHAN. And you'll sing the song you learned here . . . (*Sings a sad, heroic, Yugoslav partisan song. They join in. Stephan and the other three leave quietly. Hanna's left alone. The singing gradually fades. The door opens. Enter Rozsa, the Detective, two Guards.*)

ROZSA. So, you're ready to talk, Anna Senesh?

HANNA. (*Glowing face.*) Isn't it clear to you, Officer Rozsa that I'm not going to bend to force?

ROZSA. (*To the Guards.*) To her cell! (*They grab her. She leaves head up high.*)

ROZSA. (*To the Detective.*) Dumb like a stone! But I can make even stones speak! (*Phone rings. Rozsa rushes to answer.*) Yes, Officer Rozsa (*excited*), yes, sir! (*To the Detective.*) The Gestapo. Officer Seifert. (*On the phone, despondent.*) Yes. . . . The British paratrooper? . . . Yes, Anna Senesh. . . . We're working on her. . . . But this matter belongs to the Hungarian intelligence, sir. . . . Not yet. . . . Nothing to report. . . . Yes, we'll keep it up. . . . Yes, sir. I hope there won't be a need. . . . Yes, sir! (*Hangs up, to the Detective.*) To hell with it, they know. I was really afraid of this. They want us to tell them everything we get out of her. To hell with it!

DETECTIVE. Officer Rozsa, have you heard the news this morning? The Russians are taking Pinsk . . .

ROZSA. Yes, but we cannot be totally certain yet. (*Firm.*) We can't let her slip away from us, understood?

DETECTIVE. Understood, sir. A decisive card to trade in later. If the Allies get here . . .

ROZSA. (*Interrupts.*) That's enough. I'll break this Jew if it's the last thing I do. I'll crack her shell, or my name is not Rozsa.

CURTAIN

ACT II

(*Prison cell. Hanna sits on a bed, raises her head when hearing steps. Yanos approaches, a bunch of keys in his hands. Opens the door slightly, looks around the room. Hanna comes toward him.*)

HANNA. Found any?

YANOS. There is one, in the last cell. An English officer. They say, he's from Palestine. A spy, they say.

HANNA. His name? Do you know his name?

YANOS. No, I don't know. But I'm sure he's from Palestine.

HANNA. How can I thank you for this, Yanos?!

YANOS. No need. An old man like me will get his rewards in the world to come.

HANNA. You're wonderful, Yanos. Please see if there is one named Joel . . .

YANOS. Of course I will! In a place where there are no human beings, Yanos is a human being . . . (*After a pause.*) Where is Palestine? Very far?

HANNA. You don't know? The Holy Land!

YANOS. (*Stunned.*) The Holy Land! . . . Now I believe . . .

HANNA. Believe what?

YANOS. What they say about you. That they beat you, and beat you, that they've tortured you for over a month, and you said nothing. They threatened your mother, still nothing.

HANNA. And why do you believe now?

YANOS. Because the Holy Land is something else. Christ, too, did not say a word when they put him on the cross. Must be a good land if such people grow there. And your mother, from cell 528, she's from there, too?

HANNA. No, she's from here. Have you seen her today?

YANOS. No. (*Whispers.*) I'll arrange for you to see her tomorrow. In the bathroom. For a minute.

HANNA. Oh, Yanos.

YANOS. I'm a believer, and I remember the words of the Bible— "Blessed are they who suffer and are persecuted for righteousness sake, for theirs is the Kingdom of Heaven." . . . (*Crosses himself. Steps are heard.*) I'm going. Go back to your place. (*Closes and leaves. Rozsa and Hilda approach. Hilda opens the door.*)

HILDA. (*Orders her*): Get up! (*She does. Enter Rozsa. Hilda leaves, Rozsa examines Hanna closely.*)

HANNA. Please sit down. (*He continues looking at her, a smirk on his face.*) After all, you're my guest. Sit. . . . I see you're really interested in me if you bothered to come here . . .

ROZSA. I didn't want you to come to me after the twenty-four hours you've spent there, upstairs.

HANNA. I really appreciate that. I expect you're preparing a more enjoyable show for me.

ROZSA. I hope so. You may sit.

HANNA. Thanks. (*Sits on the bed.*)

ROZSA. (*Sits on a stool behind the table.*) I would like to tell you something I'm not supposed to, and I wouldn't do it if you hadn't stirred up in me a feeling of . . . let's call it sympathy . . .

HANNA. I must admit you show your sympathy in a very original way . . .

ROZSA. (*dryly.*) I'm performing my duty. (*After a short pause.*) Well, the Germans know about you.

HANNA. I never doubted it.

ROZSA. And since we caught you, a month, is it . . .

HANNA. A month, really? It feels like an eternity.

ROZSA. So, since your capture—they've been asking for you to be handed over to them. (*Waits for a reaction.*) You've admitted in the interrogation that the purpose of your mission was to save Jews, and smuggle them across the border, to Yugoslavia, Romania, and from there to Palestine. Isn't it so?

HANNA. Yes, I testified to it.

ROZSA. The matter of the Jews, as you probably know, is under the exclusive authority of the Germans. That is, the Gestapo. According to the law, I must turn you over to them. I was reluctant to do that till now . . . perhaps because of that feeling . . .

HANNA. Of sympathy.

ROZSA: Or respect for courage, if that's what it is. I won't be able to refuse them any longer. Have you heard of Eichmann?

HANNA. Yes.

ROZSA. Well then, he demands I hand you over, or get the information out of you, and report it to him. (*Waits for reaction.*) I promised I'll get it for him. (*Waits for reaction.*) You surely know that German justice in your case would mean the death sentence. You know that, don't you? (*Waits for reaction. Starts again, softer.*) Forget the code for a minute. We'll be happy to know other details. The Yugoslav partisans. (*Waits for reaction.*) Or the British army camp in Cairo. (*Waits for answer.*) Or, the Air Force. (*Waits for answer. Shouts.*) I must give them information—you get that? They demand that! They demand it! (*Desperate, angry.*) I'm doing it for you! (*Waits for answer. She's quiet.*) I'm offering you the most generous offer an interrogator can offer to a spy! You'll get no mercy from them! You are putting yourself—miserable girl that you are—face to face with the world's most powerful military machine! Give me one detail, any one! Who is the contact for your secret operations here? Who is he? Who is he? (*Light fades. The words "Who is he" slowly fade. She sits, head bowed. In Rozsa's place now stands Professor Molnar.*)

MOLNAR. Anna Senesh, who was the wise man who stood before

the judges and refused to ask for mercy, even after the death sentence was announced?

HANNA. (*Gets up promptly like a student being tested.*) Socrates, Professor Molnar.

MOLNAR. Do you remember the words he told the judges before his death?

HANNA. Yes. "If you're sure that justice is on your side—you must stand firm in peril, must not be swayed by death or anything else, or face disgrace."

MOLNAR. Correct. When did Jan Hus live, Anna Senesh?

HANNA. Born in 1369, and died at the stake in 1415.

MOLNAR. John Wycliffe.

HANNA. Born in 1320 and burned at the stake in 1384.

MOLNAR. Galileo Galilei.

HANNA. From 1564 to 1642.

MOLNAR. Remember Galileo's words when the Inquisition forced him to give up his beliefs?

HANNA. Yes. "*Eppur si muove.*" Nevertheless, it moves.

MOLNAR. Correct. What do all these people have in common?

HANNA. They all fought oppression, they all refused to bow to power, and gave their lives for their beliefs.

MOLNAR. What is the source of their courage?

HANNA. The certainty that in the end justice prevails, and the belief that spiritual power is greater than physical power.

MOLNAR. Could you, Anna Senesh, mention similar people from modern times?

HANNA. Yes. Garibaldi, Mazzini, Petöfi, the courageous American freedom fighter, Patrick Henry, who said: "Give me liberty, or give me death!"

MOLNAR. Now you're entering a different area, Anna Senesh—political conflicts, which is not what I meant.

HANNA. Isn't this the same war, Professor Molnar? Isn't national freedom as important as personal freedom?

MOLNAR. National freedom was won with bloodshed, and that's why it's different, Anna Senesh.

HANNA. But, it's the same war, sir! Against oppression, tyranny, against any brute force sending men to death because of their beliefs, religion, race, or the desire to live free! What is holier than fighting it, and to give one's life for it?! (*Dark. When the lights come up again, the set shifts to Hanna's Mother's cell—three beds, a low table. Her Mother sits on a bed. Opposite her, Fruma, a woman about forty.*)

FRUMA. They took her from my arms. . . . They took my husband at night, together with the rest of the men on our street. . . . I shouted, I cried, but the child was quiet. Like a deaf person. Only her eyes, they were wide open, big like the sky. Occasionally, she would ask, "Why are you crying, Mother, why?" . . . And only four years old. . . . In those moments, I thought she was the mother and I the child. . . . And in the morning, they rounded up the women. I covered her in a blanket and went out to the street. It snowed, and hundreds of women were already there. We walked. We walked about four kilometers, away from the city, and it snowed the entire time. Then we arrived in a small town, in the train station. They told us to get in. I went with the crowd, but as I reached the steps, an armed German came over to me, shouting. "You're leaving the girl here! We don't take children to labor camps!" "I won't allow it," I shouted back, "I won't!" And when he tried to take her from my arms, I held her tight, and fought like mad. Then, I felt a blow to my head and fell to the ground. They probably thought I was dead, so they left me there, on the platform. When I woke up, I saw only snow, everywhere. She was only four. What eyes . . .

MOTHER. But, they couldn't have killed her!

FRUMA. What are you saying? They kill everyone. Everyone. I saw with my own eyes how they shot a boy who was running after his father. Really, you people here know nothing.

MOTHER. And you, how did you get here?

FRUMA. I got up and started to walk. I walked. Aimlessly. I saw a carriage driven by a Polish peasant. He asked me where I was going, I said I was looking for my child. I guess he knew where I came from and asked, "Are you Jewish?" I said, "Yes." I had nothing to lose. He told me to climb in and took me to his village. He said with money they could take me over the border. "In Hungary, Jews still live," he said. I had some money in my handkerchief, I gave it to him. I arrive in Tohaly and started to look for Jews. They caught me there and brought me here. By now, I don't feel anything. Only her eyes, I see them all the time . . .

MOTHER. There are a few Polish women here, and several children. They were caught trying to cross the border.

FRUMA. Yes, I know. And they'll take them all to the same place. We'll see each other yet. . . . How long have you been Here?

MOTHER. Over a month . . . (*A moving reflection is seen on the ceiling. Gets up, smiles happily.*) It's my daughter, she got a small mirror, and this is how she signals to me . . . (*Gets on the bed to reach the small window.*)

FRUMA. Your daughter is here?

MOTHER. Yes, the cell across the courtyard. (*Waves through the bars, smiling happily. To Fruma.*) Would you like to see her? Here, come.

FRUMA. (*Gets on the bed next to the Mother.*) How? . . .

MOTHER. They caught her. She came from Eretz Yisrael . . . (*With her fingers, draws letters on the glass.*)

FRUMA. Did you say, from Eretz Yisrael?

MOTHER. Yes. . . . Look, she's waving to you. Answer her. (*Fruma does.*) Look, she's writing something on the glass.

FRUMA. *Shin, lamed, vav, mem-shalom!* (*Very excited.*) From Eretz Yisrael . . .

MOTHER. (*Slowly reads the message.*) There, she writes more. . . . "Do not despair—the war—will end soon, the Russians—at the Visla—see you." . . . She climbed down. Probably heard steps in the corridor.

FRUMA. From Eretz Yisrael—how is it possible? . . .

MOTHER. She came to save people and got caught herself.

FRUMA. Save you?

MOTHER. No. Jews.

FRUMA. From Eretz Yisrael. . . . They come here from Eretz Yisrael?

MOTHER. There, she's up again (*Reads.*) "Field—flower—tree." . . . (*To Fruma.*) She's teaching me Hebrew. I've learned, like this, fifty words (*Reads.*) "I-go-in-the-fields." (*Guard Hilda's voice is heard from outside: "Get down!" The two jump off the table.*)

HILDA. (*Opens the door, enters. To the Mother, quietly.*) Inspector Lamke is here. Careful. (*Gives her a package.*) This came from the city.

MOTHER. Thank you.

HILDA. (*Quietly.*) If you need something, two knocks on the door. (*Leaves.*)

MOTHER. (*Puts the package on the table.*) It's from my neighbor. A Hungarian actress, a wonderful woman. They allow it once in two weeks.

FRUMA. And the guard, a friend?

MOTHER. Because of my daughter, Aniko. All the guards respect her. (*Opens the package.*) It's her birthday today. I'm sure she forgot. All this time, I'm thinking how to send her my greetings and surprise her. Now I have it. I'll send her this jar of jam. Orange jam. . . . Poor girl, she doesn't get any packages.

FRUMA. From Eretz Yisrael. . . . How did she get here from Eretz Yisrael? . . .

MOTHER. Don't ask me. I don't know myself.

FRUMA. Haven't you two met?

MOTHER. Very rarely, in the courtyard. And even then, for a moment only. The guards are extremely strict, one cannot exchange a word. (*Wraps the jar in paper.*) All of us walk in twos, but she's not allowed. They only let her walk with children. She holds their hand and tells them about Eretz Yisrael . . .

FRUMA. But, why did they send her? God knows what will happen to her now . . .

MOTHER. That's the way it is. She couldn't stand by there anymore, so she came . . . (*Makes a paper flower, sticks it into the package.*) Twenty-three. . . . I never imagined I'd celebrate her birthday like this. . . . In a prison . . . (*Sits on the bed, covers her face with her hands.*)

FRUMA. (*After a pause.*) Allow me. . . . Allow me to add my present . . . (*Gets a handkerchief from the skirt pocket.*) It's all I have. (*Sticks it into the package.*)

MOTHER. Thank you. I shouldn't complain. You've lost a daughter. . . . I'm happy to be with her. (*In tears, choking.*) Yes, happy . . .

FRUMA. (*In a trance.*) From Eretz Yisrael. . . . A pioneer?

MOTHER. Yes. From a kibbutz. A fishing village. Sdot-Yam.

FRUMA. In our town, before the Germans came, there were many pioneers. . . . And now . . .

MOTHER. One night, I was lying down on this bed and could not fall asleep. Suddenly, my heart told me she couldn't sleep either. I got up to the window. It was a moonlit night, incredibly peaceful and clear. I looked at the wall across the courtyard, and there she was, sitting by the window in her blue blouse, dreaming. In that instant, she was beautiful like an angel, the moon glowing on her face. She couldn't see me since I was in the shadow. It was not a sight from this world. When she disappeared, my heart suddenly told me that I won't see her again, ever . . . (*They're quiet; steps are heard outside. The door opens. Enter Hilda the guard with Clary Benedek.*)

MOTHER. (*Gets up, gives Hilda the package.*) Please give this to Aniko. It's her birthday today. A present from her mother, and thanks from the bottom of my heart.

HILDA. (*Takes it, orders.*) And no more looking through the window if you don't want to taste solitary confinement! (*She leaves.*)

MOTHER. (*To Clary, pointing to Fruma.*) A new friend. From Poland.

FRUMA. My name is Fruma.

CLARY. Clary Benedek. How did you get to Hungary? Slipped through the border?

FRUMA. Yes.

CLARY. You won't stay here a long time. I heard that already starting today they're taking away all Poles. They're deporting them—God knows where.

FRUMA. The Devil knows and I do—to Auschwitz.

CLARY. That's not so bad. A labor camp is still better than prison . . .

FRUMA. What—you really don't know? You don't know that in Auschwitz they throw people in the ovens?

CLARY. Don't believe it! The Germans know what they want— they need workers so they're taking the Jews . . .

FRUMA. My God, really you know nothing? Not one person has returned from there! They kill them all! All!

MOTHER. That's how it is, Fruma, people refuse to believe in the worst—until they see it with their own eyes.

CLARY. The Germans themselves are scared these days. The Russians are in Kishinev and the British in Holland. Strangled. And here—they say Horthy is negotiating with the Allies. So I heard today in the Swabian Hill.

MOTHER. They interrogated you again?

CLARY. They tortured me five hours with questions, the bastards. I have no idea what they want from me. My grandmother was Jewish—so I must be a spy! "Baroness Benedek," they say, "where did you hide the gold?" "You can plow all of Hungary, but my gold you won't find," I said to them. "I sent it to Paris before the war." "So you have connections with the Allies," they say. "I wish," I said, "because I would love not to see your faces. That brought on a slap and insults, the pigs. I'm used to it already. And since six this morning not even a slice of bread.

MOTHER. (*Gives her a sandwich from the bag.*) Take it, I got this from Margit. She also sent a jar of jam, but I gave it to my daughter.

CLARY. (*Breaks the sandwich into two, gives it to Fruma.*) Take, I'm sure you're hungry.

FRUMA. Thanks, I'm not hungry.

CLARY. All right. (*Chewing.*) I heard your daughter went through it, also. Yesterday, the day before, they've interrogated her every day, the Gestapo.

MOTHER. They tortured her again . . .

CLARY. No! They wouldn't dare! They tell miracles about her there, it's hard to believe they treat her like that. Imagine, even Officer Seifert, the beast, softens up in her presence. He speaks to her like a gentleman, offers her cigarettes, orders food to the interrogation room, gives her newspapers to read. The guard says she's teaching him Zionism, and he seems convinced . . .

MOTHER. It's a trap . . .

CLARY. Nonsense! She's not telling a thing! And they know she won't. I heard a German SS officer say that she's the bravest girl he's ever seen, and if she weren't Jewish, he'd give her a gold medal! (*To Fruma.*) She dares do things no prisoner would ever dare! Everyday she informs inmates on the situation at the front by signaling through her small window. How she knows—only God knows!

FRUMA. Well, a Jew from Eretz Yisrael, is something special . . . something special . . .

CLARY. She's proud of what she does—that's the main thing! I'm telling you, the Germans respect pride more than anything else! I've found that out myself—if you're determined and fearless they retreat. But if you try to ingratiate yourself . . . (*Enter Hilda, gives the Mother a package.*)

HILDA. (*To the Mother.*) From your daughter. (*Order.*) No more loud talking! This is not a hotel! This is a prison! (*Leaves. The Mother pulls out two paper dolls: a couple of pioneers, holding hands, carrying pickaxes.*)

MOTHER. (*Lifts the dolls in the air.*) What a present! Could one wish for a nicer present?

CLARY. True artistic talent.

FRUMA. May I? . . . Just for a minute?

MOTHER. Please . . . (*Gives her.*) I never knew she was so good with her hands.

FRUMA. (*Cradles the dolls.*) Pioneers. . . . From Eretz Yisrael. . . . I had a picture like this at home, my daughter loved it so much . . .

MOTHER. Take them, Fruma. A souvenir.

FRUMA. (*Glowing face.*) Really, you'll give them to me? . . .

MOTHER. Yes, with all my heart.

FRUMA. (*Sits down on the bed, eyes riveted on the dolls in her hands.*) I'm so grateful to you. . . . My daughter . . . she used to rock her dolls like this. . . . (*Shows how.*) And would sing. . . . (*Sings quietly.*) "Sleep my baby, sleep / 'Night to you my child / Daddy will come / And bring you a red dress" . . . (*She cries. The Mother, Clary fight back tears.*)

MOTHER. (*Reads a note from the package*). She sent a note, too. "Dear mother, thanks for the present, the most precious I've ever gotten from you. The orange jam reminded me of the country I miss so much. When I look back on the twenty three years of my life, I see that I have nothing to complain about. Everything I did came from deep inside me, and I lived a full life. Forgive me for the pain I'm causing you. We may live better days" . . . (*Choking from tears.*)

FRUMA. (*Rocking the dolls.*) So beautiful dolls from Eretz Yisrael. . . . A present from Heaven. . . . I loved them so much . . . (*Rocking and Singing.*) "Sleep my baby, sleep / 'Night to you, my child" . . . (*Step are heard. They listen. Enter Hilda and Guard.*)

SOLDIER. (*announces from a list.*) Fruma Goldstein!

FUMA. (*Terrified.*) Me?

SOLDIER. Out!

MOTHER. What's this, where are you taking her?

CLARY. They're taking the Poles today.

HILDA. (*To Fruma.*) Take your stuff, and let's go!

FRUMA. (*Frozen in place.*) Where to?!

HILDA. Get up, and let's go!

MOTHER. (*Positions herself between Hilda and Guard.*) Where are you taking her?

SOLDIER. None of your business!

HILDA. (*Pulls Fruma's arm.*) Quick! We got no time!

MOTHER. (*Protects Fruma with her body.*) No, I won't let you! I won't!

SOLDIER. (*Pushes the Mother on the bed.*) Get away, you Jew, or I'll take you, too! (*Hilda and Soldier drag Fruma out.*)

MOTHER. (*Pounding on the door.*) Animals! Beasts! Child murderers! Mother murderers! (*Sound of steps fades.*) My God, what a world! What a world! And God sees it and is silent.

CLARY. Calm down, Kate, calm down. Some day they'll pay for it.

MOTHER. And I believed in them! I thought I could talk to them like to human beings! I thought they had an ounce of mercy! My dear daughter! She was so much smarter than I! How she foresaw all this, and my eyes were closed! And she asked me to go with her, she begged me! What a fool I was! This land is a cursed land! Where are the noble hearts, the intellectuals, the teachers, the poets, the revolutionaries, the noble souls?! They are dirt, all of them! Thousands are thrown into the Danube, and they're quiet! They hear the screams of death in every home—and they keep quiet! Loathsome slaves! I hope evil spirits will haunt them to their graves! (*Light fades. When it comes up again, it's Hanna in her cell, on her bed making paper dolls. Sound of steps. Enter Yanos with a tin teapot and tin plate.*)

YANOS. Paper dolls again? (*Puts pot, plate on table.*)

HANNA. Yes, Yanos. They're for the children. They're alone in the world, we must sweeten their lives a little. Will you give it to them?

YANOS. For you, Miss Anna, anything. (*About to leave.*)

HANNA. Wait, Yanos, wait a little . . .

YANOS. The supervisor is around. (*Looks up and down the corridor.*) Only a minute. (*Sits on the stool.*)

HANNA. So Yanos, what's new outside?

YANOS. Good and bad. Good—the Russians are near the border, in the Carpathians, and bad—people are still being deported by train. . . . Every day . . .

HANNA. And the Germans, going wild in the city?

YANOS. Oh, yes. A lot of shooting. Executions every day, Communists, Jews, anyone they suspect.

HANNA. But the Russians, they're bombing away, right?

YANOS. And how! They say two bridges over the Danube collapsed into a pile of rubble!

HANNA. Patience, Yanos. Patience is very important. After the war—you'll get back to your village. And I, to mine . . .

YANOS. (*Laughs.*) Miss Anna Senesh comes from a village? You must be joking!

HANNA. Not at all, Yanos. A fishing village. . .

YANOS. (*Laughs.*) Some joke! Everyone knows you're the daughter of a great writer, that you're so educated! A fishing village! Next, you'll tell me you were a fisherwoman!

HANNA. No. I was not, but I did work in the fields. In the chicken coop.

YANOS. (*Laughs.*) With chickens!

HANNA. You don't believe it, do you?!

YANOS. You're making a fool out of an old man, Miss Anna, that's slender! And the fishermen, are Jewish . . .

HANNA. What did you think? The farmers, the fishermen, the drivers, the sailors, are Jews—all of them.

YANOS. (*Stunned.*) If it were not you, Miss Anna, who says these things, I wouldn't believe it.

HANNA. And if I told you that we have Jewish soldiers, would you believe it?

YANOS. That I would. Because they say that you're a soldier. Not just a soldier, an officer! But if you tell me you're an officer who worked in a chicken coop, then my head goes around like a wheel!

HANNA. (*Laughs.*) And what if I told you that in our village we

shared everything, that no one had any private land or money—
that'll throw you off completely.

YANOS. And . . . your mother, she agreed you should live in a
crazy place like that?

HANNA. Oh, yes. In the end she agreed, of course.

YANOS. Your mother has a heart of gold. Too bad they've transferred her to Kistarcsa.

HANNA. But, it's better there, right?

YANOS. Oh, yes! It's a hotel compared to this place. One can take
walks, get food from the outside . . . But you liked it when she was
here . . .

HANNA. Soon, Yanos, I hope all doors will open up— (*Sound of
steps. Yanos gets up, scared.*)

YANOS. If they catch me here—(*Passes his hand across the throat.
Enter Hilda and attorney Devcsery, carrying a briefcase.*)

HILDA. (*To Yanos.*) You—what are you doing here?

YANOS. Me—I brought her food . . .

HILDA. Get out of here—immediately! (*He does. To Hanna.*) He's
here for you. (*Hilda leaves. Hanna gets up.*)

DEVCSERY. (*Extending his hand.*) Attorney-at-law Devcsery. Your
mother asked me to defend you.

HANNA. My mother? Is she free?

DEVCESERY. Yes. A few days already. She'll be allowed to see you
today.

HANNA. (*Takes his hand.*) I thank you so much . . .

DEVCSERY. You need not thank me. It wasn't me who freed her.

HANNA. I thank you for the good news. . . . It makes me so
happy.

DEVCSERY. Your trial is set for the twenty-eighth, a military court.

HANNA. Hungarian?

DEVCESERY. I hope so. But these days, with all the confusion, who
knows.

HANNA. And what, according to Hungarian law, may I expect?

DEVCSERY. Fifteen or twenty years in prison. If the judges are not
swayed by the defense. But it doesn't matter. . . . Anyway, the war is
almost over, they'll have to capitulate or call for a cease-fire any day
now.

HANNA. You think it's that close?

DEVCSERY. It seems so. But no one is sure. If the Germans decide
to handle the case, it could, as I said, be very bad. They're behaving
like trapped animals. They're worse than ever before . . .

HANNA. Yes.

DEVCSERY. Well I'm here to clear up some things. . . . Please sit down. (*She sits on the bed, he on the stool.*) I went over the documents, and the interrogation. The law is very strict in cases like these. You were caught with a transmitter radio, you've admitted it was yours, and it is clear your duty was to pass information to the Allies . . .

HANNA. I've admitted that the purpose of my mission was to save Jews.

DEVCSERY. First of all, this does not mitigate your crime since this is considered a subversive act against the state . . .

HANNA. I'm willing to accept punishment for this.

DEVCSERY. Second, the authorities do not believe you were not sent here to spy.

HANNA. It's not true.

DEVCSERY. The evidence speaks against you. The transmitter, for example. Can you prove it was not used for relaying information to the enemy?

HANNA. It's not true.

DEVCSERY. Anyway, your mission failed.

HANNA. Yes, it failed. This is my only crime.

DEVCSERY. Let me ask you: why not divulge the code? It could lessen the sentence. Maybe even acquit you.

HANNA. You, too?

DEVCSERY. No, no. I'm not trying to influence you. I'd like to understand.

HANNA. You want me to bring destruction on the people who sent me, and on my country.

DEVCSERY. Please consider seriously what I'm about to tell you: let's say that by telling the code you'd be making it easier on those you came to save and prevent the death of hundreds of Jews. Would you tell?

HANNA. I don't understand you, you're trying to trick me.

DEVCSERY. I'm not tricking you. This is a possibility.

HANNA. You're trying to trap me like Rozsa before you. Are you his messenger?

DEVCSERY. You're mistaken. What I said is possible.

HANNA. I don't believe you.

DEVCSERY. And if you were convinced—just for argument's sake—that what I said is true, would you tell?

HANNA. I would say that this is a dirty German trap designed to make me commit treason.

DEVCSERY. And if they told you that in return for your information such and such number of Jews would be saved—

HANNA. I'll never believe the promise of murderers.

DEVCSERY. Let's say they gave you guarantees—

HANNA. You talk to me like a horse trader, to hurt my pride! You think I would let German bombers destroy my country, betray my mission, my friends, my people—all for promises made by scum?! I don't need your defense. I can do it alone.

DEVCSERY. Don't be so rash, Miss Anna Senesh. I'm merely repeating what people who want to save you have told me . . .

HANNA. Just stop talking to me about it. I stood up against harder ordeals, and no one should hope that I would be tempted by such despicable offers.

DEVCSERY. We're talking about peoples' lives, Anna Senesh, the lives of men, women, and babies. Perhaps if you were outside you wouldn't talk like this. You would see how hundreds and thousands are led to the platforms by the river, like sheep to the slaughter . . .

HANNA. Oh, you don't get it! Not at all! Why am I here, do you think? If not to hold back this process, even a little . . .

DEVCSERY. And you think you could have done it?

HANNA. I don't know. But if I could have moved ten, five people to stand up against these murders, with might and with dignity—I would have believed that my mission has been accomplished. Can you grasp that?

DEVCSERY. I'm not sure . . .

HANNA. (*After a pause.*) Who gave you this "suggestion," that I should speak in return for lives saved? . . .

DEVCSERY. (*After a pause.*) Jews . . . (*Hanna buries her face in her hands. Enter Hilda and the Mother with a bag. Devcsery gets up. Hanna runs to her Mother, embraces her.*)

HANNA. Mother!

MOTHER. Aniko!

HANNA. Mother, you're free!

MOTHER. Two weeks, but they've let me see you only now . . .

HANNA. And I was so worried. I had nightmares!

DEVCSERY. I won't disturb you . . .

MOTHER. You've spoken to my daughter, Dr. Devcsery?

DEVCSERY. I did. I'll do my best to defend her.

MOTHER. And you . . . do you think there is any chance she may be acquitted?

DEVCSERY. Legally acquitted, I don't think so. But if she'll make such an impression on the judges like she made on me . . . I think at least they'll be less harsh. The trial is set for the twenty-eighth of the month. I'll try to get you permission to attend.

MOTHER. I'm very grateful to you. And I hope . . .

DEVCSERY. Let's hope. (*Shakes hands.*) And I thank you for the privilege of knowing your daughter. If we had many like her, maybe the world would look differently. (*Shakes Hanna's hand.*) Good-bye until the trial. Perhaps you're right—I shouldn't defend you, you should defend us instead . . . (*Leaves. Hanna and the Mother sit on the bed.*)

HANNA. Tell me, Mom, did you suffer a lot? . . .

MOTHER. Oh, no, not at all. I've only worried about you.

HANNA. I'm fine, Mom, and now—I feel great!

MOTHER. And the interrogations?

HANNA. Nothing. They gave up. And here, too, I have good relations with the guards, and manage to recruit people for Eretz Yisrael . . .

MOTHER. Careful, Aniko!

HANNA. Why? Everyone knows who I am, and what can be more serious than "treason"? At least I'll do what I. . . . If they let us out today I would take twenty girls with me to my kibbutz . . .

MOTHER. And they would go with you?

HANNA. Of course! Even the Communists are Zionists now! Don't worry, Mom, I'm not just sitting idly here, but you . . .

MOTHER. Free, as you see. Kistarcsa was a hotel compared to the previous jail. We were allowed to take walks, read, write, even receive visitors. Margit came once to see me . . .

HANNA. Margit the actress?

MOTHER. Yes. She still lives in our house. Also, she brought me a big bag of food . . .

HANNA. Oh, if only I could repay her . . .

MOTHER. Yes, she helped me a lot those days . . . Then, on Yom Kippur, they suddenly let us go and closed down the camp.

HANNA. And Jews are allowed to go free?

MOTHER. No, Aniko. Almost all of Budapest's Jews are gathered in Red Cross stations, their destiny unknown . . .

HANNA. And?

MOTHER. No one knows. We hope. Hope that things will get better.

HANNA. And no one does anything?

MOTHER. What can we do?

HANNA. Waiting? Waiting idly to be taken away?

MOTHER. Waiting. They say they're negotiating.

HANNA. With the Germans?

MOTHER. So they say. But nothing is definite yet . . .

HANNA. And someone thinks Germans will consent to spare even the life of one Jew?

MOTHER. I don't know, Aniko, it's all taking place in secrecy, I couldn't find out anything.

HANNA. And you?

MOTHER. For now, I'm free. The main thing is I got permission to see you . . .

HANNA. It's so wonderful!

MOTHER. I brought you a few things. . . . (*Bends down to get things from the bag.*) Yes, but before that—yesterday, with Margit, she gave me an envelope, with money, and said that someone had brought it for you, a certain Geri . . .

HANNA. (*Shouts for joy.*) Geri?!

MOTHER. So she said. And said to give you regards from him . . .

HANNA. (*Hugs her around her neck.*) Oh, Mom . . .

MOTHER. Who is this Geri?

HANNA. Oh, I'm so happy. At least he's free . . .

MOTHER. Who is he?

HANNA. Oh, no news could have made me happier. (*Whispers.*) We came together. On this mission. And you know nothing about him?

MOTHER. No, nothing.

HANNA. Not all is lost then. I'm so happy! (*Kisses her.*) Now show me what you have there.

MOTHER. (*Takes out things.*) Here's a cheese sandwich, some eggs, salami, too.

HANNA. How did you get all this?

MOTHER. I did. Good friends helped me. Anyone who heard of you sent something. This too—a sweater.

HANNA. Very good. It's really cold in the cell and my clothes are not warm enough.

MOTHER. I thought so. And now—(*Takes out a small sewing kit made of embroidered material.*)

HANNA. (*Shouts of joy.*) My sewing kit! (*Clutches it to her chest.*)

MOTHER. Still remember?

HANNA. How can I forget? Looking at it, I see my whole childhood pass before my eyes! What a beautiful present! (*Opens it.*) The same old thread, the scissors, and these buttons! How many toys I made with them! Remember the costume Giora and I made for a show?

MOTHER. You were two charming clowns, you and Giora! Which show was it, the first?

HANNA. An operetta, Mom!

MOTHER. Right! After all, you composed it! About two little soldiers who were sent to war, and on the way saw flowers—

HANNA. And forgot to go to the place they were sent to!

MOTHER. Oh, how we laughed when the two of you danced and sang in the middle of the room, around the flowers you had made!

HANNA. (*Sings a happy song.*) Remember?
Let's rejoice, and dance and revel
Roses, tulips, rich of petal . . .

MOTHER. (*Continues.*)
Evil we forget readily while singing, dancing merrily . . .
(*Enter Hilda.*)

HILDA. (*announces loudly.*) Two more minutes! (*Softly.*) You can stay a little longer, only be quiet. The supervisor is in the area. (*Leaves.*)

MOTHER. You were seven then, if I'm not mistaken. And you were writing plays—almost like Daddy . . .

HANNA. If I could only write here—I'd write more and more. I have so many ideas these days!

MOTHER. Soon, Aniko, it will all end, I hope.

HANNA. You know what? Sometimes I think I've accomplished less than I should have . . .

MOTHER. You've done more than I did in my whole life, and you still have a lifetime ahead of you.

HANNA. But, I have so many plans and ambitions. . . . You'll laugh when I tell you what I'm thinking of in my spare time: How to organize the work force in the kibbutz, how to improve efficiency in our clothing warehouse, how to improve conditions for workers in the chicken coops.

MOTHER. You always had a good practical mind, Aniko.

HANNA. Sometimes, I totally forget that I am in prison awaiting trial. . . . How did you find this lawyer, Mom?

MOTHER. My friends recommended him; they said he's an expert in political trials, and very successful.

HANNA. And . . . how do Jewish organizations not know about me?

MOTHER. I don't know, Aniko, maybe they don't want to know. I knocked on every door but no one answered. I've asked to see people, and got no response. . . . Perhaps they're afraid . . .

HANNA. Afraid of what?

MOTHER: Maybe it can do damage. . . . I have no idea. . . . After all . . . you were sent to them!

HANNA. (*After a pause.*) They must know what they're doing.

MOTHER. Maybe. . . . I'm very disappointed at the way they treated me.

HANNA. You should trust them, Mom. If they're doing nothing, then this is how it must be. . . . (*Three knocks. Signal that their meeting is over. They get up.*) We'll meet again before the trial, Mom?

MOTHER. I hope so, Aniko. I'll try to get permission again. What should I bring you?

HANNA. I only ask for one thing, Mom. Please bring me a Hebrew Bible.

MOTHER. Yes, Aniko, I'll do my best to get it for you. (*They embrace.*) And let's hope for the best. Only a crooked heart cannot see that in God's eyes your deeds are pure.

HANNA. Let's hope so, Mom, let's hope people still have God in their hearts. (*Long embrace. Lights dim. When the lights come up again we're in a courtroom. Three colonels at the judges' table. On one side, prosecutor Matzkas, and Simon, a military judge. On the other side defense attorney Devcsery. Opposite them, in the dock, Hanna. At some distance, away from the courthouse, the Mother sits by herself.*)

JUDGE. (*Lowers the gavel.*) The accused, Hanna Senesh! You've heard the charges, the testimonies, the prosecution, and the defense. Have you anything to say in your defense?

HANNA. (*Stands up.*) Yes.

JUDGE. Speak.

HANNA. I have been accused here of a number of crimes which I do not deny. I did cross the border from the partisans in Yugoslavia—I admit it. I was sent here by the Allies—I admit it. I carried a transmitter to relay information abroad—I admit that, too. I came to save Jews from death—I'm proud of it. But the charge that I betrayed the country of my birth and planned its destruction, I categorically deny. I grew up in this country, I was educated here. At home, in school, in society—they taught me to love this Hungary, this land that had been liberated from the foreign yoke, the Hungary of Petöfi, of Addy, the Hungary of freedom fighters. I loved this land. Its simple, good people, its intellectuals, who stood up to tyranny. In it I breathed the air of freedom. So it was—until I found out that I, the daughter of an admired writer and respected mother—was considered a second class citizen, that I'm not entitled to the same rights as anyone born in this country—all because I'm a Jew. So I left the country I loved since childhood, and the person closest to me—my mother—and traveled to Palestine. There, I found my real homeland because there I discovered that I can walk with my head held up high, without fear, breathe the air, enjoy the sunlight, without any worry. I would have never left that land—were it not for the terrible events you all know about. I risked my life to get here—to save my brothers from death. Yes, I admit to that crime. If fighting slavery, humiliation, hellish cruelty the world has not seen since the Huns, is sin in your eyes—I admit to that sin. If fighting against vicious, wild beasts who take away innocent men and women, whose only sin is—that they were born Jews—if this is a sin in your eyes—I admit to that sin. But if anyone betrayed this country—that's you, all of you . . . (*Noise in the room.*)

PROSECUTOR. I ask you to stop this! We must not allow her to turn the courtroom into a political forum!

JUDGE B. The accused forgets before whom she stands.

JUDGE C. We won't allow a spy to accuse us!

PROSECUTOR. She is taking advantage of the court's leniency! I demand that she be stopped!

JUDGE. (*Pounding the gavel.*) Since the prosecution is asking for the death penalty—I'll let her finish.

HANNA. I repeat, everyone, including you, who serves this government and does not protest, is a traitor. Look what you have done to your Hungary, to this great country that suffered for hundreds of years under foreign occupation, saved in wars by freedom fighters! Examine your self-dignity, trampled on everywhere, how thousands of your sons are fighting a foreign war, for Hungary's eternal enemy—Germany! Look at the ruin you've brought on your people! How they're haunted by fear! How law-abiding citizens are kidnapped from their homes and thrown into pigsties! How tens of thousands who worked side by side with you for the good of all—are sent to death camps, to the ovens! Could anyone truly love his country and remain deaf to their outcry? Remember! This shameful government that you're serving, its days are numbered. Its hours. Judgment day is near for those who murdered, who shed innocent blood! The day will come when you'll sit in the dock, and facing you will be the souls of all those whose lives you've cut short! What will you say? How will you defend your actions? This is your last chance to retreat! One good deed can purge you of your sins! I know my actions are pure in God's eyes, so I am not afraid of death. If I feared your verdict, I wouldn't have wholeheartedly taken on this mission. You can kill me, as the Prosecutor wants, but know that this is just another nail in your coffin, in the coffin of the order you represent! (*Quiet.*)

JUDGE. (*Gets up, pounds the gavel.*) The court will adjourn for consultations. (*All leave except Hanna and the Mother.*)

MOTHER. (*Comes over, hugs her, then fixes her eyes on her.*) You've grown so tall, Aniko, that I must raise my eyes to the sky to see you . . .

HANNA. I'm at peace with myself, as if the nightmare were gone . . .

MOTHER. (*Holds her hand, scared.*) Suddenly, I'm scared . . .

HANNA. Of what?

MOTHER. Of losing you . . .

HANNA. But you saw, Mom, how they were afraid to look at me when I spoke!

MOTHER. But your words rang to distances far away from here, from life . . .

HANNA. But I spoke of life, Mom, only of life! (*Enter Devcsery.*)

MOTHER. So?

DEVCSERY. They've decided to postpone sentencing for a week.

MOTHER. Is this a good sign or a bad one?

DEVCSERY. I think—it's good, Mrs. Senesh. They're afraid. Very much! They're afraid that judgment day is near, as your daughter has warned them! This is the first time in the history of this military court! (*To Hanna.*) They're afraid of you! (*Light dims. When it comes back again it's Hanna's cell; she sits on the bed, holds her head in her hands. She stirs when hearing a noise. Drumbeat and soldiers marching in step. Gets up, tries to get to the window, cannot. Knocks a few times on the walls, hears no answer. Knocks on the door. Enter Yanos.*)

HANNA. Why the drumbeats?

YANOS. (*Terrified.*) Executions, Miss Anna. Every hour—executions . . .

HANNA. You know who?

YANOS. I can't know, Miss Anna. They just grab people from their cells, put them against the wall, and shoot. May Jesus our Savior have mercy on their souls.

HANNA. You haven't heard even one name?

122 / Aharon Megged

YANOS. Not one. They do it without sentencing. God protect us from Antichrist, it has never been this way.

HANNA. And me—no one asked about me?

YANOS. No, Miss Anna. . . . God have mercy on you. . . . (*After a pause.*) There's a narrow gate to the Kingdom of Heaven. Only a few will enter, but I know that you'll be one of them. Yes, yes . . . (*More drumbeats, marching soldiers. Yanos closes the door, leaves quickly. A shot. Hanna hides her face in her hands. Tries again to get to the window. Brings a chair, climbs on it. Just then the door opens. It's prosecutor Simon. Hanna climbs down, retreats to the wall.*)

SIMON. (*Stands in front of her for a while, silent.*) I came to inform you that this morning the judges pronounced your sentence . . . (*Long pause.*)

HANNA. Death?

SIMON. (*Head bowed, after a pause.*) You still have one opening left—ask for mercy.

HANNA. When did they pronounce my sentence?

SIMON. An hour ago.

HANNA. That's a lie! There was no sentence! (*Shouting.*) Why didn't you call me? Were you afraid to look me in the eye? Say it! Speak! (*After a pause.*) Are you afraid of the truth, you crawling cowards?! You know you'll never be able to cleanse yourselves of the blood you're shedding! Miserable creatures! Have you no dignity? Speak! Say something in your defense! (*He's quiet.*) Oh, better to die than live like you! (*After a pause.*) Call for my lawyer, I want to appeal.

SIMON. There is no appeal here.

HANNA. A lie! You know there is a higher court! I want to appeal to it!

SIMON. There is no appeal. You can only ask for mercy.

HANNA. From you? To fall on my knees and ask you for mercy? Never! (*Shouting.*) I want to appeal!

SIMON. The sentence will be carried out in an hour. You may write letters to your family. Be ready.

HANNA. (*Shouts after him, grabs the door bars.*) Bring me my mother! My mother! (*He leaves.*) Bring me my mother! . . . My mother! . . . (*Falls on the bed, hides her face in her hands. Lights dim. Enter Eliahu. She gets up, clings to him.*) Look, what they're doing to me, Eliahu . . . (*Buries her face in his chest, cries.*)

ELIAHU. You said you were strong, remember?

HANNA. I want to live Eliahu, I want so much to live . . .

ELIAHU. I warned you.

HANNA. It's terrible dying like this, like a star in the dark. Terrible.

ELIAHU. It's the common fate of many. Predictable fate.

HANNA. I was a little girl, Eliahu, that's all. A voice called, and I went.

ELIAHU. It was a true voice, wasn't it?

HANNA. Must it be this way—that truth should lead to death?

ELIAHU. Remember? "Blessed is the match consumed / In kindling flame."

HANNA. Please console me, Eliahu.

ELIAHU. Should I tell you about your friends?

HANNA. Yes, tell me everything. (*Pulls him to the bed. They sit down.*)

ELIAHU. Three who went before you, are no more. And twenty-three who went by boat were lost in the sea. Fifteen young men fell when they got to the fortress.

HANNA. Tell me about life, Eliahu. Not about those who are gone.

ELIAHU. The living remember you, Hanna, they'll remember you forever.

HANNA. Tell me about them, I want them with me as I go. It's much easier that way.

ELIAHU. Should I tell you about your kibbutz on the seashore?

HANNA. Yes! I'm so eager to hear it—(*Opposite them, three young men, fishermen, barefoot, sit on shoulders.*)

ELIAHU. The fishermen are leaving now to faraway places . . . almost near the islands . . . and the two trees you planted by your tent have grown since you've left . . . and on the beach, little children run after the seagulls . . .

HANNA. Tell me more, Eliahu . . . (*Drumbeat. Marching soldiers.*) I must go, Eliahu, my time is up. Let me hold you to be strong. I want to look at the rifles without fear . . . (*The song "Blessed Is the Match" grows louder and louder from afar. Hanna walks toward the sound. Lights dim. Dark. More drumbeats. As the light comes back up, we see the Mother, as if lost in the streets.*)

MOTHER. (*Turning this way and that way, confused.*) Where's my daughter? (*Judge B passes by with belongings. She speaks to him.*) Where's my daughter? What happened to her? It's been ten days since the trial, and I'm not allowed to see her . . .

JUDGE B. Madam, the Russians are at the gate, everyone's fleeing. (*Runs off. Judge C passes by with belongings.*)

MOTHER. (*To Judge C.*) Why didn't I hear a thing from my daughter? I asked for permission to enter the prison, why don't they let me in?

JUDGE C. It's total chaos now, madam, no one knows anything, try the office on Conti Street . . . (*Starts to leave.*)

MOTHER. But I've been there—it's empty . . . (*He leaves. She hears drumbeats, marching soldiers. Listens until they fade away.*)

MOTHER. (*To herself.*) Are these executions? But they haven't sentenced her yet. Attorney Devcsery himself said sentencing won't happen for days. . . . Perhaps not at all! (*Judge A passes by, with belongings.*) Your Honor! I'm asking about my daughter . . . Where is she? Where?

JUDGE A. Madam, no one knows, no one knows. Everyone's leaving . . .

MOTHER. Good God! Where is my daughter? (*The scene shifts to the Prosecutor's office. Officer Simon, at his desk, packing files. Signs of destroyed documents. Enter the Mother.*)

MOTHER. Catherine Senesh. Anna's mother.

SIMON. (*Stops work a moment, looks at her.*) Yes, what's the matter?

MOTHER. I came to ask permission to see my daughter.

SIMON. (*Opens eyes wide, unable to hide his terror.*) How . . .

MOTHER. I was told that you are in charge, isn't it so?

SIMON. (*After long hesitation.*) No, the matter is no longer in my hands.

MOTHER. So, who should I ask for a permit?

SIMON. I don't know.

MOTHER. Should I ask the prison authorities?

SIMON. I don't know. Maybe.

MOTHER. (*After a short pause.*) Mister Officer! At least give me an idea, where should I turn now? I don't know why it is so difficult to get one when relatives of other prisoners visit every week! I've only gotten one permit, for ten short minutes!

SIMON. Yes? I've never issued one.

MOTHER. (*After a pause*). Why isn't the sentence known yet? The date has already passed!

SIMON. Even if it did happen—I wouldn't be able to tell you.

MOTHER. How could you hide it from me? Perhaps it did happen. (*He's quiet.*) Tell me! I have the right to know! I am her mother!

SIMON. After a pause.) Please sit down. (*She does, he sits down, too.*) Are you familiar with your daughter's case, Mrs. Senesh?

MOTHER. Yes. The lawyer explained it to me.

SIMON. Your daughter served the enemy, and her job was spying and transmitting information to the Allies. If we hadn't caught her, she would have caused a catastrophe to us all. Nothing is more serious in wartime.

MOTHER. This girl is free of sin, sir. She can only do good. I know my daughter.

SIMON. Maybe you don't consider her actions a crime. I can understand that. But in the eyes of her native country, her birthplace, these actions have only one name—treason.

MOTHER. My daughter never betrayed any humane ideals. I know that well.

SIMON. Her actions led to it. If she had succeeded—we would have had here terrible bloodshed. There is no mercy for this.

MOTHER. Sir, you know she came only to save Jews from death. She admitted to that in court. Is saving people from death a crime? You! A Hungarian just like thousands I knew in my life—wouldn't you do everything to save your son, or your brother, or your mother, if you knew that they were facing death? Don't you have a father's heart in you? Don't you know what love is? Tell me! After all, you were raised among people, not beasts! You must know what fear is! The desire to live! You must know what natural impulse is when one sees innocent people being dragged to their death! Tell me! Why are you silent? (*He's silent, turns his head away.*) Am I to understand that sentencing has already occurred?

SIMON. (*Without looking at her.*) Yes. It has.

MOTHER. (*Terrified.*) But this is impossible! Impossible! Only today I got a letter from the lawyer telling me he'll call me when it happens. . . . Is it possible he doesn't know?

SIMON. He knows.

MOTHER. If so, why hasn't he told me? Why was I not allowed to see my daughter?

SIMON. He probably felt sorry for you, so he didn't tell you.

MOTHER. (*Terrified, abruptly.*) Sorry? Why should he feel sorry? They . . .

SIMON. For the gravest of crimes—the gravest sentence.

MOTHER. (*Screams.*) No!

SIMON. And the sentence was carried out today, this morning. (*Drumbeat, marching steps sound closer and closer. Then they stop abruptly. Simon leaves. The Mother looks around; frozen look on her face. Lights fade. Enter Hanna, as an apparition. Puts an arm on her mother's shoulder.*)

HANNA. Are you sad, Mom?

MOTHER. (*Looks at her.*) You are here, Aniko! . . . I was sure you had left me . . .

HANNA. I'm with you, Mom, always. Very sad, Mom?

MOTHER. Reflecting.

HANNA. On me?!

MOTHER. Yes, Aniko. I was thinking how difficult it will be to part from you.

HANNA. (*Hugs her around her neck with joy.*) But I'm your little girl, that's what I'll always be to you . . .

MOTHER. Where do I go from here, Aniko?

HANNA. To my home, Mom. Look at my footprints in the soft sand, the two trees I planted by the tent, and listen to my voice in the murmur of the waves . . . (*Falls on her knees near her.*) These will be beautiful days. No more wars, and evil men won't howl at little girls's faces, and daughters won't part from their mothers anymore. Remember what I told you once about the stars.

MOTHER. Yes, I do. There are stars whose light reaches the earth only after they themselves are extinguished.

HANNA. Can you see this light?

MOTHER. It's near me, Aniko, very near, now . . .

HANNA. Only when a person is alone does darkness surround him. Do you know, when they put me there, against the wall, in the courtyard, there was a moment of darkness around me, and I thought I'd collapse. Then I opened my eyes—and I no longer saw the firing squad with their rifles pointing at me—I only saw you . . . you suddenly appeared, you, and all my friends, those with whom I traveled on the road of life—and there was light around me. I knew I was going to be with them forever, always, and was no longer afraid. (*The song "Eli, Eli, shelo igamer leolam" is heard from afar; the sound grows increasingly louder. Hanna gets up. Her Mother, too. They stand for a while looking at each other. Hanna begins to walk away slowly, as if ascending, until she disappears. The Mother is left alone as she follows Hanna with her eyes.*)

CURTAIN

Ben-Zion Tomer

Ben-Zion Tomer was born in Poland in 1928. He went to Palestine by way of Russia and Tehran. He fought in the 1948 War of Independence and was held captive in Jordan. Tomer studied philosophy and literature at the Hebrew University. He edited a literary journal and taught at various educational institutions. A writer of prose, poetry, and plays, Tomer won the Prime Minister's Prize for literature.

His major works are *River Returning* (1959/poetry), *On the Equator* (1969/poetry), *Via Salt* (1978/prose), and *Children of the Shadows/* 1962. *Children of the Shadows* has appeared in English, German, Spanish, and French.

Children of the Shadows

1962

(Translated by Hillel Halkin)

Characters

YORAM, twenty-eight years old.
NURIT, twenty-six years old.
DR. SIGMUND RABINOWITZ, fifty-five years old.
BALLOON SELLER, sixty years old.
BERELE, a newcomer, twenty-eight years old.
DUBI, twenty-eight years old.
HELENKA, Yanek's wife, twenty-six years old.
YANEK, Yoram's brother, thirty-seven years old.
WAITER

PASSERSBY

PARTICIPANTS IN A PARTY

ACT I

Scene 1

The roar of the sea. Sunbeams dance on the waves. The stage is empty. After a few seconds, enough to permit the audience to take in the scene, Sigmund Rabinowitz enters from the direction of the sea, his legs straddling the railing of the boardwalk. In his right hand he carries a briefcase. With one foot over the railing he turns to look back at the sea. He crosses over to a bench and sits down, producing from his briefcase a notebook and a decrepit stuffed toy dog. Enter Dubi, passing by.

SIGMUND. Shameless mortal, sinful one. Give me a pound and I'll be gone. (*Dubi brushes him off with a self-assured gesture and walks away. Sigmund returns to his bench. The waiter appears in front of the sidewalk café. From offstage come the cries of melon vendors blended with phonograph music coming from the café. The waiter goes back inside. Enter the Balloon Seller. Sigmund is busy writing. The Balloon Seller sits down on the far end of the bench. Sigmund does not notice him. The Balloon Seller inches up to him and tries to peek at the notebook.*)

SIGMUND. (*Noticing him.*) Beat it!

BALLOON SELLER. It's not your bench.

SIGMUND. It's my notebook.

BALLOON SELLER. I haven't stolen it.

SIGMUND. But you were peeking.

BALLOON SELLER. I wasn't peeking . . . (*He takes a peek. Sigmund goes on writing. The Balloon Seller peeks again.*) What are you writing?

SIGMUND. My will.

BALLOON SELLER. (*Alarmed.*) No! You're sick? Going to die?

SIGMUND. To kill myself.

BALLOON SELLER. No!

SIGMUND. Right now . . . if you don't beat it.

BALLOON SELLER. Whew, you scared me. . . . I can see you're fond of jokes. . . . Haven't we met before?

SIGMUND. (*Examining him suspiciously.*) I hope not.

BALLOON SELLER. What's the matter? It's nice to meet old friends. . . . I'm from Bezhuchovitsa. Ever hear of it?

SIGMUND. No.

BALLOON SELLER. Near Lvov.

SIGMUND. No.

BALLOON SELLER. It's a very nice place . . . (*After a pause.*) You scared me. To kill yourself. . . . Suicides don't go to Heaven. Do you believe in Heaven?

SIGMUND. As much as in this world.

BALLOON SELLER. I believe all right, even in the resurrection of the dead.

SIGMUND. Earth is Heaven enough for me.

BALLOON SELLER. You're not afraid to die?

SIGMUND. Afraid to die? Not at all, not at all—that is, I haven't been afraid up till now; but if there really were such a thing as Heaven and the Resurrection, I certainly would be.

BALLOON SELLER. I don't get it.

SIGMUND. Did I say you did?

BALLOON SELLER. Do you have a family?

SIGMUND. Would you kindly remove yourself and stop interrogating me?

BALLOON SELLER. I'm not interrogating you. . . . I saw a Jew sitting by himself, I sat down.

SIGMUND I'm not by myself.

BALLOON SELLER. You're lucky.

SIGMUND. Praise be to God.

BALLOON SELLER. Do you live in Tel Aviv?

SIGMUND. Here.

BALLOON SELLER. Here where?

SIGMUND. Here is here. (*Points to the bench.*)

BALLOON SELLER. On the bench?

SIGMUND. Under it.

BALLOON SELLER. I live in a shack . . . not far from here . . . it's fine in summer, but in winter . . . you're not afraid to sleep all alone?

SIGMUND. I don't sleep all alone.

BALLOON SELLER. I don't get it.

SIGMUND. I don't doubt that. . . . Shall I tell you a secret? You are a fortunate man.

BALLOON SELLER. Me?

SIGMUND. You.

BALLOON SELLER. I don't think . . .

SIGMUND. That's why you're fortunate.

BALLOON SELLER. I really don't get it.

SIGMUND. And so you're fortunate. It says somewhere: blessed are the poor of brain, for theirs is the Kingdom of Heaven . . .

BALLOON SELLER. Then you do believe in the Kingdom of Heaven?

SIGMUND. Listen, Reb Yid, you have your balloons, why don't you go and sell them?

BALLOON SELLER. Who to? It's autumn . . . the cafés are empty . . . in summer it's fine . . . people . . . lots of people . . . children . . . they even made up a song about my balloons . . . (*Sings.*)

> Uncle Balloon
> Has balloons to sell
> Uncle Balloon
> We think he's really swell.

Little devils. But in the winter . . . it's so depressing . . . and boring.

SIGMUND. Talking is boring.

BALLOON SELLER. If you were as lonely as I am, you wouldn't say that.

SIGMUND. You're right. . . . It's a pity you don't sell loneliness instead of balloons. I'd buy some loneliness from you. (*He gets up.*) (*Enter Yoram. He sits down in the café. Sigmund stares at him as if bewitched. He buries his face in his hands as if trying to remember something.*)

BALLOON SELLER. What's the matter with you? (*Sigmund brushes him off rudely. He gets up quickly as if to walk off, then comes back. In the meantime, the Balloon Seller moves to another bench.*)

WAITER. (*To Yoram.*) What will you have?

YORAM. Espresso. (*He takes a letter from his pocket and reads.*)

WAITER. (*Returning with the coffee.*) Here you are. . . . (*He cleans a nearby table.*) Don't I know you from somewhere?

YORAM. I used to come here during the war. During the truce.

WAITER. That's right, that's right. An officer. With a jeep. Oh, you used to enjoy yourselves. Now none of you come here any more. Maybe you'd like some music? We have lots of records—wartime hits, I don't remember the names.

YORAM. No, thanks, don't bother. (*Waiter arranging the chairs.*) You used to clear tables here, if I'm not mistaken.

WAITER. Yes, I was a newcomer then, now the café is mine, all mine . . .

YORAM. Then you've done well for yourself.

WAITER. Yes, some German compensation money and some brains. In Yiddish we say brains are a gift from God. You speak Yiddish?

YORAM. No.

WAITER. You know, sir, when one of you guys comes here, something in my heart . . . now you don't come anymore. But we're as crowded as ever. In the summer. Lots of noise, but nobody knows how to have a good time. (*Yoram looks at his watch.*) She'll come, she'll come all right. That's how girls are, they come late, but they come.

YORAM. Maybe I'm waiting for him and not for her?

WAITER. When you wait for a him, you wait differently. I'm an old pro. In the old country, I worked in a big hotel. (*He leaves. Enter Nurit. Yoram puts the letter in his pocket and gets up to greet her. They shake hands.*)

NURIT. It's strange to see you out of uniform.

YORAM. And to see you without braids.

NURIT. When did you arrive?

WAITER. (*Enters.*) Something for the lady?

NURIT. *Café au lait.* (*The waiter disappears.*) So you've really, really left the kibbutz?

YORAM. Are you surprised?

NURIT. A little . . . you were so passionately fanatic . . . like a monk.

YORAM. The . . . frock is not the man. And how are you?

NURIT. I've cut off my braids, as you see, and gave away my jumpers to the maid. How do you like my new hairdo? Is it nice?

YORAM. I'm not very good with compliments.

NURIT. I know . . . it's all written down in your personal file, Captain.

YORAM. There's a lot written down in our personal files. They'd best gather dust.

NURIT. If they become dust, what will become of us?

YORAM. That is the question.

NURIT. And what do you do now, Hamlet?

YORAM. Hamlet?

NURIT. That's what they called you, Captain. You never knew?

YORAM. Never.

NURIT. Dubi gave you the name. He said that when you studied *Hamlet* in school you had all kinds of theories about it. . . . Do you have any plans?

YORAM. I'll manage somehow. After all, I'm not a newcomer.

NURIT. Do you have a place to stay?

YORAM. Why have they chopped down the old woods by the river? Maybe at Dani's. Do you ever see him?

NURIT. Hardly at all. Every Independence Day. Wherever the coffee still flows—there you'll find Dani. Haven't you any relatives in town?

YORAM. No.

NURIT. In that case, you have even less than an immigrant—you don't even have the Jewish Agency. And money?

YORAM. Enough. For two weeks.

NURIT. And no profession, of course. A professional idealist and warrior. You should have stayed in the kibbutz, or gone back to the army. You're like a fish in water there.

YORAM. That's why I'm trying to live on land.

NURIT. You're likely to dry up.

YORAM. Hey, balloons!

BALLOON SELLER. (*Gets up off his bench, approaches.*) Balloons! Balloons!

YORAM. (*To Nurit.*) Instead of roses. How much does one cost?

BALLOON SELLER. Ten pennies.

YORAM. And how many balloons do you have?

BALLOON SELLER (*Counts them.*) Ten.

YORAM. I'll take them all.

BALLOON SELLER. All of them?

YORAM. All of them.

BALLOON SELLER. If you buy them all, what will I do all evening?

YORAM. You don't want to sell?

BALLOON SELLER. I do, it's just that when I have my balloons I can walk up to people, I can talk to them. The night is so long. (*Yoram takes out a bill.*) Here you are, mister, they're yours. (*He gives Yoram all the balloons.*) I'm all alone here. My family . . .

YORAM. All of it?

BALLOON SELLER. Yes, dead. From typhus. A wife and three children. In Samarkand.

YORAM. (*Somehow excited.*) Samarkand?

BALLOON SELLER. You know where that is?

YORAM. (*Reservedly.*) I've heard of it. Where is it?

BALLOON SELLER. Not far from Tashkent, the city of bread, they call it. Bread . . . what a famine we had there, what a famine . . . you were born here, weren't you? Can tell right away . . . the ones who were born here don't know where it is. Would you like to see pictures of my children?

YORAM. No, we believe you.

NURIT. (*She takes the balloons from Yoram, hands half of them back to the balloon seller.*) Five will be enough.

BALLOON SELLER. You don't want them all?

NURIT. What will you do all evening? (*The balloon seller takes some change from his pocket and begins to count it.*)

YORAM. You can keep the change.

BALLOON SELLER. (*Proudly.*) I'm not a beggar. Half-a-pound, please. (*He leaves the money on the table, takes five balloons from Nurit, and disappears.*)

NURIT. They're so quick to take offense.

YORAM. Each one of them has twenty pounds of TNT in his heart.

NURIT. He thought you were born here.

YORAM. They all think so.

NURIT. Do they? Why did you buy all those balloons?

YORAM. I don't remember anymore.

NURIT. In order to pop them?

YORAM. They are too lovely for that, it would be cruel and unfair. There's an alternative.

NURIT. Being?

YORAM. To keep them until they shrink by themselves. And still another: to let them fly away and disappear. Nurit, it's good to see you . . .

NURIT. Really? (*Yoram lays his hand on hers, she pulls away.*) I have to go.

YORAM. I know it's too late to ask for forgiveness.

NURIT. Forgiveness . . . after two years. . . . I believe that's a new word in your vocabulary.

YORAM. Many words have died in the meantime. Through those two years, I kept wondering.

NURIT. I can still remember that morning in the kibbutz. I came to stay with you for good. I waited for you to say just one word, but you, all you had to say was "Nurit, go home." That was all.

YORAM. I couldn't Nurit, something gave inside me, everything. . . . Suddenly you came, to my home which wasn't a home anymore and from which there was nowhere to go, which I still wasn't ready to leave. . . . I wanted to find it all over again, or to lose it all, but to lose it by myself, just me alone . . .

NURIT. And you thought that for two years I'd be a lily-white maiden, shut up in her castle, waiting for an eagle, or at least a dove, to bring her a letter from her prince charming far away . . . two hours away by bus. . . . I have to go. Someone's waiting for me at home. . . . (*Vengefully.*) Dubi! Would you like to see him? Let's go. (*Yoram gets up. He leaves a bill on the table. As they are about to go, Sig-*

mund appears. He stares fixedly at Yoram, who, unlike Nurit, does not notice him.)

NURIT. Who's that?

YORAM. Who?

NURIT. That man.

YORAM. How should I know? Some nut.

NURIT. (*Releasing the balloons, which slowly rise and disappear.*) Let's go. (*They leave. Music is heard from the café. A man enters and sits by the table, newspaper in hand.*)

SIGMUND. (*following them. To himself.*) What a resemblance! (*He follows them offstage.*)

Scene 2

Nurit's room. A bookcase featuring the collected works of various authors. A small table. Two armchairs. As the light goes on in the room the music from the café gradually fades out and some quiet music of Bach's fades in. Yoram and Dubi are seated by the table, on which there is a chess board. They are silent. Nurit enters, wearing an apron. As she approaches Dubi, he strokes her back; she slips away. Yoram notices, though his head is lowered over the chess pieces. Nurit leaves. When Yoram and Dubi speak, it is with the tone of people recollecting something from long ago.

YORAM. No, the pawn here was mine. The queen is yours.

DUBI. How do you manage to remember?

YORAM. It was one of those games that you don't forget.

DUBI. It was on Hill 74. How many years ago was that? Seven?

YORAM. The board and the pieces haven't changed at all.

DUBI. And the chess players?

YORAM. More or less the same.

DUBI. Nurit was in the next room, too. (*From the kitchen comes the sound of something heavy falling.*)

YORAM. Nurit, are you all right? (*To Dubi.*) The hut shook with every explosion.

DUBI. Shall we begin?

YORAM. We might as well. Who moved last, do you remember?

DUBI. (*After hesitating.*) . . . I did.

YORAM. Right.

DUBI. It's your move then.

YORAM. It's my move. (*He moves.*) There.

DUBI. (*Moving.*) Can I take that back?

YORAM. It's just like it was then. . . . How did I answer you? Yes, you can take it back, as long as you've got somewhere to go to.

DUBI. I had a place to go then, Green Fields.

YORAM. A lovely name, Green Fields.

DUBI. It was a lovely kibbutz. . . . I said to you, "If you ever feel like it, come join us."

YORAM. Will you have me?

DUBI. Well, you're not exactly one of the "gang," you're a little green, but we'll give it a try.

NURIT. (*Entering.*) Anybody care for some coffee? (*The two of them burst into laughter.*) What are you laughing for?

YORAM. We recalled the last game we played, up on the hill, and the conversation we had, and you came in exactly the same place you did then.

NURIT. Is the game still on?

YORAM. Uh-huh . . .

DUBI. This time we'll finish it, right Nurit?

NURIT. (*To Yoram.*) You drink it black and without sugar, if I remember correctly.

YORAM. You haven't forgotten.

DUBI. And I take milk and three spoonfuls of sugar. (*To Nurit, who is standing in the doorway.*) And turn off that Bach of yours. It makes me jumpy.

NURIT. With a whole lot of sugar. (*To Yoram.*) These kibbutz boys always need something to suck on. (*She leaves.*)

YORAM. When did you leave Green Fields?

DUBI. It's been a while. Three years ago.

YORAM. Do you ever go back to visit?

DUBI. Hardly at all. You know how it is.

YORAM. Don't you ever visit your parents?

DUBI. They've also left. My father is now a big shot in the immigration department.

YORAM. And you?

DUBI. I'm his assistant.

YORAM. (*Bursting into laughter.*) You?

DUBI. What's wrong with that?

YORAM. Nothing. . . . I only happened to remember the way you used to talk about the new pastoral age . . . about Arab dances, artesian wells, horses and camels . . . campfires. The mysterious powers of fire . . . about how one shouldn't allow anyone over the age of thirteen into the country . . . so as not to nip our reawakened primitivism in the bud. . . . Do you remember? I was fourteen years old when I came here.

DUBI. That extra year will always count against you.

YORAM. I suppose you're right. (*He laughs again.*) So now you're helping gather our Jewish brethren from the corners of the earth?

DUBI. As if I give a damn. . . . At least I can get to Europe every once in a while instead of rotting away forever in this provincial hole.

YORAM. Now that's another story! That I can understand.

DUBI. We'll be going away to Paris for two years pretty soon.

YORAM. Who's we?

DUBI. Nurit and I. (*Nurit enters with the tray of coffee. Two cups.*)

NURIT. (*Giving Dubi a cup.*) With. (*To Yoram.*) Without.

DUBI. Get dressed. We'll be late for the movie.

NURIT. I've invited Yoram for dinner.

YORAM. (*He is surprised, then understands.*) Don't put yourselves out.

DUBI. I'm sorry I don't have another ticket. (*To Nurit.*) Are you off?

NURIT. (*Angrily.*) I've invited Yoram for dinner. (*She leaves.*)

DUBI. Okay! I'm going.

YORAM. I'm awfully sorry.

DUBI. It's all right, I have to go.

YORAM. (*Looks at his watch.*) We've still got time. Come on, let's finish the game.

DUBI. (*Angrily.*) Some other time. (*In a tone ostensibly friendly, but actually haughty and ironic.*) Nurit told me you're looking for work. For someone like you, I can always find something—with you speaking a couple of languages and being acquainted with the problems of immigrants.

YORAM. No thanks, I have plenty of offers. . . . But thanks anyway.

DUBI. It's just that . . . for old time's sake.

YORAM. I know how you feel, and I'm grateful . . . really . . .

DUBI. Well, that's that. I'm going. Whose move is it?

YORAM. Mine. . . . Some other time.

DUBI. Fine, sure, it's about time we finished this game. (*He steps toward the kitchen door, then turns back and leaves.*)

YORAM. (*Following after Dubi, who leaves without saying good-bye.*) So long, Dubi. (*Dubi doesn't answer. Yoram is left by himself on stage. He plays with his and Dubi's chess pieces.*)

NURIT. (*To Yoram.*) I'll be right back. (*She leaves.*)

YORAM. (*Speaking as it were, first to Dubi's chess pieces, then to himself.*) Can you have that move back? You can have it back! If you've got somewhere to go. But you haven't, Dubi, you haven't. Yes, now you're on horseback. But it doesn't matter. I'll get you off that high horse. All the king's riders . . . (*Outside, on the boardwalk, Dubi crosses the stage. He remains standing by the darkened café. He lights a cigarette. Enter Nurit.*)

NURIT. Dubi, there's something I have to say to you.

DUBI. Me, too. I don't want to see him around here anymore.

NURIT. That's no way to behave.

DUBI. What right have you got to talk? He's always tagging after me, like a puppy. There, it was Naomi; here, it's . . . (*Nurit moves to the railing. Dubi follows her. They engage in conversation, as it were, while Yoram speaks the following monologue.*)

YORAM. I'll never forgive you that night in the dormitory. I was dreaming of Samarkand. After the typhus. I was hungry. I leaned against a wall and the wall collapsed. "Who's making that racket?," you asked. "Let him be, he's dreaming," Naomi said. "Then let him stop dreaming. I can sleep without dreams!" I was afraid to fall asleep because I might shout again. Always, whenever I couldn't fall asleep, you used to snore. You lay there and snored. Every time. You slept so soundly. At peace with yourself like a block of wood. And as stupid as a block of wood.

DUBI. (*Continuing, as it were, their previous conversation.*) No.

NURIT. Yes, Dubi. I'm not going with you to Paris.

DUBI. You mean . . .

NURIT. Yes.

DUBI. You . . . love him?

NURIT. What difference does it make? If he hadn't turned up, I wouldn't have gone with you anyhow. You were so sure of yourself, you never bothered to ask me. Good night, Dubi. (*She starts in the direction of home. Dubi takes the tickets from his pocket and tears them up. He stands there for a moment, thinking, then disappears.*)

YORAM. (*Moving one of his pieces.*) Move. Stop dreaming, Dubi. I've got myself, but where have you got to go to? You haven't got anywhere, Dubi nowhere! I've cut you down to size, Dubi, A chip off the old block. Mate! (*He scatters the chess pieces. Nurit enters.*) I'm sorry.

NURIT. Soon we'll eat dinner. (*They look each other in the eyes. Again, Bach's music.*)

BLACKOUT

Scene 3

The café. Daylight.

BERELE. How come nobody from our town knows that you're here in Israel?

YORAM. I don't know. . . . You say you saw my parents a month ago?

BERELE. Approximately. . . . They're kind of angry with you.

YORAM. With me? Why?

BERELE. They said you hardly ever write.

YORAM. You really haven't told me anything about yourself yet.

BERELE. What's there to tell? It's pretty tough being alone. . . . It's a funny thing, when I got on the boat I thought there was nothing between me and Israel but the sea. Now I know that there's still another sea that I must cross; a sea of new immigrants . . .

YORAM. You've . . . got no one? . . . I mean . . .

BERELE. It's all right. I know what you mean. I've already noticed that only here people are afraid to talk about these things, but that's obviously my situation. Obviously.

YORAM. (*Sipping his drink.*) I guess you're in need of a job. (*He takes out a pencil and notebook.*) I'll give you a note to a friend of mine—I'm sure everything will turn out all right . . .

BERELE. Thanks, Yossele, thanks.

YORAM. Don't talk nonsense. . . . By the way . . . my name now is Yoram.

BERELE. Since when? To me you'll always be Yossele. Do you know that two more of the old gang, Hersh and Wolf, are here in Israel?

YORAM. Wolf?

BERELE. What? You don't remember Wolf? The tall one . . . with the. . . . And now you, too. . . . I'm meeting them tonight, will you come along? There's so much to talk about. . . . It's been such a long time.

YORAM. I'm sorry, but I won't be in town tonight. Look, give me their address, I'll see to it that . . .

BERELE. It's a shame. . . . Your mother gave me a sweater for you. Where should I bring it?

YORAM. Could you maybe leave it . . . here? At the café? The waiter will give it to me. . . . I mean . . . well, I don't have a permanent address yet.

BERELE. Right, I understand . . . (*He sips the drink.*) Your parents must have gotten their visas by now.

YORAM. Yes, two weeks ago. They're coming soon.

BERELE. You're lucky. You always were lucky.

YORAM. Would you like another drink? . . . No . . . I'll just finish writing this note. . . . Sorry, I've got to be on my way now. . . . Try this address, and I'm sure everything will be alright . . . (*He hands over the note.*) In a couple of days I'll have the time, we'll definitely get together; in the meantime, give my regards to Hersh and Wolf. . . . I'll get in touch with you all. (*He gets up, as does Berele. Yoram accompanies him and adds, after they have already parted.*) Berele. . . . Maybe you need some money? (*Berele cringes inside, lowers his head.*) Twenty pounds, okay? (*He pushes the bills into Berele's hand.*)

BERELE. Thanks.

YORAM. Forget it . . .

BERELE. I'll let you have it back from my first paycheck. (*He turns sharply and disappears in the direction of the boardwalk. Yoram follows him with his eyes.*)

BLACKOUT

Scene 4

In this scene Yoram talks at length about his past, but this must be acted concretely, as if events were actually taking place in the present. The lights pick out Sigmund, who is staring at Yoram and Nurit's window. Noises come from the boardwalk: the sound of waves, "Hot corn!", etc. The waiter chases Sigmund from the front of the café. All this is mimed. A half-empty glass of whiskey that has been left on a table is gulped down by Sigmund as soon as the waiter disappears. As in the previous scene, the man with the newspaper is seen onstage. The light in Nurit's room is intimate and warm.

YORAM. (*As if continuing a conversation.*) So Naomi said, "Listen, Yossele, from now on your name is Yoram."

NURIT. How old were you when you came here?

YORAM. Fourteen.

NURIT. Half of what you are now.

YORAM. Half there and half here.

NURIT. When it comes to the first half, I'm completely in the dark.

YORAM. The dark side of the moon.

NURIT. Take me there.

YORAM. You'll end up like Lot's wife.

NURIT. Take me there.

YORAM. It's a long story.

NURIT. We have a long night ahead of us.

YORAM. You won't understand anyway.

NURIT. Thanks for the compliment . . .

YORAM. You know what I mean.

NURIT. I know. Tell me about it.

YORAM. The night isn't long enough. Nurit, come here. (*She sits by his side.*) Aren't you afraid to marry me? You hardly know me at all. . . . It's strange, other girls never wanted to know more than they knew, and so they only knew the second half of the story.

NURIT. Perhaps because that's as far as you ever let them go? (*She gets up.*) Now you're trying to get out of it again.

YORAM. Perhaps. Since the day I came here, I've tried to eat from the tree of forgetfulness. Do you remember your childhood?

NURIT. Everything.

YORAM. And sometimes, I remember nothing . . . isolated fragments . . . nothing whole or in one piece.

NURIT. Is changing a name enough to forget?

YORAM. No. (*He gets up.*) But it's enough to make believe. Whoever wants to change his biography in this country, changes his name. (*As if to himself.*) From now on, your name is Yoram. Yoram! Wasn't I something?! (*He laughs sarcastically, then, as it were, imitating Naomi's voice.*) You changed so much since you came. Now if you'd only learn to dance a polka you'd be just like the rest of us. Just like the rest of us! I'll never forget that evening in the dormitory. I was waiting on tables along with Dubi and Naomi. I was cleaning up. Huge amounts of food had been left on the table. Enough to have lasted my parents a whole year over there. "What should I do with what's left?" I asked. "Throw it out!" Dubi said. "I can't" I said. The two of them began to laugh as if I had told a good joke. Suddenly I started to hate myself. Them. Myself. The memories that kept me from being one of them. Do you know what Dubi was? What I wouldn't have given to have one-quarter of that? Try to imagine: the first-born child of the kibbutz. Captain of the soccer team. The best dancer around, and if that wasn't enough—a good tractor-driver and an excellent speaker. A very important person in the Jezreel Valley. The prince of the valley. And Naomi was his girl. Inside me, I began to murder Yossele. Yossele is dead! Long live Yoram! A year later, I was king, Naomi was in my arms. I learned to dance the polka. I learned the ropes. All the ropes. . . . Let's go to the movies!

NURIT. (*Going over to the pantry.*) Will you have a drink? (*She returns with a bottle and two glasses and pours drinks.*)

YORAM. Have you spoken to your father?

NURIT. Everything will be all right.

YORAM. I want to know what he said.

NURIT. That you should rejoin the army. Security, my dear, young love, my dear, but even the young need security.

YORAM. He's like all those in this generation who never played at being soldiers, now we've become their toys. Actually, I don't blame him. What have I got? A profession?

NURIT. Take Gilead's offer.

YORAM. You're kidding. You're prepared to live in a little town full of immigrants?

NURIT. I'll live with you.

YORAM. You'd be a stranger there.

NURIT. And you?

YORAM. I am already a stranger.

NURIT. Then there's nothing to worry about, stranger. The ceremony will be in two weeks.

YORAM. You have a magnificent way of putting things.

NURIT. You're not telling me anything I haven't heard before, but if you think I'm something, you should listen to my father. (*Imitating him.*) Yoram? A lovely guy. Back then, during the war, his picture was in all the papers. Yes, indeed, well I remember. . . . The special atmosphere of the Holy Land. . . . The speech that I gave the day his shipload of immigrants arrived on our shores! Published verbatim in all the papers. The special atmosphere of the Holy Land. . . . Simply marvelous. . . . Along came a bent-over refugee lad. . . . Perfectly marvelous.

YORAM. Along came a bent-over refugee . . . come on, let's have a rhyme for it.

NURIT. They bathed him all over in DDT.

YORAM. Not bad, not bad at all:

> Along came a bent-over refugee,
> They bathed him all over in D.D.T.
> And that was the last of the refugee.

(*The doorbell rings. Dubi enters.*)

NURIT. Oh, is that you?

DUBI. I can only stay a few minutes. The taxi is waiting for me. I came to get my small valise.

YORAM. I'm going down to get cigarettes. I'll be back in a minute. (*He leaves.*)

DUBI. Are you happy?

NURIT. We're getting married soon. Will you come?

DUBI. Why not? If I'm in the country.

NURIT. It's in two weeks.

DUBI. Then I can make it.

NURIT. Dubi. Try not to be mad at me. . . . I know that . . .

DUBI. Me? Mad? At you? They say one shouldn't carry coals to Newcastle or come to Paris with a woman around one's neck. There's one thing, though, I still would like to know. Why did you have to pick me, was it to get over him?

NURIT. Dubi, it's pointless to talk about it now.

DUBI. Still, I think I have the right to know, don't I?

NURIT. Maybe it was because . . . because you never liked him. I tried not to like him, too.

DUBI. You're wrong. I never hated him. I only felt sorry for him.

NURIT. I don't think he needs your pity, Dubi. . . . You always liked to call him Hamlet so you could sneer at him. But some of us possess the strength to be weak, too.

DUBI. Thanks.

NURIT. There was really no need to open up old wounds.

DUBI. I guess it would flatter you if I were sore all over, but I don't bleed so easily. . . . I have to go. (*He steps into the next room and returns with the valise.*)

NURIT. You'll come?

DUBI. Of course. Good night, Nurit. (*He leaves, Yoram returns.*)

NURIT. Yoram, come here . . . do you love me? (*He hugs her tightly.*) Yoram, the window's open. (*She slips out of his embrace and goes to close the windows.*) Come here. (*Yoram crosses over to her.*) Look down below. (*Yoram looks.*) He's looking at us again. Who is he?

YORAM. How am I supposed to know?

NURIT. He saw you and ran. Yesterday, I met him on the stairs. He was reading the names on the mailboxes. (*She looks out of the window again.*) Look, he's back.

YORAM. I'll go down after him.

NURIT. Don't go. Are you sure you don't know him? He's always hung around the boardwalk, but he's never followed me before. I don't like it.

YORAM. You're not getting superstitious, are you?

NURIT. I certainly am. . . . When I see a black cat . . .

YORAM. Don't worry about it. He's crazy-looking, all right, but he seems harmless. (*He leaves. Nurit keeps looking at Sigmund through the window. Sigmund continues to look up at her. At first he is unaware that Yoram is approaching. When he notices him, he glances at him and takes a step forward, then suddenly swivels around and disappears.*)

YORAM. (*Following Sigmund.*) Hey, you! God, what eyes, they shine in the dark like a cat's!

NURIT. (*The telephone rings. She answers.*) Hello? To whom? Yoram Eyal? There must be some mistake. . . . Who? Uzi? How are you? . . . Now what leads you to suspect that Yoram must be here? . . . (*She laughs.*) Really, I'm not kidding. . . . Okay, Uzi, I'll call him. (*She yells to Yoram as if he were in the next room, although he is by now standing beside her.*) Yoram, Uzi!

YORAM. (*As from the next room.*) Coming! (*He takes the receiver.*) Uzi? . . . Yeah. . . . Yeah. . . . Branch manager? But I. . . . How. . . . Listen, old buddy, we're going to hit every bar in town tonight, we're going to get plastered. It'll be like after—what was the name of that goddamn Arab village? . . . That's right, Abu Shusba. . . . The wedding? . . . Nurit calls it the ceremony. . . . In two weeks. . . . What time should I come over? . . . Nine? . . . I'll come right away. . . . Uzi, you wouldn't feel insulted if I thanked you, would you? See you, Uzi. (*He hangs up, goes over to Nurit, picks her up and circles the room with her.*) Did you hear that? (*They tumble onto the sofa. Nurit struggles free and sits down.*)

NURIT. And now I've got a surprise for you. Do you like this apartment?

YORAM. I don't get it. I thought you wanted me to take the job Gilead offered me.

NURIT. Father's built a private house. In a week they're flying this coop.

YORAM. Why didn't you tell me?

NURIT. I didn't want you to feel dependent on father or me.

YORAM. Nurit. (*He hides his head in his hands.*) You're. . . . I'll never forget this.

NURIT. Tomorrow we're going to order new furniture. We'll get rid of these historical relics. What am I going to do with all these collected works? (*Yoram looks at his watch.*) Which do you like better: bright furniture or dark? (*Unable to concentrate, Yoram goes over to the window. He half-listens.*) I saw some lovely African masks in the flea-market. Black. Yoram, you're not even listening.

YORAM. I'm listening, Nurit.

NURIT. No, you're not listening.

YORAM. It's late, I've got to go to Uzi's.

NURIT. I think you're in a bad mood.

YORAM. Look, I . . . I'm just not used to . . . since I was eleven, all I ever thought about was a bed to sleep in, a roof over my head. . . . And now all of a sudden, a home . . . furniture . . . I've got to go. (*He kisses her hurriedly and leaves.*)

NURIT. (*She sits on the sofa, thinking to herself.*) When he should be happy—he's sad. When he's sad—he's sarcastic. Like a Chinese doll. (*She plays with two dolls that are on the bed. To one of them.*) Isn't he a darling? Say he is! (*She brings the dolls together.*) What do you know about it, he's awfully cute. All he needs is a home. That's all.

BLACKOUT

Scene 5

On the boardwalk. The café is lit up with colorful Chinese lanterns. The stage is foggy. Two couples from the party stroll outside for some fresh air, to the accompaniment of a steamy jazz tune. Another couple slips into the café. The dance music and the noise of the party cease. The stage is now bathed in red moonlight, though still shrouded in fog. The music switches to blues. One of the partygoers, drunkenly, takes a harmonica from his pocket and blows two sad chords. Berele emerges from the café, followed by Yoram.

YORAM. Hey, Officer! Stop that thief! Berele, do you remember how we used to punish quitters when we were kids?

BERELE. We dunked them three times in water, with their clothes on.

YORAM. Well, if you quit now I'm going to dunk you in three bottles of wine.

BERELE. I've got to get back to the precinct, I'm on duty tonight.

YORAM. Don't hand me any stories, Officer, you already told me that somebody was standing in for you tonight.

BERELE. Look, Yossele, I don't feel, how would I say. . . . They're all in there. You know what I mean.

YORAM. So what if they are there? They're just like you and me, they're like everybody all over the world. Take my word for it, they hollered when they were born and they wet their pants the same as we did.

BERELE. At any rate, that's how they seem to me. My girlfriend said something smart to me yesterday: the insecure feel secure only among the insecure.

YORAM. Why didn't you bring her along?

BERELE. She felt embarrassed. To tell the truth, so did I . . .

YORAM. From a distance every cat looks like a tiger. Come in, no one's going to eat you.

BERELE. I'd better get back to work. Have you heard from your parents?

YORAM. (*He takes a letter from his pocket, shows it to Berele.*) This. They'll be here in two weeks.

BERELE. You're lucky. (*Nurit enters from the café.*)

NURIT. (*To Yoram.*) I've finally found you. (*To Berele.*) Are you leaving?

BERELE. I've got to get back to work. (*Kisses her hand.*) Once more, congratulations! (*He leaves.*)

NURIT. It's so foggy!

YORAM. Yes, it's foggy.

NURIT. You sound sad. (*She strokes his hair. He remains silent.*) Let's go inside . . .

YORAM. You go . . . I'm not . . . I'll come right away.

NURIT. But right away, all right? (*She goes.*)

YORAM. Nurit! (*She returns.*) I've something to tell you.

NURIT. Happy or sad? If it's sad—not tonight. What did you want to tell me? (*She sees the letter in his hands.*) Who's that from?

YORAM. I'll tell you when we get home.

DUBI. (*From inside.*) Nurit!

YORAM. Go on. You're being called. Go on.

NURIT. You're so strange, Yoram. What's the matter?

DUBI. (*From inside.*) Nurit! Where are you? Nurit!

NURIT. (*In the direction that Dubi's voice is coming from.*) Can't you wait a minute? (*To Yoram.*) Is it something important?

YORAM. (*Angrily.*) Not now. When we get home. (*The band strikes up a polka in the café.*)

DUBI. (*Coming out.*) Nurit, where are you? You promised to polka with me, I have a right to the last polka. (*He takes her by the waist. Before they begin to dance, he says to Yoram.*) Don't you agree? (*He polkas with her, first in the open then into the café. Yoram is left alone. He still holds the letter. Inside, an accordion continues noisily to play the polka. Sigmund enters. His face is hidden in his overcoat, an unlit cigarette is in his mouth. He approaches Yoram.*)

YORAM. Why do you follow me like a shadow? Who are you?

SIGMUND. A light!

YORAM. (*He takes out a pack of matches and strikes a match. It goes out.*

He strikes another one successfully. All this time, Sigmund does not cease staring at him.) Here. *(Sigmund walks away, then immediately returns.)*

SIGMUND. *(Extending his hand aggressively, as before.)* One pound please! *(He stares lengthily at Yoram.)* What a resemblance!

YORAM. A resemblance? To whom?

SIGMUND. Purely imaginary. . . . To someone . . . over there. *(He laughs an almost diabolical laught.)* Over there. . . . Do you know where "over there" is?

NURIT. *(She comes out of the café. At first she is not aware of Sigmund.)* Yoram, all our guests . . . *(Suddenly she sees Sigmund. She walks over to them.)*

YORAM. You're making a mistake, I was never there . . . I was born here, my whole family is here. *(He senses Nurit's presence and becomes bewildered, caught lying.)*

SIGMUND. Your whole family is here? Ha-ha-ha-ha! And mine— *(He blows smoke from his cigarette straight upwards, following its progress with his eyes.)* ha-ha-ha-ha-ha-ha!

YORAM. Who are you?

NURIT. *(Nervously.)* Yoram, let's go inside!

SIGMUND. Why so nervous, my good man? One pound—and I'll be gone. *(Yoram makes a motion with his hand as if to dismiss him. Sigmund responds by feigning as if he has really been given money.)* Thank you, madam. *(He bows to Nurit.)* Thank you, sir. *(He bows to Yoram, then to both of them, steps backward and again, from a distance, bows once more.)* What a resemblance! *(He disappears.)*

NURIT. Who is he? He looks at you as if he knew you.

YORAM. I've never seen his face before.

NURIT. Are you sure?

YORAM. One doesn't forget a face like that.

NURIT. Is he crazy or just pretending to be?

YORAM. Anyone who can pretend like that is crazy beyond all insanity.

BERELE. Why did you tell him you were born here? Maybe he . . .

YORAM. *(Nervously.)* I'm not accountable to every lunatic. . . . I wanted to get rid of him . . . that's all.

NURIT. What are you so angry about?

YORAM. I'm sorry. . . . Something in his look gives me the creeps.

NURIT. Yoram, Let's go inside. It isn't nice . . . *(She tries to pull him along.)*

YORAM. *(He speaks quickly and nervously, but it is a nervousness without irritation.)* Nurit, I have to tell you . . . now!

A VOICE FROM INSIDE. Yoram!

NURIT. They're looking for us.

YORAM. I've got to! (*He shows her the letter.*) This letter is from . . . from . . . my parents. . . . They're coming to Israel . . .

NURIT. From your parents? I was positive. . . . You never mentioned them. . . . I was afraid to ask. . . . God, how could you hide a thing like that?

YORAM. I just got it . . . this morning. . . . All of a sudden, don't you see? . . . And especially today . . . it . . . the wedding . . .

BERELE. (*From a distance.*) You see, I managed to get off, I'm back . . .

NURIT. (*Running over to him.*) Did you hear? Yoram's parents are alive! He got a letter!

BERELE. (*Surprised that she should be surprised.*) Yes . . . I know . . . I . . .

VOICES FROM INSIDE. Nurit! Where are you?

YORAM. (*Putting his arms around both of them, trying to look happy.*) Let's go in, huh? It really isn't right . . . (*Sigmund appears and stares at the three of them. They do not see him, and disappear into the café. Sigmund sits on a bench and writes. All at once, with Yoram's last words, the band bursts into a noisy melody. The doors of the café fold upstage, and the interior becomes visible through a transparent curtain. Whenever the action shifts to the boardwalk, the lights go off within the café, and vice versa. Inside—an atmosphere of dolce vita. Bohemian types. The women are partly in elaborate evening dress, partly in black slacks and black shirts. Cabaret music, a saxophone. Those present may dance or otherwise employ mimicry or mime. The atmosphere is unreal and grotesque. There is constant movement on the stage. Places and partners are changed about. There is room for continual improvisation. One of those present is wearing khaki shorts, a blue denim shirt, and an Israeli work hat. His manner is free and cynical.*)

HAGAR. (*Dancing with her bearded partner, a young poet.*) Here comes Guilt-feeling. (*She points at the man in the khaki shorts.*)

POET. Is he here? When did he arrive?

HAGAR. Tonight I'm getting drunk with Guilt-feeling.

POET. You can drink with him, but in the morning you'll sober up in my bed.

DUBI. (*To the nearest bystander.*) Do you remember the Castle? (*A girl comes up to him. He leans on her and begins to declaim.*) Those were the good old days, little sister, I was a young hell-raiser then.

HAGAR. (*To her partner.*) There's Ziva, she's crazy about your poems. I'm going to dance with Guilt-feeling.

POET. (*To Hagar, who is dressed in black.*)
A blue denim shirt
Though covered with dirt
Is worth diamonds and rubies.
The shirt on your back,
My lady, is black,
But covers two fatally sharp boo . . .
(*He tries to caress her breasts.*)

HAGAR. You're not going to stab yourself to death on me, you poet of despair. (*To Guilt-feeling, who is passing by nearby.*) Want to dance? (*She goes off to dance with Guilt-feeling.*)

POET. Two-timer, all women are two-timers.

YORAM. (*He holds a large glass in his hands. To Nurit.*) Now he'll read his latest poem. That's what always happens when she dances with somebody else. (*At the top of his voice, drunkenly.*) Stop the music! Nobelus! Read us your latest poem!

CHANTING VOICES. We don't want to go to bed. We'll make whooppee till we're dead.

YORAM. Quiet, you dinosaurs! (*Gradually they all fall silent, settling into bored poses, their eyes turned upwards, their chins on their knees. Yoram turns to the poet.*) Nobelus, read to us, Nobelus, from your songs of . . .

A VOICE. Zion.

VOICES. We want Guilt-feeling! We want Guilt-feeling!

YORAM. Quiet, you dinosaurs! Sing to us, Nobelus, from your songs of despair!

POET. (*He downs a drink, coughs. Everybody coughs.*)
The sun's like a green frog
Croaking in the mud, in the sky.
The storks in their bills carry
A child, not yet dead.
Never born.
Why?
Tell your Grandma how she came into the world.
I'm a tired man,
I'm a clock,
Whose hands
Whose hopes,
Are like ships
Wrecked at sea
All of them.
Now rain is falling

The rain is falling now
Like currency.
The last of men
Swallows his shadow's shade.

VOICES. Bravo! Bravissimo! Universal! Cosmic! Decadent! A toast to Nobelus! (*All lift their glasses. The poet leaves. The party is blacked out. The spotlight picks out Sigmund sitting on his bench, the poet on his way to the boardwalk, and the Balloon Seller, who is coming toward him. A heavy fog hangs over the boardwalk.*)

BALLOON SELLER. (*To the poet.*) Balloons?

POET. One prick and our blown-up world . . .

BALLOON SELLER. Right you are, mister. My balloons are blown up fine. They're full of air.

POET. You poor dumb thing. I was almost going to say, you blown-up bag of flesh. But you are too thin.

BALLOON SELLER. What can I do? That's how it is.

POET. Let's sell them some balloons. Maybe they're better at that than they are at poetry. (*He snatches the balloons from the Balloon Seller and pushes him in the direction of the café.*)

BALLOON SELLER. Me? In there? Oh, no . . . I . . .

POET. Shake a leg, fool!
The night's getting cool,
This bog
Of a fog . . .

(*To himself.*) Not bad! Not bad at all! (*The two of them disappear in the café. Sigmund remains on his bench, listening to the voices from inside.*)

HAGAR. Now, Guilt-feeling.

GUILTFEELING. (*Climbing on a chair.*) What have I done that I should have to speak in this sexpool? The smell of dung, the sweet incense of . . . poetry. (*Holds his nose.*) Nihilism, my friends! We cannot go on any longer like this. What will we come to, my friends?! What?, I ask. I see the pinnacles of our dreams bow down for shame. Is this what we dream of, my friends? This? It's true, I struggle with myself, but something must be done. Perhaps you know what must be done? No? Neither do I. Maybe Tolstoy. Maybe A. D. Gordon. Yes, don't laugh. A. D. Gordon. Yes. Perhaps I'm simpleminded. Granted. I'm a simpleminded man. Just the other day I ran into Yitzhak. "So what's new?," I said to him. "The refugees." There you have it. The Pan-Semitic front. I asked him, "Imperialism?" He said, "The Crusades. Sparta. Children in steel helmets." He began to cry and said, "Do you remember those surplus Czechoslovakian rifles? We sat in mourning for the Internationale." Seven bottles of brandy. We wept. It was marvelous. "O little red apple, whither wilt thou roll?" So I ask you, my friends, can it be? Is it possible? No, my friends, it cannot be! It must not be! Perhaps I'm simpleminded. Granted. It had to be thought out. There you have it. It has to be thought out. But what? Have you nothing to say? Neither have I, my friends, but it hurts me to see the way you live. . . . Granted, I live it up, too, but it hurts, my friends, it hurts me that everything should be . . . that somehow, one way or another, perhaps, in general, yes, in general it's very, very sad. Oh, you generation of iconoclasts! There you have it. It's very sad.

EVERYBODY. (*Singing.*)
Oh, how sad, how very sad,
Was the fall the apple had.
The apple exploding on the ground
Nothing of it was ever found.

(*On the boardwalk. The lighting is as in the previous scene.*)

SIGMUND. (*To the Balloon Seller, who enters from stage left carrying nothing but a stick.*) Where are all your balloons?

BALLOON SELLER. I sold them. At the wedding. Ah, what wonderful kids . . . what kids . . .

SIGMUND. Are you acquainted with the bridegroom?

BALLOON SELLER. (*Looking at his dirty clothes.*) Me? What makes you ask?

SIGMUND. A resemblance. Words. (*The sound of a foghorn.*)
Ships anchor in harbors.
Ashes float off,
Turn white the hair
A corpse in river is what I hear.

(*The foghorn sounds again. Sigmund suddenly gets to his feet and leaves. The Balloon Seller is left sitting on the bench.*)

HAGAR. Yoram, sing us a solo! . . .

EVERYBODY. Yoram, sing us a solo! . . .

YORAM. (*Drunkenly.*) Something happy? Okay, I'll sing you something happy. Happy as hell!

(*The spotlight is on Yoram. He sings.*)
Samarkand's a hot, hot city,
But then it hailed and snowed.
They call us Children of the war,
'Cause we're the donkey that it rode.
The war rode piggy-back upon us

Traveled round the world on us.
At night we sleep in alleyways.
We raid the markets when it's day.
We crawl like lizards through the stalls,
And steal and laugh and run away.
    And while the Uzbek shouts: Thief! Stop!
    We fill our bellies from his shop.
And all night long we dream and dream,
and usually the dream's the same!
The world's a mountain of fresh bread,
and all of it is ours to claim.
And usually the dream's the same!
    The more we eat, the more we crave.
And all of it is ours to claim.
Our little brothers two years younger.
Our home's the marketplace, the street.
We pick their lice. We soothe their hunger.
    And if at night they wake and cry,
    We sing to them a lullaby
So hush, my child, you cry in vain;
They say we'll go to Tehran,
And then to where the orange blooms.
So hush, we'll go to Tehran.
Hush, hush, my child, we'll soon be gone
To where it's green all winter long.

(*When Yoram is through singing his song, the stage is darkened and one hears, with increasing force, the noise of the seawind and the waves breaking. When the lights go on, Sigmund is looking at the spot Yoram occupied while singing. The Balloon Seller appears behind him.*)

BALLOON SELLER. What are you looking at?

SIGMUND. The stars.

BALLOON SELLER. There's not a star in sight. It's a hell of a night.

SIGMUND. He's right. The stars are all in hell.

BALLOON SELLER. Who's he?

SIGMUND. He is he, and I am I.

BALLOON SELLER. But you're talking to me.

SIGMUND. I'm talking to you, but he's answering me. (*He points to someone standing, as it were, behind him.*)

BALLOON SELLER. You're getting me all confused.

SIGMUND. (*Again pointing behind him.*) Now he's confusing him.

BALLOON SELLER. Who? Me?

SIGMUND. No. Him. (*This time he points to someone standing, as it were, on the other side of him.*) No matter. The winter is coming on.

BALLOON SELLER. Maybe you'd like to come live in my shack? Come on, I'll show it to you. It's a good shack. It's got a tin roof.

SIGMUND. Rain beating on a tin roof drives me crazy.

BALLOON SELLER. It's better for it to beat on a tin roof than for it to beat on your head.

SIGMUND. That depends on the head. If the head is on fire, the rain puts it out.

BALLOON SELLER. I don't get it.

SIGMUND. You don't get it? That's bad, or rather . . . very good. (*There is a sudden crash of waves.*)

BALLOON SELLER. I think there's going to be a storm. My shack is as snug as Noah's ark.

SIGMUND. Noah was a poor righteous man and you're a poor righteous man, and so God told you to build an ark like Noah's. But methinks for the righteous rich He makes more Noah-ble provision than that. And so I bid you good night. (*He takes a last look at Nurit's window, then lies down on the bench.*)

BALLOON SELLER. (*Shrugs his shoulders.*) He's crazy as a loon. But he's sure an interesting talker. I didn't understand a word. I swear he's out of his mind. (*The crash of waves. A sliver of moon. Fog.*)

SIGMUND. Give me sleep without dreams, O my Lord. All the dead rise up against me when I dream. Ever wakeful. Only no dreams, my Lord.

Scene 6

A simultaneous dream scene. Yoram and Nurit are in their room, in bed. Her face is turned toward the wall. His face is turned toward Esther, who is in the center of the stage. Sigmund lies on the bench. He, too, faces Esther. The sound of the sea. Churchbells ring. A reddish-blue moon. Esther has her back to the audience. Her voice comes over a tape-recorder, deep and distant and restrained. Her movements are rigid. In the course of the dialogue, Yoram and Sigmund sit up; they lie down when the dream is over. The light that falls on them is cold and clear. No extra effects should be added.

SIGMUND. Let me be, my wife,
Angel full of eyes.
Let me be.
Depart from me!

ESTHER. Into the water, Sigmund.

SIGMUND. Depart from me!
Remove from me your dead fish-eyes,
Remove your eyes from me!
Let me be!

ESTHER. (*To Yoram.*) Come down from the tree.

YORAM. I won't.

ESTHER. You'll fall.

YORAM. What do you care? Sister, take me to you.

ESTHER. I live in the river.

SIGMUND. I'm not to blame. Leave me be!

ESTHER. (*To Yoram.*) All right, I'll get into bed with you, move over. I'll tell you about the Eskimos and then you'll sleep. What are you looking for up in that tree?

SIGMUND. My God!

ESTHER. (*To Yoram.*) What are you looking for up in that tree?

YORAM. For the head of the rooster. The tin weathercock. They came toward the crack of dawn, just when he was about to pray the morning prayer. They came glittering like knives, angels of steel with swastikas on the wings. Suddenly they swooped over the roof and sliced off his head. Now, he's here. In the treetop. Don't touch my rooster, don't make a blood offering of him!

SIGMUND. I'm not to blame for her death. Leave me be. Why are you following me? No, I'm from Lvov, you're mistaken, you're wrong . . . no. . . . Shameless mortal . . .

YORAM. Don't make him a blood offering, don't touch my rooster.

ESTHER. He wore a gray uniform. He caught me by the leg and swung me about his head and shouted, "This very rooster shall go to its death! This very rooster shall to its death!" (*Churchbells. The sound of waves.*)

SIGMUND. I'm coming, Esther, I'm coming.

ESTHER. This very rooster shall go to its death.

YORAM. I had nothing to do with it. Why are you yelling at me?!

ESTHER. Nothing? Nothing? So why don't you lend me a helping hand? I'm cold. He undressed me. He shot me and bled my body dry. You've got the whole blanket to yourself. I'm cold.

YORAM. Is it cold inside the igloo, too?

ESTHER. Inside the igloo it's warm.

YORAM. When I grow up we'll go to the North Pole.

ESTHER. Don't grab the blanket. (*To Sigmund.*) Resign from the Judenrat. Run away.

SIGMUND. I must play a role as horrible as this bloody spectacle.

ESTHER. You're afraid for your own skin?

SIGMUND. No! I have done my best to stop the epidemic. To gain time.

ESTHER. There's not a trace left of us. When I walked in the street I was pelted with stones. I can't bear the shame of it. Join the revolt.

SIGMUND. The community is not in revolt, there are only scattered rebels. The rebel is to hasten our doom.

ESTHER. You're blind, Sigmund, our doom will not be long.

SIGMUND. Remove your eyes from me! I'm not to blame. Be gone! (*The last word he emits with a shout. A policeman appears on stage left and rouses him. He awakes at once, jumps from the bench, and says to the policeman.*) I'm not to blame! (*He starts to run and disappears. The policeman shrugs his shoulders and walks slowly after him.*)

YORAM. The ship! Esther! the ship! (*His shouts awaken Nurit.*)

NURIT. (*Shaking him.*) Yoram, you're shouting!

YORAM. (*The dialogue that follows between him and Nurit is for him, essentially, a monologue. Yoram hears her, but it is as if he doesn't see her.*) No Esther, no! (*To Nurit.*) Esther, you . . . who are you?

NURIT. Yoram, you. . . . Wake up, Yoram.

YORAM. Yoram? . . . Yoram? . . .

NURIT. You're dreaming, Yoram.

YORAM. I'm dreaming? It was only a dream? Only a dream! Only a dream!

NURIT. You don't have to tell it to me.

YORAM. I wanted it to happen! I wanted it to!

NURIT. Nobody is master of his dreams.

YORAM. The ship sank and I wanted it to! Oh, God!

NURIT. You scare me.

YORAM. Both of them scared me with their eyes. Whenever I sat down to eat I saw their eyes: "You see? You have enough to eat! You have enough to eat!"

NURIT. Forget about it, Yoram. They'll come and everything will be all right. I'm sure it will. It'll certainly be a surprise for them.

YORAM. (*As if he has just now awakened to the truth.*) They know about you, Nurit, I lied to you. It wasn't their first letter. It wasn't the first lie, either. I wasn't born in Warsaw. I was born in Goray. A dirty little town. We weren't rich—we were miserably poor. I didn't lose my parents in a railroad station and I wasn't brought up by my uncle the artist in Samarkand. I was the head of a gang. We used to steal food in the market. I fed my parents on what I got. But I remained hungry. That's why my parents put me in an orphanage. Don't do it, I begged them, I'm not an orphan! And when I came to this land and it fed me from the tree of forgetfulness, I burned my lice-infected clothes along with myself. Along with Yossele. And Esther. And my parents. And when I was through being disinfected, I was a new man, a superman like Dubi by the name of Yoram! That life-of-the-party who's making you eat his offerings of the dead. Charming, isn't it?

NURIT. I never realized you hated your new clothes so much.

YORAM. I don't feel any hatred, Nurit, only contempt, the contempt that a clown feels for his costume and his mask.

NURIT. There's no denying you've played your part well. But if you want to know why I was attracted to you in the first place, I'll tell you: because you never really managed to be Yoram to the end. (*Triumphantly.*) Now I'll make you coffee, and then we're going to stay in here and you're going to begin to peel. Peel after peel . . . until you're naked. This time, you'll talk. No more evasions.

YORAM. Spiritually naked? Why not. I think it's time. Maybe then I'll be able to find my true clothes.

NURIT. And in the meantime—coffee? (*Yoram nods in agreement. She goes into the kitchen. He lights a cigarette and smokes it, thoughtfully contented.*)

CURTAIN

ACT II

Scene 1

Twilight. The sound of the sea. The Balloon Seller appears on stage from the direction of the boardwalk. He sings a popular Yiddish song. When he is finished with his song, he sits down on a bench.

BALLOON SELLER. By the roadside stood a tree,
              Its roots were bare and jagged;
              A single tree, alone it stood,
              Its head was white and ragged.
              The tree was there hundreds of years,
              Its roots were in the water;

They say its heart was made of earth
From Jerusalem, Zion's daughter.
In this earth, so people say,
There lived a bird, a wonder!
It could not die by any death,
This bird of sand and wonder.
Then one day, the bird was killed,
A blaze reached up to heaven;
It burned the holy seat of God,
Destroyed the tree for ever.
The leaves alone, they did remain,
Like little birds a-flying;
They flew to Israel's promised land,
And there they still are lying.

(*Enter Sigmund, hurrying.*)

BALLOON SELLER. What's the rush? Sit down for a minute.

SIGMUND. I said I'm in a hurry.

BALLOON SELLER. What's on fire?

SIGMUND. The sea.

BALLOON SELLER. Sit down, sit down for a minute.

SIGMUND. I said I'm in a hurry.

BALLOON SELLER. Ah, nothing's on fire.

SIGMUND. The hat . . .

BALLOON SELLER. I don't get it.

SIGMUND. I don't get it . . . I don't get it . . . That's all you know to say.

BALLOON SELLER. I don't get it.

SIGMUND. All right, then, let's sit for a while. (*They sit down.*) Well?

BALLOON SELLER. Eh . . .

SIGMUND. Eh. . . . That's a great deal. . . . And what else have you got to say besides eh?

BALLOON SELLER. (*Sighing.*) Hhhhh . . .

SIGMUND. Now you've said it all. . . . Hhhhh . . .

BALLOON SELLER. Things are sad.

SIGMUND. You're not telling me anything new.

BALLOON SELLER. I wanted to ask you, what are you writing all the time?

SIGMUND. I am a certified accountant.

BALLOON SELLER. You're an accountant? Really? And you dress like that? I once had a friend who was an accountant for a very big firm. Boy, it was a very big firm.

SIGMUND. I'm a certified accountant for the biggest firm in the world, the biggest that you can imagine.

BALLOON SELLER. Really?

SIGMUND. That's what I said.

BALLOON SELLER. What's it called?

SIGMUND. God Almighty.

BALLOON SELLER. You're making fun of me.

SIGMUND. Making fun of you? Really, now. . . . To prove to you that I'm not making fun of you, and that we're friends, I'm going to read you something from my account book.

BALLOON SELLER. Will I get it? (*Sigmund takes a notebook from his briefcase.*)

SIGMUND. No, but that doesn't matter in the least. (*He reads the poem with the utmost simplicity, and without the histrionics that are characteristic of his manner and speech.*)

> I shut my eyes.
> The same weak voices make
> Movements without noise.
> In stockinged feet
> Children of the shadow.
> They skirt circles of the sun.
> As I skirt dead rats on the road.
> And never say a word.
> At night they come
> Stealthily through memory's thin slats.
> And always in that moment of recall
> I hear the sound of railcars
> Emptied of their children as of coal.
> Their warm, sweet smell.
> A ragdoll left behind.
> A paper boat no one will find.
> Buttons.
> And threads
> Angels with wax-colored faces.
> They're taking off. They've done it. Now they rise.
> And still upon my back I feel their eyes.

BALLOON SELLER. Are you crying?

SIGMUND. (*To Nurit who enters.*) Shameless mortal, sinful one . . . (*Nurit takes fright, drops her wallet, and quickly sinks in a chair. Sigmund picks up the wallet.*) Madam, you lost your wallet. (*She takes out a bill.*) Thank you, madam, it's not necessary. A pleasant evening, madam.

NURIT. Why are you always following me? Who are you?

SIGMUND. A rat! A rat leaving a sinking ship. A rat, madam.

WAITER. (*Entering. To Sigmund.*) Are you here again? I've told you a thousand times to stay clear of here. (*Sigmund returns to the Balloon Seller.*)

WAITER. (*Turning to Nurit.*) Where do they come from? All these nuts? It's enough to drive one crazy.

NURIT. The war.

WAITER. War. So what's war? Why don't they find work? When people work there aren't any wars. Are you waiting for Mr. Eyal?

NURIT. Yes. He's in Haifa. He went there to meet his parents.

WAITER. Back from a tour abroad?

NURIT. New immigrants.

WAITER. What? Mr. Eyal wasn't born here? I was sure . . . Coffee and a paper?

NURIT. Yes. (*The waiter leaves.*)

BALLOON SELLER. (*To Sigmund.*) First you were crying. Now I'm crying.

SIGMUND. Nonsense, I was laughing.

BALLOON SELLER. No, you were crying. I saw you crying. Maybe you'd like to sleep at my place? There's room for both of us. You don't have to pay me.

SIGMUND. I snore like a thousand trombones.

BALLOON SELLER. That doesn't bother me.

SIGMUND. And I shout in my sleep, terribly.

BALLOON SELLER. You too? That's why I wanted us to live together. . . . It's horrible to wake up shouting. It's even more horrible than dreaming . . . To wake up with nobody to touch. . . . My youngest son always used to get into bed with me. It's nice when a little boy gets into bed with you at night. . . . Did you ever have children? (*Sigmund gets up.*) Why are you leaving?

SIGMUND. We agreed that you weren't going to interrogate me.

BALLOON SELLER. I'm not interrogating, I just asked. (*Sigmund walks away, passes in front of Nurit, to whom he bows, and disappears.*)

NURIT. Hey! Balloons.

BALLOON SELLER. Balloons! Balloons! A balloon for a young miss?

NURIT. I'll buy five balloons from you every day if you tell me who was the man you were talking to. (*The man with the newspaper enters and sits down in the café.*)

BALLOON SELLER. I don't know, miss. He doesn't allow any questions. When I asked him if he ever had children, he got up and left. He was real mad. What for? I don't get it. I told him he could live with me in my shack. I've got a little shack, it's not far from here.

Over in the slums. I don't get it. He writes and writes. He's always writing. He said he was an accountant . . . for a big firm . . . for God Almighty. He cried when he read something. So did I.

NURIT. What did he read to you?

BALLOON SELLER. I swear I don't remember. Something about a rat. A railcar. A ragdoll. Angels. He's out of his mind. I don't know what's wrong with him.

NURIT. If you find out, tell me. I'll pay you.

BALLOON SELLER. No! Only balloons.

NURIT. Well, here's for five. I'll take them tomorrow. Ok?

BALLOON SELLER. Ok. (*Moves out.*)

WAITER. (*Enters.*) Another one? (*The Balloon seller moves away when he approaches, but comes nearer when Nurit calls for him.*)

BALLOON SELLER. (*To the waiter.*) You see?

NURIT. And in case you know anything don't forget to inform me.

BALLOON SELLER. Certainly, madam. (*To Yoram, who enters and appears on his way.*) Balloons?

NURIT. (*Seeing the wound on Yoram's face.*) God, what happened to you? Seems as if you came back from hell.

YORAM. No, not from hell, only from Shaar Haaliya* and this is just the first gate. (*To the waiter who remains standing on stage.*) Double coffee. Black. (*Waiter moves out.*)

NURIT. You won't be able to sleep.

YORAM. For the better.

NURIT. Are they in Shaar Haaliya?

YORAM. They are.

NURIT. I should have gone with you.

YORAM What for? (*Sips from Nurit's coffee.*)

NURIT. Don't drink, you won't be able to sleep, let's go home.

YORAM. Wait a few minutes.

NURIT. If you don't want to, you don't have to tell me now.

YORAM. And if I do want, could I? What do you know?

NURIT. I understand.

YORAM. (*Angrily.*) You don't understand a thing! Not a thing!

NURIT. I know.

YORAM. (*Still angrier.*) You don't know anything.

NURIT. How did you hurt yourself?

YORAM. On the fence. For fourteen years I haven't seen them, and when they come I'm allowed to look at them through a fence.

*Transit camp for newcomers.

There were thousands of people there, thousands. On both sides. (*The waiter brings the coffee and leaves.*) A whole hour I walked along the fence. Back and forth. I didn't recognize anyone. No one recognized me. Suddenly, someone grabbed me by the arm and pulled me toward the fence. At first I thought it was my brother. I called him by name and he let go. It was a mistake.

NURIT. And you didn't see them?

YORAM. About two hours later. Am I badly cut?

NURIT. It's not so terrible. (*She takes a mirror from her bag. He looks at himself in it.*)

YORAM. I vaulted over the fence and began to look. Block after block and tent after tent. Who here knows the Goldschmidts? Who here knows the Goldschmidts? A woman bares her breast and sticks it in the mouth of a screaming baby, and right next to her there's a couple naked as the day they were born, and they don't care and she doesn't care and I don't care. I go from tent to tent, like Orpheus in Hades. And suddenly there's a familiar smell in my nostrils, and I'm in a railroad car, and above me and below me people are eating and drinking, children crying all night, and next to me, right next to me, a couple lying down laughing: "Look, how he is staring at us! Sonny, you should be ashamed!" And I was ashamed, I wanted to scream, but the locomotive . . . the locomotive . . . the locomotive . . .

NURIT. Yoram, come on home.

YORAM. (*Sarcastically.*) Home! The railroads are my home and all the rest is a lie! God, why must I torture you? Why didn't you go to Paris with Dubi?

NURIT. You're insane.

YORAM. Yes, I'm insane. For fourteen years I didn't see them, and when they embraced me I felt as though they were embracing a statue. "He's changed," my mother said, and her voice broke. I ached to cry, to give them the feeling that I was their son. "You swine," I said to myself, "You swine, be a man!" But nothing happened inside me. Like stone! (*His head sinks onto the table. She caresses him. The light fades out slowly.*)

Scene 2

A telephone rings in the darkness. Nurit comes running into the room and switches on the lights.

NURIT. (*Picking up the receiver.*) Mother? . . . I just got in. . . . Lovely. . . . For how long? . . . Two months? . . . I wouldn't have any objections. . . . How are things there? . . . You know, it's hell. . . . But what are you talking about? . . . That's all very fine, but we're not living in the days of the pioneers and they're not eighteen. . . . His father is very sick. . . . He mustn't go on living in a tent. . . . How do I talk to them? . . . I don't talk. . . . Yoram translates. . . . Yes, his brother knows a little Hebrew. . . . It's not so nice of you not to have invited them all this time. . . . When aren't you busy. . . . Father? No, I haven't spoken to him. . . . He arranged for them to get an apartment? Are you sure? . . . Yoram? . . . He's with them now. . . . What? . . . I didn't hear. . . . Don't you think you should keep out of it? . . . If worse comes to worse, they'll live here, but they'll manage to get by. Yes. . . . Exactly . . . And when you're in South Africa, don't forget to tell the Jews there all about it, all right? . . . Since when am I such a Zionist? . . . I don't lose any sleep either over Zionism, or over the Jewish people, the way you do. . . . I'm simply his wife. . . . That's all. . . . Oh, I'm sure you are. . . . Absolutely. . . . It's all for my own good, what you're saying. . . . Yes. . . . Absolutely. . . . Someone's coming. . . . I'm hanging up. . . . (*She hangs up. Yoram enters.*) Did you talk to the doctor?

YORAM. He told me what we already knew . . .

NURIT. My mother called, she said that Father arranged to get them an apartment.

YORAM. I know. He arranged to get them an apartment that they could have had anyway. . . . They don't want it. They want to be near the city. Near me. . . . Yanek doesn't have a chance of getting a reasonable job in that hole.

NURIT. Somehow people manage.

YORAM. In your father's speeches. . . . He's got a brilliant future there, a day laborer with a university degree. It's heartwarming. (*Shouting.*) Isn't it?

NURIT. What are you shouting about? Why are you always picking on my father? I'm trying to be patient, Yoram, trying, trying, trying. . . . But if you think I am going to be a scapegoat for all your problems, you're wrong. . . . You suffer more than I do, I know that, but I haven't done anything! No one's going to wave the banner of suffering in my face all the time. . . . If you've been crucified by life, that doesn't mean you have to make me a present of your crown of thorns. I'm not to blame for anything that's happened, not to them and not to you!

YORAM. Nobody's to blame for anything, just me! They have no apartment—I'm to blame! When they get an apartment, it's out in the sticks—I'm to blame! Helenka walks around as if she's been

played for a sucker—I'm to blame! And my wife has three rooms—
I'm to blame!

NURIT. Why does your wife have three rooms and not you, too?

YORAM. Because.

NURIT. They can live here until they set themselves up.

YORAM. Never!

NURIT. Why not?

YORAM. Because. . . . So as not to have to see Helenka's eyes
every day, as if I'd stolen something from her, as if it were my fault
that I didn't go through what she went through, my fault that I
came to Israel before she did, that I'm here! . . . (*Bitterly.*) Live with
them. . . . You'll talk with your hands and I'll translate. . . . I rented a
room for them in Natanya, just for my parents. . . . If they all left
the immigrants' camp, they'd lose their right to get government
housing. . . . Someone promised me to get them a place near Tel
Aviv . . . (*The doorbell rings.*) It must be Yanek and Helenka. . . .
(*Yoram goes to the door.*) Hey, what are you doing here? (*Dubi enters.*)

DUBI. Dubi's here, Dubi's there, Dubi's everywhere. (*To Nurit.*)
How are you, *chérie?*

NURIT. *Merci, mon ami,* how's my French?

DUBI. *Magnifique, mademoiselle, ah, pardon, madame.* (*To Yoram.*)
How are the old folks?

YORAM. Who told you about them?

DUBI. I put them on the ship in Marseilles. . . . You know how it
is, people begin to ask questions: Who here knows, who's seen. . . .
Are they still in the camp?

YORAM. Yes . . .

DUBI. Is there any way I could help you? True, it's against my
principles, but . . .

NURIT. Actually, you could . . .

YORAM. No thanks, it's not necessary. . . . Are you here for long?

DUBI. No, I'm going back tonight. . . . When are you coming to
Paris? There's a lot to see in the world, a lot to see . . .

NURIT. Would you like to stay and eat dinner with us?

DUBI. Sorry, *chérie,* I've got to be at a meeting and from there
straight to the airport. (*He notices the chessboard on the table.*) It's too
bad, we could have finished the game.

YORAM. You mean we never finished it?

DUBI. Have you forgotten?

YORAM. For my part, we can call it quits. (*The doorbell rings. Yoram
goes to open it. Yanek and Helenka enter.*)

DUBI. Isnt't this your brother?

YORAM. Yes, it is. Why don't you sit down?

YANEK. Avram's not here?

YORAM. Who's Avram. (*Dubi goes into the kitchen.*)

YANEK. You don't remember Avram?

YORAM. No.

YANEK. Avram, the owner of the flour mill. I gave him your address. He was supposed to meet me here.

YORAM. I'm sorry, he hasn't come. (*Nurit enters, followed by Dubi.*)

NURIT. (*To Yoram.*) Ask them to excuse me, I'm making dinner. Ask them what they'll have to drink.

YANEK. No. . . . Thank you. . . . I, we . . . (*He smiles confusedly.*)

DUBI. So long, I've got to go. I'll give you a call before I leave. (*To Yoram.*) I can see that you're literally engaged in the absorption of immigrants. (*He leaves.*)

YORAM. Will you have something to drink?

HELENKA. Yes.

YORAM. (*To Nurit.*) Something cold for everybody. (*Nurit goes into the kitchen.*) So who is Avram?

YANEK. The one who owned the apple orchard . . . don't you remember? Your old gang used to mess it up.

YORAM. Right. . . . Right. . . . Something . . .

YANEK. Once, you really hurt him. . . . It cost papa a small fortune. Well, do you remember now, you bandit?

YORAM. Something having to do with snow.

YANEK. With snow.

YORAM. A snowball?

YANEK. That's somewhat inexact. It was a rock that you covered with snow.

YORAM. (*In a moment of recall.*) His watchdog tore my pants.

YANEK. You apple thief.

YORAM. And then I decided to avenge myself.

YANEK. And do you remember his daughter Rachel?

NURIT. (*From the kitchen.*) Helenka, could you come to the kitchen for a minute? (*Helenka goes into the kitchen.*)

YORAM. Rachel?

YANEK. You were in the same class in school.

YORAM. That's right, she had blond hair.

YANEK. She had black braids. . . . You used to pull on them, like reins.

YORAM. Is she in Israel?

YANEK. She had black braids just like our Esther.

YORAM. Yanek, I didn't exactly understand what you wrote me about Sigmund.

YANEK. Sigmund? Yes. . . . Well . . . you see. . . . After the Liberation I went to Lvov. I wasn't laboring under any illusions, but . . . I walked the streets for three days. On the third day, it was at dusk, closer to dark than it was to light, I came to a ruined street. Only one house was still standing on it. The house was dark, and then in a window a woman appeared and lit a candle. (*Helenka enters with two lit candlesticks and puts them on the table.*) Then she disappeared. (*Helenka leaves.*) All of a sudden, I saw a man standing across from the window and staring at it as though he were bewitched. I walked up to him. (*While talking he moves closer to Yoram.*)

"You're a Jew?"

"A Jew? Yes."

"From Lvov?"

"No," I answered him. And he says to me, "I thought perhaps one more Jew from Lvov had been saved." And with that, he went back to looking at the window, in which the woman had appeared again. (*Nurit comes in carrying a tray full of dishes. She puts it on the bookshelf and leaves.*) And then she was gone. "I come here every day at six," he says to me, "every day. For the last two weeks. Sometimes it seems to me that face is my wife's, blessing the candles on Sabbath eve." Suddenly, he begins to shout: "Lord of the Furnaces! So many houses were destroyed during the war, on this street there's not a single house left standing, and this house had to remain? It had to?"

"What's the street called," I asked him.

"Nickiewich."

"What's the house number?"

"Seven."

"My brother-in-law lived there, Dr. Sigmund Rabinowitz."

"Your brother-in-law?" He began to laugh hysterically. "You can find him in prison. What did he do?—He was in the Judenrat!" And then he began to laugh in a way that I'll never forget. "His wife and son are gone, too." (*Yanek completely changes his mannerisms. He goes on talking, but very softly.*) What was I supposed to do? To visit him in prison after Esther and the child. . . . No, that would have been too much, even for me. I preferred to think that I was dealing with a madman, or that even if there was a Sigmund Rabinowitz somewhere in jail, that it was someone else. . . . Do you know how Sigmund was? He had nobility. A man of intellect.

YORAM. That's exactly why I would want to find out more.

YANEK. It's easy for you to talk, you were never there.

NURIT. (*From the kitchen.*) Yoram, come help me open this can.

(*Yoram goes into the kitchen and Helenka comes out.*)

HELENKA. Talk to him. He'll be able to do something. He knows his way around here.

YANEK. But what can he do?

HELENKA. I want to live in Tel Aviv. I just have to. There must be something that can be done.

YANEK. You're hiding from reality, you're talking as though you were dreaming.

HELENKA. You promised to bring me to the land of dreams. I can't go on waking up morning after morning to the stench of that camp.

YANEK. You know very well that it's temporary, that it won't last for ever. Everyone says so. Even Yoram.

HELENKA. Yoram. Yoram. Always the same refrain: Yoram says. I have to live in Tel Aviv. In a big city. I need to have crowds around me. Crowds and crowds of people. Oh Jesus, talk to him. (*Yoram returns, carrying glasses and a bottle of cognac.*)

YORAM. (*Pouring.*) Shall we have a drink? Dinner will be ready soon. (*They drink. Helenka drinks several glasses.*)

YANEK. Helenka, that's enough.

NURIT. (*Brings a bowl of apples, and leaves.*) Helenka picks up a large apple and turns it around her hands.

HELENKA. (*To Yanek.*) What a nice apple!

YANEK. It's very nice, but it's nothing like the ones we used to have back home.

YORAM. How long before you'll learn to enjoy things here, the way they are, without always comparing them to what used to be?

YANEK. Why get angry? I happened to remember, that's all.

HELENKA. (*Listening only to herself.*) What a pretty apple—just like the ones there. In the convent.

YORAM. More memories of paradise!

YANEK. Yoram.

HELENKA. Yes, of paradise and paradise lost. At the age of six. When was that? Many, many years ago. . . . After God created the Germans and God beheld that they were good. . . . What am I talking about? Everything is suddenly all confused. . . . Maybe it's the cognac. . . . It was in the year seven according to the German calendar. (*To Yoram.*) Don't be shocked by my knowledge of the Bible, I was educated in a convent. Wasn't I? Everything there was white, like the birth of Jesus. My mother was named Mary, too. We ran away. She wrapped me in her shawl and ran all night through the snow. We're going to be caught, we're going to be caught. And afterwards . . . what happened afterwards? . . . I awoke in the cottage of an old farmer. Mother wasn't there.

NURIT. (*Entering.*) Coffee?

YORAM. That's a good idea. Make it strong, very strong.

HELENKA. Do you think I'm drunk?

YORAM. What kind of question is that?

HELENKA. In any case . . .

YANEK. It wasn't right of you, Helenka. He didn't say a thing.

HELENKA. All right. It wasn't right. He didn't say a thing. Why is Nurit taking so long in the kitchen?

YORAM. She's getting dinner ready. Besides, you forget that she doesn't speak Polish.

HELENKA. You're right, I forgot. . . . (*To Yoram.*) Will you permit me to have one more glass?

YORAM. There's no need to ask permission. (*He pours her a drink.*)

YANEK. (*Trying to take the glass away from her.*) You've had enough!

HELENKA. (*Holding on to it.*) Don't you worry! (*She drinks, then picks up the apple and begins to play with it again.*)

YORAM. And afterwards, what happened?

HELENKA. Afterwards? You mean you really want to hear more? I thought I was boring you. They put me in a convent. . . . Let's go to the movies, okay?

NURIT. (*Entering with cups of coffee.*) Soon we'll be ready to eat.

YANEK. (*To Nurit.*) No coffee for you?

NURIT. Later, I have to finish up in the kitchen. (*She leaves.*)

HELENKA. (*After taking a sip.*) It's good coffee . . . so sweet and strong.

YORAM. Nurit's an expert at making coffee from our days in the Palmach.

HELENKA. Ah, underground commando, the Palmach. (*Sings.*) "F-o-r we are the Palmach." That's the right melody, isn't it? A boy aboard ship taught it to us. You know, I think it was the fellow who was just here. . . . Maybe. . . . The other words I don't remember. Just "F-o-r we are the Palmach." He taught Israeli dancing too. . . . The polka . . . (*She bursts out laughing.*)

YORAM. Helenka, you still haven't told me what happened afterwards.

HELENKA. You're a funny one. On the one hand, it's memories of paradise, and on the other—you want to know so badly. Well. . . . It happened in the convent before the communion.

YORAM. Communion? What's that?

YANEK. It's a Catholic ceremony.

HELENKA. They starved me half-to-death. The light's too strong in here, could you soften it? (*Yoram turns out the lights. A single spotlight shines on Helenka alone. The others have disappeared, as it were, from her field of vision. She is alone with her memories and sees no one.*)

HELENKA. In the courtyard of the convent, there was an apple tree. I kept peeking at it between prayers. When it was night, I left my room and snuck out to the tree. I took off my shoes (*She unconsciously takes off her shoes.*) and tiptoed silently over to the tree. (*She picks up the apple and regards it carefully.*) The tree was heavy with apples. There was an apple there that was the biggest and nicest of them all. It hung on a low-lying branch. I reached for it, but the tree was too high. I couldn't get at it. It was so near. I looked for a stick. I couldn't find one. I tried climbing the tree. It didn't work. The tree was covered with barbed wire. Like snakes. I had an uncontrollable desire for that apple. I started to climb again. My hands and feet were bloody all over. I stood at the foot of the tree. Suddenly, I began to plead with the God of my father and mother, "Please, throw me one apple. Just one apple." But the tree was too high. And God was even higher. I got down on my knees and whispered, "Jesus, sweet Jesus, if you are really so good, please, sweet Jesus, just one apple." All of a sudden I began to laugh . . . Fingers gripped me by the neck. I went on laughing. "Jewish filth!" . . . The mother superior dragged me off to her room and beat me. She beat me and beat me. (*The lighting reverts to what it was before. Helenka snaps out of her reveries and says, calmly, quietly, half-smiling.*) And what do you think happened in the end? They starved me for three more days. (*Silence, Yoram, who has picked up an apple halfway through Helenka's story, now, in his excitement, absentmindedly bites into it. Helenka stands up stiffly, snatches the apple from his mouth, and throws it on the floor.*)

HELENKA. I want to get out of here.

YANEK. (*To Helenka.*) We'll go outside, Helenka. . . . (*To Yoram.*) We'll be back later. (*They go out. Yoram starts to go after them, then stops and comes back. He sees Nurit, who has been standing in the kitchen door and watching the proceedings.*)

YORAM. (*Losing control.*) What are you looking at me that way for?

. . . What are you . . . (*Nurit runs into the kitchen. Yoram begins to pound his forehead with his fist. He walks over to the table and turns off the light. In the darkness, one hears him strike the table with dull thuds. Muffled noises. Nurit re-enters.*)

NURIT. What are you doing? . . . Yoram! . . . (*Another thud. Nurit crosses over to him in the dark.*) Yoram! . . . (*She turns on the light.*)

YORAM. You simply must have a look at me, mustn't you? . . . I suppose I look lovely now. . . . Don't I?

NURIT. You make me sick!

YORAM. Shut up!

NURIT. What are you shouting again for? You think you're the only one who ever suffers? . . . I can't understand it any longer . . . I can't. . . . After every visit of theirs, you drive me crazy. . . . I didn't look at them the right way. . . . My gestures weren't right. . . . I didn't smile enough. . . . I wasn't nice to them when they came in. . . . What do you want from me?

YORAM. All right, it's my fault . . . just leave me alone now.

NURIT. After every visit you say it's your fault and then you go right on. . . . I've had enough. . . . I left home because I couldn't stand the way they fought. . . . Now it's the same thing all over. . . . Let's get away from here.

YORAM. Where to?

NURIT. Anywhere. . . . But if we don't leave here together, somebody's going to leave by herself.

YORAM. Nurit, I promise you that this is the last time. . . . Everybody will be all right. . . . When they get settled. . . . Right now I can't . . .

NURIT. But to make wrecks of us both, that you can? It's not they who have to get settled, you've got to decide what you want.

YORAM. I promise you that this is the last time . . .

NURIT. This is the thousandth time that I've heard that from you. . . . Try not to be naïve. . . . See things for what they are . . .

YORAM. O Lord! . . . If I only knew why I behaved this way, damn it. . . . Who am I? . . . Their tales of horror make me the guilty one. Guilty without having done anything. And then I close myself off from the world. Like a fortress. And the more they try to break their way into me, the tighter I close myself off. I close myself off, the guilt grows worse. The guilt grows worse, I close myself off. What have I done? What? . . . "You've already got roots in this country," Yanek once said to me. As if it were an accusation. And you, you're pulling me up. . . . He looked at me and didn't understand.

. . . And you, too. . . . You said to me, "Since they've come here, you've begun to escape into your past." . . . In fact, I've only now stopped escaping from it. . . . And you also looked at me without understanding. . . . You were right . . . There was no need for me to present you with my crown of thorns, but they, they present me with their thorns, day and night . . . with my past full of corpses, my past that isn't mine anymore . . . (*The doorbell rings, Yoram hastens to open it in the hope that it is Yanek and Helenka returning. All his anger and disappointment are taken out on the Balloon Seller, who enters.*)

BALLOON SELLER. (*To Yoram.*) Mister . . . (*He sees Nurit.*) Miss . . . I found this. . . . (*He is holding Sigmund's notebook.*) It's his . . .

YORAM. (*Angrily.*) You're all that was needed here—get out!

NURIT. Yoram, I asked him to investigate that man who . . .

BALLOON SELLER. That's right, mister, the lady asked me to, and so when I found this. . . . Here . . . its his notebook. (*He waves the notebook in the air.*) You can see for yourself . . .(*Yoram takes the notebook and begins to read.*) I read it. . . . I don't get it at all, but there's some horrible things written there . . . that I . . . I mean that he, together with the Germans. . . . I don't understand all the words that he uses . . .

YORAM. (*Reading aloud, but as though to himself.*) Lvov, 1942 . . . (*To the Balloon Seller.*) Do you know what his name is? I need his name, do you understand? His name?

BALLOON SELLER. I am sorry, mister, you can't get anything out of him, nothing . . .

YORAM. See if you can find out, and meanwhile—don't say a word about the notebook being here. Do you follow?

BALLOON SELLER. Sure I do, mister, I know how to keep my mouth shut. . . . What'd he write in there, huh?

YORAM. I don't think he wrote anything out of the ordinary.

BALLOON SELLER. I'll go now. If I find out anything more, I'll let you know. So long. (*As he is about to leave, Nurit puts some money in his hand. He exits.*)

NURIT. (*To Yoram, who has been looking in the notebook all this time.*) Is it interesting?

YORAM. Very. . . . At any rate, the style is unusual. And the title, it's called:

"The Heritage of Ashes" . . . (*He reads.*)
Another planet, a planet of fire.
Words that touch it are burned to ashes.
Beginnings of another creature,

A new being.
Not in the image of God, not in the image of beast.
Something new, different, new and different.
You, here to judge my deeds
On the planet of fire.
Inscribe my sentence with words that are dead
Petrified. Remnants of another age,
Like footprints of dinosaurs in rocks.

BLACKOUT

Scene 3

On the boardwalk. Sigmund is lying on the bench. The man with the newspaper is sitting in the café and reading.

BALLOON SELLER. (*Waking Sigmund.*) I'm glad I found you. I haven't seen you for a long time. People ask about you.

SIGMUND. About me? Who?

BALLOON SELLER. The boy who always sits there. (*He points to the café.*) The girl, too. She's asked about you several times. She's a good girl, she buys a lot of balloons.

SIGMUND. To hell with him and his balloons, what did he want?

BALLOON SELLER. I don't know. . . . Well, he wanted to know . . . why you're always going around with that dog. (*He points to the stuffed dog that Sigmund is holding in his hands.*)

SIGMUND. Never mind that dog, you'd better tell me everything, and not . . .

BALLOON SELLER. Well, he asked about your name. And where you came from.

SIGMUND. What else?

BALLOON SELLER. That's all.

SIGMUND. And what did you tell him?

BALLOON SELLER. I said to him, "I don't know what his name is." Now that you mention it, what is your name?

SIGMUND. Medusa.

BALLOON SELLER. Your name is Medusa? It's a nice name. Come to think of it, what kind of a name is it? I never heard of it.

SIGMUND. It's nice, yes it is. Did you ever hear a fish singing in the water?

BALLOON SELLER. No.

SIGMUND. A fish talking?

BALLOON SELLER. Never, so help me.

SIGMUND. You may tell them, if they ask you again, "He's as silent as a fish in a pelican's jaw."

BALLOON SELLER. A pelican? What's that?

SIGMUND. It's a kind of water bird. And what kind of bird are you? (*Aggressively.*) Do you have your papers?

BALLOON SELLER. My papers? Of course. What for?

SIGMUND. Permit me to examine them. (*He seizes him by the lapel.*)

BALLOON SELLER. Why?

SIGMUND. (*Slyly.*) Aren't we friends?

BALLOON SELLER. Sure we are.

SIGMUND. Well, then? Permit me. (*The Balloon Seller shows him his papers.*)

BALLOON SELLER. Does it mean anything to you?

SIGMUND. Righteous, perfectly righteous. (*He produces his own papers.*) Would you care to see mine? Help yourself.

BALLOON SELLER. Benjamin Apfelbaum. Born in Vilna. You look a lot younger in this photo. . . . Arrived in Israel: 1947. (*Impressed.*) You've been here eight years. An oldtimer.

SIGMUND. Mm-hmmm . . . I was wounded in the war. . . . Nerves. Get it?

BALLOON SELLER. You're crazy?

SIGMUND. No, no. . . . My sickness is I call myself all kinds of names, particularly those of animals. (*Confidently.*) Now you mustn't tell a soul. . . . It's strictly between the two of us, you understand. . . . I'm fondest of calling myself rat. (*He contorts his face and begins to whistle through his teeth like a rat.*) Rat! (*To the dog on the bench.*) After him! After him!

BALLOON SELLER. But that's not a real dog.

SIGMUND. There is nothing as real as unreality.

BALLOON SELLER. Why do you call yourself rat?

SIGMUND. In China they eat them for dessert. Ha, Ha, Ha!

BALLOON SELLER. Brrrr . . .

SIGMUND. Brrr . . . it's cold. . . . This rat is being called by another hole. The wind's at my back. It's time to sail.

BALLOON SELLER. To sail? Where to? Why?

SIGMUND. It's cold.

BALLOON SELLER. You may come live in my shack.

SIGMUND. There's a cat by the shack.

BALLOON SELLER. You can sleep in my bed. I'll give you a blanket.

SIGMUND. I'll lay me down in some other hole. (*To a passerby.*)

Shameless mortal, sinful one. Give me a pound and I'll be gone. (*The passerby tosses a coin on the ground. Sigmund picks it up.*)

BALLOON SELLER. It's not nice to beg. You shouldn't do it.

SIGMUND. You're wrong—anything can be done. Pettiness disgusts people. Bigness makes them want to forgive.

BALLOON SELLER. I don't get it.

SIGMUND. I'll tell you a little story: There was once a tiger who ate a whole lot of sheep. But the tiger bit off more than he could chew, and sent a challenge to the lions, too. The lions defeated him and wounded him terribly. They brought him to trial and accused him, among other things, of eating the sheep. They punished him, not too severely, to be sure, but the tiger decided that he was sorry. As for the dead—why worry? He announced that he was repenting. And then a big fat she-lamb proclaimed, "The tiger was changed. He's not the same." (*He snatches away the Balloon Seller's balloons and disappears on the run backstage.*) Balloons! Pretty balloons! They come in all colors you like! Dirt cheap! Balloons! (*The Balloon Seller runs after him.*)

BALLOON SELLER. Give me my balloons! Give me my balloons! (*From backstage comes the sound of balloons bursting and of Sigmund laughing.*)

SIGMUND. (*Returning.*) Ha-ha-ha-ha! (*He sits down and rubs his back against the bench. To the dog.*) Did you see how he ran from me? Ha-ha-ha-ha! What are you staring at me for? Run, my friend, run while there's time. (*He pets him.*) Poor thing, you're so neglected. You would have been worth hundreds of gold teeth over there. Figure it out, how many gold teeth does an average man have? . . . Four hundred people. Ridiculous! Much more than that. . . . And what are you worth here? Just another dog. You see? You've got to know where to be born. You don't understand a thing. Not a single thing. (*He continues to pet it.*) Whew . . . you have bugs. You bite (*Scratching.*) Stop biting! . . . All right. . . . All right. . . . You're forgiven. You see? Men forgive dogs, but not men. Do dogs forgive dogs? The sheep are a funny nation, they forgave the tigers, but they never forgave the tiger's stooges. Unwilling stooges. You understand me, don't you? (*He pets the dog.*) I asked you not to bite! (*He scratches himself again.*) All right, no need to be insulted. It's not your fault. You're filthy. Want to take a bath? (*He gets up.*) In the water? (*He strides toward the sea.*) No. . . . No. . . . Come to me, you good little dog, come. You have beautiful, good eyes. Why do they say that dogs have eyes like people? Don't you think that's an insult? (*A passerby appears and stands on the railing. Sigmund gets up and crosses over to him.*)

PASSERBY. (*Taking a coin from his pocket and putting it in Sigmund's out-stretched hand.*) Take it and beat it! (*He himself exits.*)

SIGMUND. Do you see how they treat me? Like a dog. No, no, a thousand thousand pardons, thou glory of creation. Are you insulted? (*He glances at the coin in his hand.*) Want some ice cream? (*He pets the dog.*) You have wonderful curls, just like Esther's. My curls were nice, too. What, you don't believe me? Get away, get away from me. I'll have nothing to do with you. (*Lets the dog drop.*) All right, you can stay. (*He picks the dog up.*) If you only knew who I was you'd run from me, too. Believe me, I'm not to blame. (*The bark of a dog is heard from backstage.*) See, now you're angry at me, too. Listen, I have an idea. You'll be my judge. Agreed? I'll be the prosecutor myself. There'll be no lack of witnesses, they'll be like raindrops in wet weather. Well, then. (*He places the dog on the beach.*) Get up on the bench. They called me a dog. . . . Should I get down on all fours? (*He gets down on his hands and feet. Another bark from backstage.*) I tell you, that's a fine beginning. You're an excellent judge. We'll begin. (*In the hardened tone of an interrogator.*) Your name?! (*Submissively.*) My name is Dr. Sig . . . (*He strikes the dog as hard as he can, then throws it over the railing.*) Come back! Come back! I have to be judged by someone, I have to be! (*Suddenly, facing the audience.*)

Shameless mortal, sinful one,
Take a pound and I'll be gone.

(*He throws, as it were, a coin into the audience.*)

BLACKOUT

Scene 4

On the boardwalk. It is Independence Day. Enter the Balloon Seller with a bunch of balloons. The noise of celebrating crowds. In the background, backstage or over the sea, fireworks are set off. Over the radio in the café come the intermittent sounds of announcers, celebrating children, ceremonial speeches, ice cream vendors, and insistent paper horns.

The time is twilight. The sky over the sea is blue and reddish gold.

BALLOON SELLER. (*Blowing a paper horn.*) Business is going to be good tonight, Mr. Greenstein . . .

WAITER. Yes, it looks like it might. God willing.

BALLOON SELLER. Two straight nights like this and you'll be a millionaire, Mr. Greenstein . . .

WAITER. God should only be so good. Amen.

BALLOON SELLER. Tell me, Mr. Greenstein, did you ever dream that we'd have a Jewish state, huh? It's a great day, Mr. Greenstein, a great day. Look at me, who am I and what am I? Just a Jew selling balloons, I have nothing to my name, I'm as lonely as a stone, but I'm a happy man. It makes me rejoice that we've lived to see this day. I tell you Mr. Greenstein, it calls for a prayer of thanksgiving . . .

WAITER. Tonight you can sell your balloons inside.

BALLOON SELLER. Is it crowded inside?

WAITER. No, not very.

BALLOON SELLER. Then, I'll wait till later. (*He notices Yoram and hurries toward him.*) I saw him . . .

YORAM. Who?

BALLOON SELLER. That man, he's up above. . . . I asked him what his name was, he said it was Medusa. But on his identity card it says: Benjamin Apfelbaum, born in Vilna, a long time in this country, an oldtimer. . . . He lied to me, he also busted all my balloons . . .

YORAM. What did you say his name was?

BALLOON SELLER. Benjamin Apfelbaum.

YORAM. Thank you very much, happy Independence Day. (*The Balloon Seller walks over to the café.*)

YORAM. (*To the waiter.*) Max, (*The waiter comes over.*) I'm waiting for a phone call. . . . I'll be out on the boardwalk. Will you call me?

WAITER. I certainly will.

YORAM. (*Crossing over to Sigmund.*) Listen, mister . . .

SIGMUND. Can I have a light?

YORAM. Sure. (*Yoram hands him his cigarette.*) Their eyes meet.)

SIGMUND. Thank you. . . . The light is so strong. . . . There's too much light, too much. . . . Do you mind if I put on my sunglasses? (*He puts them on.*)

YORAM. Why should I mind? There are many lights, all right, tonight's a holiday. Happy Independence Day . . .

SIGMUND. A holiday? . . . I completely forgot, that is, I completely didn't remember that today is a holiday . . . (*A siren sounds. Everyone stands at attention. Sigmund sits down.*)

SIGMUND. This siren—does it signal the start?

YORAM. It means that the day of mourning for the war victims is over. How come you don't know, you're not new here, are you?

SIGMUND. How simple it is. The siren blows and the mourning is over. (*The siren blows again.*) And now the holiday begins? It's brilliant, simply brilliant. . . . I should say, most impressively symbolic.

YORAM. Mister, would you mind leaving me alone once and for all? Who are you?

SIGMUND. You want to know about me? Kindly believe me, I'm not worthy of anybody's attention. . . . I am (*He points to himself.*) the equivalent of a corpse. . . . Permit me to ask whether you believe in ghosts. . . . No, of course not, well, then, think of me as a ghost; and now, since you don't believe in ghosts, I'm no longer here. . . . May I be excused?

YORAM. (*Angrily.*) Is anyone keeping you? Listen, friend, I have the feeling there's something you want to tell me, so why don't you spill it . . .

SIGMUND. Ah, but that would be unfortunate, so very unfortunate. . . . You're a young man, and I'm an incorrigible windbag. . . . If I began talking, there'd be no stopping me. . . . Should you be so kind as to lend me an ear, who knows, I might rob you of this night meant for women and wine. (*There are sudden noises of celebration.*) And should you interrupt me in the middle and leave, I'd be left without an audience, and that would distress me no end. . . . All in all, you can see that I'd best remain silent. (*More shouts.*) Well, that's how it is, isn't it? (*Shouts from afar. Voices chanting to the melody of a hora: "Everybody must be merry / Everybody must be merry".*) Words like a whiplash! . . . "Everybody must be merry." . . . But you're sad, aren't you? . . . It's a sin, you know, an unpardonable sin to be sad on a night like this. . . . Something about you, if I may say so, reminds me of something or somebody, your voice, perhaps, or your eyes. I can't place it, but it's remarkable. But our imagination forever plays tricks on us, doesn't it? Consequently . . .

YORAM. Perhaps you'll finally tell me who it is I'm supposed to resemble so much?

SIGMUND. Imaginary figments. . . . I, you see . . . sleep when I wake and wake when I would dream. There's an image another image conjures from the dead. A sin we thought went out like a candle flame, only to return. Then left the creditor aware of what lies ahead.

YORAM. You may be a newcomer, but you're a rising talent . . .

SIGMUND. Not at all, or rather yes, I have a talent for rising . . . from the grave. It's a nice phrase, "a rising talent," . . . isn't it?

YORAM. Where are you from?

SIGMUND. From everywhere and nowhere. . . . "I sleep in the East. My heart is in the West." Rabbi Judah Halevi, if I'm not mistaken . . .

176 / Ben-Zion Tomer

YORAM. Yes, but you're mistaken, it's the other way around . . .

SIGMUND. Around and around and around and around. . . . Your patience in listening to me blabber touches my heart, though my heart, as I say, burned in the West.

YORAM. And your ability to play a part is beyond all belief. A poet, an immigrant, and an actor . . .

SIGMUND. An actor? What a sharp eye you've got. . . . Allow me to compliment you. . . . I've practiced the most important act of the twentieth century, the art of staying alive . . . and as you can see, I've been a successful artist. Or have I? Are you familiar with the famous soliloquy in Hamlet?

YORAM. You mean, "To be or not to be—that is the question"? . . .

SIGMUND. Yes. . . . No. . . . Permit me to recite for you a variation on that soliloquy as Shakespeare would undoubtedly have written it had he lived in the twentieth century, "To be or not to be—some question!" . . .

YORAM. What did you say?

SIGMUND. Nice, isn't it?

YORAM. Terrible!

SIGMUND. Terrible? My dear young man, when I was your age and a lecturer at the university in Lvov . . .

YORAM. In Lvov? You were a lecturer in Lvov? What's your name?

SIGMUND. My name? 155370, and kindly note that the last digit is zero. And that, my fine fellow, is all you'll ever know. Zero.

WAITER. (*Entering.*) Mr. Eyal, telephone for you . . . (*Yoram turns to face the waiter and Sigmund disappears. Yoram enters the café. Holding his balloons, the Balloon Seller does a dance in pantomime, expressing the happiness felt by all on Independence Day. The hora music—"Everybody must be merry"—continues . . .*)

SIGMUND. (*Returning to the dog.*) Why are you sad? (*He sings to the dog.*) "Everybody must be joyful, everybody must be joyful." If he comes back, I won't have the strength to act any more. . . . Stop being sad. It's Independence Day. Come, let's dance. (*He begins to dance with the dog.*) Don't be so lazy. Can you be hungry? Come along, perhaps we'll find you a bone. A bone of joy. (*A young couple enters. The girl has long black braids. They kiss. To the dog.*) Why do you stare at me as though I were the moon? (*Again the melody: "Everybody must be merry".*) They've learned to be joyful. And to forget. And why not? Why remember? There's too much light tonight. Much too much. (*He puts on his sunglasses. The couple, having crossed the stage and exited,*) *now reappears. Sigmund springs toward them.*) Shameless mortal, sinful one . . . (*The couple disappears.*) Ha-ha-ha-ha! I made them run away. Did you see that? I spoiled their fun. (*He strokes the dog. Again: "Everybody must be joyful".*) Listen to the noise they make. Is it because they remember that they make it? What do you think, my little philosopher? Why so quiet? Say something . . . (*The couple returns, Sigmund approaches them and sings.*) "Everybody must be joyful." (*They take fright and run off. To the dog.*) Run, damn you, run . . . if you don't . . . (*Yoram returns. Sigmund leaps in front of him.*) Shameless mortal. . . . Ah, it's you . . .

YORAM. It's I, but who in hell are you?

SIGMUND. I? A debtor, a repenting sinner who has no one to repent before. Do you know what the rabbis say about repenting sinners?

YORAM. (*On the verge of hating him.*) Listen, you!

SIGMUND. It's said that, in the place where repenting sinners stand, even the purely righteous may not set foot. Why? Nothing could be clearer: because of the stench. But what I would like to know from you is: Whose stink? Complicated isn't it?

YORAM. (*Grabbing him by the lapel.*) Why don't you tell me where you're from? What's your name?

SIGMUND. My name? I've already told you. 155370. Zero, and that's all you'll ever know about me. Zero. (*Sigmund slips out of Yoram's grasp.*) Good night and happy Independence Day.

BLACKOUT

Scene 5

Quiet blues are heard from the café. It is evening. Yoram and Yanek sit at a table on which there is a large bottle of whiskey.

YORAM. Maybe you'll have a drink with me after all?

YANEK. No thanks, just some juice.

YORAM. You don't drink. . . . You don't smoke. (*He lights a cigarette.*) One might think you'd come out a sterilized bottle at some school, rather than . . .

YANEK. Have you had a lot to drink?

YORAM. Drink big—forget big. Sleep big—escape big. I've got a big mouth.

YANEK. Are you under the weather, or what?

YORAM. And what weather. . . . You'll feel it soon enough.

YANEK. I think we're in for a hot wind.

YORAM. "Then blew the wind throughout the land" . . .

YANEK. "Twelve." By Alexander Block.

YORAM. Hey, you know the poem . . .

YANEK. From my days in the youth movement . . .

YORAM. You know, sometimes you make me wonder how a person can go through so much and come out so virginal and antiseptic. . . . How's Helenka?

YANEK. It's not been easy for her. . . . She's lonely. . . . Life hasn't spoiled her any . . .

YORAM. Life's to blame for everything, isn't it? It's never anybody's fault . . .

YANEK. More or less, although . . .

YORAM. So you, too, are one of these? . . . I thought with you black was black and white was white. I am a chameleon. I take on every color and none of the colors is me. That's how it is when you try to understand everything and everybody, all the colors. . . . (*Unexpectedly.*) Have you ever killed a human being?

YANEK. Why do you ask?

YORAM. Answer me first, then you'll see why . . .

YANEK. Does that term include Germans?

YORAM. In this case, no.

YANEK. Well, I've killed two half human beings . . . collaborators. At times they weren't any better than the Germans.

YORAM. In the ghetto?

YANEK. Yes, in Warsaw. . . . Right before the revolt . . .

YORAM. The revolt. . . . Where was I at the time of the revolt? . . . (*He drinks from his glass.*) Wait a minute. . . . Let me think. . . . Right. . . . I was sitting here. . . . In this café. . . . They brought us to demonstrate. . . . That was my contribution. I had two free hours. . . . I sat down and enjoyed the sun. It was a lovely day. The girls went by and showed off what they had to show. (*Two girls go by.*) Just like now. After the demonstration, I went to the movies. The theaters were open. Just like now. The economy was booming. The war effort. Yes, things were good. Like now. Only no German reparations. Concerts. Culture. Like now, only on the news broadcasts they played different background music . . .

YANEK. You can't tell me that that's the historical truth . . .

YORAM. Do me a favor and don't speak to me about that whore. . . . Historical truth! I don't give a damn about her—or she about me. . . . It comes to the same thing. . . . You're right about one thing, though; I'm trying to look smart in retrospect. And I don't give a damn about retrospective wisdom. . . . Listen, if someone presses a button and three-quarters of the human race (*He makes a liquidating motion.*)—the quarter that's left will go right on, it'll mourn a while or a little longer and it'll go on, and the poets will immortalize all those brave bearers of tradition, of mortality, of culture, of. . . . Right after the war was over, when the first of you people began to arrive and tell us what happened, I too began to ask: "Why didn't you rise up?" And with an accusing finger! Do you get me? With an accusing finger and with more than faint contempt. But of course it wasn't meant for people like you. You saved your honor . . .

YANEK. We asked the very same question over there.

YORAM. (*Angrily.*) You had the right to! I didn't!

YANEK. It was possible to remain human even there. That's a fact.

YORAM. You're talking about the ones who were strong.

YANEK. Lets drop the subject.

YORAM. But what kind of a world is this where you always have to be strong? Do you know what mistake the strong always make? They overestimate man's resources . . . and man is weak . . . weak. . . . (*He drinks.*) That weakness mustn't be put to the test, it mustn't be . . . (*At this moment, Sigmund appears. Yanek doesn't notice him. Yoram does, and his face shows apprehension. Sigmund approaches Yoram resolutely, as though to have it out once and for all. He sees Yanek and turns, disappearing in the direction of the boardwalk.*)

YANEK. What's wrong?

YORAM. Nothing. . . . Nothing. . . . Its from the . . . (*He points to the glass and takes a breath of air. He passes his hand over his forehead and says, suddenly and quietly.*) Sigmund's in Israel.

YANEK. (*Taken by surprise.*) No!

YORAM. Yes, Yanek, yes . . .

YANEK. God!

YORAM. It's true.

YANEK. What will we do?

YORAM. You mean, what will you do. It's your decision, not mine.

YANEK. Why mine and not yours?

YORAM. Because having the right not to forgive, you have the right to forgive, too.

YANEK. Yossele, are you sure?

YORAM. I'm sure, Yanek, I'm sure.

YANEK. You never knew him, how do you know? . . . Maybe . . .

YORAM. I think he recognized me; and besides, (*He takes a photograph from his pocket.*) I went through your belongings and found this in Mom's album . . .

YANEK. Mama destroyed all his pictures. (*He studies the photograph.*) She left this one because it was taken at the wedding. . . . Look what a noble face that dog has . . .

YORAM. You should see what that dog looks like now . . .

YANEK. Do as you like. . . . Kill him. . . . Get rid of him. . . . Let him go. . . . As you like . . . but not me . . . not me . . . (*Enter Nurit. From a distance, she seems happy. Then, as she approaches and hears Yanek's last words, her expression changes. The photograph is on the table.*)

NURIT. What happened now? (*They don't answer. She sees the photograph and picks it up.*) Whose photo is this?

YANEK. Esther and Sigmund.

NURIT. Wait. . . . He's. . . . I know him from somewhere. . . . I've seen him . . .

YORAM. Yes, you've seen him . . .

NURIT. It's not . . . (*She points toward the boardwalk.*)

YORAM. Yes . . . it's him . . .

NURIT. That man is your brother-in-law? . . .

YORAM. Yes! Yes! Yes!

NURIT. I understand what resemblance he was talking about. (*To Yanek.*) Have you seen him?

YANEK. Have I? No. . . . He has. (*He points to Yoram.*)

NURIT. (*Suspiciously.*) Who is he?

YANEK. He's. . . . Don't ask me. . . . I've done my share. . . . I have a right to rest, too.

NURIT. (*Losing her temper at Yanek.*) What do you want from him?

YORAM. (*Trying to quiet her down.*) Nurit!

NURIT. They're ruining you, you know they are?

YORAM. Go home!

NURIT. Don't you send me to a nunnery, or to the kitchen either. Why should it be you and not him? (*She points at Yanek.*) You weren't there . . .

YORAM. (*Sarcastically.*) No, I wasn't . . .

NURIT. I know . . .

YORAM. Something has to be done about him . . .

NURIT. Something has to be done. . . . What? . . . And meanwhile you make a mess of everything . . .

YANEK. I'm sorry, the mess has been our doing . . .

NURIT. I didn't mean to hurt your feelings, but I know him . . . how sensitive he is . . .

YANEK. I never said to him that he should . . .

YORAM. Whether I should or shouldn't—that's my business. Stop pitying me the two of you, quit worrying about your precious darling . . . (*To Yanek.*) Yanek, go home.

YANEK. (*Getting up confusedly.*) Yossele . . .

YORAM. (*Angrily.*) Good-bye, Yanek. (*Yanek leaves.*)

NURIT. Yoram, what are you going to do? Turn him in?

YORAM. (*Echoing her.*) Turn him in? I don't know. I don't know. I wish I did. . . . I have to understand it. . . . I have to . . .

YANEK. (*Returning.*) Perhaps . . .

YORAM. (*More gently.*) There's no need to justify yourself, Yanek, you're the last one here who has to do that. . . . You'd better leave us alone . . . (*Nurit attempts a confused, apologetic smile. Yanek leaves.*)

NURIT. Let him go.

YORAM. (*Echoing her.*) Let him go.

NURIT. He's an unfortunate man.

YORAM. Unfortunate! They're all unfortunate! . . . (*After a short silence.*) Esther couldn't have loved . . .

NURIT. What can we know about it?

YORAM. Because we can't know anything about it, we have to proceed with the agenda, is that it?

NURIT. I didn't say we have to proceed with the agenda. Why do you think that none of this matters to me? It matters a great deal, but what matters to me now is you. For God's sake. . . . How can people live like this? . . .

YORAM. Like what?

NURIT. In constant hell . . .

YORAM. That's how it is, either you live in paradise or you knock about in hell, and I like it better in hell.

NURIT. Why do you think I'm less sensitive than you?

YORAM. I never said that . . .

NURIT. You don't always have to say something in order to say it. . . . There's no reason why I should feel guilty or make a saint out of myself . . .

YORAM. Am I to take that as a hint? A saint? It's barely possible to be a human being.

NURIT. You know very well that you like to torture yourself, to feel guilty . . .

YORAM. I know, but something . . .

NURIT. Leave him alone . . .

YORAM. Leave. . . . Run away. . . . One day, when I was a child, it was a sunny day, I noticed my shadow. It was gigantic, long, black, behind me. I turned around and it turned around, too. I had a wooden sword in my hand. I began to strike at it. The sword broke. The shadow was still there . . . (*He looks at the photograph.*) I have to see him . . . to understand . . .

NURI. To understand. . . . Understand everybody. . . . All of them, Helenka, and now Sigmund . . . and me, me you understand?

YORAM. You I love, Nurit. (*Sigmund enters. Nurit bows her head and leaves. Yoram walks over to Sigmund, who stands as if awaiting sentence.*)

YORAM. (*From a distance.*) And so, shameless mortal, sinful one . . .

SIGMUND. (*He approaches.*) I must say you're very clever . . . that is you, isn't it? It's not right of you, not right at all, you're causing me deficits. A light, please. (*He becomes aware of the tension in Yoram's face.*) I believe I'll light it myself.

YORAM. Come with me.

SIGMUND. Where?

YORAM. To have a drink.

SIGMUND. Am I hearing things? You're asking me to join you for a drink? You must be joking. You might as well have said that the mountain really came to Mohammed.

YORAM. I'm probably no mountain, but you're certainly not Mohammed.

SIGMUND. You're quite right, allow me to present myself: Dr. Medusa . . .

YORAM. Listen, you . . .

SIGMUND. Perhaps you've changed your mind?

YORAM. Come on! . . . There is no one here. . . . Can we talk?

SIGMUND. Ah, as long as there's no one here, you're not embarrassed to share a table with Medusa.

YORAM. (*Dragging him forcefully.*) Move! Sit!

WAITER. (*Entering.*) But Mr. Eyal . . .

YORAM. He's my guest. (*To Sigmund.*) What will you have, cognac?

SIGMUND. Yes . . .

YORAM. (*To the waiter.*) Two doubles. (*The waiter remains standing.*) Two doubles! (*The waiter goes off.*) Now, then, Dr. . . . .

SIGMUND. Medusa.

YORAM. I've never heard a Medusa who sold his soul to the devil!

SIGMUND. If there is a God, there is a devil, too, and he's the whip in God's hands! (*Deprecatingly.*) God . . .

WAITER. (*Returning with two glasses of cognac.*) Here you are . . .

SIGMUND. (*Putting a bill on the tray.*) For your gracious service. (*The waiter leaves.*) Here's to you, you needn't drink to me. (*He drinks.*)

YORAM. Want another? (*Sigmund drinks Yoram's glass. Yoram goes inside and returns with a bottle. In the meantime, Sigmund gets up as if to leave. He stops, comes back, and sits down in another chair, all before Yoram reappears.*) I'm waiting for an answer.

SIGMUND. I've already answered you about where repenting sinners stand.

YORAM. I'm still waiting for an answer.

SIGMUND. You're a very stubborn fellow, my good man, and I'm soft . . . soft as a Medusa. . . . What's already been broken is no longer breakable . . .

YORAM. I take it that you were a Medusa even in Lvov.

SIGMUND. I thank you, and now if you'll kindly permit me to be on my way . . . (*He tries to go. Yoram forcibly restrains him.*)

YORAM. Sit down, we're not through yet. (*He takes out the photograph.*) Do you recognize this photograph? Do you?

SIGMUND. I do, Yossele. I recognized you from the very first. By the eyes, the shape of the . . .

YORAM. Do you know that my parents are in Israel, and Yanek? . . .

SIGMUND. I know. . . . I've wanted more than once . . .

YORAM. Then how could you go on pretending all the time to be . . .

SIGMUND. Mad? By virtue of that madness, I've somehow managed to preserve my last shred of sanity. . . . Well, what are you waiting for? Call the police. Why don't you call them? Are you afraid? I can do it for you . . . (*Shouting.*) Hey! (*Yoram covers his mouth.*) So that you can remain the immaculate virgin that you are. You effeminate soul . . .

YORAM. And what if this virginal, effeminate soul should tear you into little pieces?

SIGMUND. So much the better, why don't you?

YORAM. I always knew I would do nothing . . . nothing . . . nothing. . . . "True conscience does make cowards of us all." Conscience. . . . If that's the proper name for this swamp (*He passes his hand over his forehead.*) into which one sinks and sinks, in which nothing is ever clear. . . . But how could anybody sink as far as you have, you mad dog? . . .

SIGMUND. (*To his dog.*) Is that you, thou glory of creation? (*To Yoram.*) Don't you think there's a resemblance between us?

YORAM. Stop acting!

SIGMUND. What is it that I'm supposed to do? Tell you how it was there? . . . Burst into a Dostoevski-like confession? . . . Beg forgiveness? What do you understand about all this?—Zero!—You understand Zero! Forgiveness? From whom? From the enlightened world? At least I know who I am: I'm a Medusa, a kind of jellyfish. Do you know why I insist on being a jellyfish? Because jellyfish have no words, they don't even have a voice. All they have is memories for which there aren't any buyers in this world of forgetfulness. Fill up my glass. (*Yoram pours him a drink.*) What do you want?

YORAM. To understand. . . . To understand how a man like you, a man of principles, a humanist, Yanek told me about you—could end up the way you did. . . . To understand.

SIGMUND. You want to understand, to understand. . . . And if I were to tell you that in more than one way I was their biggest victim, would you understand? That silences you. . . . You want to understand, what you want is to understand. . . . (*He suddenly takes out some papers and gives them to Yoram.*) Here. Take them. Read them. Perhaps you'll understand. . . . Here you'll find the life story of Medusa, erstwhile doctor of philosophy, authority on Renaissance art, fervid believer in humanism. Take them! Take this, too. . . . (*He pulls out another notebook.*) Here you'll find the story of a certain commandant of a concentration camp. . . . A boyhood friend of mine. . . . A good friend. . . . A German. . . . We studied together at Heidelberg. . . . A humanist. . . . He had a special way of torturing me. Once a week, he would invite me to discuss with him the future of humanity. Once he said to me, "You Jews have given us Marx, Freud, Einstein, Heine. . . . But only Heine grasped the essence of the German temperament . . . that we've remained fire-worshippers to this day." "In the end you'll be burned to death," I told him, "we'll consume you yet." "No one will consume us," he said to me, "we'll leave behind us a world so stripped clean of everything, that there won't be a rag of an ideal to cover the nakedness with." . . . And he was right. . . . (*After a pause.*) He mustn't be right! He mustn't be! Do you hear me, he mustn't be! I want you to understand that I was a human being, and the most terrible thing of all was that they were human, too.

YORAM. (*Shouting.*) Everyone is human! You! Me! THEM! So what is a human being? What?

SIGMUND. Whoever still asks that question. They only knew how to execute, not how to ask!

YORAM. To ask. That's the most that can be. Never to understand . . .

SIGMUND. You're so much like Esther now. She loved you. Very much. . . . I have to go. . . . (*He begins to walk away.*)

YORAM. Where are you going, Sigmund? . . . Wait . . . I . . .

SIGMUND. Do me a favor, a favor I don't deserve; don't ask . . . don't talk. . . . Anything you might say to me, I've already spent many long nights saying to myself. . . . So many times I've wanted to end it. . . . To. . . . To end it. . . . But I've gone on, as flesh-and-blood will go on. . . . Now, too, I've gone on because I couldn't forgive. To die, to sleep, no more . . . is to forgive. . . . There must be no forgiveness! None! I have to go. . . . Take good care of yourself. (*He rises suddenly, turning his back on Yoram. He sees Nurit standing, half-hidden, in the corner.*) Here is your wife. . . . She's waiting for you. (*He walks toward the sea. Crash of breakers. The stage is slowly darkened. Yoram picks up the notebook, looks at it, and then to Sigmund. Nurit comes up to him. Both are looking at Sigmund as he disappears.*)

CURTAIN

Motti Lerner

Motti Lerner was born in Zichron Yaacov, Israel, in 1949. He studied theater at the Hebrew University, in England, and in the United States. He directs his own and other playwrights' plays.

Lerner writes only plays: *Kastner* (1985), *Waiting for Messiah* (1987,) *Exile in Jerusalem* (1990), *Golden Age* (1991), *In the Dark* (1992), and *Temporary Kingship* (1993).

Exile in Jerusalem, Waiting for Messiah, and *Kastner* have appeared in English. *Exile in Jerusalem* has been produced twice in America.

Kastner

1985

(Translated by Imre Goldstein)

Characters

THE JEWS

SHAMU STERN, BARON, head of the liberal faction of the Jewish Community in Budapest; later, head of the Judenrat.

FOLÖP (PHILIP) FREUDIGER, head of the Orthodox faction of the Jewish Community in Budapest; later, member of the Judenrat.

OTTO KOMOLY, chairman of the Zionist Federation in Hungary; head of the Zionist Rescue Committee.

RUDOLF (REZSÖ) KASTNER, vice-chairman of the Zionist Federation in Hungary; member of the Rescue Committee.

JOEL (YENÖ) BRAND, member of the Rescue Committee.

HANSI BRAND, Joel Brand's wife; member of the Rescue Committee.

ELIZABET (BOGYO) KASTNER, Kastner's wife.
HELEN KASTNER, Kastner's mother.
IMRE VARGA, member of the Revisionist (Zionist) movement in Budapest.
MIKLÓS BENEDEK, Jewish journalist (A fictitious character).
MALCHIEL GRÜNWALD, Hungarian Jew, resident of Jerusalem. Following his several publications about Kastner's activities, a libel suit was brought against him by the Israeli government's legal advisor.

THE GERMANS

ADOLF EICHMANN, head of Section IV B4 of the Reich Security main office (in charge of Jewish Affairs).
HERMANN KRUMEY, Eichmann's deputy.
DIETER WISLICENY, Eichmann's assistant.
HELMUT, Eichmann's personal attendant. (A fictitious character.)

THE HUNGARIANS

LÁSZLÓ ENDRE, secretary of state for Jewish Affairs. A fascist.
LÁSZLÓ BAKY, commander of the Hungarian Gendarmerie. A fascist.
DR. SCHNELLER, Hungary's finance minister. A former liberal.
LULU, a prostitute. (A fictitious character.)

Place and Time

Budapest, between March 19, 1944, and July 1, 1944.

The Prologue, and most of the Epilogue, take place in the District Court of Jerusalem in 1954.

PROLOGUE

RÜNWALD. Your Honor, all my family, the Grünwalds, a very large family, was killed in the war along with most of Hungary's Jews. Luckily for me, I was already here in Israel at the time. To this very day, Your Honor, I cannot comprehend, neither logically nor emotionally, how the members of my family and those 700,000 other unfortunates got on the trains that took them to Auschwitz. I have been asking, Your Honor, and will keep on asking whether this terrible murder was really unavoidable?

Consider, Your Honor, that by the summer of 1944, when the Germans invaded Hungary, the Russians had already reached the Carpathians, the Americans had captured Italy, and the Third Reich was in a state of collapse. Was it not possible to save 700,000 Jews from the claws of the defeated Nazis?

(*Komoly's apartment. Violent knocking at the door.*)

KOMOLY. Who is it?

BRAND. It's me, Brand. (*Komoly opens the door.*) The Germans have invaded the country.

KOMOLY. Invaded the country?

BRAND. Yes. The army has surrendered. In two hours they'll be in Budapest. (*Blackout.*)

GRÜNWALD. Your Honor, I know that the free world did nothing to help, it remained indifferent to the end. But that is not the only explanation for the terrible genocide. My own investigations have led me to the shocking conclusion that there were guilty ones among our own people. People who were ready to collaborate with the Nazi murderers. Some did it to save their own skins, some did it for profit, and some to satisfy their delusions of grandeur and hunger for power. And the man the Nazis made the most use of in order to carry out their crimes, was, without the slightest shadow of a doubt, Dr. Rudolf Rezsö Kastner!

(*Kastner's apartment. Brand is knocking on the door.*)

BRAND. Rezsö, Rezsö . . .

KASTNER. What's the matter?

BRAND. The Germans have invaded the country.

KASTNER. When?

BRAND. This morning. The BBC is talking about seven divisions. (*Blackout.*)

GRÜNWALD. I know what people involved in this trial say about me. They say: "Malchiel Grünwald is a psychopath." It seems that *psychopath* means someone who insists that we must get at the truth. And I do insist, not for myself, but for the sake of our national conscience and honor. No one will silence me until the terrible crimes of Dr. Kastner come to light, crimes for which he is still wanted in Hungary as a war criminal and collaborator. The people must know the truth.

(*Stern's apartment. Kastner is knocking on the door.*)

SERVANT. Whom would you like to see, sir?

KASTNER. Baron Stern, please.

SERVANT. Your name, sir?

KASTNER. Kastner, Dr. Rudolf Kastner. I must speak with the Baron. It's very urgent.

SERVANT. You had better come back in an hour, sir. On Sundays, the Baron sleeps until eight o'clock. (*Blackout.*)

GRÜNWALD. Do the people know that Dr. Kastner saved his family for the price of keeping the truth from his fellow Jews about Auschwitz and the gas chambers? Do the people know that only because of that, did hundreds of thousands of Jews get on the trains, in complete ignorance, on the way to Auschwitz? Do the people know that only because of that, did those same hundreds of thousands go quietly into the showers, without a word, without the slightest resistance? Are the people aware of Eichmann's proposal to Joel Brand? The proposal that could have saved all of Hungary's Jews, had it not been for Kastner's collaboration with the Germans, and for the helplessness of the Jewish Agency here, in this country?

Do the people know that after the war Dr. Kastner interceded with the Allies for the Nazi leaders who had destroyed the Jews of Poland, Hungary, and Slovakia? That he worked for the release without punishment of such murderers as Kurt Becher, Hermann Krumey, and Dieter Wisliceny?

Do the people know that those few refugees who did manage to get here from Hungary have been trying to take revenge on this man, the cause of their unspeakable sufferings? Your Honor, the stench of a carcass assails my nostrils. This will be a happy and joyous funeral, indeed. Dr. Kastner must be destroyed!

ACT I

Scene 1

Offices of the Jewish Community in Budapest. Stern, Freudiger, Krumey, and Wisliceny. In one corner stands a German Soldier with his weapon at the ready.

KRUMEY. Don't be alarmed. This is only a courtesy visit. We thought we should get to know each other. To reassure you. Frightened leaders can bring disaster on their community. Notice, gentlemen. We did not break into your place, and we have no intentions of confiscating any documents. You are surprised. You can see for yourselves that all those rumors about us are simply not true. Especially those about Obersturmbannführer Eichmann. By the way, Obersturmbannführer Eichmann has already arrived in Budapest, and this meeting is taking place at his request. (*Clicks his heels.*) May I introduce myself: I'm Obersturmbannführer Hermann Krumey, his deputy.

WISLICENY. (*Clicks his heels.*) Obersturmbannführer Dieter Wisliceny. Judenkommando.

STERN. This is Philip von Freudiger, head of our Orthodox Community. (*Freudiger bows.*)

KRUMEY. Aren't you going to offer us something to drink, Baron Stern?

STERN. But of course, Herr Obersturmbannführer. Right away (*Rings bell.*)

KRUMEY. We are very keen on a purposeful and relaxed atmosphere. It's a lot easier to reach understanding in a pleasant atmosphere, don't you agree?

STERN. Yes, I do, Herr . . . (*Enter Servant.*) Wine for my guests. (*Exit Servant.*)

WISLICENY. Nice office you've got here, Baron Stern. Comfortable, still with servants and old-fashioned formalities.

STERN. The war hasn't affected us yet, sir.

KRUMEY. And I hope it won't either. It's all up to you.

FREUDIGER. What exactly do you mean, sir, that it's all up to us? (*Enter Servant, serves wine. Exit.*)

KRUMEY. Naturally, we do not expect cooperation from you. We are not that naïve. (*No reaction.*) We expect only a dialogue. If we can talk to each other, we may reach an understanding. (*Motions to Wisliceny, who hands him a sheet of paper.*) On this list, you'll find the names of about five hundred Jews. Leaders of institutions and organizations here in Budapest. Obersturmbannführer Eichmann would like to meet them, to get to know them. Tomorrow. At four in the afternoon. (*Hands list to Stern, who looks at it.*)

STERN. You want us to invite all these people to the meeting?

KRUMEY. Why not? Opposite each name you'll find the address as well.

STERN. That's a rather difficult task for us to . . .

KRUMEY. We don't want to waste any time. Look, we're still busy setting up our own offices. Yours are well equipped, you've got secretaries, messengers. You can start right away.

FREUDIGER. We can send out the invitations, sir, wire some people and make telephone calls, but I'm not sure that those invited will come.

WISLICENY. If you want my advice, tell them that it's for their own good; that Obersturmbannführer Eichmann would like to talk things over with them.

FREUDIGER. You must understand, sir, people are afraid. We're in an emergency situation, there are curfews. War is raging at our borders, and there are rumors of a strong-hand policy . . .

STERN. Fifteen hundred people were arrested this morning, sir.

WISLICENY. Arrested?

KRUMEY. You mean those arrested at the railway station?

WISLICENY. Oh . . . those . . .

STERN. Yes.

KRUMEY. They've been temporarily interned at Kistarcsa. These are simple, preventive detentions. They'll be released right after having been interrogated, the moment the emergency situation is lifted.

STERN. Those on your list will ask for a guarantee of their safety at the meeting. What can we tell them, Herr Obersturmbannführer?

WISLICENY. What sort of guarantees would you like?

KRUMEY. There's no need for guarantees. We understand your apprehensions. We'll take no steps against those who won't show up.

FREUDIGER. Perhaps we could have this meeting the day after tomorrow, Herr Obersturmbannführer? That would give us time to talk with most of the leaders personally and convince them to come.

KRUMEY. Why waste time? Every passing day only adds to the confusion and anxiety. Between now and four tomorrow, you can talk to all of them. (*Pause.*) Tomorrow at four then?

STERN. We'll do our best, but we can't give you assurance that all of them will come, sir . . .

KRUMEY. You don't have to; we understand. (*Gets up.*)

WISLICENY. The wine was excellent. A bit too sweet, but with body. And the bouquet . . .

KRUMEY. Baron Stern, I'd very much like to pay a visit to your community's museum. I've heard so much about it. Perhaps tomorrow after the meeting with Obersturmbannführer Eichmann, if it's convenient for you . . .

STERN. By all means, sir. I'd be glad to show you around. (*Turns to see the Germans out.*)

KRUMEY. Don't trouble yourself, we'll find our way out. Heil Hitler! (*Stern and Freudiger mumble some kind of reply. Exit the Germans.*)

FREUDIGER. (*Excited.*) We can't invite our people for them! If anything happens to them, God forbid, their blood will be on our hands.

STERN. It's better that the invitations come from us. That way attendance is optional. Anybody who doesn't want to come will have time to draw his own conclusions.

FREUDIGER. People will honor invitations signed by the head of the community. They trust you.

STERN. I'll talk to the Interior Minister. I'll ask him to send a representative to the meeting. I can't believe the Germans would do anything in the presence of a representative of the Hungarian government.

FREUDIGER. This same Wisliceny made a deal with the Chief Rabbi of Slovakia two years ago. Maybe we can work something out with him . . . with gifts . . . money. We have to make a deal with him to reduce this list.

STERN. This is not Slovakia, Philip. And here we won't have deals like that. We have laws, and there is still a government here. So long as the law hasn't collapsed, we won't make any illegal deals. (*Enter Servant.*)

SERVANT. Two people wish to see you, sir. They wouldn't tell me their names. (*Enter Endre and Baky.*)

STERN. (*To Servant.*) It's all right. (*Exit Servant.*)

ENDRE. How are you, Baron?

STERN. I'm well, thank you. (*Points to Freudiger.*) Philip Freudiger, head of the Orthodox Community. (*Freudiger bows; his bow gets no response.*) What can I do for you?

BAKY. What's the rush, sir? We're not in a hurry.

ENDRE. We haven't seen each other for a long time, Baron. Not since that nasty little affair in the Interior Ministry. Right, Baron? (*To Freudiger.*) The Baron here suggested they fire me. The Baron has excellent connections in the Interior Ministry.

STERN. Mr. Endre, that affair was over ten years ago.

ENDRE. Now it is, Baron, now, at last. Your friend the Interior Minister, Ferenc Fischer, was fired.

BAKY. I took him to the railway station myself this morning. Destination Dachau.

FREUDIGER. Dachau?

BAKY. Oh yes, yes. He sends you both his best. He hopes to see you soon. Obersturmbannführer Eichmann personally waved goodbye to him from the platform.

ENDRE. And your other good friend, Prime Minister Kállay, isn't with us anymore either. He's also realized that the affair was over and asked for political asylum in the Turkish Embassy.

BAKY. The Foreign Minister, although he wasn't personally involved in the affair, put a little bullet through his own head. Imagine that. Right in his own office. In front of his staff. The funeral is tomorrow. We'll all be there, shedding crocodile tears. (*Pause.*)

STERN. (*Totally unmoved.*) What can I do for the two of you?

ENDRE. Oh. . . . Thank you so much for your good intentions. For the moment, however, we've come only to present ourselves. (*Points to Baky.*) László Baky, Commander of the Gendarmerie. (*Points to himself.*) László Endre, Secretary of State for Jewish Affairs. These appointments have been in effect as of this morning.

BAKY. (*To Freudiger.*) Nice to have met you.

ENDRE. Please don't let us disturb you any further. You probably have lots of things . . . to think about. Just wanted to take the opportunity to let you know that we are now in charge of all problems concerning Jews. All the problems. From beginning to end. I'm sure you'll be ready to cooperate with us, won't you? Heil Hitler! (*Blackout.*)

Scene 2

Kastner's apartment. Kastner, Komoly, Brand. Komoly is trying desperately to get a line on the telephone.

BRAND. We can't go to this meeting with Eichmann. He knows we're Zionists. He also knows about all our activities. Will he let us smuggle people into Romania? Or hide Polish refugees? And most likely the Gestapo knows about our connections with the Jewish Agency in Istanbul. We go to that meeting and they'll just arrest us.

KASTNER. If they know so much about you, why don't they just come and arrest you? Why should they organize this ceremony?

BRAND. They want to save themselves the trouble of looking for me. They know I won't wait for them at home. We must find a way to hide and continue our activities . . .

KOMOLY. Hide where? Have we prepared hiding places? Food? Bunkers? Hello . . . hello . . . we've had five years to prepare and we've done nothing. Hello . . . hello . . .

KASTNER. This isn't the time to dwell on the past. Otto, please, let's try to understand why they want us at this meeting. Why the meeting at all?

BRAND. I've told you. They want to arrest us.

KASTNER. (*Angry.*) So that's why they gave us a thirty-hour advance notice? That we'd have time to escape?

KOMOLY. What I don't understand is how we've managed to convince ourselves that the Germans wouldn't invade the country. The signs were so clear. Hello . . . hello? . . . Yes, yes . . . Otto speaking. Komoly. 4781 please. (*To Kastner.*) It's Deputy Foreign Minister Meszek.

KASTNER. You'll see he knows less than we do.

KOMOLY. Hello . . . yes . . . Otto Komoly speaking. . . . Yes, it is very urgent indeed. . . . Tell him I'll hold on. Tomorrow? I can't wait until tomorrow. . . . Disconnected again. (*Pause. Knock at the door.*)

VARGA. (*From outside.*) Kastner . . . Kastner . . .

KASTNER. Who is it?

VARGA. Dr. Varga.

KASTNER. (*Opens door.*) Come in. . . . What's the matter?! (*To Komoly.*) Mr. Komoly, what are you planning to do?

KOMOLY. We're discussing it right now. (*To Brand.*) Try this number . . . maybe he's at home . . .

VARGA. Mr. Komoly, discussions will get you nowhere. I've come to tell you that the Revisionist movement is seriously considering going underground. The leadership hasn't made a final decision but . . .

KOMOLY. (*Cutting him off decisively.*) An underground of fourteen people?

VARGA. There are more . . . but I won't tell you how many. (*Pause.*) Mr. Komoly. . . . This is an emergency situation. We're all Zionists. We must pull together and act together. I've heard that Baron Stern has already met with the Germans. We know how they operate. They'll set up a Judenrat, and I'm willing to bet my life that Baron Stern will be made head of the Judenrat. This must not happen. The Zionists must remove him and take over the leadership of the Community underground.

KOMOLY. Varga, the Germans have the name and address of every one of us. If they find out we set up an underground movement, we'll be arrested in five minutes.

VARGA. That's why we must hide. Mr. Komoly, if you decide to go underground and personally lead the movement, many people will join you . . . from the Revisionists, the Hashomer Hatzair, and also some of the Polish refugees who have never questioned your leadership.

KOMOLY. Varga, we are a Zionist Rescue Committee, not a "Zionist Opposition Committee," and our task is to rescue people, not to resist. Maybe there's still a chance to save people. Resistance means suicide. Do you understand? So please stop running around and spreading such wild ideas before having checked them out. (*Exit Varga angrily.*)

BRAND. Varga's gone off his rocker. (*Enter Bogyo.*)

BOGYO. More coffee, anyone?

BRAND. Not for me, thanks. Hansi's waiting for me with breakfast. (*Exeunt Komoly and Brand. Blackout.*)

Scene 3

Stern and Dr. Schneller, in their respective offices, are talking to each other on the telephone.

STERN. Still, Mr. Minister, I implore you, there should be a representative of the government at this meeting. If not a senior representative, at least a junior one.

SCHNELLER. I'd very much like to send one, Baron Stern, but as I've told you, I'm not at all certain I'm still authorized to give such an order. I'm not even sure I'm still the Finance Minister.

STERN. Perhaps you could check with Admiral Horthy, sir. According to the latest rumors, he is still Head of the State. I'm sure he'd agree to send a representative, if only you asked him. I wouldn't want to bother him on a day like this.

SCHNELLER. According to the rumors I've heard, I'm not sure the Admiral is still authorized to give orders. I beg you to wait until the overall picture clears up a bit. For the moment, I'm sorry. . . . I'd like to help . . . if only I could. (*Blackout.*)

Scene 4

Kastner's apartment. Kastner and Bogyo.

BOGYO. Would you like something to eat?

KASTNER. Yes.

BOGYO. You were talking so loud, I've heard everything.

KASTNER. Otto's got me worried. Suddenly, he's wavering. He won't manage alone. I must go with him tomorrow.

BOGYO. Go where?

KASTNER. To that meeting with Eichmann.

BOGYO. How can you even think of such a thing? I'm sure Otto isn't planning to go either.

KASTNER. He has no choice. They called him. You think he can say no?

BOGYO. Let Otto do what he pleases. But why should you be pushed around?

KASTNER. Otto won't manage without me. He's become so cautious he can't make any decisions . . .

BOGYO. You must be cautious, too. First thing in the morning we're going to the Romanian Embassy to see about visas.

KASTNER. And what should I say if somebody asks why the visas?

That we're going on a holiday, right? Come on, I'll make the coffee, you make us something to eat. (*Blackout.*)

Scene 5

Lights on in Stern's office and in Freudiger's apartment. Late at night. Stern and Freudiger are talking on the telephone.

FREUDIGER. Yes, yes, almost all of them got it. I think most of them will show up. Maybe all. . . . Except for Komoly.
STERN. (*Surprised.*) Komoly won't come?
FREUDIGER. Not sure. The Zionists may try to do all sorts of things on their own . . .
STERN. That worries me a lot, Philip. Would you please tell Komoly for me that, if he's planning something irresponsible, we will not support him. We'll do more than that; we'll try to stop him. We shouldn't do anything to provoke them. . . . That's all we need now! (*Blackout.*)

Scene 6

Noon. Brand's apartment. Preparing for the meeting with Eichmann, Brand is packing a small suitcase. His wife, Hansi, is in the kitchen, offstage.

BRAND. Please don't hold me up any longer, Hansi . . . Eichmann is a stickler for time. . . . All I need is to be late for this meeting . . .
HANSI. (*From the kitchen.*) Coming . . .
BRAND. Hansi . . . Hansi . . . enough. . . . I have no appetite, anyway. . . . You think Eichmann will wait until you finish making my sandwiches?
HANSI. (*Enters.*) Here you are. . . . I wrapped a loaf of bread in brown paper . . . there's some smoked meat in this box . . . and two bottles of cognac . . .
BRAND. All right . . . thank you . . . (*Puts provisions into suitcase.*)
HANSI. Your coat . . .
BRAND. No more room. . . . (*Takes out a bunch of keys.*) This is the key to the cash box . . . must be kept somewhere safe . . . this is the one to the mailbox . . . I'm leaving you my telephone book . . . these are the numbers in Istanbul . . . these are the ones in Zurich . . . take special care of this . . .
HANSI. All right. . . . Keep the house keys. . . . Here, put on your coat . . .

BRAND. It's warm outside. I can't wear an overcoat on a day like this. . . . Hansi, if anything should happen, first of all report it to the committee in Istanbul. . . . If Rezsö hadn't asked me, I'd have stayed home.

HANSI. You've said that about five times. . . . Take the coat . . .

BRAND. No room.

HANSI. Take it in your hand . . .

BRAND. Stop it, Hansi. . . . Oh . . . almost forgot. . . . The car keys . . . take them . . . don't forget to keep the tank full at all times . . . that's it . . . I'm going . . .

HANSI. Where are you going? I'm taking you . . .

BRAND. What do you mean you're taking me? I don't want you anywhere near there.

HANSI. Stop wasting time, nothing will happen . . . come on, I'll take you. Give me the coat.

BRAND. Hansi I beg you . . . stay here . . .

HANSI. Don't worry, I'll wait for you outside . . .

BRAND. Don't try to fool me, I know you won't wait outside . . . besides, they can arrest people outside, too.

HANSI. Nobody will notice me . . . (*Taking his coat.*)

BRAND. Leave that coat alone. I won't take it. Rezsö will die laughing if he sees me show up with a coat and a suitcase. And please, stay home.

HANSI. I'm coming with you. I want to see this man Eichmann. Let's have no argument about it.

BRAND. Hansi!

HANSI. Shall we go? (*Telephone rings. Brand picks it up.*)

BRAND. Yes, Otto . . . I see. . . . (*Slams receiver down.*) It was Otto. . . . We're not going to the meeting. The Germans will announce the establishment of a Judenrat today. If we go to the meeting, we'll have to be a part of it . . . (*Blackout.*)

Scene 7

About five hundred leaders of various Jewish organizations are gathered in the assembly hall of the Jewish Community in Budapest. Armed soldiers are stationed at the corners of the stage. Enter Krumey and Wisliceny, take their places on the stage. Short pause. Enter Eichmann.

KRUMEY. Heil Hitler!

EICHMANN. Heil Hitler! (*Looks at his audience for a few seconds then speaks.*) I'm glad to see that most of you have answered my invitation.

There was no need for you to bring suitcases. The moment I finish what I have to say, you will all return, safely, to your homes. I am fully aware of the vicious propaganda conducted against me in the last few years. It's only natural that you, too, should be affected by it, yes? I am ready to challenge anyone who claims that I have ever harmed a single Jew. Is there anyone in this hall with such a claim? Is there anyone here who has ever seen me harm a Jew? Or a non-Jew?

(*Transition to Kastner's apartment. Morning. Kastner, Helen, and Bogyo are sitting around the breakfast table.*)

KASTNER. They were all stunned, Mother. And he went on and on and on . . . and they believed him. If he had continued for another fifteen minutes, he would have been unanimously elected head of the Judenrat. What naïveté! What do you say, Mother, maybe we'll ask him to come with us to the opera tomorrow?

HELEN. You're always trying to be smarter than everybody else, Rezsö. I've heard that some of the arrested people have actually been released. Exactly as he promised. Just as we got through the last war, we'll get through this one, too.

EICHMANN. (*Back to the assembly hall.*) We are at the peak of our mighty efforts on the Eastern Front. The *Wehrmacht* has entered Hungary in order to protect her from the Russians. The entire Hungarian nation is mobilized for the war. We expect Hungarians of the Mosaic faith to do their share, too, in this crucial effort. We need the Jews now more than ever before. And I promise you right here, in the presence of my assistants, that for those who join us in this work, our war production, not a hair on their heads will be harmed. Of course, we have no cure against natural balding.

BOGYO. (*Back to Kastner's apartment. To Kastner.*) I still don't think we'll lose anything by applying for visas to Romania, Rezsö . . . (*Exit to kitchen.*)

KASTNER. It's just the other way around, Mother. Now, after Eichmann's promises, Romanian Jews will ask for visas to come here. (*Enter Bogyo.*)

HELEN. (*To Bogyo.*) If you think it would be better in Romania, you're mistaken. If they've got this far, they'll get to Romania, too. And if not the Germans, then the Russians.

BOGYO. Did I say I loved the Russians? But from Romania we can go to Switzerland . . .

EICHMANN. You have to explain these things to the members of your respective communities and reassure them. Our experience in organizing relationships with Jewish communities is most extensive. We shall soon submit to your authorized institutions several plans at the core of which is the establishment of a Central Jewish Council, the Judenrat, yes? Let me conclude with the words of a great Hungarian Jew who once lived among you, Dr. Theodore Herzl: "Each man will do his duty to his nation, his homeland, and his beliefs." Let us all act according to these words. (*Blackout.*)

Scene 8

Krumey and Stern, on their way out of the Jewish Museum in Budapest.

KRUMEY. A very impressive museum, Baron. But these were not the pictures I've been looking for. I'm almost sure, sir, that most of your friends didn't obey the Führer's orders to destroy their paintings. In their cellars and basements, we can probably find other names as well, like van Gogh, Paul Klee, Gauguin, Cézanne, and that Spanish genius . . . Pablo Picasso . . .

STERN. I wouldn't know, Herr Obersturmbannführer, I've never rummaged through the private basements of my friends.

KRUMEY. You should start then, sir. Sending my own men to do the job could be very unpleasant for your friends. I want a detailed list. Within a week, if possible.

STERN. What list, sir?

KRUMEY. Of paintings, Baron, paintings. . . . One more thing, sir. . . . I'd like two or three, actually four or five pianos. Bechsteins, of course. Please see to it that they're in my office by tomorrow . . . is that clear?

Scene 9

SS offices. Wisliceny is eating; a bottle of beer and a large mug in front of him. Enter Freudiger, followed by an armed Soldier.

SOLDIER. Heil Hitler!

WISLICENY. (*With his mouth full.*) Heil Hitler!

SOLDIER. He was armed, Herr Obersturmbannführer.

WISLICENY. Armed? With what?

SOLDIER. (*Produces a penknife.*) With this, Herr Obersturmbannführer.

FREUDIGER. It's a penknife to clean my fingernails with, sir . . .

WISLICENY. (*Laughs.*) Your fingernails get dirty sometimes, too, eh? (*Motions for Soldier to leave. Returns knife to Freudiger.*)

FREUDIGER. Excuse me, sir, I didn't mean to disturb you in the middle of your meal . . .

WISLICENY. You're not disturbing me at all. (*Pause.*) I hear you . . .

FREUDIGER. I'm here about the arrest of my brother . . .

WISLICENY. Moritz Freudiger . . .

FREUDIGER. Yes. . . . Obersturmbannführer Eichmann has promised . . .

WISLICENY. Yes, I know. . . . He's got a big problem, your brother. I'd be glad to help, but there seems to be clear evidence that he's stashed away foreign currency. Normally, people like that are shot on the spot. If he's lucky, he'll only be sent to a labor camp . . .

FREUDIGER. Exactly, sir. If he gets lucky. . . . About the labor camp. . . . If you'd be willing to hire somebody else to do my brother's work . . . naturally, I'd be ready to cover all the expenses such a replacement might entail. (*Pulls out a wad of bills.*)

WISLICENY. Such a possibility hasn't occurred to me, Herr Freudiger. It's an interesting idea. And just on my birthday, too. It's a pleasure doing business with you.

FREUDIGER. My brother's name is . . .

WISLICENY. Moritz Freudiger. . . . He just got lucky . . . your brother . . . (*Blackout.*)

Scene 10

A street in Budapest. Varga and Kastner.

VARGA. They've already arrested 3,000 Jews . . . Who knows how many of them are still alive. . . . I told you they'd set up a Judenrat, remember? Otto is kaput, Rezsö . . . sits around the house doing nothing but talking on the phone. Talks, talks, talks. Otto must be removed, and you have to take over. I'll take care of our leadership. . . . We'll contact the Hungarian underground, even the Communists. You are the man . . .

KASTNER. The whole Hungarian underground is in Dachau already, Varga. And only you told me about a Communist underground . . .

VARGA. All right, let's leave Otto where he is . . . as a cover. . . . But you should give the orders . . . we'll obey you unconditionally . . .

KASTNER. My first order, Varga, is for you to go home, take a tranquilizer, and stop roaming the streets, stirring up trouble. Your blabbering does nothing but give excuses for the Germans to arrest and kill Jews. Do you understand? (*Exit Varga angrily.*)

Scene 11

Offices of the Jewish Community. Stern, Freudiger. Enter Varga.

VARGA. (*Rushing to Stern, brandishing a newspaper.*) What is the meaning of this notice, sir? What does it mean that "All instructions given by the Germans should be carried out promptly and most conscientiously." If they tell us to get on the train to Auschwitz, we should get on?

STERN. This is the official newspaper of the community. Do you think that in it we can print a notice *not* to obey the Germans?

VARGA. If you hadn't set up the Judenrat, you wouldn't have to publish this paper in the first place, and you wouldn't have to tell people to obey the Germans . . .

STERN. We set up a Central Council, not a Judenrat, Varga . . .

VARGA. A Judenrat . . . Judenrat. . . . I want to call this abomination by its name . . .

STERN. We have set up a Central Council. . . . And we have elected its members, Varga. This is not Poland. I specifically requested that our council not be called Judenrat in order to emphasize its independence . . .

VARGA. Independence? "Only strict adherence to German instructions will ensure the continuation of our existence." Allow me to ask you, sir, is this what you call independence? This is surrender . . .

STERN. What would you have done in my place, Varga? If I had refused to head the council, they would have appointed somebody else. Believe me, Varga, with my poor health and at my age, I would have been glad to retire. But then they would have picked someone with a lot less experience, and certainly with a lot fewer connections in the right places, than I have. This Central Council is the lesser of two evils. We must obey the Germans until the new Hungarian government begins to function. In Poland, there was simply no government. Here we do have one, and it will protect us from the Germans as it would protect all Hungarian citizens . . .

VARGA. The Hungarian government will not protect us. . . . No government in any state has protected a single Jew. . . . We must protect ourselves . . . get hold of weapons . . . go underground . . .

STERN. I'm warning you, Varga. Provocation against the Germans is sheer madness. Stop spreading such ideas . . .

VARGA. (*To Freudiger.*) Sir, you have to talk to your rabbis. . . . They should warn people in the synagogues about the German plans, explain to them about Auschwitz and the gas chambers.

FREUDIGER. How can one explain things like that, Varga? And who would believe it? Is it possible to believe? We know they stopped operating the gas chambers a year and a half ago.

STERN. Rumors, nothing but rumors. . . . There are no confirmations of any of these rumors . . . besides, they have nothing to do with us.

VARGA. The world is going up in flames and you want me to be quiet? Those who don't know, the ignorant, will get on the trains to Auschwitz like sheep. . . . Just as it happened in Poland and Slovakia. No, I'll take to the streets by myself and scream Auschwitz! . . . Auschwitz! . . . I won't let you hide the truth. I hereby declare war on the Judenrat, sir, and on you personally . . . (*Exit. Music. Varga meets a man on the street.*)

The rebels in the Warsaw ghetto held out for a month and a half . . . they were just a few hundred against ten thousand Germans. There are several thousands of us here, and the Germans have no more divisions to send against us . . . (*Man leaves, Varga meets a second man.*)

Silence means accessory to murder, don't you understand? If you don't do something, you are responsible for everything that happens here . . . a terrible Holocaust. . . . We must let them know . . . sound the alarm . . . shout it from every corner . . . otherwise the guild will be ours, too. (*Second man moves on. Varga returns to his apartment, pulls a revolver out of his pocket. Simultaneously, two uniformed and one civilian policemen enter. The civilian points to second man. One of the uniformed police asks second man to come along. The argument is not heard, but second man refuses. Policeman drags him along by force. As they leave the stage, a shot, Varga's suicide, is heard.*)

Scene 12

Offices of the Jewish Community. Wisliceny and Freudiger.

WISLICENY. You do read Hebrew, don't you, Herr Freudiger?

FREUDIGER. Yes, sir . . .

WISLICENY. (*Handing Freudiger a letter.*) Translate this into a civilized language, will you . . .

FREUDIGER. (*Surprised.*) It's addressed to me . . .

WISLICENY. That's why I've brought it to you. You know the Chief Rabbi of Slovakia, right? He's asked me to deliver this to you personally. . . . Go on, read it . . .

FREUDIGER. (*Reads.*) "Obersturmbannführer Wisliceny, who stopped the Jewish transports from Slovakia to Auschwitz, is now working with us on a plan to save all the Jews of Europe . . . for a ransom. . . . It is possible to work with him and save the Jews of Hungary, too . . ."

WISLICENY. What do you say to that, Herr Freudiger?

FREUDIGER. This is something well worth considering, sir. . . . A very serious offer. . . . We are very interested in just such a plan.

WISLICENY. Interest alone is not enough for me, Freudiger. . . . I want cooperation . . .

FREUDIGER. But of course, sir. . . . To cooperate in a rescue mission is our duty . . .

WISLICENY. We want two million dollars.

FREUDIGER. Two million?

WISLICENY. For starters, of course. Get your people to start collecting the money, and I'll be in touch with you. (*With a lighter, he sets letter on fire.*) You realize, of course, that the Hungarians mustn't know about this. They don't understand anything about deals like this . . . (*Blackout.*)

Scene 13

Kastner's apartment. Freudiger, Kastner, and Komoly.

KASTNER. (*Seeing Freudiger to the door.*) I hope we'll be able to give you an answer within a day or two, sir.

FREUDIGER. I'd like an answer by tonight, if possible. (*Addressing both Kastner and Komoly.*) The Judenrat meets tomorrow. If you're going to be part of this deal, you'll have to be at that meeting.

KOMOLY. We'll do our best, sir.

FREUDIGER. I'll hear from you then . . . tonight. (*Exit.*)

KOMOLY. (*Aggressive.*) Why lead him on, Rezsö, we're not getting into this deal.

KASTNER. You can't dismiss a deal like that out of hand.

KOMOLY. We know some Judenrat leaders, and Zionists, too, in Poland, who got similar offers from the Germans, and how they started, gradually, to collaborate. I don't want to find myself in a few weeks on the same railway platform with Eichmann, deciding for him who gets on the train to Auschwitz and who stays alive.

KASTNER. Maybe this same Wisliceny who was ready to save one third of Slovakia's Jews would be willing to do more here? And even if he could save only one third, wouldn't that be worth it?

KOMOLY. If he really means to save anybody, the Judenrat will come to terms with him. Why should we get involved?

KASTNER. Because at the moment we can't do anything else.

KOMOLY. Why not make a deal with the Hungarians who have supported . . .

KASTNER. All the Hungarians who have supported us are already in Dachau or Mauthausen. The new Hungarian government will do nothing to protect us.

KOMOLY. We can smuggle people into Romania . . . give out forged papers, hide people in bunkers. We could . . .

KASTNER. That's absurd, Otto . . . continuing to smuggle three or four people a week to Romania won't amount to much.

KOMOLY. Let's step up the tempo.

KASTNER. If we want to rescue people on a large scale, we have to talk to the Germans. No getting around that. And you shouldn't let Freudiger do the job. You have to talk to them.

KOMOLY. Don't underestimate Freudiger, Rezsö. He's proved himself to be pretty good at deals like that.

KASTNER. At most, Freudiger will save his own family, and maybe a few other, religious ones close to him. He couldn't cope with a serious, major rescue operation. You have to take the initiative.

KOMOLY. I can't talk to the Germans, Rezsö. I'm just not cut out for it. How can I face a German like Wisliceny? His hands are still dripping with the blood of Greek and Yugoslav Jews. He did all the dirty work for Eichmann in Poland, too. I can't talk to a murderer like that.

KASTNER. I've got an idea, Otto. What if we approached the Germans unofficially? I would do it, not you. Just to find out what their true intentions are. If I see that they're serious, then you'll join in.

KOMOLY. And if they're not?

KASTNER. Then we break off contacts with them. But at least we'd have gained some time. And time works for us. This war will be over in a few months.

KOMOLY. Don't be naïve, Rezsö. Making contacts is easy. Breaking them off afterwards is what's really hard.

KASTNER. The committee wouldn't be involved at all. I'd endanger only myself, Otto. You know I can handle such risks.

KOMOLY. And how would you explain later to Freudiger and Stern that we acted behind their backs?

KASTNER. If they see that we only helped to implement their own plan, they'll ask no questions. (*Blackout.*)

Scene 14

An interrogation room of the Hungarian Police. Enter Endre, Baky, and Freudiger.

ENDRE. (*To Freudiger.*) Sit down. (*Freudiger sits down. Bloodcurdling screams are heard from outside where other prisoners are being tortured.*) We could use similar methods with you, too, Freudiger . . . unless you're ready to be a little more cooperative.

FREUDIGER. I'll cooperate in any way you want me to.

ENDRE. Good. In that case, perhaps you can tell us what you were doing in the offices of the SS on the twenty-third of March, at nine in the morning?

FREUDIGER. I went there to ask for the release of my brother, Moritz, who was put in prison in Kistarcsa.

ENDRE. Who did you see?

FREUDIGER. Obersturmbannführer Wisliceny.

BAKY. Why did he hurry so much to release your brother?

FREUDIGER. I explained to him that my brother's arrest seriously affects the work at our textile plant, and the financial loss to the State would be very great . . .

ENDRE. And you really believe that Wisliceny cares about the great financial loss to Hungary caused by the arrest of your brother? Wisliceny cares only about the SS . . . and about himself . . .

FREUDIGER. That's all I told him, sir . . .

ENDRE. Let me suggest to you an alternate scenario. . . . We have already seen the German's penchant for making financial deals with Jews. A week ago, for example, Manfred Weiss transferred his steel plants to the SS, and yesterday his whole family miraculously turned up in Portugal. Hungarian property worth billions has found its way into German hands. . . . That is the great financial loss to Hungary, Freudiger . . .

FREUDIGER. Indeed it is, sir . . .

ENDRE. Perhaps you'd tell me who the Freudiger brothers mean to transfer their textile plant to? . . .

FREUDIGER. God forbid; how can you think of such a thing, sir? . . .

BAKY. Don't try to be wise with us, Freudiger! Wisliceny didn't release your brother for nothing. What did you give him?

FREUDIGER. Nothing, sir . . .

BAKY. Did you promise him anything?

FREUDIGER. I told him that if my brother wouldn't be released, I'd have to resign from the Judenrat and run the textile plant . . .

BAKY. And you want us to believe that Wisliceny worries more about the Judenrat than about his own pocket? . . .

FREUDIGER. That's what he said . . .

ENDRE. And what do you say?

FREUDIGER. It's possible that he wants to maintain a good working relationship with me and the Judenrat.

BAKY. Why would Wisliceny need good working relationships with you, goddamn it? . . . You think we're idiots? He can string you up any time he wants to . . .

FREUDIGER. God forbid! . . .

ENDRE. I want a more logical answer from you, Freudiger. . . . Why would Wisliceny want good working relations with you?

FREUDIGER. As I've said, to improve the relationship between us in general . . .

ENDRE. (*Motions to Baky. Exit Baky.*) You'll have a whole night to think about improving your relationship with the SS. Also I give you somebody to commiserate with. (*Baky returns, dragging a prisoner, tortured and covered with blood, nearly beyond recognition. Baky throws the prisoner at Freudiger's feet.*)

FREUDIGER. (*after a few seconds.*) Moritz . . . Moritz . . . Moritz . . . (*Blackout.*)

Scene 15

In his private room, Eichmann is sitting on a chair; Helmut is shaving him.

EICHMANN. Budapest is the only city in Europe where you can still go to a nightclub. The trouble is, Helmut, we don't have much time to enjoy luxury.

HELMUT. Yes, sir . . .

EICHMANN. You know we're losing the war, don't you, Helmut.

HELMUT. Yes, sir.

EICHMANN. Have you ever thought about the reason why we're losing?

HELMUT. Yes, sir.

EICHMANN. Let's hear your conclusions, Helmut.

GUARD. Heil Hitler! (*Enter Krumey to SS office and waits for Eichmann.*)

HELMUT. It's the Hungarians' fault, and the Italians'. Their armies are too weak, sir.

EICHMANN. You're wrong, Helmut. It's your fault.

HELMUT. Mine, sir?

EICHMANN. That's right, Helmut. Yours and everybody else's who think like you: that it's not our fault.

HELMUT. I don't get your meaning, sir.

EICHMANN. Helmut, Helmut, if you weren't my nephew I'd send you to the Eastern Front so fast. . . . You haven't the slightest sense of humor. (*Enter Guard, tells Helmut about Krumey.*)

HELMUT. Obersturmbannführer Krumey, sir.

EICHMANN. Tell him to wait. (*Wipes his face, enters his office.*)

KRUMEY. I'm sorry to disturb you at this hour, *Obersturmbannführer*, but we've just got a call from a Jew named Kastner.

EICHMANN. Kastner?

KRUMEY. Yes. He's a member of the Zionist Rescue Committee.

EICHMANN. Yes, yes, I remember. He is what's his name's assistant . . . Komoly. . . . Yes, what does he want?

KRUMEY. He wants to know if we'd be ready to negotiate with them about softening the measures taken against the Jews . . . in return for material gains.

EICHMANN. He doesn't know about our offer to Freudiger?

KRUMEY. Yes, he does, but he chooses to ignore it. That's why I thought I'd better tell you, sir.

EICHMANN. You've been with me long enough, Hermann. Think for yourself. He wants to upset our deal with Freudiger, this Kastner. Or, maybe he wants a separate deal for the Zionists?

KRUMEY. I'm not sure, sir. The Zionists are only about 5 percent of the Jewish population, but we could make use of their contacts with the Jewish Agency in Istanbul and with the British.

EICHMANN. That doesn't interest me that much, Hermann. You

haven't answered my question. Are they coming to us now to cover up some brewing disturbance, like the one we had in Warsaw, or because they swallowed our bait and think that we want their money?

KRUMEY. That's what I meant, sir; we should find out what their real intentions are. I've been trying to guess . . .

EICHMANN. No guessing, Hermann. We must know. We have to learn their particular ways of thinking. This is not the first time we're dealing with Zionists. In the Bialystok ghetto, for example, they did a pretty good job for us. In the Vilna ghetto, they helped us organize the transports.

KRUMEY. Apropos of transports, sir, I suggest we act with moderation. Allow me to remind you of Reichsführer Himmler's plan, which we're supposed to be carrying out. I'm sure he will want to keep some Jews in reserve for the negotiations with the British and the Americans. May I also remind you, sir, of the situation at the front . . .

EICHMANN. It's unbelievable, Hermann, isn't it? We throw these Zionists a few extra privileges, maybe a few gifts, and they'll set up ghettos for us, load their fellow Jews on the trains, even throw them into the gas chambers. It's going to be a great success. . . . (*To Helmut.*) Now do you understand, Helmut, why Germany is going to be defeated in this war?

HELMUT. No, sir . . . not exactly. . . . But I'm thinking about it.

EICHMANN. Because some Germans are not dedicated to the Führer's vision, that's why. (*To Krumey.*) Call in Kastner for tomorrow. We must act fast. (*Blackout.*)

Scene 16

Kastner's apartment. Morning. At the table Kastner is preparing several lists. Enter Bogyo.

BOGYO. How do you like that, no rolls this morning. They closed the grocery. It's terrible. Soon there will be no Jewish stores open in the city.

KASTNER. We can eat bread. Lots of people would be grateful for a few crumbs.

BOGYO. You know that non-Jewish stores won't sell us on credit anymore, don't you? . . . Make me something to drink, please. Oh, what a scatterbrain I am, I forgot to tell you . . . a cousin of mine was looking for you yesterday.

KASTNER. (*Preparing something for her to drink.*) What did he want?
BOGYO. He wants to go to Cluj. To hide out there, near the border. Maybe you can help him.
KASTNER. He's old enough to buy himself a train ticket, isn't he?
. . . (*Gets up.*) Where is my lighter, damn it?
BOGYO. Where are you going? Here it is.
KASTNER. I've got a meeting.
BOGYO. But I thought we were going to the Romanian Embassy today . . .
KASTNER. I won't have time for that today. I'm taking a few of your cigarettes . . .
BOGYO. I thought we said today . . .
KASTNER. I've got a very important meeting. We'll go tomorrow.
BOGYO. I don't want to meddle in your affairs, but why is this meeting so important?
KASTNER. I have to meet Otto . . .
BOGYO. Maybe it can be postponed. (*Goes to the telephone.*) I'll ask him . . .
KASTNER. No point asking him. (*Takes receiver from her.*) He doesn't know yet that I'm going to meet him.
BOGYO. Great. In that case, don't meet him and come with me.
KASTNER. No, no. . . . Yenö knows. . . . Yenö was supposed to let him know last night, but couldn't find him, and I don't know if he's managed to get hold of him this morning. That's why Otto doesn't know. Maybe.
BOGYO. Rezsö, are you hiding something from me? I don't like this at all. What's bothering you? And since when do you eat only chocolate for breakfast? You'll ruin yourself this way. . . . Your hands are shaking . . .
KASTNER. Yes, chocolate is a dangerous thing. See how many Jews die because they eat chocolate . . .
BOGYO. I won't let you off the hook; I'm just going to change, and we're going to the Romanian Embassy. After that you'll go to any meeting you want to. (*Exit to an inner room. Kastner walks over to the next scene in the offices of the SS.*)

Scene 17

Offices of the SS. Enter Krumey, Wisliceny, Kastner, and Brand.

KRUMEY. What is it exactly that you want from us, Kastner?
KASTNER. We would like, Herr Obersturmbannführer to extend

the scope of the offer Obersturmbannführer Wisliceny has made to Freudiger, and to work out a plan together . . .

KRUMEY. (*Cutting him off.*) Whom exactly do you represent here, Kastner? Freudiger?

KASTNER. The Jewish Community, Herr Obersturmbannführer . . .

KRUMEY. It seems to me that Freudiger represents the Jewish Community. As far as I can see, Kastner, you represent only the Zionists.

KASTNER. We are working together toward the same goal, Herr Obersturmbannführer, in mutual cooperation . . .

KRUMEY. (*Cutting him off.*) Mutual cooperation is not representation, Kastner. There is no point in talking to you so long as you represent only yourselves, right, Dieter?

WISLICENY. Absolutely. My impression was that Freudiger represented the Jewish Community very convincingly.

KASTNER. Your plan, Herr Obersturmbannführer, can be carried out only by people experienced in organization, and with the appropriate contacts that could . . .

KRUMEY. What kind of contacts do you have, if I may ask?

KASTNER. We have the closest ties with the World Zionist Federation, the JOINT . . .

BRAND. Sir, you probably know about our contacts with the Rescue Committee of the Jewish Agency in Istanbul . . .

WISLICENY. We're talking about ransom, gentlemen. You think your international connections could produce money, too?

KASTNER. Of course, sir . . .

WISLICENY. How much?

KASTNER. The entire sum you've asked for, sir. Two million dollars.

WISLICENY. For starters, don't forget.

KRUMEY. Good. . . . In that case, we'll give you a chance to prove your competence in money matters.

KASTNER. Will one hundred thousand, as an advance, prove our competence?

WISLICENY. Two hundred thousand. Ten percent. As in any business deal.

KASTNER. Very well. Two hundred thousand.

WISLICENY. Within a week. The rest in equal payments on the first of every month.

KRUMEY. In dollars, Kastner. I want to be sure those connections you've mentioned really work. And I want the dollars from Washington, not the black markets of Budapest.

BRAND. That might take two weeks, even three, sir. If you're willing to accept pengös, we can pay you in a week.

KRUMEY. I can wait another week. Dollars, please.

KASTNER. Of course, sir.

KRUMEY. Good. Will you have something to drink? (*Servant offers drinks.*) To the Führer's health! To the Reich! (*They drink.*)

KASTNER. We've brought along a memo, sir. (*Brand takes a document from his briefcase.*) In return for our payments we'd like you to guarantee that Hungary's Jews will not be kept in ghettos or sent to camps like Auschwitz, and to allow the emigration of Jews who possess appropriate visas.

KRUMEY. No need for such a memorandum. As long as the payments reach us on time, we won't ask the Hungarians to set up ghettos or send Jews to camps . . . unless the Hungarians will act on their own initiative . . . in which case we can't stop them, of course.

KASTNER. Nevertheless, sir, I'd like very much to have these promises in writing.

WISLICENY. You'll get nothing in writing until we see the money.

KASTNER. Herr Obersturmbannführer, a commitment in writing would make it a lot easier for me to gain authorization for our future negotiations . . .

KRUMEY. Well, now, Kastner! Here I was, naïvely thinking that your extensive contacts gave you enough authority. Now I see that you need my written word, right? Kastner, I'm interested in people whose authority comes from my written word. Lots of those around. (*Pause.*) When you bring the money, you get the guarantees.

KASTNER. Am I to understand, sir, that until then there would be no turn for the worse in the situation of the Jews?

KRUMEY. That's correct. So long as the matter depends on us. (*He indicates that the conversation is about to end.*)

BRAND. What about the emigration of Jews with valid visas, sir?

KRUMEY. I'll check on that with Berlin. It doesn't seem to me impossible to allow such emigration. To neutral countries only, of course. Is that clear? (*Blackout.*)

Scene 18

The entrance to Kastner's apartment.

KASTNER. Send the report to the Jewish Agency in Istanbul first thing in the morning.
BRAND. We're meeting Stern in the morning, aren't we?
KASTNER. I'll see him alone. It's most important that the report goes out in the morning. (*Exeunt.*)

Scene 19

Krumey, Wisliceny, Baky, and Hungarian Policemen are standing in front of Budapest's central synagogue.

BAKY. (*Trying unsuccessfully to open the door.*) This isn't a synagogue, it's a fortress. What are these locks for, goddamn it?! . . . Locking their synagogue like a jail. (*He loses his patience, motions to a policeman, who breaks the glass in the door.*)
KRUMEY. (*Failing to stop the policeman.*) Just a minute. . . . Pity . . . such beautiful stained glass . . .
BAKY. Plenty more like that in the windows . . . (*They enter the synagogue.*) You can fit at least twenty cars and fifty motorcycles in here. . . . The horses you can put in the rear wing . . .
WISLICENY. I want this opening widened a little . . . the Daimler won't get through the door. (*A Policeman comes out of the synagogue dragging along an old man covered with blood.*)
POLICEMAN. (*To Baky.*) He cursed my mother, sir . . . (*Blackout.*)

Scene 20

Offices of the Jewish Community. Stern, Freudiger, Komoly, and Kastner.

STERN. (*To Komoly, indicating Kastner.*) He shouldn't have negotiated with them about ransom. That's a matter of life and death. We must be extremely careful about that. It's unthinkable that anybody who feels like it just goes ahead and discusses matters of life and death with the Germans. (*To Kastner.*) As far as I'm concerned, any agreement you've made with the Germans, that wasn't in my name, has no validity whatsoever.

KASTNER. But of course I acted in your name, sir. . . . I specifically told them that anything I had agreed upon with them would have to be approved by you.

STERN. But who authorized you to tell them *that?*

KASTNER. It was the Germans who suggested the deal, Baron Stern, and I seized the opportunity to further our common cause. I had no intention of doing anything behind your back. It is a fact, is it not, that we are here right now, discussing the future steps to be taken in the negotiations.

KOMOLY. Baron Stern, let's assume that Kastner has made a mistake. A mistake that I may have had something to do with as well. But ultimately he's achieved a lot. I suggest you reconsider your stand, sir.

STERN. There's nothing to reconsider. Things are very clear. Who are you to act in my name, Kastner? Even if you did achieve something, you've also seriously damaged the authority of the Community's leadership.

FREUDIGER. With your permission, sir, this isn't the time for hairsplitting. . . . Personally, I don't think one can blame Kastner. I couldn't have obtained better terms myself. True, it wasn't exactly proper not to consult with us in advance, but that doesn't negate the agreement Kastner has reached with the Germans. (*Stern does not reply.*)

KOMOLY. I promise you, sir, that we've learned our lesson from this misunderstanding and will act more correctly in the future.

FREUDIGER. Fine. That's fine with me. *Shoyn.* Let's be grateful for what's been accomplished and start collecting the money.

STERN. The money will be ready the day after tomorrow.

KOMOLY. (*Shakes Stern's hand.*) Good-bye. (*Exit.*)

KASTNER. (*To Stern.*) I'll be at your office, sir, the day after tomorrow . . . first thing in the morning . . . (*Exit.*)

STERN. Philip, make sure everything Kastner does is coordinated with you. You'll go with him to the Germans; I want you to be a full partner in every phase of the negotiations.

FREUDIGER. With your permission, sir, it would be better if Kastner went to them alone. He is right, you know, with the Germans one must deal in devious ways. It seems to me that he is better versed in these ways than I am. I don't understand the Germans. Kastner speaks fluent German. When I speak to them in Yiddish, they claim I soil the purity of their language. (*Blackout.*)

Scene 21

Kastner's apartment. Enter Kastner. There is no one at home.

KASTNER. Bogyo? . . . (*No reply.*) Bogyo? . . . (*Worried.*) Bogyo?
(*Goes to phone. Dials. Waits. Puts receiver down. Pause. Door opens. Enter
Helen and Bogyo.*) Where have you been?

BOGYO. You'd better tell us where you've been all day. We've
looked for you all over the place. (*Helen sits down, exhausted.*) I'll bring
you a glass of water, Helen. (*To Kastner.*) Why do I have to get so
nervous about you every day? Where have you been for a whole
day?

KASTNER. I told you I was going to be busy. (*Exit Bogyo.*) What's
wrong, mother?

BOGYO. (*From the kitchen.*) You told me you'd come with me to the
Romanian Embassy . . .

HELEN. She made me go with her to the Embassy. Don't ask what
went on there. There must have been three hundred people there
. . . yelling and screaming, crying, pushing and shoving. . . . Four
hours we waited in line. People were going mad. Somebody wanted
to rob me . . .

KASTNER. What can they still rob from you?

HELEN. My ring. One of the clerks wanted me to sell it to him for
five pengös. I paid six hundred for it thirty years ago. "They'll confiscate it, anyway," he said. (*Points to her necklace.*) He wanted this, too
. . . and the earrings. . . . Given half a chance, he probably would
have wanted my gold teeth. (*Bogyo returns with a drink.*)

BOGYO. We waited five hours before they let us in. And then that
idiot clerk said that nothing could be done for us without you. "A
woman can't leave without her husband." So, if you had been there,
as you promised, we'd have our visas by now . . .

KASTNER. We'll just have to wait with these visas. I couldn't tell
you this morning, but a lot of things are happening. We'll have to
stay. There's been a very important development today. I can't afford to leave now.

BOGYO. And I can't afford to stay. Just looking out the windows
gives me the shivers. Jews are being thrown out of their jobs, stores
are being closed. . . . What are we waiting for?

KASTNER. What are we waiting for? I'll tell you what. If we don't
stay here, a lot worse things than closing stores will happen. Total

liquidation. Like in Poland. I don't think you'd be happy with the knowledge that I could have prevented such a liquidation except that I chose to run away to Romania . . .

BOGYO. (*Very angry.*) What is it that you can prevent? Who are you, anyway, to think that you can prevent anything? You can't even look after your own wife and elderly mother who need your help.

HELEN. Why are you shouting? All you need is for your neighbors to hear you want to run away and then report you. That would be better? (*To Kastner.*) Try to calm her down, will you? (*To Bogyo.*) The last war was a lot worse, and still here we are, alive . . . (*Suddenly, air raid sirens are heard, then planes overhead, and bombs. Bogyo is frightened.*)

KASTNER. (*Soothing Bogyo.*) If these are Russian bombers, that means they're on their way here. . . . Let's get down to the shelter . . . (*Blackout.*)

Scene 22

Offices of the Jewish Community. Stern is at his desk. Enter Endre accompanied by a Policeman.

ENDRE. I guess you toasted the American bombers last night, didn't you, sir?

STERN. I had no reason to celebrate. All the windows in my house were shattered.

ENDRE. I am truly sorry about that, sir, but if you had lived in a Jewish neighborhood, you would have been unharmed.

STERN. What are you insinuating, sir?

ENDRE. I'll bet some enterprising members of your Community marked out all the Jewish neighborhoods for the Americans to miss.

STERN. That's an unfounded accusation, sir. We are all Hungarian citizens and have nothing whatsoever to do with the Americans.

ENDRE. And we happen to have proof to the contrary. Therefore, the government has decided to take over five hundred Jewish apartments in which to house those unfortunates who got hurt in the bombings. As a gesture of goodwill, we'll let you prepare the list of apartments.

STERN. This is strictly against the law, sir. We shall turn to the courts this very day.

ENDRE. I have thirty thousand homeless Hungarians on my hands. The courts will favor us.

STERN. What are you implying, sir? That Jews are not Hungarians? That they need no homes? That they don't get wet in the rain? What law allows confiscation of Jewish apartments, sir?

ENDRE. I know you well enough, sir; you'll look out for the welfare of your Jews. You've always known how to take care of your own. Even at the expense of others. I want the list by two o'clock.

STERN. Sir, I demand a written order from the Interior Minister. Does Admiral Horthy know about this? I'm sure he wouldn't allow it . . .

ENDRE. I don't think we should trouble the Admiral with such trivial matters. The list at two o'clock. Five hundred apartments. Good morning. (*Exit.*)

Scene 23

Kastner's apartment. Morning. Kastner and Bogyo.

KASTNER. I'll be back at six. Hopefully, not later.

BOGYO. Would it be too much to ask you to call me before you go in to see them?

KASTNER. I don't know. There's no public phone at the Gestapo.

BOGYO. Do you ever think about me when you're with them?

KASTNER. No. But you can take comfort in that I don't even think about myself when I'm with them. I can't wear this tie, it's got a stain on it.

BOGYO. (*Angry.*) Maybe you shouldn't go then. Why do *you* have to go all the time? Are you their messenger boy? Let Freudiger go.

KASTNER. (*Even angrier.*) All right. I won't go. (*Sits down.*) What now? Is this what you want me to do? Sit in the house all day? I want to understand; you want me to sit at home all day pretending that nothing's happening out there? (*Knocking at the door. Kastner recognizes Brand's signal, motions to Bogyo, who opens the door.*)

BRAND. Good morning, Bogyo.

BOGYO. Good morning.

BRAND. Good morning Rezsö.

KASTNER. Lovely morning.

BOGYO. Would you like some coffee?

BRAND. Yes, thank you. I have to talk to you, Rezsö . . .

KASTNER. Go ahead, I'm listening. (*Brand hesitates.*)

BOGYO. Don't mind me, Yenö. I don't understand what there is to talk about so much, anyway. (*Exit to kitchen. Pause.*)

BRAND. I was at Otto's last night. I don't think he knows what exactly happened with the Germans. And I gathered from him that Stern and Freudiger don't know either.

KASTNER. Of course they do. I told them about it myself.

BRAND. In a very ambiguous way. Why play a double game with them, too?

KASTNER. Don't you teach me how to conduct negotiations. I had to get the money from them.

BRAND. Rezsö, this isn't poker. You know what this agreement is all about. Krumey said that if the Hungarians decided to set up ghettos, the Germans wouldn't be able to stop them. You didn't tell anybody about that.

KASTNER. I know exactly what Krumey said, you don't have to remind me.

BRAND. But I do, because I'm worried. I think that Wisliceny and Krumey are making a private deal with us. Maybe the money goes right into their own pockets? That's why they can't stop the Hungarians.

KASTNER. A very interesting thought, Yenö. Too bad you don't take it a tiny step further.

BRAND. Well, look, tonight they've confiscated five hundred apartments from us and Krumey did nothing to stop them. I suppose the Yellow Star was originally a Hungarian idea, too!

KASTNER. If Eichmann is present at this meeting, then the deal won't be such a private deal with Krumey . . .

BRAND. Eichmann?

KASTNER. Yes, Eichmann. If he . . .

BRAND. Have you gone out of your mind, Rezsö? We shouldn't go anywhere near Eichmann. He's not a man we can talk to. He can shoot you just for coughing . . .

KASTNER. We have to go to him and try not to cough.

BRAND. Be reasonable, Rezsö. I do admire your courage, really, but this isn't courage. It's plain idiocy. And, with all due respect, I don't believe you can get to him.

KASTNER. If you won't hold me up here too long, I'll get to him. It is Eichmann who decides the fate of Hungary's Jews. If he is a party to the agreement, we can ask him to make the Hungarians honor it.

BRAND. All right, let's assume you get to see him. What will you tell him about the ninety thousand dollars we are short? With Krumey, we could possibly work something out. Eichmann is not Krumey. . . . When he finds out that nearly half the sum is lacking, he'll blow up the whole deal.

KASTNER. About the money, I've got at least seventeen different answers for Eichmann. But first, we have to make sure he comes to the meeting. And you, instead of wasting your energies on blaming me, would do better to come back here at two o'clock and help me pick out the best answer.

BRAND. What if Eichmann doesn't like any of your answers? I won't take that responsibility on myself alone. Let's go talk to Otto. We'll postpone the meeting with the Germans. We'll also consult Stern and Freudiger. They have every right to know what we're doing with their money.

KASTNER. You can consult anyone you like. I won't. And I won't postpone the meeting, either. I'm going to meet Eichmann. With you, or without you. (*Exit Brand.*)

BOGYO. (*Enters.*) What's going on? What was that shouting about?

KASTNER. Good-bye . . . (*Exit. We see Brand getting drunk in his apartment.*)

Scene 24

Krumey and Stern in the offices of the Jewish Community.

KRUMEY. (*Hands Stern a list.*) I want all these people to report to the Central Railway Station tomorrow morning at ten o'clock sharp. It would be best if their families did not accompany them. The station will be crowded enough without them. And another thing, Baron . . . this time we'll have no excuses or evasions. Eight hundred people. At Krupp Industries they need every one of them. We'll personally take care of anyone who doesn't show up. Is that clear?

STERN. Yes, sir.

KRUMEY. Heil Hitler! (*Stern hesitantly raises his hand, does not repeat the words. Exit Krumey.*)

STERN. (*To audience.*) I didn't make up the list, I was only the mailman. They could have delivered the orders themselves. And if not them, then the Hungarian Police, who would have been glad to call up even more. Not eight hundred, maybe a thousand . . . or thousands . . . not to mention those whom they would have "injured by accident" while delivering the orders. I had no illusions about Krupp Industries: what would lawyers, accountants, doctors, journalists, actors, and opera singers do in a Krupp plant? Did Krupp have the time to turn them into steel workers? The war was about to end. . . . What was I to do? Refuse to deliver the orders and throw these people, and many others, at the mercy of the Germans? Or, turn in those on this list and thereby delay, even if for a little while, the calling up of others? Common sense could supply no answers to these questions. . . . A moral sense? In the name of what morality could anyone call on "moral sense" in those days?

Scene 25

A café in Budapest. Kastner and Wisliceny are playing cards and drinking beer.

WISLICENY. That would mean a great effort on my part.

WAITER. (*Enters.*) Would you like anything else?

WISLICENY. Bring me a cream puff, an apple strudel, and ice cream . . .

WAITER. And for you, sir?

KASTNER. Nothing, thank you. . . . (*Exit Waiter.*) Five hundred dollars.

WISLICENY. Obersturmbannführer Eichmann is not an easy man . . . very hard to convince. Besides, he's very busy.

KASTNER. Eight hundred. . . . The meeting will take place, anyway. All I ask is that Obersturmbannführer Eichmann be present.

WISLICENY. You have no idea how difficult it would be to ask him to come.

KASTNER. A thousand dollars . . .

WISLICENY. And what am I supposed to say to Obersturmbannführer Krumey? He'd be insulted. He'd think that he wasn't good enough for you.

KASTNER. Obersturmbannführer Krumey knows very well that, without Obersturmbannführer Eichmann, the deal can't go forward.

WISLICENY. I just can't, Kastner. There are things you don't understand. Not everybody in the SS is as good to you as I am.

KASTNER. That's why we've come to you, sir. Because of your special relationship to us. You, sir, are clear minded, understanding

. . . twelve hundred now, and another five hundred after the meeting.

WISLICENY. It's a pleasure doing business with you, Kastner. Eichmann will be at the meeting. (*Enter Waiter with refreshments. Hands Wisliceny a small plate with the bill on it.*)

WAITER. The bill, sir. (*Wisliceny pushes the plate toward Kastner.*)

WISLICENY. Thanks for the treat, Kastner. (*Fade to blackout.*)

Scene 26

Brand in his apartment, alone, drunk. Enter Hansi.

BRAND. Where have you been?

HANSI. At Rezsö's. What are you still doing here?

BRAND. Waiting for you.

HANSI. For me? You should be at Rezsö's, with the money.

BRAND. I won't go to Rezsö until I talk to Otto. And I want you to come with me.

HANSI. There's no time for talking, Yenö. You've got to meet the Germans in an hour and a half. Look at yourself. You've got stains all over your shirt.

BRAND. I understand he couldn't get Eichmann to come.

HANSI. You're wrong. He bribed Wisliceny, and Wisliceny will take care of Eichmann.

BRAND. I don't believe it. This man is simply . . . And you . . . you don't care that I'm going to Eichmann with only half the money . . .

HANSI. Rezsö has a few ideas. And he wants to talk to you about them. Have some coffee before you go. You stink of cognac. (*Exit to kitchen.*)

BRAND. (*Calls after her.*) He's always got ideas, Rezsö does. If he thinks Eichmann will be as excited about those ideas as you are, then he is sadly mistaken. When Eichmann finds out we don't have all the money, he'll put a bullet in our heads before listening to a single idea of Rezsö's. Rezsö and his ideas. He's also told Otto that the Germans were willing to issue emigration permits. That's a lie. They're willing only to talk about it. But *that* is Rezsö's idea.

HANSI. (*Has in the meantime returned with a cup of coffee.*) Stop wasting time, Yenö. Maybe Rezsö was wrong, and the two of you should have consulted Otto. But these minor points can be settled after the meeting with the Germans. Drink this . . .

BRAND. Minor points? Let the Hungarians set up ghettos and Krumey tell us that he knew nothing about it, is that what you call minor points?

HANSI. All right. You're right, Yenö. But don't you see that's exactly the reason why Rezsö wants Eichmann to be at this meeting?

BRAND. What's the matter with all of you? Since when can one believe that Eichmann will keep his promises?

HANSI. That's why you should go to the meeting and get a written guarantee.

BRAND. I'm not going. I'm not Rezsö's servant. He wants me around when he needs me. When he doesn't need me, he throws me out of his house. He sent me to take care of the mail during the meeting with Stern so he could tell him anything he wanted to.

HANSI. You're working together. Somebody had to take care of the mail, too . . .

BRAND. For half an hour I've been trying to explain to you that it's impossible to work with him. Once he makes up his mind, nobody can stop him.

HANSI. Good! At last we've got somebody who can't be stopped. Somebody who can go to the Germans and talk to them without shaking in his boots. And instead of helping him, you get insulted, polish off a bottle of cognac, and sit around moaning and groaning.

BRAND. And you're shaking in your boots when you talk to him. He's blinded you completely. If he can do anything, as you say he can, then what does he need me for? He told me he'd go to the Germans with me or without me. So let him go without me.

HANSI. He can't go without you. He knows that and you know that. I'm sure he's very sorry about that outburst of his. Go to him, he needs you.

BRAND. When he needs me he sends you to make his apologies . . .

HANSI. You know Rezsö. He can get so carried away by his great ideas, and then overlook the one small detail that could bring him down. Come on, get up, he's waiting for you. You have to decide what to tell the Germans about the money. Here's the suitcase. I've ironed the bills we bought on the blackmarket. They look as good as new. I hope they won't suspect anything. And throw some water on your face before you go. (*Hands him the suitcase. Blackout.*)

Scene 27

Eichmann, Krumey, Wisliceny, Kastner, and Brand in the offices of the SS.

EICHMANN. I see you've brought the advance . . .
KASTNER. Yes, Herr Obersturmbannführer.
EICHMANN. Good. . . . Good . . . there's still money left in your safes, eh? Behind paintings, in flower pots, in the sewage pipes. . . . Those bills should be aired out so they wouldn't stink . . . open it.
BRAND. This money got here only yesterday, from Istanbul, sir . . .
WISLICENY. Brand new bills, straight from the Government Printing Office in Washington.
BRAND. They're arranged in packets of one thousand dollars each, Herr Obersturmbannführer. There are fifty packets in this suitcase.
EICHMANN. We can dispense with the actual counting, eh? If I were in your place, I'd make no mistake either. Obersturmbannführer Krumey, these people have made extraordinary efforts to obtain this money. Should we reciprocate, eh? What do you say?
KRUMEY. By all means, sir . . .
EICHMANN. First of all, we'll relieve you of these. (*Tears off yellow stars.*) I get goose bumps when I see yellow stars around me. And, Herr Obersturmbannführer Krumey, I'd also suggest we help Dr. Kastner and Mr. Brand carry out their tasks as efficiently as possible. . . . So what do you say we let them keep their telephones, yes? And their cars? That would help you a lot, Dr. Kastner, would it not?
KASTNER. Oh, yes . . . greatly, Herr Obersturmbannführer.
EICHMANN. (*To Krumey.*) Issue the appropriate permits.
KASTNER. Herr Obersturmbannführer, there are a few more people . . . very helpful to us in these contacts with you. It's hard for them, too, with these stars . . .
EICHMANN. Submit a list, Kastner. We'll consider each case on its own merits. (*He glances at the suitcase, does a quick calculation in his head.*) Fifty thousand in the suitcase . . . (*Turns to Brand suspiciously.*) How much money have you brought, Herr Brand?
BRAND. One hundred and ten thousand, sir.
EICHMANN. You promised two hundred thousand, no?
BRAND. Yes, sir.
EICHMANN. The way I figure it, we're missing ninety thousand dollars. Isn't that right, Hermann?

KASTNER. (*Interferes.*) Of course, we've wanted to give you the additional ninety thousand, Herr Obersturmbannführer, but the leaders of the Jewish Agency have refused. They hadn't received from us, after we talked to these gentlemen, (*indicating Krumey and Wisliceny*) a definite guarantee that no ghettos would be set up, and no transports be sent . . .

EICHMANN. But you did receive the word of a German officer, didn't you? The word of an Obersturmbannführer is a word, Kastner; we're not Jews!

KASTNER. I don't doubt that, Herr Obersturmbannführer; but contrary to the promises given us, rumors that have reached us from several cities . . .

EICHMANN. (*Cutting him off.*) Dr. Kastner! It's you who hasn't kept his promises, not him. (*Points to Krumey.*) This fact notwithstanding, Kastner, I'll continue to be fair with you. I won't cancel our deal. And to prove to you my good intentions, I'm giving you a week's extension to come up with the rest of the money. What do you think, Hermann? Can we really afford to be that fair?

KRUMEY. Yes. I think so, Herr Obersturmbannführer.

BRAND. With your permission, sir, the leaders of the Jewish Agency in Istanbul are very worried. They know about the yellow stars and have heard rumors that Jewish houses will be marked yellow, too . . .

EICHMANN. I suggest you don't let rumors guide your actions, Brand. I have just made a rather generous gesture to you, and if our negotiations continue the way we want them to continue, it won't be the last one.

KASTNER. (*Insistent.*) Herr Obersturmbannführer, I repeat, our people want no gestures, but guarantees that Jews will not be herded into ghettos . . .

EICHMANN. (*Cutting him off, screaming.*) Kastner!! (*Pause, Eichmann calms down.*) Kastner . . . you're walking on very thin ice. Don't take advantage of my good heart. I'm offering you two choices: either you take the money and leave right now, or you come back here with the rest within a week. Is that understood?

KASTNER. There's another possibility . . .

EICHMANN. I've given you only two!

KASTNER. (*Relenting.*) Will I get your guarantee in a week?

EICHMANN. Our word is a word, Kastner. (*Blackout.*)

Scene 28

General Headquarters of the Hungarian Police in Budapest. Gathered in the hall are several hundred officers. Enter Endre and Eichmann.

ENDRE. Heil Hitler! (*The audience replies.*) Gentlemen, Officers of the General Staff. Tonight we mark the beginning of the largest, most comprehensive operation in the history of the Hungarian Police. In only three weeks we shall separate 700,000 Jews from the Hungarian population. In only three weeks we will confiscate all their properties amounting to billions of pengös. I promise you that in three weeks, when I'll be standing here before you once more, we'll be able to say proudly, "Never have so few Hungarians got rid of so many Jews in so short a time." And now allow me, on this festive occasion, to present to you the man who has initiated this operation and has cooperated with us in every stage of its planning. Obersturmbannführer Adolf Eichmann. (*Tumultuous cheers. Transition to Scene 29.*)

Scene 29

The last segment of Scene 28 is shown in the background. The dialogue is not heard. (Kastner's apartment. Kastner is typing up a report. Bogyo is backstage. The door is forced open. Enter a Sergeant and two Hungarian Policemen.)

SERGEANT. Hands up!
KASTNER. What's going on?
SERGEANT. Shut up! (*The Policemen move about the house. One discovers Bogyo asleep. Rudely, he drags her into the room.*)
FIRST POLICEMAN. Stand on your own legs, filth bag!
KASTNER. What do you want from her? She's ill.
SERGEANT. (*Hits Kastner with the butt of his pistol.*) I told you to shut your trap, didn't I? (*Bogyo is stunned.*)
FIRST POLICEMAN. You get your hands up, too! (*Bogyo raises her hands. Policeman shoves her toward Kastner.*)
BOGYO. Rezsö . . .
SERGEANT. (*Hits her.*) Shut up! (*Policemen finish their search.*)
SECOND POLICEMAN. Nobody else. Just them two.
SERGEANT. Check out everything. The floors. They probably hide them under the floor, the pigs.

KASTNER. There must be a mistake, sir. You've got the wrong apartment.

SERGEANT. Will you shut up!

KASTNER. Excuse me, sir, we're not hiding anybody. I'm Dr. Kastner . . . (*Back to Scene 28.*)

EICHMANN. (*Shakes Endre's hand and turns to his audience.*) The Führer has personally asked me to convey to you the great admiration he has for you. With your devotion and dedication, you are paving the way toward Hungary's liberation from the Jews. Until now, we have removed them from 180,000 key positions, well-paying jobs, here, in Hungary. Just imagine what would have happened had we delayed. I'm sure that during your upcoming operation you will discover for yourselves that it's the Jews and the Bolsheviks who are responsible for this terrible war. The Red Army wanted to enter your land and be welcomed with open arms by these Jews and Bolsheviks. Luckily, we uncovered the plot in time and took appropriate countermeasures to foil it. Gentlemen, Officers of the Police. The success of this operation depends on you; on your carrying it out to the last detail. Well, I admit, I've kept one little detail a secret—only to reveal it to you now, at this great moment. If you keep to the timetable we've set for you, if you succeed, you too will have your share in the confiscated Jewish property. Each and every one of you will get at least 75,000 pengös. (*Blackout. Back to Scene 29. Kastner's apartment.*)

FIRST POLICEMAN. (*Enters, carrying a suitcase.*) A packed suitcase. They wanted to run away, or they got guests.

SERGEANT. You've been hiding guests from Kistarcsa!

BOGYO. No, no . . . the suitcase is ours, sir.

SERGEANT. Why is it packed?

BOGYO. We were going to visit my parents.

SERGEANT. (*Hits her.*) You were going to run away! (*Opens suitcase, spilling its contents to the floor.*)

KASTNER. It's all a mistake. I'm Dr. Kastner . . .

SERGEANT. (*kicks him.*) Up against the wall! (*Enter Second Policeman.*)

SECOND POLICEMAN. Nothing.

SERGEANT. They got away. . . . Bastards! (*Exeunt Sergeant and Policemen.*)

KASTNER. (*Bending over Bogyo.*) Oh my God, what these animals have done to you! (*Bogyo recovers quickly.*)

BOGYO. We're getting out of here right now. I'm not staying in this house another night. I told you that one day this would happen to us, too. What would I have done if I'd been here all by myself? I don't want this to happen again. You can't make me stay here.

KASTNER. I'm sure they didn't mean us. Just some dumb Hungarian policemen who came to the wrong address, Bogyo . . . (*He is wiping her face.*)

BOGYO. Don't touch me. And start packing. We're getting out of here right now, and don't think I'm going to pack your suitcase for you, either.

KASTNER. I can't go anywhere now. I've got a meeting at Stern's and this report has to be typed up. I'm late as it is.

BOGYO. Even if they had killed me just now, you'd still go on typing that report, wouldn't you? If you don't come with me right this minute, I'm going without you. (*Blackout in the apartment. We see Bogyo running across the stage with two suitcases. Kastner moves directly over to the offices of the Jewish Community.*)

Scene 30

Offices of the Jewish Community. Freudiger, Stern, and Kastner are waiting for Komoly and Brand.

KASTNER. Eichmann has explicitly told me that they would reconsider the question of the yellow stars for the whole community. In the meantime, I suggest we prepare a list of those who should get immediate exemption. My feeling is that the good atmosphere at the talks may bring additional practical results. (*Enter Komoly and Brand, supporting Miklós Benedek, who seems to be in very poor physical condition.*)

KOMOLY. (*His manner suggests the horror of his message.*) The transports have started. One left Kistarcsa last night for Auschwitz . . . (*Pointing to Benedek.*) This is Miklós Benedek. He managed to jump off the train near the German border.

STERN. This is Benedek? Editor of *The Nation?* (*Benedek comes to.*)

KASTNER. Can you tell us exactly what happened?

BENEDEK. They tricked us. Last night, they led us out of the barracks and told us we'd be going to a labor camp. Most people were ready to get on the train. We'd had a very hard month at Kistarcsa. Nobody thought anything could be worse. . . . Some people, who didn't believe we'd be going to a labor camp, refused to get on the train. They laid down on the ground. The police just shot ten or twenty of them; then everybody got on the train. We were shocked. There was a woman in labor pains. She couldn't stand up. She began giving birth on the platform. The police stood around her, laughing. I asked a Hungarian officer what this woman could do in a labor camp? He said that at her husband's side she could boost his morale. . . . And I believed him. . . . When she gave birth, they kicked her, trying to make her get up. She couldn't move . . . she was having twins. After she gave birth to the second baby, they grabbed her by her hands and feet and threw her into the freight car . . . then they threw her babies after her. I don't know how we could have believed them. . . . Nobody even wanted to talk about other possibilities. . . . They were afraid to say the word *Auschwitz* . . .

KASTNER. How do you know that this train was going to Auschwitz?

BENEDEK. After about five hours, the train stopped. I heard two Germans talking just outside our wagon. It was clear from their conversation that we were going to Auschwitz, to a "salami factory." (*The door bursts open, enter Baky with two Hungarian Policemen.*)

BAKY. (*Approaches Benedek and shoots him at close range.*) I should shoot all of you. Hiding escaped prisoners! You too, Baron Stern? I thought you were a Hungarian patriot . . . (*Blackout.*)

ACT II

Scene 31

Thunderstorm. Lightning. The home of Dr. Schneller, finance minister of Hungary. Stern is knocking at the door.

SCHNELLER. (*Opens door.*) Baron! To be out on such a night!

STERN. I'm terribly sorry to bother you at such a late hour, sir, but I've had no choice. I've been trying to reach you by telephone every day for a whole week, but your clerks have refused to put us in touch. (*Transition to Scene 32.*)

Scene 32

Kastner's apartment. Thunder, lightning, rain, Kastner, Komoly, and Brand, all exhausted, are waiting for Hansi. Knocking at the door; Brand rushes to open it. Enter Hansi.

BRAND. Hansi . . . (*Helps her off with her shoes.*) Your shoes are full of water. (*Kastner is bringing her a drink.*)

KASTNER. Here . . . drink this.

BRAND. We didn't know what to think. What happened?

HANSI. We didn't make it. All the messengers have come back from the ghettos . . . with the money, with the forged papers . . . everything. Nobody wants even to hear about Auschwitz. People are suffering from hunger . . . disease. . . . They're overcrowded . . . they're too weak to listen. . . . They say we're spreading rumors. . . . We? The Hungarians are spreading rumors. . . . The rumor circulating in all the ghettos is that the Hungarians are transferring people to agricultural work in the South. That's more convenient for them to believe. In every ghetto, people are lining up to register . . . they all want to be the first on those trains. . . . They can't think of Auschwitz at all, and they don't want to escape either. Children and the elderly are afraid they wouldn't make it in the cold; and the younger ones, who could make it to the border, don't want to leave their families. . . . There's nobody to talk to . . . nobody. . . . We didn't think about this. . . . You were right, Rezsö . . . we have to get back to negotiating with the Germans. (*Return to Scene 31.*)

SCHNELLER. What can I do for you?

STERN. That train out of Kistarcsa, sir. We know it got to Auschwitz.

SCHNELLER. Auschwitz?

STERN. Yes. Somebody who had jumped off that train managed to reach us eight days ago.

SCHNELLER. Miklós Benedek. Yes. I did get a report on him. . . . He escaped from a labor camp in Southern Germany. This story about Auschwitz is just his excuse for running away.

STERN. Benedek used to be the editor of *The Nation*. If he hadn't been telling the truth, the police wouldn't have shot him right in front of our eyes.

SCHNELLER. Benedek was fired from *The Nation* for disseminating hostile propaganda. And you should have turned him over to the police the moment he got to you . . .

STERN. The man escaped from Auschwitz. How could we have turned him in?

SCHNELLER. I'm not talking about just this one man. We hear daily rumors about the ever increasing web of contacts between the Jewish Community and the SS, contacts that you yourself know about and support with money. The government cannot help people who break the law.

STERN. (*Furious.*) Is that so? We are breaking the law? And all those operations in the provinces, according to what law are they being carried out? And what law calls for the confiscation of Jewish property? According to which law have all the Jews of Budapest been fired from their jobs? Which law requires the closing of Jewish businesses? According to what law are we to wear the yellow stars? Mr. Minister, Jews are being shot on sight in the streets, without trials. According to what law? And the transports to Auschwitz? According to what law are they being sent? What law? And you dare accuse *us* of breaking the law?

SCHNELLER. My dear sir. *We* didn't ask the Germans to invade Hungary. *We* are not sending the transports to Auschwitz. We are an occupied country. The Germans have sent more Hungarians than Jews to their camps. It's they who set up the new government, and I only take care of this government's money. (*Blackout.*)

Scene 33

SS offices. Enter Krumey, Wisliceny, Kastner, and Brand.

KRUMEY. You can put the suitcases on the table. (*Brand and Kastner are hesitating.*)

WISLICENY. What's the matter?

KASTNER. Our agreement is still not being carried out properly.

KRUMEY. What do you mean?

KASTNER. I mean that despite all your guarantees, and despite all your promises that those guarantees have some force, despite everything, transports are being sent to Auschwitz.

KRUMEY. Auschwitz?

KASTNER. Yes, Auschwitz.

KRUMEY. Dear Dr. Kastner, not a single Jew is being sent to Auschwitz. I've told you this several times before. We have absolutely no interest in sending valuable Jewish manpower to Auschwitz when we need it for our war effort elsewhere.

KASTNER. Two weeks ago, fifteen hundred Jews were taken from the prison in Kistarcsa and sent to Auschwitz. Who knows how many others have been sent from there to other places.

WISLICENY. Is that what that Benedek has told you, the one who jumped off the train?

KRUMEY. But you've got letters from them, don't you?

KASTNER. Letters?

KRUMEY. (*To Wisliceny.*) You didn't give them the letters?

WISLICENY. I only got them yesterday. (*Takes out a bunch of post-cards from a desk drawer.*)

BRAND. (*Reading.*) "We are working and happy here. There is enough to eat." Where were these sent from?

KRUMEY. It says there. "Waldsee."

BRAND. Waldsee?

KRUMEY. Yes. It's in Southern Germany.

BRAND. I've never heard of it.

KASTNER. I'd very much like to visit these people and see what they're doing there.

KRUMEY. There are factories there, and the people are working. Exactly as they've written to you.

BRAND. I grew up in Germany. I don't recall a place like that.

WISLICENY. You can look it up on the map. (*He is looking at a map.*)

KRUMEY. Dr. Kastner, this suspicion is really unnecessary. I can understand your fears. I'm not trying to deny that we, including myself, have not treated the Jews with kid gloves during the last few years. But the situation has changed. There are quite a few people among the SS who no longer support the harsh treatment of Jews. Reichsführer Himmler is behind this new attitude which Dieter and I are representing here.

KASTNER. I'm delighted to hear that the Reichsführer has changed his attitude, but how does it square with the fact that almost all Hungarian Jews are now kept in forty-three ghettos, in shameful and inhuman conditions? That's not exactly a new attitude.

KRUMEY. The ghettos have been set up by the Hungarians, Kastner, not by us. They claim that you people are a security risk and must be isolated so you won't aid the Russians the way you did in 1918.

BRAND. According to the information we have, the SS has taken part in every action of the Hungarians. SS men have supervised and instructed the Hungarians every step of the way.

KRUMEY. Hungary is an ally of the Reich against the Russians, Brand. Our presence has been representational only. We've had explicit orders only to be present at these actions.

KASTNER. The explanations we've been getting, sir, may be correct, or, just as easily, incorrect. In Poland, too, Jews were told that they'd be sent to labor camps. If the Reichsführer is indeed behind this new attitude we're hearing so much about, then I'm sure he could easily arrange to have those detainees returned from Waldsee to Hungary . . .

KRUMEY. Hungary is helping German industry with manpower, Kastner. It's a political agreement.

KASTNER. Which means, sir, if I've understood you correctly, that the deportations will continue?

KRUMEY. The supply of manpower, according to industry needs, will continue. Even the Reischsführer can't stop that.

KASTNER. In that case, there's no point in having these meetings. (*Rises, picks up suitcase.*) Not until the deportations are cancelled, and the detainees from Kistarcsa are returned to Hungary.

WISLICENY. Kastner . . . Kastner . . . what are you doing? (*To Krumey.*) He forgets who he's talking to.

KRUMEY. Kastner, don't make us change the cordial atmosphere of these negotiations. Under the circumstances, impulsive action can be dangerous. Be reasonable. All of you.

BRAND. What kind of reason would help the lamb in the slaughterhouse?

WISLICENY. I don't understand what's going on here.

KASTNER. I thank you for your cooperation.

KRUMEY. I suggest you hear me out to the end . . . if you really want proof of our new attitude. If you'd let me finish what I was saying earlier, you'd have it by now. Obviously, the Reichsführer can't send the Jews from Waldsee back to Hungary, but he's willing to grant one of your earlier requests: to allow emigration from Hungary for a limited number of Jews.

KASTNER. The Reichsführer is ready to do that?

KRUMEY. Yes . . .

KASTNER. When?

KRUMEY. Immediately. The minute you find a country willing to accept them.

BRAND. We have entry visas to Palestine.

KRUMEY. Very good. How many?

BRAND. Six hundred.

KRUMEY. Prepare a list of six hundred, and they'll go.

BRAND. We'll give you a list of six hundred families, sir, within a week.

KRUMEY. Six hundred individuals.

BRAND. Every visa is good for a whole family.

KRUMEY. Six hundred persons, I've said. And this whole matter is a state secret. The Hungarians must not get wind of it. Is that clear, Kastner?

KASTNER. Yes, sir.

WISLICENY. The suitcases. (*They put suitcases on the table. Exeunt Krumey, Kastner, and Brand. Lights on Eichmann, speaking with Wisliceny on the telephone.*)

Scene 34

SS Offices. Eichmann and Wisliceny are talking on the telephone.

EICHMANN. You two are getting no commission. I need this money for other purposes.

WISLICENY. What sort of purposes, may I ask?

EICHMANN. Somebody has to pay the Hungarian Railways for transporting the Jews to Auschwitz. The financial situation of the Reich doesn't allow a budget for this purpose. Every train costs me 42,000 pengös. You'll have to get more money out of them.

WISLICENY. But, sir, aren't we overdoing this just a little? We don't know how the war will end. We may need the money for ourselves. Maybe we should transfer part of it to South America. Our families . . .

EICHMANN. Loyalty, Dieter, is measured precisely at moments like these. Don't be a worm. You could learn a lot from this Kastner. All those large sums passing through his hands and nothing sticks to him. Pity he's a Jew. He could be one of us. And if you so much as mention commission to me again, you'll find yourself in Auschwitz. They need officers there. (*Blackout.*)

Scene 35

Helen Kastner's apartment. Helen, Bogyo.

HELEN. Go to the store on the corner, if you have to. I wouldn't leave our street though, not even for cigarettes.

BOGYO. You really think it's more dangerous on the street than in here?

HELEN. Our street is not so dangerous. The Germans won't bother with it. But to go out on the avenue, just to buy cigarettes? Why look for trouble? (*The door opens. Enter Kastner. Helen starts.*) Rezsö! . . . I didn't know you had a key to my apartment.

KASTNER. Well, I do. Hello.

HELEN. Still, you could have knocked. You gave me such a fright.

KASTNER. I did knock. Nobody answered. (*Turns to Bogyo.*) How are you, Bogyo? (*Bogyo does not reply.*) How are you?

HELEN. She's better.

KASTNER. Could I talk to her alone for a few minutes?

HELEN. Don't be impertinent, Rezsö. First you come in here without knocking, and now you're chasing me out.

KASTNER. Mother, please. Just for a few minutes, that's all . . . please, Mother.

HELEN. That's better. I'll make you both some tea. The kettle's hot. And don't you two fight in my house.

KASTNER. Two sugars, Mother.

HELEN. Stop pampering yourself. You'll get one. (*Exit.*)

KASTNER. Feeling better?

BOGYO. I didn't realize you were so interested in my feelings.

KASTNER. I've come to take you home.

BOGYO. Thank you, but I'm just fine right here. (*Takes a cigarette out of her pack, lights it.*) At least here I could stop talking to myself.

KASTNER. No reason why you should stay here. I've checked with the police. They had the wrong address, just as I told you. The whole thing was a mistake.

BOGYO. A mistake?

KASTNER. Yes. And it won't happen again. Obersturmbannführer Krumey spoke to the Chief of Police and the matter is taken care of.

BOGYO. I can't believe my ears. What a funny setup: you're running around all day to your meetings, and I'm sitting at home with the Gestapo guarding me.

KASTNER. Krumey has good reasons to protect me. We've made serious progress in the negotiations. We've even managed to get six hundred emigration permits from them. Krumey realizes that I need my freedom of movement. Here . . . this is yours . . . exemption from wearing the yellow star. Take it . . .

BOGYO. (*Takes it.*) You've got six hundred emigration permits?

KASTNER. Yes . . .

BOGYO. Are you sure now, Rezsö? Because if you're not absolutely sure, I don't want to hear about it. I don't want to live with deceptions.

KASTNER. I should hope not.

BOGYO. I have to know. Do we have an emigration permit? We can leave here at last?

KASTNER. (*Realizing her meaning.*) Bogyo, we haven't made up the list . . . or actually thought about who would be leaving.

BOGYO. What do you mean you haven't thought about it? You didn't think that I'd want to leave? Or your old mother? And what about my parents? They wouldn't want to leave?

KASTNER. Of course, I thought you'd want to leave. But it hadn't occurred to me that you'd leave without me. You have no idea of what I've been through. I need you to be with me. I do expect you to stay with me, even it it's a little hard for you. It's hard for me, too . . .

BOGYO. Don't preach to me.

KASTNER. I didn't mean to preach.

BOGYO. What's all this righteousness all of a sudden? And coming from you . . .

KASTNER. Bogyo, I've come to take you home, not to give you a license to run away from here by yourself . . .

BOGYO. I don't want to run away by myself. I want to leave with you. Am I supposed to be ashamed of wanting to live? I don't care what people say about me, or about you, for that matter.

KASTNER. You've never cared about anything except polishing your nails and having an ample supply of cigarettes. And yes, having a pillow under your fanny while playing cards.

BOGYO. You're a fool. You'd better take a good look at yourself and see how everybody is using you. How naïve can you get? Your best friends will get their families out of the country, and in the end they'll spit in your face. They'll let you stay behind and play with the castles you've built in the air. You're out of your mind. Just what do you think you can really do? With your stupidity you won't be able to save even a . . .

KASTNER. You'll be able to get out. I'll put you on the list, and I'll put you on the train myself. Just get out from here and do whatever you want to. (*Exit. Goes directly to the offices of the Jewish Community.*)

HELEN. (*Enters.*) Where are you going? (*To Bogyo.*) You've had a fight again?

BOGYO. I'm going out to get cigarettes. (*Exit.*)

Scene 36

On the street, a terrible sight confronts her. In a group of Jews, wearing yellow stars and mostly very old, some are on their knees while others are leaping over their heads. (Hungarian Policemen are standing around, laughing boisterously. A shocked Bogyo runs back to Helen's apartment slamming the door behind her.

Scene 37

Offices of the Jewish Community. Stern, Freudiger, Hansi, and Kastner.

FREUDIGER. If we all agree that the Szatmár Rebbe has to get out, then let's put him on the list today.

KASTNER. We can put him on the list right now, but then we won't have room for Leo Goldberg and his family.

STERN. There's room for both of them if you leave out Gyuri Wessely.

KASTNER. Why Gyuri Wessely?

STERN. I know that Wessely is a very active Zionist, Kastner, and that he's very close to you. But Leo Goldberg has given us a lot of money. One and a half million pengös last month alone.

HANSI. Maybe the Szatmár Rebbe's group should be reduced. Twenty-seven persons for one family is a little too much.

FREUDIGER. But he's got nine children. He and his wife; his mother-in-law and father-in-law; his brother-in-law and their respective parents, plus his sister and her husband, and another eight children. You wouldn't want to separate small children from their parents, would you?

KASTNER. Wessely must get out, sir. The police have been after him for weeks.

STERN. How can you compare a minor Zionist functionary to Leo Goldberg or the Szatmár Rebbe? What right does he have?

HANSI. Just as you wish, sir. He is only a minor Zionist functionary, as you say, but when you, sir, needed a forged passport for your sister's grandson, you were willing to pay a lot for it to this same Wessely . . .

KASTNER. And what right does Leo Goldberg have? His money? For three whole years he didn't give a single pengö to our rescue activities. He's always denied he's a Jew at all. Now that the Germans have reminded him that he is one, he is willing to admit it. Now that he knows that either the Germans or the Hungarians are bound to take away his money, he's ready to give it to us. Leo Goldberg and all the rest of the great benefactors that you work so hard for, sir, now ask for favors and offer money.

STERN. They ask for favors, Kastner? You're spitting in the faces of those who have financed your activities! It is with their money that you've bought the privilege of preparing this very list. Don't forget that! These same people can pay for the trains you say are about to leave, or they can refuse. They're not licking your boots, Kastner. You are licking theirs.

KASTNER. I thank you all, very much. (*Gets up, gathers his papers and leaves angrily.*)

Scene 38

A street. Kastner is hurrying along. Music. First Man stops Kastner.

FIRST MAN. Dr. Kastner . . .

KASTNER. Yes . . .

FIRST MAN. I wanted to ask you . . . about the list of emigration permits. . . . I've always been a Zionist . . . (*Music intensifies, the conversation cannot be heard. Kastner refuses and continues on his way. Second Man stops him.*)

SECOND MAN. Dr. Kastner . . .

KASTNER. Yes?!

SECOND MAN. Don't you recognize me? I'm . . .

KASTNER. Yes . . . yes . . . I remember . . .

SECOND MAN. The police are looking for me. I'm sorry to bother you, but I can't go home. . . . My friends are afraid to hide me . . .

KASTNER. How can I help you?

SECOND MAN. I've heard about this train going to Palestine . . . (*Music intensifies, the argument between two men is swallowed up. Kastner leaves angrily, Second man is alone for a moment, then three Hungarian Policemen come up to him.*)

FIRST POLICEMAN. Hey . . . you! . . .

SECOND MAN. Me?

FIRST POLICEMAN. Papers! (*Second Man produces his papers.*) Günther Jötner?

SECOND MAN. That's me . . .

FIRST POLICEMAN. (*Sarcastic.*) Günther Jötner?

SECOND MAN. Yes . . .

FIRST POLICEMAN. (*Takes his canteen and pours water over Second Man's head, rinsing out the blond dye, revealing black hair underneath.*) Günther Jötner . . . ha . . . (*To the other two Policemen.*) The pants. . . . Pants-check. (*They force him out of his pants and ascertain that he is circumcised.*)

SECOND POLICEMAN. A work accident, eh? Your prick got caught, and right at the tip, too! (*Policemen laugh. Blackout.*)

Scene 39

A street. Komoly and Brand.

BRAND. You've always had a way with Stern, Otto . . .
KOMOLY. I can't make decisions like that, Yenö. I'm willing to do anything to have anyone we can, but to pick whom to save . . . I just can't. Rezsö is less sensitive than I am. I hope he understands.

Scene 40

Eichmann, Endre, and Baky in a night club. They're quite drunk. Music and singing in the background.

EICHMANN. And what's the difference between a fat Jew and a skinny Jew?
BAKY. A fat Jew stinks more . . . (*Endre laughs.*)
EICHMANN. A fat Jew burns longer . . . (*Baky and Endre nearly burst with laughter.*) And what's the difference between a loaf of bread and a Jew?
ENDRE. What?
EICHMANN. (*To Baky.*) Well?
BAKY. What?
EICHMANN. A loaf of bread doesn't scream when they put it in the oven . . . (*They all roll with laughter.*) And how can you fit fifty Jews into a small Opel?
ENDRE. Fifty???
EICHMANN. Two in front, three in back, and the rest in the ashtray . . . (*General hilarity.*)
BAKY. But tell me, Herr Obersturmbannführer, . . . sir, . . . if that's so, then why do you deal with them . . . and let them get out on that train . . . we know everything, you know. . . . No, really . . . tell me . . . and you take all their money . . . that's Hungarian money, you know, for yourself. . . . Why? . . . That's our money . . . no? . . .
EICHMANN. (*Gaffaws.*) The train? László Baky, you don't even begin to realize how much *you've* been taken for a ride. . . . I'll collect all those dirty Zionists in one train and send them to Auschwitz . . . one big package . . . all of them together. (*They laugh wildly. Music.*)

Scene 41

In his apartment Kastner is dozing in an armchair. Around him a pile of newspapers. Knocking at the door. Kastner recognizes Brand's signal. Rises to open the door.

KASTNER. Just a minute, Yenö . . . just a second. (*Opens the door. To his surprise it's Hansi.*) Oh . . . Hansi. . . . (*Fastens the belt of his robe.*) I thought it was Yenö. . . . I haven't had a chance to put away these newspapers. . . . Come in. . . . I dozed off a little . . .

HANSI. Where is Bogyo?

KASTNER. She's not here.

HANSI. Not here? Has anything happened to her?

KASTNER. No. She wasn't feeling well and went to stay overnight with my mother. . . . Would you like something to drink? Coffee?

HANSI. Yes, thank you. Actually no, no. Don't bother. I just wanted to talk to you for a moment.

KASTNER. Sit down. . . . Not there, the leg is broken. (*Hansi sits down . . . Kastner is looking for his lighter. Hansi gets up.*)

HANSI. (*Giving him the lighter.*) Here you are . . .

KASTNER. (*Plops down listlessly.*) You're sure you don't want something to drink?

HANSI. Yes, I'm sure, thanks. I wanted to ask you . . . Krumey has agreed to issue six hundred permits, right?

KASTNER. Yes . . . (*Lights up.*)

HANSI. Why exactly six hundred?

KASTNER. That's how many entry visas we have.

HANSI. And if you had said eight hundred? Only fifty of those visas are real, anyway. Another two hundred could have been forged in a day.

KASTNER. Just a minute. . . . I'm not quite awake yet. . . . What are you getting at?

HANSI. Maybe you want something to drink. Coffee. I'll put on the water. Have you had anything to eat?

KASTNER. Yes . . . thank you. . . . I don't know if we have any coffee . . . (*Hansi goes into kitchen and comes back with a glass of water.*)

HANSI. Water. (*Kastner drinks.*) If six hundred is an arbitrary number, we could ask Krumey for another six hundred.

KASTNER. I don't know. We've already failed to turn those entry visas into six hundred family permits. Maybe we'd better wait and see that this first group really leaves . . . and gets to Palestine, and not some other place . . .

HANSI. Look, if they get to Palestine, we have saved them. And if not . . . what have we lost?

KASTNER. I can't go to Krumey again, Hansi. If I ask for additional permits, he's likely to consult Eichmann. Eichmann would be furious and might cancel the permits already issued . . .

HANSI. You've told me yourself that they've got good reasons for giving us these . . .

KASTNER. I can't play this game anymore. Let somebody else go. I've done my share. Instead of being grateful for the six hundred permits I've got out of the Germans, people are spreading the rumor that I've been handing them out to whoever I please.

HANSI. That's not true, Rezsö. Nobody's spreading rumors about you. On the contrary. Otto himself has said that, without you, this first group could never have arranged.

KASTNER. People attack me in the street because of these permits. If they hear there are six hundred more, they'll set up a blockade around the house. . . . One Jew stopped me on the street: "Kastner, the police are looking for me. If you don't give me a permit, I'm finished." What could I say to him? Why do I have to make these decisions? Why do I have to do it alone? (*Gets up.*) Why are you all attacking me? You've given me all the dirty work to do and left me to myself. I'm not doing anything anymore. Get someone else. . . . Let Yenö go. . . . Or Otto. . . . I've had it. (*Blows up.*) Leave me alone! I want to rest, I want some peace and quiet. Enough! I'm fed up with these people. I don't want to see anybody anymore! (*Pause. Hansi starts out. Kastner, contrite, calls after her.*) Hansi . . . Hansi. . . . Don't go . . . I'm sorry, I got carried away. . . . I'll be all right. . . . You have to stay with me for a little while. Bogyo's left me. She's moved in with my mother. . . . I've been alone for the last two weeks. . . . I've nobody to fight with; you're the only one who can understand that. Stay a while . . . (*Hansi, already at the door, turns and walks toward Kastner.*)

Scene 42

Offices of the SS. Late at night. Wisliceny, Kastner, and Lulu.

WISLICENY. (*Counting dollar bills.*) Ten thousand dollars for two hundred permits? Any way I figure it, Kastner, it comes to fifty dollars per skull. Isn't that right, Lili?

LULU. Lulu . . .

KASTNER. You've forgotten the dessert.

WISLICENY. She won't ask me for anything extra in the morning, will she?

KASTNER. Refreshments are on the house. (*Hands a bill to Wisliceny who sticks it into Lulu's bra.*)

LULU. *Danke, bitte.*

WISLICENY. When my main course is in Hamburg, I can't be too choosy about my dessert . . . (*Laughs.*)

LULU. *Ish liebe dish . . .*

WISLICENY. Couldn't you get one that speaks German?

KASTNER. This one has other, more outstanding, qualities, sir.

WISLICENY. Kastner, Kastner, always one more joker up your sleeve. (*Seriously.*) Still, I would have thought that you valued Jews in, shall we say, rounded figures . . .

KASTNER. When we get the permits, we'll double the amount, sir.

WISLICENY. That's a very wise idea, Kastner. But it's not enough. You already know Obersturmbannführer Eichmann. He's a thorough man. (*Indicating Lulu.*) Gifts like this don't influence him.

KASTNER. That's all I have at my disposal, sir.

WISLICENY. I'm not talking about money, Kastner. You're a man who understands delicate matters, and as you can see I'm not an idiot, either. We both know that the Reich will not last a thousand years. If the Russians attack us in the Carpathians, we may not last a thousand hours. Let's think about that, Kastner, shall we?

LULU. *Bitte, bitte, danke. . . . Ish liebe dish . . .*

KASTNER. (*Silencing her.*) What do you mean, sir?

WISLICENY. We could help each other, Kastner. After the war, a lot of fingers will be poking around, checking into our activities among the Jews in Poland, Greece, Yugoslavia. I'll give you two hundred permits, and you give me a piece of paper.

KASTNER. Paper?

WISLICENY. Yes. Something short. Simple. In it you will put down the things I've done for all of you. The main thing is that my good intentions be very clear. Do you get my meaning, Kastner?

KASTNER. Indeed I do, sir. The moment I get the permits, you'll get the paper from me.

LULU. *Bitte, bitte, Wisly . . . danke. . . . Ish liebe dish . . .*

WISLICENY. To your health, Kastner.

LULU. *Skol!* (*Adds a juicy Hungarian curse.*)

WISLICENY. What did she say, Kastner?

KASTNER. She's already in love with you, sir.

WISLICENY. (*Laughing hard.*) Good for her . . . right. . . . Bravo.

. . . When you come to get her in the morning, bring her something else to wear. She can't walk out of my office like this.
KASTNER. Just leave it to me, sir. . . . Good night. (*Exit Kastner, with dancing steps, Wisliceny and Lulu retire to a side room. Blackout.*)

Scene 43

Offices of the Jewish Community, Freudiger, Stern, Komoly, Kastner, and Brand.

STERN. (*To Kastner.*) A very admirable achievement, Kastner . . . these two hundred additional permits. I hope they'll help us out of our predicament. In my congregation alone, I have 147 people I simply can't refuse.
KASTNER. Wisliceny has also given me a few hundred more postcards from Waldsee. (*Gives a small package to Freudiger.*)
STERN. Very good. (*To Freudiger.*) I want these distributed immediately. Good news should not be delayed. (*To Kastner.*) Out of the two hundred additional permits my congregation should get, according to these lists . . . (*Counting names on the list.*)
BRAND. (*To Komoly.*) Here's one addressed to you, Otto.
KOMOLY. To me?
FREUDIGER. I suggest we divide the permits in proportion to the size of each organization, as usual . . .
BRAND. Yes. Somebody named Oshbeno Witztimberg . . .
KOMOLY. Witztimberg? (*Looks at the postcard.*) Oshbeno Witztimberg. . . . I know somebody called Timberg. Beno Timberg. In fact, he was imprisoned in Kistarcsa, then sent to Waldsee . . . (*He screams.*) Oh my God! God! Beno Timberg did send this postcard. He's trying to tell us about Auschwitz. He's added letters to his name. Together they make up Auschwitz. . . . Here. . . . *Osh*Beno *Witz*Timberg. . . . Oshwitz. . . . Auschwitz . . . (Kastner *scrutinizes the postcards.*)
STERN. Who is this Timberg?
KOMOLY. A lawyer. Active in the Young Maccabee movement.
FREUDIGER. (*Shouting.*) Auschwitz here, too. (*Holding up a postcard.*) Somebody has tried to erase the letters, but you can still make it out: Auschwitz.
STERN. (*Looking at the postcard.*) Ernö Kohn. That's Kohn, the eye doctor from Rök Szilárd Street. (*Looking at the other postcards.*) Hirsch, curator of the Museum. . . . The lawyer Fabian. . . . Mrs. Weisz, Mrs.

Reiner. . . . The engineer Gabor. . . . Greenberg. These names were on the lists Krumey's given me. (*Long pause.*)

FREUDIGER. Maybe trains have gone out from other towns, too. Budapest may be the only place with Jews left in it. We just don't know. . . . These damned Germans have been deceiving us all along.

KOMOLY. If we give them these new lists, they'll send all these people to Auschwitz too . . .

FREUDIGER. I'll have nothing to do with these lists. I won't give them a single name from my congregation. We can't put up with these lies anymore. (*To Stern.*) Perhaps you could talk to Admiral Horthy, sir. . . . He's still the Governor of this country.

STERN. And who can guarantee that he isn't a part to all these lies? Is there anyone left in Hungary one can trust?

FREUDIGER. You're right, sir. We can't go on functioning like this. We can't save anybody. Now we have to spread the word, we must warn people. Every Jew has to save himself; find a way to escape, or go into hiding.

KASTNER. Everybody will use his own connections to get away, right? And what about those who have no connections, what will they do? Look, we still have the promise of those eight hundred permits. . . . Maybe, despite everything, we should find out just what is behind that promise.

KOMOLY. No more meetings with the Germans, Rezsö. From this moment on, we're breaking off all contacts with them, and that includes contacts about those permits.

BRAND. How can you break off contacts with them? It they call us, we won't go? But, if we don't lose our heads, maybe we can benefit from what we've just learned and be more careful. What if we turned this list over to the Red Cross?

KOMOLY. Since when do the Germans pay any attention to the Red Cross?

KASTNER. Otto, let's be logical about this. I suggest we do give these postcards to the respective families and also tell them the truth. With the Germans, we pretend we don't know anything. Maybe they'll be less cautious. If they find out we're on to them, they'll come up with new tricks . . . and they might even speed up the rate of deportation. Later we'll check . . .

STERN. (*Angry.*) Are you trying to compete with them in cunning, Kastner? With them? There's no limit to their trickery. The more cautious we are, the more underhanded they become. Look where this method has gotten us. They've lied to you. You've believed them, and we've all been taken in right along with you. The Judenrat has become a tool of the Germans. We've called their meetings for them, we've turned apartments over to them, and we have published their proclamations. Now we must stop. (*Pause.*) Tomorrow we'll assemble all the leaders of every Jewish organization and announce the dissolution of the Judenrat. From now on, each of us must worry about his own fate. (*Blackout.*)

Scene 44

Offices of the Hungarian Police. Endre is sitting at a desk, busy with paperwork. Enter Baky dragging Bogyo along.

BAKY. Mrs. Kastner, sir . . .

ENDRE. Oh. . . . Hello, Mrs. Kastner. . . . (*Offers her a chair.*) Sit down. . . . How are you? I'm László Endre, secretary of state for Jewish affairs . . .

BOGYO. How do you do, sir. . . . My husband has mentioned your name on several occasions . . .

ENDRE. (*Offering her a cigarette.*) In my work, I come across Dr. Kastner's name just about everyday. (*To Baky.*) Can I be of any assistance?

BAKY. Madam's been arrested by the railway station. She wasn't wearing her yellow star and was carrying a forged exemption certificate . . .

BOGYO. Forged? Impossible, sir. I got the certificate from . . .

BAKY. (*Cuts her off and hands Endre the certificate.*) That's not my signature. . . . (*To Bogyo.*) One of your people has tried to forge my signature. . . . A period is missing in the lower right hand corner. I am very careful about the period.

BOGYO. My husband gave me this certificate. It can't be forged . . .

ENDRE. If the Colonel here says the signature is forged, it's forged. . . . After all, it's his signature. I'm surprised that of all people you got a forged one from your husband . . .

BOGYO. I beg you, sir, please talk to my husband. . . . I'm sure he can explain everything.

ENDRE. I'd be happy to talk to your husband, only I don't see how he could help us. . . . (*To Baky.*) Perhaps you could do something?

BAKY. The penalty for this offense, according to the law, is ten years imprisonment. And, of course, detention while awaiting trial. . . . There's nothing to be done. The law is clear.

BOGYO. There must be a mistake, sir. . . . Maybe you could reach my husband by telephone. . . . I'm sure the mistake would be all cleared up. . . . I've never forged anything in my life. Anybody who knows me can tell you that. . . . Maybe you can talk to Obersturmbann-führer Krumey, sir. . . . He could give you an explanation, too.

BAKY. I'm very sorry, madam. (*Motions to a guard to drag her out.*)

ENDRE. Just a minute, Colonel. . . . Maybe there is one little thing that would let us overlook her offense . . .

BOGYO. Yes, sir . . .

ENDRE. There was a meeting this morning in the offices of the Jewish Community. Your husband was there. Immediately afterward the leaders of Jewish organizations were notified of an emergency meeting tomorrow. What's happened? Why the panic?

BOGYO. I don't know, sir . . .

ENDRE. I'm trying to help you. . . . Your husband has done business with the Gestapo before, right?

BOGYO. Yes . . .

ENDRE. He's transferred money to the Gestapo, hasn't he?

BOGYO. Yes . . .

ENDRE. How much?

BOGYO. I don't know.

ENDRE. Approximately?

BOGYO. A hundred thousand dollars?

ENDRE. More. . . . More . . .

BOGYO. I don't know. . . . Really, I don't . . .

ENDRE. I suspect they're about to decide on another deal tomorrow . . . an especially big financial deal. . . . Maybe you could make an effort to refresh your memory. It would help you a lot . . .

BOGYO. I don't know . . .

BAKY. (*Kicks her.*) Talk!

ENDRE. (*Stopping Baky.*) Your husband is organizing the meeting, and he hasn't told you what it's all about?

BOGYO. No . . .

ENDRE. This is not a petty hundred-thousand-dollar deal. . . . Something a lot bigger than that. . . . And your husband has already started wasting away some of the money he's made on the deal . . .

BOGYO. He's got no money. . . . I've never seen him with money . . .

ENDRE. He's got no money? Then how can he afford a different nightclub every evening? How come he plays cards with Obersturm-bannführer Wisliceny, and loses sixteen thousand dollars in a single game? . . . Where does all that money come from?

BOGYO. I've no idea what you're talking about, sir. . . . I didn't know he was going to night clubs. . . . He hasn't told me . . .

ENDRE. And all kinds of other places, too . . .

BOGYO. What kind of places?

BAKY. (*Kicks her.*) Don't you play games with me! Start talking, or else you may never get to your own trial.

ENDRE. The gentleman is not joking. . . . We have to know what sort of deal is about to be negotiated. In wartime, deals like that are tantamount to treason. If you won't tell us everything you know, you become an accessory to treason . . .

BOGYO. I don't know anything . . . really I don't . . .

BAKY. We're wasting our time. . . . I'll take her down to the cellar. . . . In ten minutes, we'll know everything . . .

BOGYO. I don't know anything. . . . My husband and I separated two weeks ago. . . . I don't see him at all. . . . I've been living with relatives . . . with my mother-in-law . . .

ENDRE. Separated?

BOGYO. Yes . . .

BAKY. (*Strikes her.*) Why didn't you tell me that when I arrested you, you dirty bitch? . . .

ENDRE. (*Stops Baky.*) Get her out of here. . . . Go find her husband. I want to question him, and I don't care if the Germans go complaining to Horthy. . . . (*Baky throws her out of the room and returns.*) Go find him. What are you waiting for?

BAKY. Leave Kastner alone. He's too important to Eichmann. (*Blackout.*)

Scene 45

Kastner's apartment. Kastner and Hansi are having tea. A frightened Bogyo approaches. Opens door. Looks at Kastner and Hansi. Draws her conclusions and leaves, slamming the door.

KASTNER. Bogyo! . . . (*She's gone. Blackout.*)

Scene 46

Offices of the SS. Eichmann, Krumey, Wisliceny.

EICHMANN. You're sure they mean to stir up all the ghettos?

WISLICENY. Absolutely sure. They've already told all their leaders to start some sort of resistance in every ghetto in Hungary.

EICHMANN. We can't afford a second Warsaw. Trouble in one ghetto alone can upset our timetable. I've got no time for this kind of nonsense. I've promised the Führer a smooth and clean operation. We've got to stop them. (*To Krumey.*) First of all, take care of the censors who checked the postcards. (*Shouting.*) The Reich will fall because of negligent clerks. The whole war, all the sacrifices, everything will go down the drain because of these nobodies!

KRUMEY. I've already taken care of them, sir. Our problem now is how to calm the Jews down.

EICHMANN. That's right.

WISLICENY. We could imprison all their leaders before the meeting.

EICHMANN. (*Furious.*) Idiot! That's the best way to get a million Jews to rise. Do you know what it's like to have a million nauseating rats scurrying around you, biting the soles of your boots? (*Pause.*) The fish did not bite. We have to throw out another bait. A more tempting one. (*To Wisliceny.*) Don't touch their leaders. Not one. And tell the Hungarians to stay away from them, too, for a few days. They mustn't find out that we know about the postcards.

KRUMEY. May I suggest, sir, that we give them the exit permits now, ahead of time. That would soften them up a little.

EICHMANN. Absolutely, Hermann. You can give them a thousand, if you like. . . . The question is whether that will do the trick. . . . (*To Wisliceny.*) Get me the Reichsführer in Berlin.

WISLICENY. (*Into the telephone.*) Get me Reichsführer Himmler, urgent.

EICHMANN. Now we'll offer them the "Big Deal." The Reichsführer has been pressuring me for some time to start it, anyway. He'll be glad to hear we're making contacts for him with the Americans, right, Hermann? That way we might calm the Jews down for a few weeks. (*To Krumey.*) I want Brand. Find him. Turn Budapest upside down, but bring him to me right away.

KRUMEY. Brand, sir? Not Kastner? Kastner is a lot more efficient.

EICHMANN. I've said Brand. He'll travel to strike the deal. I want Kastner here. Kastner is strong. He'll stay here and help me finish the job. Find Brand. (*Blackout.*)

Scene 47

Stern's office. Stern and Freudiger.

FREUDIGER. I hope they'll all show up. They were very worried when I told them about the meeting.

STERN. They must know the truth, the whole truth, no matter how bitter. I'll make a short announcement about the dissolution of the Judenrat, and we'll disperse immediately afterward. There will no discussion, no debate . . . (*They continue their conversation. Light fades.*)

Scene 48

Offices of the SS. Eichmann, Krumey, Wisliceny, and Brand.

EICHMANN. Sit down. (*Brand sits down.*) You know me, Brand, don't you?

BRAND. Yes, Herr Obersturmbannführer . . .

EICHMANN. I've solved the Jewish problem in Germany, Austria, Poland, Czechoslovakia, et cetera. Now it's Hungary's turn, eh?

BRAND. What do you mean, Herr Obersturmbannführer?

EICHMANN. I've had my eyes on you for several weeks now, Brand. And also on your Rescue Committee. . . . And I've come to the conclusion that you people, as opposed to the Judenrat, are ripe for our Big Deal . . . a deal a lot bigger than any we've made with you so far . . . a deal that will solve more than just the problem of Hungary's Jews.

BRAND. Yes, Herr Obersturmbannführer . . .

EICHMANN. I am prepared to sell you one million Jews.

BRAND. One million?

EICHMANN. One million Jews, wherever they may still be found. . . . We'll get them from Hungary, Poland, Austria, Theresienstadt, Auschwitz, any place you wish. You may take women who can bear children and men who can sire children . . . you pick them. Blood in return for merchandise . . . merchandise for blood. . . . What do you say?

BRAND. What kind of merchandise do you have in mind, sir?

EICHMANN. Ten thousand trucks, one thousand tons of coffee . . . and a few hundred tons of soap . . .

BRAND. You think we can get hold of ten thousand trucks, sir?

EICHMANN. Of course you can, Brand. If we burn twenty thousand Jews every day in Auschwitz, you'll try very hard to get them, won't you? And if you try very hard, the Americans will give them to you. You are the man. The deal is up to you.

BRAND. Me? You want me to get ten thousand trucks, sir? I can't take on a mission like that . . . surely not on my own responsibility. . . . The Rescue Committee has to decide . . . who will act on its behalf . . .

EICHMANN. But you'll be talking to the Americans on my behalf, too. And I decide who acts on my behalf, don't I Brand?

BRAND. I'm only a member of the Rescue Committee . . . not even a senior member. . . . The Committee won't agree that I should represent it. . . . I can't negotiate with border guards . . . the tax people . . . the police. . . . I've no experience in such missions. I've got no connections. This is a job for somebody a lot higher up than . . .

EICHMANN. I see no difficulty whatever, Brand. You'll fly to Istanbul; the Jewish Agency has a branch of your Rescue Committee there, doesn't it? They'll put you in touch with the American Ambassador . . . Steinhardt . . . a Jew. He'll take the matter to Roosevelt.

BRAND. Sir, I'm not the right man. . . . Nobody will even talk to me. I've got no chance to see the American Ambassador . . .

EICHMANN. Tell him, this Jew Steinhardt, that the trucks have to be equipped with winter gear . . . snow chains, tow bars, tarpaulin tops . . . and promise him, on my behalf, that we'll transfer them immediately to the eastern front . . .

BRAND. (Gets up.) Sir, I'm fully aware of my own limitations, I'm only a junior member of the Committee. I can't take upon myself this mission without the authorization of the Committee. The most I can do is take your request to the Committee for discussion, maybe . . .

EICHMANN. (Shouting.) Listen to me, Brand! . . .

BRAND. We have a lot of people much better qualified . . . like Dr. Kastner, for example . . .

EICHMANN. (Screaming.) Sit down!! (Brand sits down. Pause. Eichmann calms down.) You are an honest man, Brand . . . serious and responsible. I need a man like you. You'll leave tomorrow morning. (Pause. Brand is nonplussed. When he realizes he has no choice, he turns to Eichmann.)

BRAND. When I talk to the Americans, what guarantees can I give them that you will in fact release one million Jews?

EICHMANN. They won't need any guarantee. The moment you return with an agreement in principle, I'll release a hundred thousand Jews. Only then will I get a thousand trucks. When I release another hundred thousand, I'll get another thousand trucks and so on. . . . Pretty fair, eh?

BRAND. Yes, sir . . .

EICHMANN. You'll leave tomorrow. You've got two weeks. Your wife and children will stay here until you come back. (To Krumey.) Prepare a German passport for him. Tonight.

KRUMEY. The passport is ready. (*Takes a passport from his pocket, hands it to Brand.*)

EICHMANN. Tell your friends on the Committee, and the Americans, too, that starting tomorrow four trains loaded with Jews will leave for Auschwitz every day. Three thousand Jews on each train. Take this into account, Brand. The sooner you get back, the more of your friends you'll save . . .

BRAND. (*Puts the passport on the table.*) That's impossible, sir. If the transports start tomorrow morning, there is no point in my going. Nobody will be ready to negotiate with me while Jews are being sent to Auschwitz. . . . Everybody knows what happens in Auschwitz . . .

EICHMANN. What is it you want, Brand?

BRAND. To hold the transports until I come back.

EICHMANN. Out of the question.

BRAND. Then I won't go. You're making me fail in advance, sir. And you, sir, if you are really interested in the success of the mission . . .

EICHMANN. (*Cutting in.*) Don't go! Tomorrow morning four trains will leave for Auschwitz, and you'll be on the first one! . . . (*Angrily he starts for the door.*)

KRUMEY. Obersturmbannführer Eichmann . . . permit me, sir . . . (*Approaches Eichmann, whispers into his ear.*)

EICHMANN. (*To Krumey.*) Out of the question. (*Krumey whispers to him again. Conciliatory, Eichmann returns to Brand.*) The transports will start for Auschwitz tomorrow morning, just as I've told you. But we'll keep the people there in the cooler for two weeks. If you come back without an agreement, we'll throw them into the ovens. Is that clear?

BRAND. Yes, sir . . .

EICHMANN. I'll see you in two weeks. For the moment we can dispense with the handshake. Ultimately, we do have a common purpose, don't we, Brand? (*Blackout.*)

Scene 49

Stern's office. Freudiger, Stern, and Kastner.

STERN. (*Angry.*) I don't believe in any German proposal any more, Kastner. We've decided to dissolve the Judenrat, and I will make the announcement in less than an hour.

KASTNER. But we've already sent a telegram to the Jewish Agency in Istanbul, sir, and they've accepted this proposal on the spot. Dr. Chaim Weizmann himself has left for Istanbul to meet Brand. This telegram came twenty minutes ago. (*Produces telegram.*) "Joel should leave. Chaim is waiting for him."

STERN. Allow me not to share your enthusiasm, Kastner. Frankly, I don't believe Weizmann can pull off such a deal. And I have even graver doubts about Brand's abilities.

KASTNER. It is precisely because of those doubts that he must be helped. If you give him your authorization, too, his mission will carry a lot more weight. What have you got to lose, sir?

FREUDIGER. Kastner, we don't want another deal with them. We've decided to disband. Within a day or two, we won't even be in Budapest.

STERN. I won't authorize a deal I don't believe in. We'll have no more deals with the devil.

KASTNER. (*Addressing both Stern and Freudiger.*) You won't make any more deals with the devil? You? It's me who's knocking on his door every day. It's my throat he's holding in his claws. It's me who has to humiliate himself before him. I am the one who is contaminated with his slime when I come to offer you things in his name. I'm doing all that, not you! But when he offers to release Jews, I'm willing to do business with him, even for a single Jew. And when he offers me a chance to save a million Jews, who am I to say "no more deals with the devil"? You, who are supposed to be the leaders of these Jews, who gives you the right to say a thing like that? Who gives you the right to refuse an offer like that? "No more deals with the devil!" (*Turns to leave.*)

FREUDIGER. (*To Stern*). If you will allow me, sir, I don't think anything terrible will happen if we wait a couple weeks. Kastner! Kastner! (*Blackout. Freudiger turns to Audience.*) In the end, the Judenrat was not dissolved, and we continued to negotiate with the Germans. We sent out no warnings, sounded no alarm. It's hard to say whether we believed in Brand's mission. Still, we held on to it as to a lifebelt. . . . With all our doubts, we held on to it. Maybe there is a contradiction there . . . it's possible. . . . Many have accused us that we were afraid for our skins and of breaking off contacts with the Germans. . . . That, too, is possible. And who among us was not afraid? I don't know what made Kastner run. Surely not fear. His courage has always been a puzzle to me. We wanted to gain time. We knew that in order to gain time, we had to keep things quiet . . . we figured that panic would help no one . . .

Scene 50

Helen Kastner's apartment. Knocking at the door. Helen hurries to the door but hesitates to open it.

HELEN. Who is it?

KASTNER. What's happened to the door, damn it? I've just broken my key!

HELEN. Who is it?

KASTNER. It's me, Mother!

HELEN. (*Opens door.*) Rezsö . . . at last. . . . Why are you so late?

KASTNER. What's wrong with the door?

HELEN. I had to have the lock changed. I couldn't calm her down. Now I carry the key on me all the time so she can't leave the house. I can't keep on watching her, Rezsö.

KASTNER. Why should you keep on watching her?

HELEN. You have to take her home. She's talking about you all the time. Since that interrogation by the police, she's been talking in her sleep.

KASTNER. What kind of things does she say?

HELEN. All kinds of things, but I can't possibly repeat them. She's restless. She's chain smoking all day long. That's not healthy. She's really suffering. You have to take care of her. She's your wife.

KASTNER. Mother, can't you help me a little. I've got a million people to take care of.

HELEN. You know her. We've never gotten along.

KASTNER. Just a few more days, Mother. Two weeks, maybe three, but no more. There are new developments. Very involved business. I just won't have time for anything else. Thousands of people . . . hundreds of thousands. I've got to get them trains, boats . . . take them abroad . . . help them settle . . . take care of food, shelter. I don't know if I'll be at home at all.

HELEN. She's been here almost a month. I can't any more.

KASTNER. She'll get over things in a few days, I'm sure, Mother. I beg you. (*Enter Bogyo. Pause.*) Bogyo . . .

BOGYO. What's he doing here, Helen?

HELEN. He's come to visit you, right, Rezsö?

KASTNER. I've come to talk to you. . . . I know what you've been through. I'm truly sorry . . .

BOGYO. I don't want to talk to you. Go talk to the people you hang around with day and night. Talk to those you spend your time with in nightclubs, the ones you play cards with. I've heard about the money you take from the till and lose on cards . . . even the police know about . . . (*To Helen.*) I couldn't even afford a roll; I had to fight the grocer to sell me cigarettes on credit, and he goes and loses twenty thousand dollars on cards in a single night . . .

KASTNER. Bogyo, what's all this nonsense? You don't trust me? You'd rather believe what those bastard Hungarians tell you? You believe Endre?

HELEN. Anybody want tea? I've got some cake, too, . . .

BOGYO. You get money to save people and you spend it on whores. You don't think I know about it? Of course, you tell everybody that you've got no choice, that you do it for the contacts you need. I know you. You're doing it because you've got no inhibitions at all, because your thirst for adventure has no limit. (*To Helen.*) I was a fool, I didn't believe these stories. I thought he did everything for the good of the people. And all the time, I was sitting at home, waiting for him.

HELEN. Bogyo, what's gotten into you? (*To Kastner.*) Do something, Rezsö, she doesn't know what she's talking about . . .

BOGYO. He thinks he's some sort of national hero . . . they'll erect a statue for him . . .

KASTNER. I'm spending money on whores? What are you talking about? If you just calm down a little, I'll tell you exactly . . .

BOGYO. What am I talking about? I'm talking about those dirty little deals of yours. And with whom? With the lowest of Germans, with the worst of these mad killers. You hang around them all day hoping they'll throw you a bone. Is that how you save people? And then you go out with them at night . . . get drunk with them.

HELEN. Bogyo, that's enough.

BOGYO. (*To Helen.*) No, Helen, he'll hear me out to the end. They pick up a bunch of whores and party with them all night. And don't tell me you're not enjoying, Rudolf Kastner. . . . You forgot a long time ago why you've stayed behind in Budapest. Then I come home to find you with that other woman.

Scene 51

A street. Kastner, Brand, and Hansi. Brand is ready for his journey.

HANSI. (*Indicating Brand's overcoat.*) I've sewn the Hungarian passport into the left side, the Swiss one into the right. The stitches are loose, you can tear them easily.

BRAND. All right.

HANSI. The list of phone numbers and addresses are sewn in the left sleeve. Shall I go over the code again?

BRAND. No, you don't have to. (*To Kastner.*) What if I can't get the agreement in two weeks? The transports did start this morning. Twelve thousand people every day . . .

KASTNER. Send *something*, anything . . . doesn't matter what. An interim agreement . . . new proposals. The main thing is for us to have something to talk to them about. Send telegrams. Even to Eichmann himself.

HANSI. Don't worry. Weizmann's already in Istanbul, waiting for you. Show him Stern's letter . . .

BRAND. The letter. . . . Where is it?

HANSI. I put it right into your hand . . .

BRAND. Oh, yes, it's in the passport . . . the Hungarian one . . . if only I had another week . . . ten days . . . I'd feel a lot more relaxed. (*Enter SS Agent.*)

AGENT. The car's here. Round the corner. (*To Brand.*) Ready?

BRAND. Yes.

AGENT. Let's go. (*To Kastner and Hansi.*) Don't follow us. (*They all stop.*) And without too much emotion, please. (*He retires politely.*)

BRAND. (*To Kastner.*) The *chutzpah!* They've made me pay for his flight, too . . .

KASTNER. Never mind. Good luck, Yenö. . . . Don't forget to get me Darling cigarettes.

BRAND. Good-bye, Hansi.

HANSI. Good-bye.

BRAND. (*To Kastner.*) Bye. Look after Hansi and the children. (*Warmly, he shakes Kastner's hand, then turns to Hansi again.*) Take care of yourself . . . (*Exit Brand.*) (*A group of Jews, wearing yellow stars and carrying suitcases moves slowly along the street, accompanied by Hungarian Police. Hansi and Kastner watch the group, then quickly leave.*)

Scene 52

Interrogation room at the Hungarian Police; Komoly stripped to the waist, is sitting, tied to his chair. Standing next to him are Endre and a Hungarian Policeman, the latter has a club in his hand.

ENDRE. Where did he go?

KOMOLY. To Romania.

ENDRE. What's he got to do in Romania?

KOMOLY. He went to buy shoes . . .

ENDRE. That's a lie. He's left on a mission for Eichmann. Baron Stern said at your meeting that an emissary would be leaving. He meant Brand . . .

KOMOLY. He went to buy shoes . . . (*Endre motions to Policeman who strikes Komoly. Blackout. Lights on another part of the stage, where Baky is interrogating Kastner.*)

BAKY. Don't tell me again about the shoes, Kastner. . . . I want the truth. Whom is he meeting in Romania?

KASTNER. A shoe merchant from Bucharest . . .

BAKY. A shoe merchant or an American agent?

KASTNER. A shoe merchant.

BAKY. Then why did an SS agent go with him?

KASTNER. Maybe the SS want to buy shoes, too . . .

BAKY. Since when do you people buy shoes together with the SS?

KASTNER. We don't buy shoes together with them . . .

BAKY. What do you do together with them? (*Blackout. Lights on another area of the stage, where Endre is interrogating Hansi. A Policeman strikes Hansi whenever instructed to do so.*)

ENDRE. Why does he have to buy shoes in Romania?

HANSI. There was a chance to buy large quantities . . . cheap . . .

ENDRE. For whom?

HANSI. Whoever wants to buy . . .

ENDRE. Who is buying shoes today?

HANSI. Those who walk barefoot . . . (*Endre signals, Policeman hits Hansi.*)

ENDRE. What was the name registered in his passport?

HANSI. His name . . .

ENDRE. Until this very moment, nobody called to say Brand has left the country . . .

HANSI. He has . . . (*Endre sticks a lighted cigarette into her neck.*)

ENDRE. What was the name in the passport?

HANSI. (*Screaming.*) His own name . . . (*Blackout. Lights on Baky interrogating Komoly.*)

BAKY. Brand is a Communist. . . . He's already done time for that. Now he's gone to meet Communists in Romania. . . . The Jews are preparing a Communist revolution again . . .

KOMOLY. Brand is a Zionist socialist. . . . We've got nothing to do with the Communists . . .

BAKY. Communists, socialists, it's all the same thing, Komoly. . . . No court would bother with the differences between them. . . . Did you know that most of the partisans were Communists?

KOMOLY. Yes . . .

BAKY. Either you turn over Brand, or I'll charge you with aiding the partisans . . .

KOMOLY. Why bother charging me? You do what you want without a trial, anyway . . . (*Baky signals. Policeman hits Komoly. Blackout. Lights on Endre interrogating Kastner.*)

ENDRE. Kastner . . . nobody knows you're here. . . . We could tie a stone to your feet and let you sink quietly into the Danube. . . . What would happen to Brand's mission if you were to disappear? Think about that.

KASTNER. What do you want?

ENDRE. Where is Brand? Whom is he meeting?

KASTNER. He went to Romania . . .

ENDRE. Come on, we both know that he's not in Romania, and he didn't leave Hungary to buy shoes. . . . Kastner . . . we're wasting time. . . . Let's make a deal . . .

KASTNER. What deal?

ENDRE. You give me the details of Brand's mission . . .

KASTNER. And you?

ENDRE. And I give a few Jews in Budapest permission to leave the country . . .

KASTNER. How many?

ENDRE. A thousand. . . . We'll recruit them into labor battalions . . . send them to build fortifications on the eastern front, and they'd walk over to Romania. . . . The Germans wouldn't even feel it . . .

KASTNER. It's a pretty tempting deal. Too bad Brand's already gone to buy shoes . . . (*Blackout. Lights on Baky interrogating Hansi.*)

BAKY. Too bad about your delicate skin . . . (*Policeman strikes her.*) You'll be limping for many years if you don't talk. . . . (*Policeman strikes her.*) I wouldn't have believed a Jewess like you could really take it. . . . (*Policeman strikes her.*) Nobody would know you talked. . . . A border guard would identify him . . . by accident . . . that's all. . . . I'll give you a written guarantee that he'd be released right after questioning. . . . (*Hansi is silent.*) You'll leave me no choice. Your children will be here soon. (*Hansi is silent.*) You've got fifteen minutes to rest before they get here. You should look a little better for them. (*Blackout. Lights on Endre interrogating Komoly, whose condition is quickly deteriorating.*)

ENDRE. (*Impatient.*) I'll bring a hundred Jewish kids in here and kill one a minute right in front of your eyes until you talk. . . . (*Policeman hits Komoly.*) Their fate will be on your conscience . . .

KOMOLY. And what will be on your conscience?

ENDRE. Shut up! . . . (*Policeman strikes Komoly.*)

KOMOLY. Brand is buying shoes in Romania . . . (*Policeman strikes him.*) Filthy Nazi dogs . . . (*Policeman strikes him.*)

ENDRE. (*To Policeman.*) Look what you've done! You finished him off, idiot! (*Komoly collapses, Policeman is bending over him.*) He's dead. . . . Throw him in the Danube . . . (*Blackout. Lights on Baky interrogating Kastner.*)

BAKY. I'm giving you a chance to save a thousand lives. . . . The Germans would send them to Auschwitz, anyway. . . . (*Kastner is silent.*) I don't understand you, Kastner. . . . If it comes to light one day that you could have saved a thousand people and didn't, you'd have to pay dearly. . . . Instead of saving Jews, you're buying shoes in Romania together with the Germans?! One fine day, a Jewish patriot may put a bullet in your head . . . (*The door is thrown open, enter Krumey with a German soldier.*)

KRUMEY. Release him! . . . I told you not to touch this man, didn't I? (*Blackout.*)

Scene 53

Krumey's apartment. Kastner and Krumey.

KRUMEY. Wine from the Rhein Valley, Herr Kastner. I hope you can appreciate a good wine. To the health of the Führer and the Reich. (*Indicates to Kastner that he does not have to repeat these words.*) You don't have to. With me, it's already a habit. (*They drink.*)

KASTNER. Vintage '41, isn't it, sir?

KRUMEY. Right. The summer of '41 was relatively hot. That's why the touch of sweetness. (*They sit. A Servant brings in a tray of assorted food.*) By the way, I want to thank you and members of your Committee for not revealing to the Hungarians the details of Brand's mission. And please convey, if possible, my condolences to the Komoly family . . .

KASTNER. I'll do that tonight, sir . . .

KRUMEY. I'm sorry about what these animals have done to you. By the way, I've kept your mail while you were all gone. Eighty thousand dollars has come from Zurich. I hope you'll find good use for that money. There's also a telegram from Brand. He's already met the American Ambassador in Ankara.

KASTNER. (*Looking at the telegram.*) That's a very positive development, sir.

KRUMEY. Indeed, it is, Herr Kastner. I'm very pleased. This will surely strengthen the ties between us. (*Raises his glass.*) To your good health!

KASTNER. To the success of the deal.

KRUMEY. Reichsführer Himmler wishes to thank you for your dedicated work, and in addition to the eight hundred permits you've already received, he has granted another two hundred. You're a native of Cluj, Herr Kastner, are you not?

KASTNER. Yes, sir, I am.

KRUMEY. These permits are for the members of your family and your friends in Cluj. The moment you let me have the list of their names, the permits will be issued.

KASTNER. In the name of my family and friends, I am most grateful, sir.

KRUMEY. Don't thank me now, Kastner. I hope one of these days you'll have a chance to be as generous to me as I am to you now. I trust your sense of fairness.

KASTNER. You can count on it, sir, absolutely. I'm aware of the possible difficulties you may have to face after the war, and I'll do my best to help you. But you could make my job a lot easier, sir, if you were to do something now about the transports. They are being carried out in a most cruel manner, sir. Truly inhuman. Without food, without water . . .

KRUMEY. I'm sorry, Kastner, but I'm not the only SS officer in Budapest. There are a lot of things I don't like, either. The only way to stop the transports is with our Big Deal. This deal, Kastner, is crucial for you, and it's crucial for us as well.

KASTNER. What exactly do you mean, sir?

KRUMEY. Well, you know so much already, I'm willing to risk telling you this: Reichsführer Himmler is about to get rid of the Führer and start negotiations with the Americans about winding down the war. Our Big Deal will be the access channel to the Americans. Now you see why this deal is crucial for us.

KASTNER. Yes, I do, sir . . . (*Pause.*) But in that case, I hope we can expect more effective help from you personally, sir.

KRUMEY. I promise to help you all I can, Kastner.

KASTNER. Promises will not do any more, sir. You and I together will visit all the places in Hungary and Germany where you are still in command. And if I see any group of Jews, or even a single Jew, that you could save but don't, I'll be free of any future obligation to help, either you personally, sir, or the Reich.

KRUMEY. Agreed, Kastner, absolutely. I need you as much as you need me. (*Blackout.*)

Scene 54

BRAND. (*To Audience.*) This morning, I left my hotel for the railway station in Istanbul to go to Ankara to meet the American Ambassador Steinhardt. I had a feeling I was being followed. While standing in line to buy tickets, a policeman asked me for my papers. He looked at me for a few long seconds, then nodded to his men. I got away from him and managed to get lost in the crowd. When I went back to the hotel to collect my things, plainclothes men were waiting for me at the entrance. They let me go in the evening, but I didn't get to see Steinhardt.

Scene 55

Eichmann in his private room. Enter Wisliceny.

WISLICENY. Heil Hitler! (*Eichmann replies in kind.*) Telegram from Berlin. Reduction of manpower in all nonessential units. They want officers on the front.

EICHMANN. Don't worry, Dieter. They won't take officers your age.

WISLICENY. With the Americans already in Paris, nobody will consider my age, sir.

EICHMANN. There are still four hundred thousand Jews left in Hungary that the Führer is determined to get rid of. He won't let you leave even if the Americans enter Germany. (*Enter Guard.*)

GUARD. Heil Hitler! (*Eichmann replies in kind.*) The Jews are here, sir . . .

EICHMANN. Tell them to wait. . . . (*Eichmann goes into the offices of the SS, where Kastner and Hansi are waiting for him. He gets straight to the point.*) All emigration permits are canceled, Kastner. You can tear up the lists you've submitted and throw them in the garbage. That's what I'm doing with the telegrams I get from Brand. The two weeks I gave him were up ten days ago.

KASTNER. But, Herr Obersturmbannführer, the Americans are not willing to start negotiations because you've increased the number of transports to Auschwitz.

EICHMANN. I made no secrets about the transports. But I also promised that I'd keep them in the cooler. I've kept my end of the bargain, but you, in your conniving despicable Jewish ways, are now trying to be wise, eh? The permits are canceled.

KASTNER. But, sir, we did have an agreement. There's a signed protocol of our meeting, and we prepared the list at your request. We also paid you. And now you tell us that the agreement is canceled?! This can't go on like this, sir . . .

EICHMANN. Your nerves are about to give out, Kastner. You probably need a vacation. How about Theresienstadt, eh? Or, perhaps you'd prefer Auschwitz?

KASTNER. I won't give in to threats, sir. Whatever may be waiting for me in Auschwitz, could be waiting for me behind that door right now.

EICHMANN. Don't put me to the test, Kastner!

KASTNER. We both know, sir, that nobody else is willing to negotiate with you.

HANSI. If we don't get the emigration permits today, sir, I'll notify my husband in Istanbul to stop the negotiations at once. But if we do . . .

EICHMANN. I see that Mrs. Brand is in fact Mr. Brand, eh? If your husband stops the negotiations in Istanbul, the meat grinders will start up in Auschwitz, grinding up twenty thousand Jews every day . . .

HANSI. But if we do get the permits, my husband would have solid proof for the American Ambassador that you could be trusted. It's the only way we can make progress with the Big Deal, sir . . .

EICHMANN. You'll get the permits. You'll have your train, but on one condition. You tell me, once and for all, when will your husband be back with an agreement signed and sealed.

HANSI. Within a week.

EICHMANN. A week. Very well, one week it is. If he is not here by then with an agreement, the chimneys of Auschwitz will start spitting you out, all of you, up to the sky. And I am known as a man of my word. (*Exit Eichmann. Blackout.*)

Scene 56

BRAND. (*To Audience.*) Like a trapped animal I've been roaming the suburbs of Istanbul for a whole week . . . waiting for the "Head of the Political Department of the Jewish Agency," Moshe Sharett. How long does it take for a man like him to get a visa to Turkey? Doesn't he understand that every day twelve thousand Jews are sent from Hungary to Auschwitz? Doesn't he understand that only Eichmann's word stands between them and the gas chamber? And I don't believe that the British refuse to let him out of Jerusalem. . . . That makes no sense. . . . All the excuses, pretexts, and explanations I've been getting from representatives of the Jewish Agency sound absurd, bordering on madness. . . . What the hell is going on here?

Scene 57

Kastner's Office. Kastner and Hansi.

KASTNER. (*Exhausted.*) One day, when it's all over, I'll meet this man somewhere, and I'll . . .

HANSI. Rezsö . . . if you don't get hold of yourself, you'll ruin everything. You mustn't show him the slightest sign of weakness.

SECRETARY. (*Enters.*) Baron Stern wants to see you, Dr. Kastner . . . (*Enter Stern, exit Secretary.*)

STERN. Kastner, I hear that besides the twelve hundred places for the Budapest communities, you're keeping another three hundred for your family and friends in your home town . . .

KASTNER. That's no secret. It was Krumey's decision. I didn't ask him for anything for myself.

STERN. You mean to tell me that Krumey has forced you to keep three hundred places for your family?

KASTNER. I didn't ask him for it. He knows that I'm from Cluj, and he's suggested that a whole group could emigrate from there. Not only my family.

STERN. Mr. Kastner, I can accept your explanation because I know you. But all over Budapest they're saying behind your back that you've deserted the Community and worry only about your own family.

KASTNER. Let them say whatever they like.

HANSI. Your family will be on that train, too, sir. And most of the families of the whole Judenrat. . . . Many industrialists and bankers, plus fifty people in the Szatmár Rebbe's group. . . . What's the difference between them and our families and friends?

STERN. I'm very sorry, but the number of people who are getting out because of their personal connection with me is no more than six or seven. . . . The bankers and industrialists on the lists are the people who are paying for the train itself. You're taking three hundred people from Cluj who have paid nothing.

KASTNER. You're wrong, sir. They have promised, in writing, to pay us the moment they're safely out. They all have some capital abroad . . .

STERN. I'm a man of experience, Kastner. Let me give you a piece of advice. The moment you make private use of your right to lead the community, you will lose that right.

KASTNER. I don't need that right. My conscience is clean. If there is anybody in this room who can manage things better, well, let him, more power to him. I'd be glad to join my family on that train . . . (*Enter Freudiger, ashen faced. Pause.*) What's the matter?

FREUDIGER. Two refugees from Auschwitz just got here. In twenty days, more than three hundred thousand of our people have been killed in the gas chambers. Eichmann didn't keep his promise. He didn't keep anybody in the cooler. From the day Brand left, Eichmann had the meat grinders going. Without selections. They didn't even bother to make them undress, or to separate men from the women. Walked them right into the showers. Until they ran out of cyanide. The ovens worked day and night until they cracked because of the tremendous heat. Hell! Hell! Three hundred thousand men, women, and children.

KASTNER. How can that be? How could they have kept this a secret until now?

FREUDIGER. These refugees have prepared a report complete with numbers, dates, and names of the different communities. (*Holds a sheet of paper in front of Kastner and Stern.*)

KASTNER. (*Looking at the sheet.*) How can it be? I spoke to Eichmann two days ago. He gave us a week. I've got the minutes of that meeting; Krumey himself signed it. Where are these two refugees? I want to talk to them.

FREUDIGER. They're hiding.

KASTNER. I've got to talk to them. . . . The facts I have are very different. Brand's already in Ankara; he's talked to the American Ambassador. We're expecting a draft of the agreement any time now. Where are these refugees hiding?

FREUDIGER. They're afraid to be seen. They wouldn't talk to anybody.

KASTNER. All right, then I'm going to see Eichmann.

HANSI. Eichmann? Wait a minute. What do you think he's going to tell you?

KASTNER. (*Coming back.*) Let's not jump to conclusions so fast. This whole thing could be a leak arranged by the Hungarians. They know about Brand's mission, and obviously they want it to fail. That's why they've fabricated this report. Baron Stern, I suggest you sound out the Hungarians, I'll check with the Germans. I sure hope I'm not mistaken. (*Exit.*)

FREUDIGER. That man is lost. We're all lost.

STERN. Three hundred thousand people . . . women . . . the elderly . . . children . . . marching into the long building . . . into the showers. . . . I can see them . . . they're walking in . . . then the furnaces . . . here, they're throwing bodies in. . . . I can hear the voices . . . the shouts of the guards . . . the crackling noises of the flames . . . they're burning in the ovens . . . the smoke . . . (*Blackout.*)

Scene 58

Eichmann's private room. Eichmann and Krumey.

EICHMANN. What's happened to you, Hermann? You've become a Jew lover? You've exterminated two million Jews in Poland, almost without any help from me? Has Kastner managed to turn your head?

KRUMEY. Sir, with your own hands you've destroyed our last chance to negotiate with the Americans. Nobody's going to believe us any more. Because of this stupid fanaticism, they won't leave a stone standing in the whole Reich.

EICHMANN. Don't try to fool me, Hermann. You're not so worried about the Reich, only about yourself. You think that, if you help Kastner save a few Jews, they won't hang you after the war?

KRUMEY. Loyalty to the Reich is not measured only by the extermination of the Jews, sir. (*Exit.*)

Scene 59

BRAND. (*To Audience.*) At last I've met Moshe Sharett. For eighteen hours straight, I sat and talked. I told him everything. He listened and took notes. A few British officers were also present. They took notes, too. They were all shocked. None of them had any idea of the extent of the horror. I hope that things will happen fast from now on. The British have promised to relay their notes to the Americans. . . . Sharett has promised to fly to London and talk with government officials there. He's asked me to accompany him to Jerusalem. Later, I realized that the British had made their assistance conditional on my staying in their hands. I knew what was waiting for Hansi and the children if I delayed. . . . But I had no choice . . .

Scene 60

Eichmann in his office. Helmut knocks on the door.

HELMUT. Kastner wants to see you, sir.

EICHMANN. Tell him to come back tomorrow.

HELMUT. He says it's urgent, sir. Something about a secret of the Reich.

EICHMANN. Tell him to wait. (*Eichmann goes down to the offices of the SS.*) What's so urgent, Kastner?

KASTNER. We've got a report from Auschwitz, sir. Until now, three hundred thousand of Hungary's Jews have been killed in the gas chambers. You've deceived me all along. You started sending Jews to the gas chambers the very day Brand left for Istanbul. You've never intended to let one Jew escape your clutches. Brand will be back in three days with an agreement. How many Jews can you give him? How many?

EICHMANN. Brand will not come back, Kastner. This very moment Brand is in a Cairo jail and your people at the Jewish Agency can't or don't want to do anything to free him. And it seems that neither the British nor the Americans are too keen on having a surplus of Jews on their hands.

KASTNER. Brand will come back. I've got a telegram about an interim agreement. The agreement itself will be sent by mail.

EICHMANN. Brand will *not* come back, Kastner. He's been imprisoned, charged with being a German agent. Funny, eh?

KASTNER. He won't come back?

EICHMANN. No. Nobody was willing even to listen to him.

KASTNER. That's why you sent *him.* You knew all along that Brand was not the right man for this mission. If I had gone, the agreement would have already been signed by Weizmann.

EICHMANN. This deal is dead, Kastner. Weizmann didn't even bother to go to Istanbul, despite your beautiful telegrams.

KASTNER. If this deal is dead, as you say, we'll find another one. This war is just about over. In a few months, the situation will be very different. People who've been responsible for all sorts of deeds will be brought to justice. If you give me Jews now, I'd be ready to . . .

EICHMANN. You want Jews on credit, Kastner? Eh? On account? You'll pay me in six months? I'm not your man for a deal like that . . .

KASTNER. Let's play with all the cards on the table, Herr Eichmann. I know you'll do everything to send as many Jews as possible to Auschwitz. But I also know that you have to make a deal with me. I've got my own sources of information. You've got orders from the Reichsführer, and you've got no choice. You have to carry out these orders.

EICHMANN. In my own good time.

KASTNER. Auschwitz is all filled up. You have no more gas. You must make a deal now.

EICHMANN. We'll throw the Jews into the ovens alive.

KASTNER. You may have enough people to throw dead Jews into the fire, but not enough to throw in live ones. The deal I have for you is the easiest way to get rid of Jews.

EICHMANN. What deal is that?

KASTNER. There are still four hundred thousand Jews left in Hungary. Let them get out of here. Instead of trucks, you'll get tractors, bulldozers, heavy equipment. All your roads are ruined, you need that sort of machinery.

EICHMANN. What assurances do I have that you can get hold of such equipment? Once you promised me trucks, remember?

KASTNER. This time I'll take care of everything myself. You know what I'm capable of doing.

EICHMANN. Yes, I do. But time is running out. And Jews are running out, too. I don't know if you'll have any left by the time you get back. Not even the fifteen hundred you want to send out by train.

KASTNER. (*Calmly.*) Those are not part of this deal. The Red Cross already has their names. If any one of these people is harmed, the Red Cross will abandon your POWs in the hands of the Russians.

EICHMANN. The train will get out. I won't touch it.

KASTNER. I'll go to Zurich to see about the heavy equipment. I'll need proof for the Americans that this deal is really going through.

EICHMANN. What kind of proof?

KASTNER. A hundred thousand Jews will be let out of Germany.

EICHMANN. A hundred thousand?

KASTNER. They'll leave within a month, under my personal supervision. Until I see them with my own eyes safe in a neutral country, there won't be any deal.

EICHMANN. I want two hundred dollars per skull to cover travel expenses.

KASTNER. One hundred dollars. And you'll get that only when they reach a place where you can't get at them.

EICHMANN. A hundred and fifty.

KASTNER. A hundred and fifty for every healthy Jew. Fifty each for the old and the sick.

EICHMANN. Seventy-five for the curable sick. (*Blackout.*)

Scene 61

HANSI. (*To Audience.*) There were those who said that Rezsö had thought of himself as the Savior . . . an angel . . . just a little less than God. Others said of him that he was the Angel of Death. . . . Let them say what they will, it cannot be denied that Rezsö saved thousands . . . maybe tens of thousands. . . . I don't have too much faith in history either. History's verdict will be pronounced by those who'll write it, and not by those who have made it . . .

EPILOGUE

KASTNER. (*Ironic.*) During the course of my negotiations with Eichmann, I cooperated with him in the extermination of Hungarian Jewry. So claimed the prosecution, and everybody who had been looking for explanations for the Holocaust held on to that accusation. Of course, Kastner's collaboration made the destruction possible. Kastner is the explanation for the Holocaust.

And, as opposed to Kastner, there arose a number of people who had sole rights to heroism. Without a shadow of a doubt, during the war, the Jewish people produced great heroes. Their names have been inscribed in our national honor rolls in golden letters. But how many Jews did these heroes save? What was the purpose of their heroism? And the man who managed to wrest a whole train from the claws of the Nazis, with 1,684 live Jews on it, that man is a collaborator. (*Transition to the train station. Enter Helen and Bogyo.*)

HELEN. I've heard so many stories about this train, Rezsö. Why can't we go to Vienna by car, we could get on the train there . . .

KASTNER. You're not the only one, Mother. We can't take everybody by car.

HELEN. Maybe you should get on with us, Rezsö; who knows where we might wind up without you . . .

KASTNER. Don't worry, Mother, you'll get to Zurich. Your passport is in the bag. I put your medicine in your pocketbook.

HELEN. The eye drops, too?

KASTNER. Yes, yes, of course. (*Train whistle is heard.*)

BOGYO. I don't know what to believe anymore, but look, this train is leaving, just as you said it would.

KASTNER. I'll have to see about the other trains. I hope to get to Zurich in a few days.

BOGYO. You won't forget to bring the suitcase with my coats, will you, Rezsö?

KASTNER. No, no. . . . I've made a special note of that. How could I forget something like that?

BOGYO. Good-bye. (*They hug.*) Take care of yourself, Rezsö.

KASTNER. Good-bye, Mother. (*They hug. Kastner hugs Bogyo again. Exeunt Helen and Bogyo.*) (*Ironic.*) In return for this train, I kept the truth about Auschwitz from the Jews in the ghettos, and that is why they boarded the trains as meekly as sheep go to slaughter. So claimed the prosecution. Your Honor, the only ghetto in all of Europe whose population stayed alive was the Budapest ghetto, despite the lack of acts which people would now consider heroic.

The ghetto was saved because of my connections with Hermann Krumey and Kurt Becher. With their help, I sent four additional trains to Vienna and also managed to put a stop to further extermination of people at Bergen-Belsen and Theresienstadt. Because of these connections, the prosecution called me "the best agent of the Nazis." Many whose families I could not save thought the same. (*Transition to railway station. Enter Freudiger.*)

FREUDIGER. I've tried to get permits for my family. With my poor connections, I couldn't. Yours are so much better, Kastner, please . . .

KASTNER. Right now?

FREUDIGER. Yes. My wife and children are waiting just outside the station.

KASTNER. I don't know what to tell you. You know very well yourself. There's a list. I can't make changes now.

FREUDIGER. Only five permits, that's all. A drop in the bucket. I'll pay any amount of money. I beg of you . . .

KASTNER. The train must leave any second. I can't hold it up for five permits. Who knows what might happen here in the meantime!

FREUDIGER. Kastner . . . only my wife and kids . . . (*Kastner does not reply.*) Kastner . . . (*Exit Freudiger.*)

KASTNER. (*To Audience.*) Eventually, all leaders of the Jewish Community got out. I stayed. Until the very end. When I came here, to Israel, after the war, I got a very cool reception, to put it mildly. The heroism of those who had fought in the ghettos doesn't need my praises. Had I perished in the Budapest ghetto, I'd be counted among them. But Kastner is a traitor. The District Court of Jerusalem ruled that I "sold my soul to the devil." My life has become hell. On the third of March, 1957, just before midnight, I was returning from the editorial offices of *Uj Kelet*.* Near my house a young man approached me and asked: "Are you Dr. Kastner?" I said, "Yes. . . ." He pulled out a gun, aimed it at my temple and pulled the trigger. The gun did not go off. I ran into the house and got as far as the staircase when I heard a shot. The bullet bounced off the iron railing. I kept on running. Then I heard a second shot. This time he got me. In the back. (*Blackout.*)

THE END

*Israel's Hungarian newspaper.

Joshua Sobol

Joshua Sobol was born in Tel Mond, Palestine, in 1939. He lived on Kibbutz Shamir and in Haifa before moving to Tel Aviv, his present residence. He studied philosophy at the Sorbonne. He is a director as well as a playwright and has staged many of his own plays in Europe, Israel, and the United States.

Sobol has written over thirty plays, including *The Night of the Twentieth* (1976), *Soul of a Jew* (1982), *Ghetto* (1984), *The Palestinian Girl* (1985), *Jerusalem Syndrome* (1987), *Adam* (1990), *Underground* (1991), *Solo for Spinoza* (1991), *Eye to Eye* (1992), and *Schneider and Shuster* (1993).

Sobol's plays have been translated into more than a dozen languages and have been staged throughout European and America. The National Theater production of *Ghetto*, the first of his trilogy of plays about the Vilna ghetto, won the London Evening Standard Award and the London Critics Award for the best play of 1989.

Adam

1989

(Translated by Ron Jenkins)

Characters

OLD NADYA, seventy years old.
YOUNG NADYA, twenty years old.
SEP, seventy years old.
ADAM, forty-five years old.
GENS, forty-three years old.

KITTEL, twenty-six years old.
LEV, twenty-five years old.
LACHMAN, thirty-five years old.
ZALTSMAN, thirty-five years old.
ROZIN, forty years old.
NIUSSIA, twenty-five years old.
MIRA, twenty-three years old.

Place and Time

The play takes place today in old Nadya's apartment in Tel Aviv as well as in her imagination and memory. She has actually experienced some of the scenes. Others, she has heard, read, or recounted so many times that they, too, although fictitious, have become part of her memory.

The acting area is surrounded by total darkness. The characters emerge from the darkness to act out their scenes in the light and then vanish again into the darkness. Places should be indicated by one motif, which should be dimly lit throughout the scene. For instance, Gen's office is characterized by a map of Europe, which should always be lit dimly whenever a scene takes place there.

EPILOGUE PLAYED AS PROLOGUE

Total darkness. A concentrated beam of light focuses on a human figure. It is Adam. He is sitting on a chair upstage, elbows on knees, head buried in the palms of his handcuffed hands. The voice of a woman screaming is heard from nearby. This screaming, which is accompanied by the constant sobbing of a child, will be repeated throughout the scene. Adam lifts his head and listens. He stands up. He puts his ear to the wall and listens carefully.

CHILD'S VOICE. (*Sobbing.*) Mama . . . Mama . . . (*A Nazi officer in uniform appears from the darkness. This is Kittel. He approaches Adam stealthily, observes him for a while, then speaks.*)
KITTEL. Fascinating, isn't it. Sit down. There's nothing quite as riveting as human suffering, is there? I mean, of course, the suffering of others. (*He opens the file he is holding.*) Adam Rolenik? (*Adam nods.*) Age forty-five, married, father of . . .
ADAM. A childless widower.
KITTEL. You mean Kaslaskas was lying?
ADAM. He met my wife before the war. She's dead now.

KITTEL. The children too, I presume?

ADAM. I never had any. (*The screaming and crying are heard once more.*)

KITTEL. (*Referring to the scream.*) Listen carefully. You know the woman?

ADAM. No.

KITTEL. Of course not. Any idea why she's being tortured? No . . . like a guess? No . . . listen carefully, comrade Rolenik. That woman is innocent. The little girl is her daughter. Why is her mother being tortured before her eyes? She doesn't know. Neither does her mother. She's innocent and as pure as spring snow . . . not a member of the underground, not a freedom fighter. Why then, you ask, is she being so cruelly tortured? She's being tortured because of you. The moment you open your mouth and start cooperating, she'll be released. Where are your wife and children hiding?

ADAM. I am a childless widower. (*Scream.*)

KITTEL. You really don't give a damn about her suffering, do you? You're the one who's torturing this woman, you and your stubbornness. I'm sure she's praying to God for mercy, not knowing that you're her God now, and you don't care. What's it feel like being God? Up on those lofty heights? Oh, I am enjoying your performance. Thank you so much. I look at you and see the universe. You are offered the chance to save a life, and what do you do? You thank the stars that you're not in her place, that you've saved your own children from the fate of that poor woman's daughter. (*Screaming and crying.*) All right, I'll make it easier for you. This woman isn't even one of your people. She's a foreigner. Does that ease your conscience? You must be wondering why I'm telling you all this? Well, because I don't give a shit about the "information" you're withholding. I don't care whether you have a wife and children or not, and I care even less who rescued you from our police. I only want one thing: to show you that you're no better than I am, because if you're honest, you've got to admit that foreigners mean less to you than your own people, and your own people mean less to you than your comrades, and your comrades mean less to you than your children. (*Adam lifts his fingers to his mouth and seems to be biting his nails.*) You can bite your nails as much as you like, but you can't help admitting that you've never been and can never be a friend of Mankind, because he who is indifferent to the fate of one human being justifies man's universal indifference to his fellow man, and that's exactly what you're doing now. Where are your wife and children hiding, and who grabbed you away from our police? Probably, the same ones who decided to hand you over when they realized it was either them or you. Correct me if I'm wrong. (*Screaming and crying.*)

ADAM. Stop torturing her.

KITTEL. Who were those men? . . .

ADAM. (*Taking his fingers from his mouth.*) I'm not a member of any underground. I'm a criminal. I was in a gang. We'd been committing crimes. Smuggling. Killing. Stealing. That's why I tried to get guns. (*He speaks with growing difficulty.*) The men who helped me escape were members of the gang . . . I have no wife . . . no children . . . I'm childless . . . a widower . . . "Adam"'s my nickname in the gang; my real name's . . .

KITTEL. (*Shouting*) STOP IT. ENOUGH OF THIS CHILDREN'S GAME. IT DOESN'T SUIT YOU, OR ME. NOW LISTEN CAREFULLY. I KNOW EXACTLY WHO YOU ARE. BUT SO FAR, I'M THE ONLY ONE WHO KNOWS. TOMORROW WE'LL HAND YOU OVER TO OUR "SPECIALISTS" WHO WILL CONFRONT YOU WITH KASLASKAS; AND WHEN THEY DISCOVER THE TRUTH, YOU'LL BE RESPONSIBLE FOR THE ANNIHILATION OF THE GHETTO. SO PLEASE HELP YOURSELF . . . (*He offers Adam some pills.*) "FRIEND HAST THOU NONE." *Measure for Measure,* act 3, scene 1. IF I WERE YOU, I'D TAKE THESE PILLS AND GO TO SLEEP. GOOD NIGHT. (*Blackout.*)

Transition to Scene 1

Old Nadya's voice is heard in the dark. First whispering, then getting louder, her muttering brings a gradual brightening of the light, which transforms the stage into an Israeli midsummer night under a full moon. The roof appears as an island floating in an ocean of night. Mountainous landscape in the distance. Scores of lights from farms and villages shine and twinkle on the mountain peaks. On the other side of the mountain, some eternal Middle Eastern war is being waged. Its echoes roll like thunderstorms in the distance.

Scene 1

Darkness. Old Nadya's voice.

OLD NADYA. No. . . . No. . . . Please don't. . . . No . . .

SEP. Nadya? (*He puts on the light.*)

OLD NADYA. (*Sitting in an armchair, trembling.*) Bastards . . . bastards . . . you're all bastards . . .

SEP. (*Shaking her.*) Nadya . . .

OLD NADYA. Adam?

SEP. Not Adam. It's Sep. Me, Sep! (*He caresses her hair. He is seventy. Tall, slim, well-groomed, a playboy past his prime.*)

OLD NADYA. What is it, where am I?

SEP. Don't upset yourself, Nadya. We're home.

OLD NADYA. Where?

SEP. Our house in Tel Aviv.

OLD NADYA. What am I doing here?

SEP. You fell asleep. (*He takes off her shoes.*)

OLD NADYA. What are you doing?

SEP. Come to bed.

OLD NADYA. What time is it?

SEP. Past midnight.

OLD NADYA. Oh my God, we've missed our performance again.

SEP. Which performance?

OLD NADYA. We should have been there by eight.

SEP. Our performance is on Sunday, Nadya. Today's only Friday.

OLD NADYA. He came out of the office. He was tall, straight as an arrow. We were all standing around. (*Sep, who is hearing the story for the n'th time, doesn't even pretend to listen anymore; he starts humming a tune and dancing to it, which doesn't stop Nadya, who goes on telling her story to her imaginary audience.*) No one dared look him in the eye. We all lowered our heads. He took off his gun holster and handed it to Lev. "Here. Now you're in command." Then he looked at us all. (*She plays Adam.*) "If you think that sacrificing me will win the masses over to the uprising, you're wrong. Forget the uprising. The people won't follow you. Everyone's out to save his own skin. Their motto is: 'As long as I'm all right, to hell with the others.'" (*Now as Nadya.*) That was the philosophy.

SEP. Yah, how about a vodka?

OLD NADYA. Vodka's fine. "We have failed, comrades, we have failed. When the last day comes, they'll all go meekly to the trains, without the slightest resistance. They'll just line up and get into the wagons like good children going to bed." . . . And that's exactly how it was. We stood on the rooftops, clutching our guns, while the people walked to the trains like they were walking to the movies. He saw it all coming. No mistake.

SEP. (*Handing her a glass of vodka.*) Here, sweetheart.

OLD NADYA. Thanks, dearie. Cheers.

SEP. Cheers, my love . . . (*They drink.*)

OLD NADYA. They just sacrificed themselves.

SEP. That's the way it was.

OLD NADYA. No chance now for a good night's sleep.

SEP. Sunday, you'll tell them all.

OLD NADYA. Yeah, I'll tell them. I hope it's a youth club this time.

SEP. No, it's an old people's home.

OLD NADYA. Oh no, they start snoring after fifteen minutes . . .

SEP. Then old Sep will wake them up with his tricks: HOP! (*Throws up his handkerchief, which turns into a stick, which he catches and throws once more.*) HOP! (*Explosion. A cloud of smoke. Part of the wall turns and brings in Kittel. He is standing close to the wall with his back to the audience, facing a map of Europe on the wall.*)

Scene 2

Kittel's office. Kittel studies the map of Europe. Gens enters.

GENS. Good evening. (*Kittel does not answer or turn, so Gens tries again, raising his voice.*) Good evening.

KITTEL. (*Turns, faking astonishment.*) What brings you here?

GENS. I was told you wanted to see me.

KITTEL. Walk out through that door, close it behind you, then knock and wait till I say "come in." Then open the door, stand at attention, salute, and say, "Good evening, sir, may I come in, sir?" Only then, and only if I say yes, close the door behind you, and enter. Is that clear?

GENS. Yes, sir. (*Turns to the door.*)

KITTEL. Gens! What are you doing?

GENS. Following your orders.

KITTEL. Have you lost your mind? What's wrong with you? Can't you take a joke anymore? Come on, old man, come here. How are you?

GENS. Fine.

KITTEL. And your beautiful wife, and your daughter?

GENS. They're fine, thank you.

KITTEL. Good, good. You know what I've noticed? You never ask me how I am.

GENS. I'm your subordinate.

KITTEL. That's not a reason, Gens. You Jews. You grovel if someone's got you by the balls, but as soon as you taste freedom, you become arrogant pigs. You don't know how to give . . . yes! That's the problem. You just don't know how to give.

GENS. What do you want me to give you?

KITTEL. No, please, not like that. You see. You've already spoiled everything. Give me something without asking. Learn from us Christians. I have a Lithuanian cook. A simple man. He went to his village for Christmas; and when he returned, he brought me a bottle of homemade vodka, brewed by his mother. And let me tell you. He didn't feel that giving me this bottle was like selling his mother, or some part of himself, compromising his existence or integrity. You see? It's precisely this Christian generosity that you Jews are missing. When you're asked to give something, you suddenly feel a threat to your very existence, as if every small present expected of you is meant to rob you of your soul.

GENS. The day I have a country of my own, with vineyards and wine cellars, I'll be delighted to offer you a case of wines, from the best of my collection.

KITTEL. You see. You immediately translate everything into materialistic terms.

GENS. Tell me what you want, and I'll do my best.

KITTEL. Who's the manager of the public bath?

GENS. The public bath? . . . Rolenick . . .

KITTEL. Adam Rolenick?

GENS. Yes. Adam Rolenick.

KITTEL. Give him to me.

GENS. What?

KITTEL. You promised to give me everything I asked for.

GENS. Yes.

KITTEL. I want to open a bath in my headquarters.

GENS. I see.

KITTEL. So will you give me the man?

GENS. Of course, with pleasure. (*He pulls out a small agenda and examines it.*) Let me see . . . the Board of Managers meeting . . . next Sunday. . . . I'll notify him. Should I tell him to be at your office on Monday, or will you send a car to pick him up.

KITTEL. I need him tonight.

GENS. Tonight? Is the bath so urgent?

KITTEL. Terribly urgent. I'll be in your office tonight at 11:15 to pick him up.

GENS. Anything you say.

KITTEL. So, what should we drink? I have vodka, some excellent Hungarian Baratz, French Cognac . . .

GENS. I'll have strychnine, if you don't mind . . .

KITTEL. What's this? . . .

GENS. Or cyanide, or I could shoot myself in my office, without your permission, but then you'd take revenge on innocent people, so I'm requesting permission to blow my brains out here and now, sir.

KITTEL. Are you sick?

GENS. Sick to death.

KITTEL. What are you suffering from?

GENS. You.

KITTEL. I beg your pardon?

GENS. You want to see me, I come . . . and you act like a sergeant with a new recruit. You lecture me on our lack of generosity, I try to take you seriously, and then you ask me to give you a man's head.

KITTEL. Who asked for his head?

GENS. You're making a fool of me. I'm not a court jester, and with all due respect, I won't put up with this treatment.

KITTEL. Watch your tongue.

GENS. Kill me now. I will not live one minute past the liquidation of the ghetto anyway.

KITTEL. Who wants to liquidate the ghetto?

GENS. You do.

KITTEL. What makes you think that?

GENS. I'm the only person who can control the ghetto and give the people a sense of security, some hope for survival. As long as you needed me, you treated me with respect. Now I can only conclude that you don't need me anymore. So arrest me. I won't fool my people into believing there's a chance of survival when there isn't.

KITTEL. (*Interrupting.*) If I wanted to liquidate the ghetto, I'd let you choose immediately: death by your gun or ours. And you know damn well why. You're the only one capable of leading an armed uprising, and I know you would if you thought the end were near.

GENS. That's as true as I stand here.

KITTEL. So let me tell you the truth. I'm very interested in the survival of your lousy ghetto because as long as this goddamn ghetto is here, I'm here; and as long as I'm here, this ghetto will exist, if you cooperate.

GENS. I've always done what I can, and I'll keep on doing it, but I'm not omnipotent.

KITTEL. Neither am I. There's been a lot of evidence lately linking the partisans in the forest to certain ghetto elements. I want you to know this could lead to the end. That's been our policy since the uprising in Warsaw. If I get an order to liquidate the ghetto, I'll have to carry it out. Is that clear?

GENS. Yes. That's the kind of language I understand.

KITTEL. So what do you say?

GENS. We have a common interest.

KITTEL. If you were born German, you'd be a general . . .

GENS. Given the circumstances, forgive me for preferring to be a Russian.

KITTEL. Still, if you were German . . .

GENS. I'd find a way to contact the leaders of the Communist Party.

KITTEL. The Communist Party does not exist.

GENS. The leaders do. If I had the means at your disposal, I'd have found them. I'd think only of the future.

KITTEL. With my kind of past?

GENS. Every regime needs and uses people with your kind of talent and experience. Now's the time to start using 150 percent of your intelligence.

KITTEL. This Adam Rolenick is a Communist, isn't he?

GENS. Before the war, I think he was an important member of the party.

KITTEL. I'll be in your office tonight at 11:15.

GENS. You're always welcome. Feel free to enter without knocking.

Scene 3

Old Sep and Old Nadya.

SEP. HOP! (*He makes some magic. Kittel and Gens disappear into the darkness. It's once more the Israeli summer night with war waging in the distance. Sep reacts to the remote audio-visual presence of war.*) FIGHTING. FIGHTING. ZA RA ZA. YOU IDIOTS. ZA RA ZA ZAM. GO ON, KILL ONE AN OTHER ZA RA ZA. HOP! *ET VOILA* . . .

OLD NADYA. THEY'RE SHOOTING AGAIN.

SEP. BARBARIANS. ZA RA ZA. LET THEM CUT ONE ANOTHER'S THROATS FOR ALL I CARE. ZA RA ZA. ZA RA ZA ZAM. *ET VOILA.*

OLD NADYA. I FEEL PRESSURE ON MY HEART. (*Sep stops his tricks and approaches her.*) THE AIR IS SO HEAVY. (*Sep puts his hands on her neck and starts massaging. She puts her hand on her breast.*) WHEN I BREATHE DEEPLY, IT HURTS.

SEP. IT'S NOTHING.

OLD NADYA. I'M NOT AFRAID OF THE END. I ONLY HOPE WHEN IT COMES, THERE WON'T BE TOO MUCH SUFFERING.

SEP. THE END IS ALWAYS WITH US, FROM THE BEGINNING. IT'S AT OUR SIDE ALL ALONG THE WAY. IT'S JUST A MATTER OF STEPPING TO THE SIDE, AND HOP! (*He performs a trick.*) HOP! . . .

OLD NADYA. Come here, my devil. (*He comes from behind her back, puts his hands on her breasts, and plays gently, extremely tenderly, with her breasts. She moans with pleasure.*) Oh, Sep . . .

SEP. Yes, darling?

OLD NADYA. None of my lovers fondled my breasts like you do, my Clark Gable . . . and I had plenty of lovers in my day . . . (*In Yiddish.*) *Oy hob ich gehat kavalirn. . . . Avu-hin zeinen zei alle avek?* (*She starts humming to herself.*)

> Wenn mentsh bist yung
> un full mit schwung . . .

(*She goes on singing the song "Ich benk n heim." The song will be heard during the rest of the scene. Adam and young Nadya emerge from the darkness. They're wrapped in a blanket. They move slowly to the song sung simultaneously by both Nadyas, one humming while the other talks and vice versa.*)

OLD NADYA. I remember the first time . . .

ADAM. Not now, Nadya. (*Now Young Nadya sings, while dancing in Adam's arms.*)

OLD NADYA. Sex. That was what kept me alive. (*Sep goes on massaging her neck and shoulders, and Adam answers her while dancing with Young Nadya.*) You won't believe it, I'd already been in the organization for a month, and I didn't know who our commander was.

ADAM. That can't be true. When we first met . . .

OLD NADYA. I'd never been a party member, so I had to find things out for myself. (*Now she starts humming, and Young Nadya picks up the dialogue.*)

ADAM. When we first met, you were already a unit leader.

YOUNG NADYA. That was thanks to my pretty face.

ADAM. Yes, what a face, and what an irresistible charm.

YOUNG NADYA. Of course, that's how I hooked you.

ADAM. That's not true. The moment I saw you . . .

YOUNG NADYA. I noticed you before you knew I existed. I remember . . .

OLD NADYA. The day we first came to the ghetto, they were chasing us through the streets. It was raining, and we were soaked to the skin. We ran to escape their blows, holding hands to keep from losing one another in the crowd. My father, my mother, my sister with her baby, and me. I was seventeen, but I looked fourteen. We were swept along by a human whirlpool, and a current of people pushed us up a staircase into a room. The air was damp and heavy with steaming wet clothes and warm sweating bodies. The whole floor was covered with bodies and more bodies, men and women moaning, groaning, gasping, and yelling, a human floor breathing like some huge sea animal thrown ashore, heaving and panting with legs flailing in the air, and bodies melting into legs, and bodies sinking between extended legs, and bodies. . . . They were all doing it, everybody screwing everybody, men, women screwing, man and wife or just man and woman, and me standing there to this day wanting someone to take me and lay me down on this human floor and screw me, but no one pays attention to me. . . . It was my baptism by fire . . . as if the people felt deep down inside that this was it, that one world was gone, and whoever wanted to live. . . . So they did it together like some kind of ritual to declare that here was the brave new world, or maybe it was out of naked fear that people clung together, and someone started it, and it caught on like brush fire . . .

YOUNG NADYA. In two years, we'll get married; and in five, I'll have your baby.

ADAM. Nadya! . . . Stop it. I have to go.

YOUNG NADYA. I hate you. I hate you.

ADAM. Nadya, what's come over you?

YOUNG NADYA. Come back to me please . . .

ADAM. (*Breaks away from her.*) Of course I will. (*As Adam and Young Nadya embrace, Old Nadya speaks.*)

OLD NADYA. That was Adam. He cut quite a figure. Most people's faces are depressed and beaten, marked by expressions of defeat that say, "We're lost." But your face always burns self assurance. He was so handsome. One day I came to rehearse in the theater and you were there talking to Gens. That's when I first knew that our future was in your hands, not Gens's. That was the night of the unit commanders meetings, and you came to tell us your plan for breaking out of the ghetto, and I finally realized you were our commander. At that moment I lost all doubts. I was proud of belonging to the United Partisans' Organization, and I felt so sure. Yes, the UPO. I felt secure. I just wanted to feel those strong arms embrace me . . .

YOUNG NADYA. You know, you really could have been a movie star.

ADAM. Do you realize how superficial you are?

YOUNG NADYA. Of course I do. I'm vain and superficial. I love you. And one day when you realize how shallow I am, you'll leave me.

ADAM. And one day you'll find out that my looks are a lie.

OLD NADYA. I wasn't the only victim. Every girl in the UPO was in love with him.

YOUNG NADYA. I love you. (*They kiss. Old Nadya sings.*)

OLD NADYA. *Ich will noch ein mall sehn mein heim* . . .

YOUNG NADYA. You remember that first night at the "Jugent Klub" when I asked you to dance?

OLD NADYA. A great dancer he was not . . .

YOUNG NADYA. When we went out to the cold, dark street I was next to you, and Niussia was walking behind us. I didn't know she was in love with you . . . and I whispered in your ear: "If we were alone I'd warm you." . . . So who started it, me or you?

ADAM. But, I hugged you.

OLD NADYA. Yeah, yeah, that's how it was . . . (*She stops humming. Adam gets out from under the blanket he was wrapped in with Young Nadya. He is naked. He pulls on his shorts and starts putting on his clothes, which are spread all over in disarray.*)

YOUNG NADYA. (*Wrapping the blanket around her.*) What if you didn't go?

ADAM. I've got to go. You heard Niussia. Gens called all the HQ members to an urgent meeting. But I'll be back soon, and we'll have the rest of the night to ourselves. (*He picks up an artificial beard.*) Can you help me put this thing on?

YOUNG NADYA. Sit down. (*She sticks the beard to his face and places a white wig on his head.*) You know, people really believe you've left the ghetto. My mother told me there was a rumor you'd disappeared. She was so happy when I said, "I don't know where he is. Haven't seen him since last week." Can't you stop hiding now? It's been a week since they arrested that Lithuanian Communist.

ADAM. Kaslaskas?

YOUNG NADYA. Yes, and nothing's happened.

ADAM. Yeah . . . but you can never be sure. It's better to be safe. I hope nobody recognizes me on the street.

YOUNG NADYA. Even I wouldn't. (*She looks at him.*) My grandfather! You could play King Lear.

ADAM. Then you'd better get rid of me.

YOUNG NADYA. Any other ideas?

ADAM. You're only nineteen.

YOUNG NADYA. Twenty. In eight months I'll be twenty.

ADAM. You're so young.

YOUNG NADYA. You think if I left you it would make me older?

ADAM. I could be your father.

YOUNG NADYA. You remind me more of my mother.

OLD NADYA. (*Playing her own mother.*) How old is he?

YOUNG NADYA. Half past forty, Mama.

OLD NADYA. How dreadful. What's his status?

YOUNG NADYA. Excellent, Mama.

OLD NADYA. I mean bachelor, widower, divorced?

YOUNG NADYA. Married, Mama.

OLD NADYA. That's bad. I hope there're no kids.

YOUNG NADYA. Only two.

OLD NADYA. That's very bad. You'll neglect your career.

SEP. Which career?

OLD NADYA. Acting. In the theater of the ghetto. (*To Young Nadya.*) You'll neglect your career, and he'll leave you to go back to his family.

YOUNG NADYA. I won't neglect my career. I'm playing a lead in our next show.

OLD NADYA. Pray to God. Maybe he'll forgive you.

YOUNG NADYA. I wonder what she means: that God should forgive me for loving a married man, or for helping her less now that I have you to take care of me?

ADAM. Probably both. People usually think of themselves when they start preaching.

OLD NADYA. (*Laughing.*) His wife complained to my father, "Your Nadya is destroying a family." "Nadya is a grown girl," said my father.

BOTH NADYAS. "She can destroy families, she can build families" . . . (*Adam departs into the darkness.*)

YOUNG NADYA. I want to live.

OLD NADYA. (*Clutches Sep's hand.*) Adam! . . .

SEP. Not Adam. Sep. Sep! (*Starts performing a trick.*) Ra cha ra cha / cha ra cha cham / Hop! / Hop! . . .

Scene 4

Gens office. Eleven o'clock at night. A door appears in the darkness, deep upstage. Someone is knocking on it. There is no answer. The door is pushed open slightly, and Rozin's head appears in the opening. He peers carefully into the light, then tells the people behind him:

ROZIN. The door's open.

ADAM. Go in!

ROZIN. (*To empty space.*) Good evening.

ADAM. For God's sake, go in, will you?

ROZIN. (*Enters squeezing his hat.*) Gens? . . . (*To his friends.*) That's strange. No one's here. Maybe we shouldn't be in here.

ADAM. (*Enters, pushing Rozin aside.*) Don't be ridiculous. (*Takes off his wig and beard.*) He'll be here in a minute. (*Niussia, Lev, and Lachman enter behind Adam.*)

LACHMAN. (*To Gens's empty chair.*) His Majesty, Jacob the First, King of the Ghetto! (*He sits in the chair and plays Gens.*) Honorable Ministers, Governors of State, I have invited you to this extraordinary cabinet session to discuss our five-year plan to improve the standard of living in this, our blossoming cemetery.

ROZIN. Lachman, please, he could come any minute.

LACHMAN. (*Stands up and examines the room.*) Something's different.

NIUSSIA. It's the first time we've been here at night.

LACHMAN. It's this drape on the wall. (*He draws an imaginary sword and challenges the carpet, which is now barely revealed, dimly lit, hanging in the darkness.*) How now! A Pat? Dead for a ducat, dead! (*Zaltsman emerges from the darkness. He joins them, panting.*)

ZALTSMAN. What's wrong?

ROZIN. (*Frightened.*) Ha! . . . Zaltsman? . . .

ZALTSMAN. Something about the arrest . . . that Communist . . . what's his name?

LEV. Why? Who told you? Gens?

ZALTSMAN. Averbuch. (*He speaks in single words, wild syntax and grammar. This is part of his character and temperament and has nothing to do with his education, which is in no way deficient.*) Said something. Came running. Any news? Dragged me from the party. What's the matter?

ROZIN. We don't know. That's the problem. That's why Gens called us . . . to ask us . . . isn't it? I don't know . . .

ADAM. Please, don't get so worked up. This isn't the first time Gens has called us here.

ROZIN. At eleven o'clock at night? It is a bit unusual, isn't it?

ADAM. Averbuch's been talking.

ZALTSMAN. Got your pistols on you?

NIUSSIA. We've got two troops on alert.

LEV. Shhhh . . . not so loud.

ZALTSMAN. On alert? Two troops?

NIUSSIA. Mira informed us that Dessler left the ghetto. He's probably gone to the Gestapo and we don't know if it's just to play cards with his friends, as usual, or if he's been called there for a reason.

LEV. Hush, the walls have ears.

ZALTSMAN. (*Thinking aloud.*) Dessler to the Gestapo . . . we to Gens . . . urgent . . . something's up . . . tell me next time . . . I'd have stopped the party . . . put my men on alert.

ADAM. Your group did a terrific job with the train. Let them celebrate.

ZALTSMAN. Celebrate? No. You need support, Adam.

ADAM. There's no need to stir up panic. If anything happens, thirty people on the street are enough for now. (*Gens enters, talking to Mira behind him.*)

GENS. What's today's date?

MIRA. July 15.

GENS. There's no rush. We can put it off till August. (*They enter the lit space. Gens yawns and stretches. Mira writes in a big notebook. Mira is a beautiful blond, stunning, Aryan-looking. She's well dressed with a terrific hairdo. It's as if she'd come from another planet. No one would guess she was Jewish.*)

GENS. (*Discovering the group.*) Oh! . . . (*Covers his yawn.*) Sorry. You're here already? What time is it? (*Looks at his watch.*) Oh, it's eleven. . . . Why so formal? Make yourselves at home. Mira, would you be so kind?

MIRA. What'll you have? (*She goes to the bar, i.e., into the dark.*)

GENS. (*Calls after her.*) Make it vodka. (*He walks toward the drape, gestures as if to push it away with his hands. The drape disappears into the darkness and in its place appears a map of Europe.*) Have you heard the latest news? Radio Moscow reports that the Red Army has taken Krinichky . . .

ROZIN. No! Where's that?

GENS. Well, it's . . . you can't see it on this map . . . it's somewhere over there . . .

ROZIN. And where are we?

GENS. We're . . .

LACHMAN. Up to our ears in shit.

GEN. (*Ignoring the remark.*) . . . There.

ROZIN. No! That means they're not far. The question is what'll they do next?

GENS. All signs suggest that they're preparing an offensive.

ROZIN. No! Did you hear that? The Russians are preparing an

offensive. (*Mira brings a tray with glasses of vodka and passes it around.*) When do you think they'll be here.

GENS. If they keep up their present pace, we should see them here in four, five months.

ROZIN. Well, this is a reason to celebrate!

LACHMAN. Five months? I'll drink to that now, cause in five months we won't be around to welcome them.

NIUSSIA. Spare us.

GENS. I think I can reassure you. I had a revealing talk with Kittel today. The German HQ, on the local level at least, has a keen interest in the ghetto's continued existence.

ROZIN. Of course. As long as we're here, they won't be sent to the front. So can we spread the news in the ghetto?

GENS. Of course.

ROZIN. That's very important, I say, very, very important! Isn't it?

LEV. Now that we're here, we'd like to make a request.

GENS. (*Magnanimously.*) Please, go ahead.

LEV. You should brief us more often, and you should consult us more often, because after all . . .

ROZIN. After all, we are the leaders of the underground, and the UPO represents the full spectrum of political currents in the ghetto from right to left.

GENS. Of course. That's exactly what I'm doing.

ROZIN. That's very important, very, very important. I say, this vodka is really something. I mean, this is real vodka. Where'd you get it?

GENS. That's a long story. You see, Kittel has a Lithuanian cook, and . . .

ADAM. Excuse me. I'm sure you didn't call us here at eleven o'clock at night just to tell us the Russians have taken some godforsaken village in the middle of nowhere.

GENS. No. The matter I wanted to discuss . . .

ROZIN. Excuse me. Don't you think that's important?

GENS. Excuse! (*Rozin shuts up.*) The local German command is of course dependent on orders from above. Their policy, since the uprising in Warsaw, is to liquidate all ghettos where they find evidence of an armed underground movement.

ADAM. You mean blowing up the train? We've covered it up. They've punished that Lithuanian village, haven't they?

GENS. That was perfectly conceived and carried out, I admit. But sometimes you don't take enough precautions and carelessly expose the entire organization.

ADAM. I don't think we've given the Germans any reason to suspect the existence of the UPO.

GENS. There was the incident of your man caught at the gate with a pistol.

ADAM. You shot him dead on the spot.

GENS. What if Kittel had taken him alive.

ADAM. The matter ended there. There were no questions.

GENS. You know that the Germans arrested a Lithuanian Communist named Kaslaskas?

ROZIN. No . . .

GENS. You were informed by Averbuch. I ordered him to tell you. You even took precautions. (*To Adam.*) You vanished from the ghetto for a week. I'm not sure that was a good idea. It attracted attention and caused unnecessary gossip. I, for instance, heard about it from Dessler.

ADAM. Well. . . . What about Kaslaskas?

GENS. Does he know about the UPO?

ADAM. No. He doesn't know a thing.

GENS. Good, because if you'd had contact with him, I'd be worried. The Gestapo broke the man down, and he's delivered a full aria plus recitative. (*Adam and Lev exchange glances.*)

LEV. We had no dealings with him.

GENS. Good. Excellent. In that case, we really can have a drink. Mira, another round, will you? (*Mira, starts pouring the vodka. Sound of a door being kicked open. Kittel emerges from the darkness with two Gestapos pointing machine guns at the group.*)

KITTEL. Who is Adam Rolenick? (*All stand except Adam, who remains seated. Short chuckle, then to Rozin.*) Are you Rolenick?

ROZIN. No, I am not. I am Rozin, Kalman Rozin, teacher and manager of . . .

KITTEL. (*To Lev.*) Are you Rolenick?

LEV. No.

KITTEL. (*To Zaltsman.*) You? (*Zaltsman shakes his head. Kittel turns to Lachman.*) Are you Adam Rolenick?

LACHMAN. No, I am not. I'm so sorry. (*Kittel appreciates the humor, chuckles, examines Niussia, Mira, and Gens, then points at Adam and orders his men.*)

KITTEL. There's your man. (*The Gestapos take Adam and exit. Kittel casts an amused glance at the perplexed group.*) Ladies and gentlemen, thank you for your splendid cooperation. (*Exits.*)

LEV. (*To Mira.*) You traitor!

GENS. Leave her alone. She's innocent. It's all your fault. Irresponsible, stupid liars. Why did you lie to me? It's obvious that Kaslaskas did work for you. (*Silence.*) Now get the hell out of here fast, before they come back to arrest you all. (*They exit. Gens is left with Mira. He collapses into his chair, burying his head in his hands.*)

MIRA. (*Standing on the edge of darkness.*) Adam . . . I'll kill you for this.

GENS. (*Hands his pistol to her.*) Go ahead. Expose the UPO and give Kittel another clue.

MIRA. What are you talking about?

GENS. So you are a double agent! That arch genius Lev exposed you with one word . . . *traitor*. (*Laughs.*) So it was the underground that planted you in Dessler's bed. I always wondered what a smart, beautiful, high-class girl like you was doing with an ugly pig like Dessler. (*Alarm, shouting, beating.*) What's going on?

OLD NADYA. It was us attacking the Gestapo. We threw blankets over them, and bags of sand. We beat them with sticks and stones. Then the Gestapo ran away. Adam was rescued. We took him back.

GENS. Why did they do that? It's irresponsible.

MIRA. You expected them to let the Germans take him away? You don't know our boys.

GENS. If Kittel didn't know who Adams was, he does now! They've given him the information on a plate, "your boys" . . .

MIRA. Oh, God . . .

GENS. It's going to be a long night. Twenty thousand people at risk. What can I do? What should I do? Listen. Tonight, you'll work for me, and not the way you've been working for Dessler. Is that clear?

MIRA. Perfectly.

Scene 5

Old Nadya is humming, almost whispering, the partisan's song "Zog nit keinmal az du geist dem letztn weg." Sep, busy with his cards, is answering in counterpoint by humming a few bars of the song "Zu eins zwei drei." This musical struggle underlines the scene.

OLD NADYA. They were both in love with him: Niussia and Mira. They were both jealous of me. They couldn't understand how they'd been outclassed by a frivolous featherbrain like me. After all, they were his party comrades, and what was I? An upstart actress. . . . But they didn't give up. They used to visit him when he was hiding in my room, after Kaslaskas's arrest. And one day, it was the fifteenth of July, the day before that horrible night, they both came to brief him about the situation outside. Mira brought news she'd squeezed out of Dessler or one of her German lovers about Kaslaskas's interrogation. Her assignment was to be Dessler's lover, but she'd given up caring about herself and screwed around with German officers and what not. Sometimes, I was afraid she was going crazy. That day, Niussia brought a new song. (*Lights up on Adam, Young Nadya, Niussia, and Mira. They huddle in a corner around a candle, concentrating on a sheet of paper, humming the song as they try to learn it.*) The song was still unknown then. Hirsh Glick, the poet, wanted to cheer Adam up and gave the poem to Niussia so she could sing it to our "commander." We were all sitting there forcing ourselves into another world, trying to learn the song. But Adam's voice betrayed him. His eyes were wet. (*While the four hum the song, Sep is growing more restless and hostile, as if irritated by the sentimentality of the group image. He hates its smugness, so he protests by adding a note of discord with his singing and talking.*)

SEP. *Zu eins zwei drei.* (*Repeats the song.*) It's a German song. They used to sing it in the machine room. The sailors. *Zu eins zwei drei, zu eins zwei drei* . . . in the ship. In the terrible noise of the machines. *Zu eins zwei drei.* And vrrrrrrrrmmmmmm. The British bombers over our heads. Raging. Roaring. Dropping bombs. *Zu eins zwei drei.* They thought I was Polish. The bombs in the water. All around. Brruuum' Brruum'.

OLD NADYA. The next day all hell would break loose.

SEP. (*Starting to walk around the square lit area, shouting.*) *Zu eins zwei drei.* . . . Let every ship be hit by a bomb / But not my ship! Let every ship be hit by a bomb / But not my ship!

OLD NADYA. Sep!

SEP. Let every ship be hit by a bomb / But not my ship!

OLD NADYA. Stop it, Sep! Why are you shouting like that?

SEP. I never learned to pray.

Scene 6

Gens, Kittel, and Mira emerge from the darkness. Again we see the carpet hanging in the air. We are in Gens's office. Kittel sits at the piano, striking a few notes.

KITTEL. Adam Rolenick is the administrator of the public bath?

GENS. Yes.

KITTEL. And what else?

GENS. He's a leather worker, and as far as I know, he was a member of the leather workers' trade union before the war.

KITTEL. Really! Can you also tell me what he was in his previous life?

GENS. I'm sorry, I don't believe in reincarnation. One has this life for eternity.

KITTEL. The public bath must be a very important institution in your ghetto.

GENS. Under the prevailing conditions, yes.

KITTEL. So much so that your peaceful populace mounts a perfectly orchestrated military maneuver to rescue its administrator. Come on, Gens, who is Adam Rolenick?

GENS. He's the administrator of the public bath.

KITTEL. Get me his wife and . . .

GENS. He's a childless widower.

KITTEL. And commander of the underground movement.

GENS. There is no underground movement in the ghetto.

KITTEL. Who were the people in this room with him?

GENS. Managers of various institutions . . .

KITTEL. Do you believe in utilitarian or heroic ethics?

GENS. I don't understand your question.

KITTEL. If you had to choose between Kant and Spinoza . . .

GENS. I'd leave both of them on the bookshelf.

KITTEL. Believe me, Gens, the war of the weak against the strong is utterly immoral. It brings unnecessary suffering to the innocent. Imagine your boys pitifully armed with pistols, sticks, and stones, attacking our soldiers equipped with machine guns, artillery, and tanks. It would have to end in the bloody slaughter of civilians. Furthermore, the battle between the powerful and the powerless is doomed to liquidate the feeble and strengthen the mighty. Believe me, I abhor our regime and despise our leaders from the bottom of my heart. But what would I achieve by fighting them openly? They would kill me and my poor old parents as well, and would it weaken the regime? Not a bit. Therefore, I carry out orders, the dumber— the better. I never overdo my duty, and when I have the opportunity, I do less. Believe me, I am delighted to waste our badly needed forces on absurd tasks like the search for Adam Rolenick. You see? I can employ a company, or even an entire regiment to catch the manager of some public bath, instead of sending those young soldiers to the real battlefield where the outcome of the war is being decided. (*Laughs.*) This is my humble contribution to our defeat. My dear Gens, there is no alternative. When a nation goes crazy, and hands over power to a bunch of fanatics, then clear-thinking men like you and me can't stop them from the frenzy of self-destruction. A whole generation must perish in war. The country must be devastated, whole towns ground to dust, and the criminal state itself must be dismantled. That's the only way to cure a nation's insane megalomania. You see, underground activity gives psychological satisfaction to the childish participants, but it endangers the whole community. Therefore, if you hand over the leaders of the underground, you will prevent the powerless from committing a suicidal act that can only strengthen the mighty. And so you will be acting morally, at least according to Spinoza's utilitarian Jewish ethics, unless you prefer the heroic, suicidal moral code of our Teutonic Kant.

GENS. If you think there is an underground movement in the ghetto, and if you suspect that I'm concealing it, then arrest me, and put me on trial. If you find me guilty, punish me according to the laws of war.

KITTEL. You're very regal all of a sudden.

GENS. I am the representative of this ghetto's autonomous government.

KITTEL. You forget who appointed you.

GENS. I am at your mercy, but as long as I am head of this ghetto, no one tells me how to use my power.

KITTEL. Well, well . . . what shall I do with you, Gens? I'll tell you what I'll do. I'll take your word that there is no underground movement, but you will deliver Adam Rolenick to me, alive, and if I find out that you've lied, the entire population of your "kingdom" will be annihilated—because of you, and your lie.

GENS. I am dying of cancer, and you threaten me with a common cold.

KITTEL. I beg your pardon?

GENS. You've murdered fifty-five thousand Jews in Vilna.

KITTEL. I did?

GENS. You've murdered millions all over Europe. What difference does another fifteen thousand make? (*They look each other in the eye.*)

KITTEL. You think I wouldn't do it because it conflicts with my self-interests. I don't give a damn for my self-interests.

GENS. Then do it.

KITTEL. I am kaput. I know damn well there's no hope for me or my self-interests.

GENS. Herr Kittel, you don't believe a word you're saying. You have no hope? You're a victim of hope, just as tormented by it as the Jews of this ghetto. You do believe, on the other hand, every word you said about your leaders and what they've done to your people. Herr Kittel, you're an intelligent man, only twenty-three years old, at the threshold of your life, and you must be tortured by the unforgivable absurdity of losing your one and only life to the insanity of those miserable half-witted leaders who dragged you down into this bloody swamp. You do hope. You hope to get out alive from the wretched reality you've created to bring my people and yours to ruination.

KITTEL. Why provoke me like this? You really are looking for trouble.

GENS. "Trouble." I can't take anymore of the filth you feed me. I can't digest it anymore. I'm tired. I can't forgive myself, and my people won't forgive me for what I've been forced to do by you.

KITTEL. Come on, Gens. "Your people." Really . . .

GENS. That's something you'll never understand. You despise your own people. But you know they'll forgive you for turning them into beasts. Some will even admire you for it.

KITTEL. Enough. Shut up!

GENS. Come on, kill me. Exterminate us. Finish your job and go fight the Russians.

KITTEL. Ha! Ha-ha. . . . Come on, Gens, I was joking, all along. Of course I want this ghetto to exist. Of course it's in my interest, I mean morally, as a human being, it's in our common interests. I don't have to tell you the moral meaning of saving fifteen thousand people in criminal times like ours. What's that Hebrew saying, "Kol Hamatsil nefesh ahat, ke-illu hitsil alam umlooh." That's a lesson you taught me, Gens: saving one soul means saving the whole world. Come on, old man, cheer up. You have three hours to deliver Adam Rolenick. I'm sure you can do it. You've done much tougher jobs before.

GENS. I'm not sure I can find him. I'm afraid those criminals who grabbed him from your police might have killed him already to cover their tracks.

KITTEL. In that case I'll make an unusual concession: the four gentlemen and the lady who were in the room with Rolenick . . .

GENS. You mean the managers . . .

KITTEL. You know damn well who I mean. It's them or Rolenick. You have three hours.

GENS. I'll do my best. (*Kittel exits. Mira emerges.*)

MIRA. You are crazy.

GENS. He really doesn't want to expose the resistance. He wants the ghetto to go on.

MIRA. Gens.

GENS. No. (*He's engrossed in his thoughts, thinking aloud, not hearing what she says.*) The moment the UPO is revealed, he will get an order to liquidate us, and that will be the end of Kittel's kingdom.

MIRA. With my own eyes I saw him pull out his pistol and shoot a hairdresser because he didn't like the haircut the poor man had given me.

GENS. (*Still ignoring her.*) Yes, he has a problem. He knows who Adam is, and he's afraid the truth might come out. He definitely has a problem.

MIRA. (*Shaking him.*) Don't you care about your own life?

GENS. What's wrong? (*Noticing her, a delayed reaction to the hairdresser story shocks him.*) How old are you?

MIRA. I'll be twenty-two this autumn.

GENS. Not yet twenty-two. Good God. This is unforgivable. It's a crime. You—with that pig, Dessler. And your friends save you the job . . .

MIRA. What do you mean "my friends"? I volunteered. It was my decision.

GENS. Dessler?

MIRA. What's wrong with Dessler? You think you're any better?

GENS. That's enough, girl.

MIRA. "Girl?" Look at me. You think I'm still a virgin?

GENS. Take it easy. Come on, let's have a drink. (*Pours vodka for two. They drink.*)

MIRA. Thanks. I'm sorry. I didn't mean it. It wasn't fair to compare you with Dessler. He was just the beginning, Dessler. My "job." My "mission" for the UPO. I did it for "ideological reasons" . . . sure. . . . It's past that now. (*She displays her gold rings and bracelets.*) Maurer is my food. Herring . . . my clothes. Kittel . . . Kittel . . . King Kittel . . . my life insurance. You want to take me out for dinner? My Friday nights are still free.

GENS. Please, stop it.

MIRA. Adam's not completely lost.

GENS. What do you mean?

MIRA. (*Thinking out loud.*) You've got to squeeze a promise out of Kittel, for the underground. Or else they won't hand Adam over. They can't. You've got to get Kittel's word to let him come back to the ghetto.

GENS. You think his friends would hand him over?

MIRA. If they get a promise that he'll come back alive? That's a ploy they're bound to fall for.

GENS. A ploy?

MIRA. Kittel has to arrest him, but if he doesn't want the UPO to be discovered, he'll eliminate Adam before the real interrogation begins. That'd be the best way to cover up the whole thing.

GENS. Don't you think Lev, Lachman, and Zaltsman will work that out for themselves. They're no fools.

MIRA. When they have to choose between him or them? No, they're not fools, but they are human.

GENS. Humans sometimes transcend themselves.

MIRA. Only when they're left with no alternative.

GENS. You're full of admiration for humanity . . .

MIRA. Admiration and . . . reverence. The human being really is a superior creature. When he's above, he treats you like a pig. When he's underneath, you're the pig.

GENS. There's another possibility, of course. To take up arms and start an insurrection.

MIRA. When there's no shred of evidence that the Germans are planning to liquidate the ghetto?

GENS. If I were commanding the UPO, that's the order I'd have given.

MIRA. You are not Adam. (*She becomes increasingly ironic.*) You are an "individualist," and "adventurer" (*sarcastically*), "a lonely wolf riding a tiger on a tightrope over a yawning abyss, as solitary as . . .

GENS. (*Enjoying it, he laughs.*) . . . as you?

MIRA. Me. I'm a prostitute. (*Same self-mockery.*) "A whore on a sacred mission." (*Laughs.*) A banal slut. (*She shows off her jewelry.*) But an expensive one, at least. . . . (*Laughs.*) Look. Costs them a lot of money . . . (*Suddenly she's not joking anymore.*) I'm going to commit suicide.

GENS. Stop it. Come here . . . (*He takes her in his arms. She hides her face, crying.*)

MIRA. God forgive my friends. They don't know what they've done to me.

GENS. I hope Adam wouldn't consider it.

MIRA. Adam? (*Laughs.*) Don't worry. He won't commit suicide, unless he's ordered to.

GENS. But if he's left without support? After all, he's "number one." I know the feeling.

MIRA. (*Still in his arms.*) Well, he's not.

GENS. What do you mean "he's not"? He's the commander . . .

MIRA. He's not number one in the Communist Party.

GENS. Oh, really. Who's number one?

MIRA. Somebody else.

GENS. I'm ready to play poker with the devil for my soul, but I won't risk the survival of twenty thousand people until I'm convinced I have a good card. If this "number one" is a real leader, a cold blooded ace, then I have a card . . .

MIRA. Play it.

GENS. You see the point I've reached. If you offer me a shoulder, I warn you, I'll lean on it.

MIRA. Lean all you want.

GENS. Go to the UPO headquarters.

MIRA. I know where to go and what to say. Count on me.

GENS. Wait. See to it that Adam's wife and children . . .

MIRA. I heard what you told Kittel. They'll disappear. (*She kisses him.*) That's for the lonely rider . . . (*Mira exits.*)

GENS. Averbuch! Follow her. (*Gens too disappears into the darkness.*)

Scene 7

Sep stands on the edge of the roof feeding crows. He talks to them in a wild blend of languages. The horizon is sporadically lit by flashes of distant explosions.

SEP. Grrr . . . grrr . . . veni-veni-veni.
    Grrr, grrr, . . . puchke. . . .
    Ahoi, Ahoi, grr-grr-grr . . .
    Dessert, dessert s'il vous plait, fromage, fromage
    Apres le carnage. veni, veni, puchke.
    You've had enough meat, enough cadavers.
    Na, na have some cheese, na, na dessert, dessert.
    What was today's main course?
    Iranians-afghanians-pakistanians-kurdistantians
    turkistanians-shiistanians-sunistanians-jewistanians-

arabistanians
Come ayatolla, come, enough you eat human meat
come come have cheese
fress a bissl kez
fromage apres le carnage
grrr grrrr grrrrrr . . .

(*Adam enters. He stays on the border between light and darkness, addressing Old Nadya, who sits in her armchair looking at an album.*)

ADAM. Nadya . . . (*She doesn't answer.*) Nadya . . .

OLD NADYA. I can hear you.

ADAM. May I come in?

OLD NADYA. But you come in whenever you want. You follow me on the street. You stand behind my back in the kitchen when I wash the dishes. You wake me up in my bed whenever you want, and all of a sudden you ask permission?

ADAM. (*Pointing to Sep.*) Well, he doesn't like me too much.

OLD NADYA. Sep?

SEP. Shshsht! Grrr . . . Grrrr . . . Puchke . . . ahoi, ahoi . . .

OLD NADYA. What does he care? He's feeding his crows.

SEP. veni-veni-veni-grrr . . .
    kot-kot-kot-kot-kot . . .
    kom-kom-kom-kom-kom-kom . . .

(*The crows answer him, and there is a dialogue between Sep and the crows.*)

OLD NADYA. "The old crow man," that's what the children call him. "Here comes the old crow man" . . . (*She laughs. Adam approaches her, stands behind her back, looks over her shoulder at the album.*)

ADAM. Show me. When was it taken?

OLD NADYA. Just after the liberation. A year after you died.

ADAM. The whole group's there: Velvele Sharashovsky, Niussia, Lev . . .

OLD NADYA. The whole group . . .

ADAM. Mira's missing.

OLD NADYA. She was killed on the way to the forest. With Zaltsman. They met a German ambush.

ADAM. You're right. Zaltsman's missing, too.

OLD NADYA. And Lachman.

ADAM. What happened to him?

OLD NADYA. He was hanged by the Germans.

ADAM. When?

OLD NADYA. The day the ghetto was liquidated. Two months after you died. Everything happened just the way you predicted.

ADAM. Why was he the only one hanged?

OLD NADYA. He was the only one they caught. The rest of us made it to the forest.

ADAM. They knew who you were. They knew everything about us.

OLD NADYA. Why did you kill yourself? They hadn't even started to torture you.

ADAM. How do you know?

OLD NADYA. When they brought your body, there were no traces of violence. Not a scratch on it.

ADAM. They were torturing a woman behind a wall. I could hear her screaming.

OLD NADYA. Yes. Mira told me.

ADAM. You must tell my story.

OLD NADYA. Why me?

ADAM. Everyone tells my story to suit themselves.

OLD NADYA. You said, "Take my story and do with it what you like."

ADAM. And they did, without shame.

OLD NADYA. Everyone tells what he remembers.

ADAM. Only you keep silent. And you're the one who knows the truth.

OLD NADYA. Oh, I am, am I? Thanks to you? You told me everything? I don't know what I know anymore. Why didn't you tell me the truth about Sharashevsky, when it still mattered? I could have saved you.

ADAM. That was a secret even the headquarter members didn't know.

OLD NADYA. And you put me on the same level as them? Me, the only person who really cared about you, who tried to save you when your friends were hunting you down like an animal. I had to hear it from an American film maker who met Sharashevsky and Niussia . . .

ADAM. They're alive?

OLD NADYA. No. She was widowed two years ago.

ADAM. They married?

OLD NADYA. Yeah, just after the war.

ADAM. Mazel-tov. I thought Sharashevsky would stay a bachelor all his life. He was a born bachelor if I ever saw one . . .

OLD NADYA. After forty years I had to hear it from an American film maker . . .

YOUNG NADYA. (*Enters and picks up the sentence.*) . . . where's Mira going? And what were you two whispering about?

ADAM. (*To young Nadya.*) I told you, she's just come from Gens and is going to the UPO headquarters.

YOUNG NADYA. Is that the truth?

OLD NADYA. It's a goddamned lie.

YOUNG NADYA. Why don't you tell me the truth?

ADAM. But I am. I told you . . .

YOUNG NADYA. What did you tell me? When did you tell me?

OLD NADYA. Never. I had to find out everything myself.

ADAM. (*To young Nadya.*) Don't you remember?

YOUNG NADYA. I want to believe you, but . . .

OLD NADYA. I don't know what I remember anymore, what I've been told, what I read, what really happened . . .

YOUNG NADYA. Me, the one by your side through all of this . . .

OLD NADYA. I have to look through other people's memories . . .

YOUNG NADYA. What is the truth? . . .

OLD NADYA. . . . to find out the truth, after forty years? . . .

YOUNG NADYA. Where are you going?

ADAM. To the meeting at headquarters. I have to . . .

OLD NADYA. Go if you have to.

YOUNG NADYA. Wait. I'm coming with you.

ADAM. You can't. It's a closed meeting. Only HQ members . . .

OLD NADYA. Go to your "members."

YOUNG NADYA. I'm coming with you.

ADAM. They won't let you in.

YOUNG NADYA. I'll wait for you outside.

ADAM. Nadya, try to understand . . .

OLD NADYA. Adam! Don't go!

SEP. Stop it.

OLD NADYA. Let's run away, Adam!

SEP. (*Bursts out.*) "Adam-Adam-Adam-Adam." All my nights are adamadamadamadamadamadam! I don't want to hear it anymore, got it? Adam is dead, got it? Dead, dead, dead, dead, got it?

OLD NADYA. Aren't you ashamed of yourself, Sep?

SEP. Go on, say it. I know. I'm a third-rate survivor. Say it!

OLD NADYA. Are you mad, Sep? You're losing your mind.

SEP. Adam's a first-rate survivor, I know. He's a national hero. You're a second-rate survivor, because you saved our honor. And I'm third-rate because I only saved myself. Say it!

OLD NADYA. How dare you, Sep?! Adam a survivor? He died a hero.

SEP. Not a hero! Got it? Not a hero! A man! A man, a man, a man, not a hero.

OLD NADYA. He died a hero.

SEP. A man. Nothing but a man. And I don't want him in my house anymore.

OLD NADYA. He'll stay in this house as long as he wants.

SEP. No. I've had enough, all right? I won't have him in this room or in my bed anymore.

OLD NADYA. (*Grasps the absurdity of the situation and starts laughing hysterically.*) "I won't have him in my bed."

SEP. Exactly. I'm fed up with your "cavalier."

OLD NADYA. (*Laughing hysterically.*) My "cavilier" . . . (*In Yiddish.*) *Oif alle meine soynim gezogt gevorn . . . hi!*

SEP. (*Imitates her laughter.*) Hi! It's him or me!

OLD NADYA. Help! I'm wetting my pants . . . ha!

SEP. Ha! (*He runs to the door.*) Adieu! (*He slams the door and disappears. The slamming of the door indicates a change of scene, which is actually only a change in lighting.*)

Scene 8

2:00 A.M. Lev, Niussia, Lachman, Zaltsman, and Rozin are assembled at the UPO headquarters. Adam enters.

ROZIN. Adam. Finally. Did you hear about the ultimatum? It's either all of us or you. We don't know what to think. The situation is very . . .

ADAM. The situation is very simple. They learned their lesson in Warsaw. They want to cripple our organization and liquidate the ghetto without resistance.

ROZIN. So they know we head the underground?

ADAM. I don't know what they know.

LEV. You haven't talked to Mira. Gens has a different opinion.

ADAM. Since when does he share his "opinions" with Mira?

ROZIN. She overheard a conversation between Kittel and Gens, and it seems . . .

ZALTSMAN. (*Mutters in his monosyllabic, heavy, instructed, grammarless language.*) Crazy. Enough. Speculations. Speculations. Stupid!

ROZIN. Well, at least you've got it all straight, haven't you?

ZALTSMAN. Adam, listen. Give an order. Immediately. To the forest. Join the partisans. Tonight.

ADAM. To the forest? Tonight? You think that's still possible?

LEV. (*Mockingly.*) "To the forest, to the forest." . . . Have you sent a patrol to make sure the way is clear? Have you checked the water level in the sewers? Have you posted guards at the exits? "To the forest." . . .

ZALTSMAN. Listen. We go. Here . . . it's over.

LEV. We didn't found the UPO to save our own skin. We built this organization to . . .

ZALTSMAN. Fight. We collected guns. We trained people. Here there won't be any fight. Here it's always "don't endanger the ghetto." That's it.

LEV. Our goal is to stir up the entire population for an armed insurrection and revolt.

ZALTSMAN. Illusions. What insurrection, what revolt? Men think only of themselves. To be, to be, nothing but to be. They have no honor. Somebody else paying the price? Fine. He won't fight.

LEV. You underestimate man.

ZALTSMAN. Don't make laugh. "Man."

LEV. Whoever sees the light has to spread his knowledge and share . . .

ZALTSMAN. Action. Only Action. Period.

LEV. Without the backing of the masses, a revolt has no meaning. It'll just be a token gesture from an elite group. We still want to save the dignity of the community.

ROZIN. Of our people: the dignity of the human being! No? . . .

ZALTSMAN. Dignity. What dignity? Mothers abandon their children. Dignity. Fight. Take arms and fight. Dignity. Blow up bridges. Trains. Set ambushes. Set fire. Kill! . . . Dignity. . . . One percent of the population. . . . Take arms and fight!

LEV. "Kill, kill" . . . if that were our ideology . . .

LACHMAN. Two Jews fall from an airplane. As they fall past the clouds, one asks the other, "What should we do?" "Nothing," answers the other, "So far, so good, as long as it stays like this."

NIUSSIA. Lachman!

LACHMAN. If there's time to discuss ideology, the situation may be catastrophic, but by no means serious. (*Mira enters breathless.*)

MIRA. Where's Adam? He disappeared . . .

ADAM. Not yet . . .

MIRA. Oh . . .

ADAM. What's wrong?

ROZIN. Any news from Gens?

MIRA. He called a meeting of the work-group foremen in the Judenrat.

ROZIN. A meeting at two o'clock in the morning? Why?

MIRA. I don't know. (*To Adam.*) Adam. . . . (*He goes with her to the side.*) Did you have any contact with Vitas?

ADAM. Why is Gens interested in Vitas?

MIRA. I just left Sharashevsky. He's been arrested.

ADAM. Sharashevsky?

MIRA. Vitas. Sharashevsky asked if Vitas knows anything.

ADAM. Absolutely nothing. I never spoke to Vitas.

MIRA. Stall the decision.

ADAM. I can't.

MIRA. You've got to. I'm going back to Sharashevsky.

LACHMAN. If we're disturbing you, we can always leave . . .

ADAM. There've been more arrests.

MIRA. Gens wants to know if Adam had anything to do with them.

ZALTSMAN. And?

MIRA. I'll be back in a minute. (*Exits.*)

ADAM. I only had contact with Kaslaskas.

ROZIN. I don't understand why Kittel's interested in us? (*To Adam.*) I'm going to have to ask you straight. In these dealings you had with Kaslaskas, did you say anything that might have led him into thinking there's an underground organization with a collective leadership and headquarters? I'm just trying to work it out.

LACHMAN. He gave him our names and photos.

ROZIN. Who?

LACHMAN. Kaslaskas. Didn't he ask you for an autographed pinup?

ADAM. (*Explains to Rozin seriously without irony.*) Kaslaskas is an experienced conspirator. I told him I needed arms, and he asked no questions.

ROZIN. (*Trying to calm himself.*) I tell you, it's all Gens's idea. The Germans can't know anything about us. They couldn't have come up with an ultimatum like that on their own: "Adam or the rest of us," no? . . .

LEV. (*To Adam.*) Send someone to the foremen's meeting. We've got to find out what Gens is telling the Judenrat.

ADAM. No need. Blum must be there.

LEV. Yes. (*He's disappointed with the way Adam's handling things.*) Yeah, yeah. . . . Well, well . . .

ROZIN. I tell you Gens is just trying to put pressure on us. It's obvious, isn't it? He wants to disrupt us, tear us apart, and make us split with Adam. He's trying to make us betray our leader, I tell you. I can feel it. This isn't Kittel. It's Gens. We should just reject the ultimatum. We should stand up as one and proudly declare . . .

LEV. Bullshit.

ROZIN. What? . . . Why? . . .

LEV. That ultimatum means that the UPO has been exposed, which means we would have no alternative but to reach for our arms and fight. No underground movement ever surrendered themselves to the enemy without fighting. Gens would never invent a lie like that. It doesn't serve his ultimate goal, which is to avoid armed revolt for as long as possible. Gens is no fool.

ZALTSMAN. The ultimatum . . . the Germans . . .

LEV. Of course.

ZALTSMAN. Right. That's the moment. Attack. Fight. Flee.

LEV. (*To Adam.*) Why don't you send someone to this meeting to see what Gens is up to? Rozin!

ROZIN. Yes! (*To Adam.*) Should I go to the Judenrat?

ADAM. Just a minute. (*To Zaltsman.*) Fight? Against who? You have a target to attack now? How will you get away? Where do you think you'll get away to?

ZALTSMAN. Blow up the gates. The wall. Break out. Scatter all over town. Cut lines. Electricity. Telephone. Bomb the water pipes. Gas pipes. Set fire. Burn the town. Poison the water. Create pandemonium. Disappear. To the forest. Your plan. Do it.

ADAM. You're sure it's the right moment?

ZALTSMAN. Yes.

ADAM. You forgot one thing. The plan had a purpose: to offer the ghetto population a chance to run for it, for everyone to save his skin as best he can.

ZALTSMAN. I know.

ADAM. You think the population is ready to follow up our action? We blow up the walls, scatter all over town, and set everything on fire. You know what will happen then? The people will hide under their beds waiting with pillows on their heads for the Germans and Lithuanians to come and slaughter them in their holes.

ZALTSMAN. Goddamnit! It was your idea! . . .

ADAM. Between the idea and the act . . .

LACHMAN. . . . lies an abyss called "the human soul" . . .

NIUSSIA. Lachman, we're trying to be serious here.

LACHMAN. You could have fooled me.

NIUSSIA. When will you stop joking?

LACHMAN. Soon, Niussia, when I die. My friends, we're turning handsprings to avoid reality. (*Young Nadya comes running in, breathless and agitated.*)

YOUNG NADYA. Sorry . . . what can we do? Everyone's confused . . .

ADAM. Do about what? What's happened?

YOUNG NADYA. Gens has been stirring up the gang leaders.

LEV. (*To Adam.*) I told you we should have been there. He's bringing those lowlife scum into the game.

YOUNG NADYA. He told them the ghetto was in danger of you. He said if you weren't delivered to the Germans by dawn, they'd set fire to the ghetto.

LACHMAN. Hah! While we're sitting here having a cozy chat, Gens is launching into action. What's wrong with us? Are we paralyzed?

YOUNG NADYA. The whole population's out on the streets looking for you. What should we do?

ROZIN. At two thirty in the morning?

YOUNG NADYA. What do we do if those bullies try to break in and take you by force?

ADAM. Take the weapons out of storage. If they try to use force, threaten to shoot.

YOUNG NADYA. And if that doesn't stop them?

ADAM. Use force.

YOUNG NADYA. You mean open fire?

ADAM. No. Just threaten them. Not one shot. Is that clear?

YOUNG NADYA. Yes. (*She leaves.*)

LACHMAN. My friends, the ghetto seems to be against us.

ZALTSMAN. There's no other way to stop them.

LACHMAN. The ghetto's turned against us, my friends.

NIUSSIA. We heard you.

LACHMAN. Funny, I thought you didn't. (*To Zaltsman.*) You want the Germans to come to the ghetto and help our own people finish us off?

ROZIN. That will never happen.

LACHMAN. Why? Because it's "not nice"?

ZALTSMAN. That's enough. Tell us what to do, or shut up.

LACHMAN. Let's not act as rashly as we did when we grabbed Adam from their hands in the first place.

LEV. You'd rather have left him?

LACHMAN. I didn't have time to ask myself, and neither did you. We acted on impulse, without thought. And our action revealed the following facts: A. There is organized military resistance in the ghetto. B. Adam's importance to this organization makes it worth risking the existence of the ghetto to save him. C. . . .

ZALTSMAN. That's enough.

LACHMAN. Can I ask a question? (*Silence.*) Given we acted irresponsibly, does anyone regret having rescued Adam? (*Silence.*) No one.

NIUSSIA. I get the feeling that you do.

LACHMAN. I'm not proud of having acted without thought, but I take full responsibility for what we did.

NIUSSIA. We all take responsibility. What the hell are you getting at?

LACHMAN. I'm trying to cope with the consequences of our action. Listen, we exposed the organization. We did it, we're responsible. All of us. Except Adam.

NIUSSIA. What do you want us to do? Turn ourselves in to the Germans?

LACHMAN. Exactly. It's the only honorable thing we can do. And the smartest, too. Listen. The Germans know there's a resistance in the ghetto, but they don't know that we're its collective leadership. You heard Mira. Gens told Kittel we were the managers of the ghetto institutions.

ZALTSMAN. Get on with it!

LACHMAN. What's your hurry? Don't push, said the man to the guy behind him in line for the guillotine. As I was saying, we should grab the ultimatum with both hands. We give ourselves up quietly to Kittel, let them interrogate us, say we have no connection to each other, no connection to Adam, and none at all with the gang who grabbed him from the Gestapo. Who is this Adam anyway? Probably the head of some gang of smugglers. That explains the attempt to steal weapons. And we've got another thing in our favor. When Kittel appeared with his gunmen, our behavior was, thank god, "I'm not Adam," we made it look like we had nothing to do with him. No attempt to cover up for him. Not the slightest expression of solidarity. We all behaved faultlessly.

ADAM. Except you. You said, "I am not Adam," and added, "I'm so sorry." Kittel heard that. He laughed.

LACHMAN. Yes, I'm sorry. I couldn't resist. In any case, if we hadn't rescued you, it would have been a lot easier for you to get through an interrogation and deny everything. As things stand now, that would be impossible. (*A shot. The voice of a girl screaming.*)

ROZIN. What's that? (*All freeze. Old Nadya intervenes.*)

OLD NADYA. It was terrible. The agents and Jewish police had led the crowd to our headquarters. The frenzied mob is besieging the entrance. We're downstairs guarding the staircase, a handful of boys and girls with hand pistols, holding back a gang that's brandishing sticks and iron bars. One of them's a provocateur named Shapira, who pulls out his gun and fires a shot. (*The shot and screaming voice are heard again.*)

ROZIN. What's that? (*Young Nadya enters the room, holding a pistol, covered with blood.*)

ADAM. What happened? I ordered you not to shoot.

YOUNG NADYA. It wasn't us. It was Shapira.

OLD NADYA. The provocateur, Shapira. Lev ordered me and Rozin to execute him. After the liberation. We caught him hiding. Rozin . . .

ROZIN. Yes . . .

OLD NADYA. All of a sudden, you got hysterical. You emptied your machine gun into him.

LEV. . . . Did he hit anybody?

YOUNG NADYA. He wounded Rashka.

OLD NADYA. I was upset because I wanted to kill him, too, but now I'm glad it wasn't me who did it.

YOUNG NADYA. What should we do?

LEV. Adam, give the order and we'll fight.

ADAM. Against Jews?

LEV. If they shoot first? . . .

ADAM. They've lost control. They don't know what they're doing.

YOUNG NADYA. Our people are waiting for orders. What should we do? (*Adam doesn't answer.*) Adam?! . . .

ADAM. (*Helpless.*) What? . . .

YOUNG NADYA. Our fathers. Our mothers. They're all out there.

OLD NADYA. (*Playing her own mother, turns to young Nadya.*) Nadinka, my child, what are you doing?

YOUNG NADYA. Mama, go away, please . . .

OLD NADYA. Nadinka, you're bringing doom to us all. The ghetto will be burned to the ground for this man of yours . . .

YOUNG NADYA. Mama, you don't understand. They want to liquidate the ghetto anyway.

OLD NADYA. Leave him. I told you at the start it would end up badly.

YOUNG NADYA. Mama, we're in the ghetto. I'm in the resistance, and he's my commander.

OLD NADYA. (*In Yiddish.*) *Oy mein gott, bistu meshugge, meidelle!* You're destroying us all.

YOUNG NADYA. It's people like you who are destroying our last chance to fight.

OLD NADYA. Your Adam has driven you mad.

YOUNG NADYA. Mama, it's not "Adam or the ghetto." It's whether we die like sheep or human beings.

OLD NADYA. *Meidelle*, what's the difference? . . . (*Old Nadya turns and leaves crying. Mira appears. She stops on the threshold and makes signs to Adam.*)

YOUNG NADYA. Adam, we can't wait any longer.

LEV. It's a terrible decision, I know, but we're all backing you up, we'll all share the responsibility. Give an order, and we'll shoot. It's justifiable self-defense.

ADAM. (*Reaching Mira with his eyes.*) She nods no. "Justifiable self-defense" . . . and our first victims will be Jews . . .

LEV. We can't stay passive any longer. You're the commander. It's your duty to command. Give an order and we'll act. (*Mira nods no again.*)

ADAM. Do you realize what you're asking me to do? You want me to order our children to open fire on their own flesh and blood, to shoot their fathers, their mothers, their brothers? You forget who those people are out there. Are they our enemies? . . .

YOUNG NADYA. Yes!

ADAM. Nadya . . .

YOUNG NADYA. They want your head, Adam.

ADAM. I know.

LEV. Adam, this indecision is subjecting our fighters to intolerable pressure. We have no right to do that.

ADAM. I know.

LEV. They won't stand for it. It's a commander's duty to . . .

ADAM. Is it a commander's duty to order children to open fire on their own blood? Isn't that the easy way out? Please, all of you, ask your conscience and be honest. Is that really what we should do, or is that just the simplest way of avoiding what has to be done?

ZALTSMAN. Make yourself clear.

ADAM. I can't, Zaltsman. My head's at stake. My tongue is nailed to my mouth. If it weren't me they were after, it would be easy to be clear; but it is me they want, and that makes all the difference. Everything's been said. Please, don't ask me to be clear.

MIRA. (*Half asking, half dictating.*) You're thinking of giving yourself up?

ADAM. Is that what you want?

MIRA. Well . . . I have to, ummmm. . . . It's not me, it's ummmmmmm . . .

ZALTSMAN. Who?

YOUNG NADYA. What does it matter what she wants or doesn't want? (*Turns to Mira.*) You have no right to take part in this debate. You're not an HQ member!

MIRA. Excuse me, you're not either, and I don't know what you're doing here in the first place.

YOUNG NADYA. All right, say it. I'm his lover, but I'm also a unit leader, and my fighters won't permit anyone to betray their commander and deliver him to the enemy.

LEV. Betray?! . . . I forbid you to use that word! . . . What's going on here? Neither one of you is an HQ member. Adam, I'm sorry, but this can't go on. You've got to do something!

ADAM. What do you want me to do?

LEV. First of all, we've got to find you another hiding place.

ADAM. Why?

LEV. To gain time, ease the pressure. Mira!

MIRA. Yes?

LEV. Just a minute. . . . Nadya, Niussia, dress Adam, disguise him. (*Nadya and Niussia take Adam aside and start disguising him as a woman with parts of their dresses. Lev continues giving orders.*) Mira, go to Gens. Tell him we need another six hours.

MIRA. What if he can't get Kittel to agree?

LEV. Then there'll be bloodshed. Now go. Wait. Tell him to stop inciting the mob. Tell him it's in his interest to defuse this bomb before it blows up his whole kingdom. Tell him one more provocation from his agents and we open fire.

LACHMAN. (*Goes downstage right.*) Lev.

MIRA. (*While Lev goes to Lachman.*) Any other message?

LEV. No, you can go. Be back as soon as you can.

MIRA. I will. (*Exits.*)

LACHMAN. (*To Lev, who approaches him now.*) Where is she going?

LEV. To Gens.

LACHMAN. Are you sure? (*Pause.*) Send Nadya after her.

LEV. Nadya, come here a minute.

YOUNG NADYA. (*Goes to Lev.*) What is it?

LACHMAN. (*Passing her on his way to Adam.*) We won't betray him. (*He approaches Niussia and Adam to help with the disguise.*)

LEV. (*To Nadya.*) Follow Mira. Find out who she really reports to. Find out what her game is. Wait. Leave the key. I want Niussia to take Adam to your room.

YOUNG NADYA. Here's my key. (*She gives him the key and runs out.*)

LEV. (*On his way to Adam.*) Zaltsman, go out to the street, speak to the people.

ZALTSMAN. What are you talking about? What people?

LEV. We have to distract the rabble while they get Adam out of here. Just to say a few words. You know.

ZALTSMAN. No, I don't. You go say a few words.

LEV. Rozin!

ROZIN. Yes!

LEV. Go to talk to them.

ROZIN. What should I say?

LEV. Whatever comes to your head. Good God, do I have to spell out every word.

LACHMAN. Are you a teacher or aren't you? You've got to have some fodder to feed them for five minutes. (*Rozin goes downstage and addresses the audience, while Niussia, Adam, and Lachman load their guns and disappear with Lev and Zaltsman following them into the darkness.*)

ROZIN. My friends . . . all of you . . . what's going on? . . . Are we your enemies? . . . Us? . . . Have we laid a finger on anyone? I have something important to tell you, my friends. Look here. We have arms. But did we shoot anybody? Who fired a gun just now, who? (*Hysterically, not knowing what to say next.*) Who fired a gun, tell me! You know who did it. And we know who did it. The public record is open, and there is a hand that is writing, and there is a law, and there is a judge, and no one will escape justice. The man who shot my dear student Rashka Novak today—his name is on the record and he will not escape his destiny as long as my name is Rozin. . . . He who runs away from death, will have death running after him, so where are you running to? Shame on you! Your beloved have gone the way of all flesh, and it was you who let go the father's hand, the mother's hand, the grandmother's, and the child's. . . . He who no longer feels that hand burning in his palm with pain, he who no longer remembers turning his back on the beloved he abandoned to death, seeking instead life for himself . . . let him, let him dare raise his hand! You think you will live forever? So why the noise? Why the panic? Why the uproar? (*Roars.*) You blockheads! Open your eyes before you die like drunken fools. Have you not yet seen enough? You want more of this foul life, more and more? To stay a few more minutes in this valley of tears? The earth is drenched with your kinsmen's blood . . . and you jump around like wild goats? Shame on you! Our enemies tell you your crime is to have been born, and you want to prove them right by turning your very existence into a crime? Or do you have another word for a life gained at the price of another's death! Men! Perhaps we cannot save our lives . . . our bodies . . . but every one of you has the chance to save his soul. And you want to sell yourselves? For what price? For an illusion! Listen to me, all of you. The soul of every one of you, the human soul, is worth being saved!

OLD NADYA. Bravo! Bravo, Rozin, bravo! (*Rozin disappears. Sep reappears, but she goes on talking without paying attention to the change.*) How did you do it? You hypnotized them for half an hour, at three in the morning, on the cold street, in the middle of a tragedy, you stopped the flow of time. "The human soul is worth being saved." . . . Where did you find those beautiful words?

SEP. (*Resigned, resentful, plays now Rozin, now Lev.*) The need, Nadinka, the sheer need . . .

OLD NADYA. You know where Mira went?

SEP. To Velvele Sharashevsky's.

OLD NADYA. To Velvele Sharashevsky's.

SEP. Ai-ai-ai . . . you don't say? One of your soldiers! . . .

OLD NADYA. One of my soldiers. And he gives Mira orders for Adam.

SEP. It's scandalous.

OLD NADYA. I ran back to Lev immediately.

SEP. (*Playing Lev.*) "Nadinka" . . .

OLD NADYA. . . . he says . . .

SEP. . . . "This is a *casus extremus*" . . .

OLD NADYA. . . . and . . .

SEP. . . . "Nadinka" . . .

OLD NADYA. . . . he says . . .

SEP. . . . "Not a word to anybody."

OLD NADYA. "Anything you say, Lev, but I've got to talk to Adam."

SEP. . . . "Nadinka" . . .

OLD NADYA. . . . He put his hand on my shoulder . . .

SEP. (*Puts his hand on her shoulder.*) . . . "I understand, Nadinka. It's only human. I don't want to interfere in your personal relationship, but when it comes to the organization" . . .

OLD NADYA. "Lev, I promise, I'll tell you everything I know, because it's a" . . .

SEP. . . . . "A *casus extremus*" . . .

OLD NADYA. "A *casus extremus*." . . . What is a *casus extremus*?

SEP. A borderline case is a . . . well, it's a . . . *casus extremus*.

OLD NADYA. Yes. . . . I ran to my room right away. Adam and I had a code signal. (*Knocks three times on the table, or clicks with his tongue.*)

OLD NADYA. "The Prison Waltz" . . . (*Sep repeats the three beats. Light changes to memory scene. Adam enters dressed as an old woman, followed by young Nadya.*)

Scene 9

Young Nadya's room in the ghetto. Adam is dressed as an old woman.

YOUNG NADYA. Tell me the truth, Adam. Who is Velvele Sharashevsky?

ADAM. I've told you all I know. He's one of the five fighters under your command . . .

YOUNG NADYA. Adam, tell me the truth.

ADAM. I don't know what you mean . . .

YOUNG NADYA. You think I'm just here for you to screw and throw away.

ADAM. Nadya.

YOUNG NADYA. How come Lev trusts me, treats me as his equal, gives me responsibility . . . how come all the others rely on me, and you don't? . . . I don't understand!

ADAM. You think I would stay in this room for one minute if I didn't trust you? Nadya . . . do you know how isolated I am.

YOUNG NADYA. Then why don't you talk to me? You know Mira meets secretly with Velvele Sharashevshy. Do you know she talks to him about what to do with you?

ADAM. Who told you that?

YOUNG NADYA. Trust me . . . she gets orders from Sharashevsky about what to do with you. It's a nightmare . . . as if you weren't yourself all of a sudden, as if the man I love is not the man I see. . . . What's going on Adam?

ADAM. I'm playing a part . . .

YOUNG NADYA. What?

ADAM. Maybe it's all about playing parts. Nadya . . . (*He tries to pull her close to him, but she won't let him embrace her.*)

YOUNG NADYA. Don't touch me.

ADAM. Nadya . . . please . . .

YOUNG NADYA. (*Pushes his hand away.*) No. Get out.

ADAM. Where?

YOUNG NADYA. You have a wife. Go to her. Let her hide you for a change.

ADAM. You know they're waiting for me there.

YOUNG NADYA. Then go to your friends.

ADAM. What friends? . . .

YOUNG NADYA. Go to Mira.

ADAM. Nadya! . . . Listen . . . I shouldn't tell you this, but . . . Velvele Sharashevsky is the general secretary of the Ze-Ka.

YOUNG NADYA. Of what?

ADAM. Of the Central Committee of the Communist Party.

YOUNG NADYA. How dare he butt into your business.

ADAM. He's my superior.

YOUNG NADYA. Sharashevsky . . . your superior?!

ADAM. In the hierarchy of the party, yes.

YOUNG NADYA. Are you telling me you take orders from this baby?

ADAM. He's no baby.

YOUNG NADYA. That "schlimazel" with ten thumbs and two left hands?

ADAM. Sharashevsky is an ideological genius. He's the brains behind . . .

YOUNG NADYA. He's a half-wit. . . . You mean to tell me that he's the one making decisions around here? (*Adams nods.*) . . . Then why isn't he commander?

ADAM. This way he can't be exposed.

YOUNG NADYA. And the other HQ members? Do they know?

ADAM. Nadya, what I just told you is top secret.

YOUNG NADYA. Who decided to make you commander?

ADAM. All the UPO movements agreed that the commander should be a Communist, for the day when we're liberated by the Red Army.

YOUNG NADYA. But who decided to make you, in particular, you the general commander?

ADAM. Well . . . the Ze Ka . . .

YOUNG NADYA. Sharashevsky. I see. And now he can decide to give you up to the Gestapo.

ADAM. He'd never make a decision like that. Sharashevsky's a comrade . . .

YOUNG NADYA. A "comrade"? Someone who sends you to die in his place. Is that what you call a "comrade"?

ADAM. He'd never do that . . .

YOUNG NADYA. Of course not. I won't let him.

ADAM. Where are you going?

YOUNG NADYA. To Sharashevsky.

ADAM. Are you crazy?

YOUNG NADYA. "My dear Velvele," I'll say to him, "if you're convinced that someone should go and deliver himself to the Gestapo, please go and do so yourself!"

ADAM. I won't let you do it.

YOUNG NADYA. No? Why not? Because he's your party superior? For me he's just one of the five fighters under my command. For me Velvele Sharashevsky is . . .

OLD NADYA. . . . and always will be . . .

OLD AND YOUNG NADYA. . . . A "Pisher"! (*Yiddish for bed-wetter.*)

ADAM. Nadya, you're only twenty. You're an intelligent girl, and I love you. But I don't know if we'll ever talk to each other again, so listen to me. I'm afraid. This life . . . I'm losing it because of a part I have to play . . . there's nothing above or beyond it. So what can I do? Should I play my part to the end and give them a hero to worship? Inside me there's just emptiness . . .

YOUNG NADYA. You're afraid of death?

ADAM. (*Stares at her as if he hasn't heard the question.*) . . . What? . . . No . . . no-no . . . not at all, no-no. . . . Once when I was sixteen I wrote a poem: "I want to die / Surrounded by friends" . . . (*Laughs.*) . . . It was just after the October revolution and the party was underground. We used to meet in a cellar . . . to read *The Communist Manifesto* . . . to learn revolutionary theory. . . . I came from a poor family. My father was a cobbler, he could barely read a newspaper. My mother was illiterate . . . the party gave me hope . . . something to believe in . . . my first love . . . became a man. . . . I grew up in the party . . . so when I was sixteen I wrote a poem:

> I want to die in battle
> Surrounded by friends . . .

But to be handed over, all alone? . . .

YOUNG NADYA. They won't do it to you. They can't do it.

ADAM. No?

YOUNG NADYA. Lev won't let them. (*Light on Old Nadya and Sep.*)

OLD NADYA. (*Echoing young Nadya, but with the bitter knowledge of what happened.*) Lev won't let them . . . (*She sighs.*)

SEP. (*Arranging his magician's props and gadgets on his magician's table.*) Well, we've finished. (*He places the cylinder on the table and sits the rabbit inside it. He puts the cane next to the rabbit, arranges the magic coins in a special container, hangs the magic umbrella on the edge of the table, observes it all and starts to sing contentedly.*)

> We've finished, we've finished, the end
> Konnietz, finito, la fin!
> All's ready for Sunday hip
> We're going, we're going to sleep!

OLD NADYA. We had a radio in the theater . . .

SEP. (*Detects a new wave of memories, which he desperately tries to ward off.*)

> We've finished, we've finished, the end
> Konnietz, finito, la fin . . .

OLD NADYA. He used to read poetry on radio Vilna. Kittel did . . . damn him.

SEP. (*Imitating her.*) . . . "and he was handsome, he was" . . .

OLD NADYA. And he was handsome, he was . . .

SEP. (*Puts on an improvised mock uniform of an SS officer. He continues mimicking Nadya's words just before she speaks them.*) "Always dressed to the T's in his uniform" . . .

OLD NADYA. Always dressed to the T's in his uniform. Damn him.

SEP. (*Puts on a Nazi hat.*) Damned be his name forevermore.

OLD NADYA. Always elegant and civilized.

SEP. "Elegant, civilized." . . . Used to come to the radio station in the middle of the night . . .

OLD NADYA. At three in the morning.

SEP. (*Burning with jealousy.*) Ay-ay! . . .

OLD NADYA. Who could say no to him?

SEP. "King Kittel"!

OLD NADYA. And he would sing, or read poetry . . . broadcasting into the night. Sometimes he'd suddenly show up at the theater in the middle of a rehearsal and show us how to walk and talk on stage. I remember his voice . . . (*Kittel appears from the darkness in front of a forties radio microphone. He sings Goethe's "Erlkonig" in a pathetic, sentimental interpretation or is parodying the Nazi style of interpreting the German classics. His singing is accompanied by someone on piano, but both the piano and pianist remain unseen. Old Nadya is humming the song as Kittel sings, nestling quaintly against her horrible memories. Sep, whose jealousy and anger are ablaze, starts to parody Kittel's performance.*)

SEP. (*Half Yiddish, half German.*)

> *Wer reitet azoi schpet durch nacht und wind?*
> *Doss iz der vater mit zayn kind.*

er hot dem zindl vol in dem arm
er fast im sicher, er helt ihm varm . . .
OLD NADYA. He was a kind of Rudolf Valentino.
SEP. Rudolf Valentino de la Schmattee.
OLD NADYA. A Nordic Rudolf Valentino.
SEP. What Nordic. A quarter Jewish Austrian bastard.
OLD NADYA. What quarter Jewish? He was a Nordic Aryan type . . .
SEP. Aryan - Schmaryan - Baryan - Charyan - Nordic - Schmordic fucking bastordic!
OLD NADYA. He was Aryan, pure Aryan.
SEP. (*Explodes.*) Voila. Here is your Aryan. Here is your Nordic. Here is your Kittel! A groisee maisee, ay. Only Nordics give them. Only Aryans. *Andersh past nit.* (*A series of explosions on the horizon. Sep turns his rage against the whole Middle East.*) Barbarians. Primitives. Only fight. Only kill. Only murder one another. Booby-trapped cars. Arpigi's, Razookas, enough! I want calm. I want to get up in the morning and drink a glass of mango juice. Why mango? Just azoi! Because! Served in the garden. In a white silk morning gown. And two Aryan servants. And coffee with schlagshane, and horse races and a soft boiled egg three and a half minutes boiled and not one second more. Because I want. And Viennese operettas. The Charadash princess. Les Miserables. The baron of the gypsies. I want a civilized life. And no more pro-sunites, proshiites, pro-sciutto. A Kittel, that's what they need, and Schnell Beheilung, Yalla. On the wagons. All terrorists on the wagons. Hop! Whoever picks up a stone I make of him pasta. Pastrami. Steak tartare. That's what they deserve. Porridge I make of him. Gehakte-leber, paté-de-la-maison to feed the pigs, and clean the country and the region. Hygienic sterile umwelt. Barbaren-rein. Sauber. No foreigners. No others. Clean and empty. (*In German.*) So! . . . (*All through Sep's monologue, Kittel's romantic-saccharine performance continues. As Sep finishes his part, light goes up on the pianist accompanying Kittel's singing. Sep and Old Nadya disappear, and their disappearance leads into Scene 10.*)

Scene 10

Gen's office. 3:00 A.M. Mira plays a Chopin nocturn on the piano. Kittel address Gens.

KITTEL. Do you realize what time it is?
GENS. You want the institutional managers? I'll have them in fifteen minutes. Mira . . .

KITTEL. Let her be. She's an artist. Go on playing, my dear. (*He offers her his glass, she drinks. He recites while gazing at her.*) "Was man nicht weis, das eben hrauchto man, und was weis, kann man nicht brauchen.*" You know it?

GENS. I heard you on the radio.

KITTEL. Tomorrow I'll read a few lines of my own:
And first man created God,
And the soul was Tohu-va-Roho
And the spirit of man suspended over the abyss . . .

GENS. Beautiful, beautiful. . . . Mira, would you . . .

KITTEL. I said let her be! Your managers can wait. I'll see them some other time. But I have to say, this Adam Rolenick fascinates me more and more.

GENS. I have to say the same.

KITTEL. I should have had him (*he takes Mira's hand off the piano and looks at her watch*) . . . two minutes ago. Well?

GENS. I'd deliver him to you gladly, if I knew where the hell he was.

KITTEL. I beg your pardon? I must have misunderstood.

GENS. The man's disappeared.

KITTEL. In that case, let us help the ghetto find him.

GENS. I'm doing my best.

KITTEL. You don't understand. Let us motivate the people. Put it this way: Either Rolenick or the ghetto. You have . . . (*picks up Mira's hand again and looks at her watch*) . . . fifty-eight minutes. (*He kisses Mira's hand then puts it tenderly on the keyboard, whispering in her ear.*) Go on, my beauty, *allegro ma non tropo. Cantabile* . . . (*he sings a few bars*) . . . *cosi.*

MIRA. *Si, maestro* . . . (*She plays.*)

KITTEL. (*To Gens.*) Italian is the language of love.

GENS. Just let me . . .

KITTEL. Don't argue with me.

GENS. I'm not arguing. Just offering advice. Before the war, I was director of a small prison. An ultimatum must be reasonable, and more importantly (*in French*) executable. Otherwise it has no effect. Now if you'll just listen . . .

KITTEL. (*Conducting Mira's playing as he continues to flirt with her.*) Go on, speak up . . .

GENS. The man's got to be hiding in the ghetto. I can start a massive manhunt, but that reduces the chances of catching him alive. He'd probably commit suicide. In fifty-eight minutes, I can give you his corpse (*exchanges glances with Mira*), if that's enough for you. (*Mira stops playing.*)

KITTEL. I want him alive. (*Mira starts playing again.*)

GENS. Then you've got to promise him something. You've got to give him a chance.

KITTEL. How will he know, if you can't contact him?

GENS. The ghetto telephone, world's fastest: word of mouth.

KITTEL. Beautiful.

GENS. What's the deal?

KITTEL. I'll confront him with Kaslaskas. If he was really just trying to get guns for a gang of smugglers, I'll hand him over to you. Criminal matters don't interest me. I've never been director of a small prison.

GENS. You'll have him in twelve hours.

KITTEL. Tell me one thing. Why should he believe me?

GENS. Because he'll have my word.

KITTEL. Why do you believe me?

GENS. You're interested in the ghetto's continued existence. I can testify to that.

KITTEL. Testify? . . . Where? . . .

GENS. We will all stand trial. After the war. (*Kittel chuckles.*) We have a saying in Yiddish: "As long as you're alive, you always have a chance to save your soul."

KITTEL. Eight hours. And I want him alive.

GENS. You'll get him.

KITTEL. (*To Mira.*) Don't forget Saturday night. I have a little surprise for you: the notes of Davidsbundler-Tanze. Schumann. (*He exits.*)

GENS. Okay. Now let's talk about Sharashevsky.

MIRA. Who?

GENS. You're a smart girl, but I wasn't born yesterday either, so let's get down to business. On your way to the so-called UPO "headquarters," I suggest you pay a little visit to Sharashevsky, . . . just as you've done on all your other little errands . . . and make it clear to him that if Adam doesn't show up in my office by 7:00 A.M., I'll see to it that his identity as your network's real commander is spread all over the ghetto. So don't be surprised if Kittel suddenly loses interest in Adam and sets his sights on the real kingpin: Velvele Sharashevsky. Let me make myself clear. I won't sacrifice twenty thousand people for any one man, and especially a straw man like Adam.

MIRA. Adam's not a straw man. He's the true commander of the resistance.

GENS. If he's such a great leader, let him sacrifice himself and give your party, the UPO, and the people of Israel a hero. This is the moment for it. I'd tip my hat to him, shut my mouth forever, and conveniently forget about Mr. Sharashevsky. That's his alternative.

MIRA. You son of a bitch.

GENS. You innocent lamb. (*Mira takes her fur coat and fur hat and exits.*)

Scene 11

Outside. An alley in the ghetto. 4:00 A.M. Mira walks stealthily from shadow to shadow. Two figures emerge and block her path. They are Lev and Lachman. The action takes place in darkness. It is difficult to make out faces.

LEV. Mira? (*She stops.*) Where have you been?

MIRA. Gens's office.

LACHMAN. Since when has his office been in this alley?

LEV. And in the middle of everything we discover that our leader takes orders from a comrade who's in turn taking his orders from a girl! . . .

LACHMAN. Who also happens to be the mistress of our supreme leader . . .

LEV. I thought we were all supposed to be equals in this organization? No secrets among the factions of the UPO. Isn't that what we agreed? But you damn Communists have to have secrets even from the members of your own party. This is serious, a *casus extremus*, in fact it's a scandal . . .

MIRA. Get off your high horse, Lev. You're not addressing a flock of your admirers, you're talking to Mira Kazovsky, the girl you ordered to become Dessler's whore. So stick your rhetoric up your ass. I'm sick to death of it all.

LEV. I'm waiting for an explanation. I want to know what's going on.

MIRA. Don't give me that. You know damn well how the Communist Party is organized.

LACHMAN. Give us a refresher course.

MIRA. Ha-ha-ha. What do you want to know? Does one have to pay to fuck you now?

LACHMAN. There's only one thing to do. Tell all the HQ members the truth.

MIRA. And that is?

LACHMAN. That you've been running your own underground within the underground. That Adam's been taking orders from Sharashevsky who, in turn, gets them from who-knows-where.

MIRA. After what's happened tonight? Isn't this enough? You self-righteous pricks! You and your truth! Go ahead. Let the shit hit the fan. What do I care!

LEV. You're right. This isn't the time for a public debate. The United Partisans' Organization must appear united in this crisis.

LACHMAN. I beg to differ. The problem here is not one of tactics, but ethics (*to Mira*) whether you like it or not.

LEV. You're right. . . . (*To Mira.*) How could they hide the truth from their comrades? How?!

LACHMAN. (*Whispering.*) Easy. The step to prostitution is a short one. (*He steps away from both Mira and Lev.*)

LEV. How can we discuss issues of life and death, knowing that your party is hiding vital information? How can we look each other in the eye?

LACHMAN. (*Aside.*) A most unpleasant affair, but we'll get over it. One forgives oneself so easily.

LEV. No. No. We can't avoid the facts. (*To Mira.*) You've got to find a way . . . (*can't find the right word*) to let your comrades . . .

MIRA. You expect me to stand up and declare that the Ze Ka has examined the matter and reached the following conclusion . . .

LEV. I don't expect a public confession, but . . .

LACHMAN. Wait a minute. Whose "conclusion"? . . . What "conclusion"?

MIRA. The Ze-Ka is convinced that Adam should give himself up.

LACHMAN. Oh, the Ze-Ka is convinced, is it? Well, I don't give a damn what the Ze-Ka thinks.

MIRA. Do what you want for all I care.

LACHMAN. We will. We are still the HQ, and Adam is still our only chief commander.

LEV. But it is important to know what his party comrades are thinking.

MIRA. There's a technical problem. I'm not a member of the HQ. I can't take part in your debate.

LEV. Niussia can.

MIRA. She wasn't at the consultations.

316 / Joshua Sobol

LACHMAN. With Velvele?

MIRA. She's not a Ze-Ka member, and besides, she was at your meeting all night.

LEV. You can brief her.

MIRA. Yes, well . . .

LACHMAN. Niussia is a smart girl.

MIRA. Yes, she is . . .

LACHMAN. One code word from you and she'll get the picture fast as you can say Velvele Sharashevsky. . . . (*Switches to a sharper tone.*) I want the two of you to know I have my own opinions, and . . .

LEV. (*Even sharper.*) I, too, have opinions, but we can't be tempted to exploit the situation for ourselves. If we don't overcome our pettiness, and transcend our limitations tonight, we're lost.

LACHMAN. Beautifully said.

LEV. Let's get back to our comrades. They're waiting.

Scene 12

UPO Headquarters. Zaltsman, Rozin, Niussia, joined by Lev, Lachman, and Mira.

LEV. Comrades, there've been some crucial developments. Mira, please.

MIRA. Gens sent me. I was there at his last meeting with Kittel. Gens carefully tested an idea about Adam committing suicide and the Gestapo getting his corpse, but Kittel wouldn't buy it. He wants Adam alive, or he'll destroy the ghetto.

ROZIN. So it's not "us or Adam" anymore. It's "Adam or the ghetto."

MIRA. Right. The population has already been informed.

LEV. I've been on the streets. The mood is ugly. They're calling us "murderers." The mob's accusing us of being the people's worst enemy. They're shouting, "the resistance is our SS."

ZALTSMAN. So it's betray Adam or kill fifteen thousand people?

LEV. That's the situation.

ZALTSMAN. (*Roars.*) No! . . . (*Silence. All look at him.*) I refuse.

LEV. What do you refuse?

ZALTSMAN. It's a crime. Even to think of it. A crime.

LEV. You want someone else to make the decision for you?

ZALTSMAN. It's filthy. Untouchable. The only ethical possibility: refusal. Total. War. No compromise. To the death. That's the situation. Be aware. Stop playing the Kittel-Gens games.

ROZIN. Who do you want to fight? The whole ghetto's against you.

ZALTSMAN. To hell with the ghetto!

ROZIN. To hell, to hell! Where will it lead? The Germans protecting the ghetto against you?

LACHMAN. Don't worry about that. They're not stupid. They'll let us fight one another and have a good laugh watching the show.

LEV. (*Trying to unarm Lachman.*) What's your proposal?

LACHMAN. I don't have a proposal. I want to have all the facts first. Mira, is this all the news, or do you have more information?

MIRA. Well, Gens got Kittel to make a promise: if Adam stands up to a confrontation with Kaslaskas and can prove he was after the arms for his own criminal purposes . . .

ROZIN. Criminal? What does he mean by "criminal"? . . .

MIRA. A thief or a smuggler: then he'll be handed over to Gens, who'll be free to do with him what he sees fit, because Kittel . . . quote . . . "is not a director of a small prison" . . . unquote, and he's not interested in petty criminals.

ROZIN. You heard that with your own ears?

MIRA. Yes.

ROZIN. This changes everything.

LACHMAN. Since when do you trust Kittel?

MIRA. Gens threatened that if he didn't keep his word, it would be their last transaction. Kittel didn't like it, but he gave in. At least for the moment, he seems interested in the ghetto's survival.

ROZIN. (*To Lachman.*) Did you hear that? Gens threatened him!

LACHMAN. Since when do you trust Gens?

LEV. It's got nothing to do with trust. It's about self-interest. But before we decide about sending Adam, I want to know more about this Kaslaskas. Who is he? What is he?

LEV. Lots of people changed their identities and loyalties under the German occupation. How do we know Kaslaskas is not a provocateur, that we're not sending Adam into a trap?

MIRA. We can't be absolutely sure, but we have investigated the matter through our channels . . .

ROZIN. (*Frightened and panicky.*) "Channels"? What "Channels"? . . .

LEV. The Communist Party's.

ROZIN. (*Relieved.*) Ahhhh! . . . Well? . . . And? . . .

MIRA. Kaslaskas is not a provocateur. He always was, and still is, a loyal party member. He was tortured, and he broke down. He told them what he knew, which is almost nothing.

ZALTSMAN. How do you know?

MIRA. Two different sources. Primo: Dessler, and don't ask me how I got him to open his big fat lips. Secundo: the party's made a thorough analysis and concluded: Kaslaskas only knows Adam, and that he was a Communist before the war. That's all he could have told the Germans.

ZALTSMAN. Were all your party members at the meeting?

MIRA. No.

ZALTSMAN. You talk about the "party." Are you a representative of your party?

MIRA. Let me explain . . .

ZALTSMAN. Who is "the party"?

MIRA. The central committee.

ZALTSMAN. Names. Who are the men?

NIUSSIA. Why do you want to know? You could be arrested to-morrow. The less you know, the better.

ZALTSMAN. We're talking about a man, about whether or not to betray him. I want to know who the man is who tells me to betray another. He has a name. He has a face. Who is the man?

NIUSSIA. You can rely on what you're told. I promise you that all the facts were taken carefully into consideration.

LACHMAN. How do you know? Were you there?

NIUSSIA. No, I was here, but I know and trust the comrades as I trust myself. (*She makes eye contact with Mira.*) And if the secretary of our central committee reached the conclusion that the risk should be taken (*Mira nods approval to her*) and that Adam should accept the confrontation with Kaslaskas (*Mira approves*), then I for one accept his opinion.

LACHMAN. What is your opinion?

NIUSSIA. My opinion?

LACHMAN. We're still a sovereign body, and we're not obliged to take orders from any Berl, Velvel, or Shmerl, even if he is secretary of the central committee.

NIUSSIA. My opinion is that we're in a crisis. We're cornered. We're being asked to hand over our leader . . . and at this same moment we discover that the masses are not with us. That's the real tragedy. If we could just count on the masses, we'd have no problem putting up a fight. But we've remained an elite group divorced from the people and that, in my opinion, is the biggest flaw in our organization.

LACHMAN. I'm still waiting to hear what the hell in your opinion we should do!

NIUSSIA. In my opinion there's no justification for sacrificing the entire ghetto when there's every possibility of getting Adam out alive.

LACHMAN. In short, you think we should hand Adam over to the Gestapo?

NIUSSIA. I think we've got to take the risk. It will prove that the UPO is not cut off from the masses. It could even be a turning point in the relationship between the masses and the resistance. When the right moment comes for armed revolt, the masses will be on our side.

ROZIN. Exactly.

LEV. You have something to say?

ROZIN. I just wanted to say . . . Niussia took the words out of my mouth.

LEV. Zaltsman?

ZALTSMAN. No, no. I get the feeling everything's already been decided, in some other place. The devil knows where.

LEV. What's your opinion?

ZALTSMAN. My opinion. My opinion. Dirty. The whole business. My opinion. Na. No-no. I hear "Secretary." "Central Committee." Who? What? Why? Bad. Bad. This whole business. Bad. Suddenly things come out. The heart doesn't speak to the mouth. What can I say? . . . (*Moans.*) Ai-ai-Adam! . . . (*A ghastly, gasping laughter.*) Crazy. You could go crazy. (*Suddenly realizes that everyone's waiting for him to say something. He shouts.*) What are we waiting for, the messiah? . . . Vote and finish! . . .

LEV. Then, let's vote.

LACHMAN. Just a minute. What is all this? What about us? Are we or are we not a collective organization? Have we or have we not been functioning on the principle of collective responsibility? Has Adam or has he not been put in this trap by a policy of our own making? If we betray Adam, we betray ourselves.

LEV. Allow me . . .

LACHMAN. You allow me! You were the one going on about connections with the outside world, "without which" . . . your words . . . "our entire enterprise is doomed." So we decided that each party would make contact with equivalent political movements outside the ghetto. Every one of us did our best to establish those contacts, and when the Reverend Mother of the convent brought you three Polish hand grenades, we all rejoiced, so now that the Gestapo's caught Kaslaskas, we all have to share the consequences. None of us can try to shake off responsibility . . .

LEV. No one's trying to shake off responsibility, but the question is . . .

LACHMAN. The question is, how do we make our people understand the situation and lead them to general insurrection? To fight,
that's what this organization was founded for. I say we can still influence the outcome of this hideous affair if we just go about it the
right way. The people are against us? I say we can turn the whole
situation around with one bold move, and then we can force the
ghetto to fight.

ZALTSMAN. What move? Speak up. Finally something interesting.

LACHMAN. Gens is always saying that, at the moment he sees the
Germans about to liquidate the ghetto, he'll lead the people to an
armed revolt. We can create that moment and force Gens to keep his
word.

ZALTSMAN. How?

LACHMAN. We appoint a new HQ. Give them command of the
UPO. Then we all go out on the street with Adam and say to the
people: the Germans want to get Adam so they can destroy the UPO
and (*his voice breaks*) annihilate the ghetto without resistance. Here's
Adam. He is one of us, and we (*tries to control his breaking voice*) we
will not betray our comrade. Join us, and we'll go together to our last
battle. If we can't be the masters of our life . . . no one . . . (*he cannot
control himself anymore and starts sobbing*) no one in the world can de-
prive us of the right and honor to be masters of our death. . . . (*He
sobs and curses himself for sobbing.*) Shit! . . .

ROZIN. No one will listen. The mob will attack you.

LACHMAN. Then we'll take out our guns then and there, in front
of the crowd, and we'll blow our brains out.

VOICE. (*From a distance.*) Jews in the houses. Jews in the hideouts.
Listen! Help us find Adam Rolenick. Save the ghetto! Look around
you in your houses, your hideouts, your shelters. He may be among
you. Jews, save yourselves.

ROZIN. What's that?

MIRA. The Jewish police. They're searching for him.

NIUSSIA. We've got to vote.

LACHMAN. (*To Lev.*) What about you? What do you have to say.

LEV. Nothing.

LACHMAN. You said, "if we don't transcend our limitations tonight, we're lost."

LEV. They were pompous, empty words. We're being forced to
make an impossible decision. It's just as immoral to betray a friend
as it is to cause the death of twenty thousand people. We are weak,
and our enemies are strong. They've forced us into a situation that
leaves us with no moral choice. It defies all moral teachings. The

Bible says "love thy neighbor as thyself" and "thou shalt not kill."
And we have to choose between betraying a friend and killing myr-
iads of men, women, and children. And if we commit suicide? That
might be easy, but it's just as rotten a solution as betraying a friend
or letting thousands die.

ROZIN. How will you vote?

LEV. I'm not saying. I know whatever decision I make is bound to
be a bad one, so I don't want to influence anybody else. (*He laughs.*)
"Morals" . . . what a terrible weapon in the hands of the oppressor to
crush the humanity of the oppressed. Only the powerful are morally
responsible. The weak cannot afford the luxury of being moral. No
authority in the world could give the right answer to our dilemma.
Each of us is the ultimate authority. No one in the world has the
right to ask anyone of us for explanations or reasons. Therefore I
demand for myself and for every one of you the right to vote secretly. And these are the options: 1. Hand over Adam. 2. We all
commit suicide. Any other propositions? (*Silence.*) All right then. Let's
vote. (*They scribble notes on pieces of paper and throw them into a hat.*)

LEV. Please, Mira. As an outsider . . .

MIRA. (*Unfolds the notes.*) For the first option, three. Collective
suicide, two.

LEV. Now we have to tell Adam . . . Rozin!

ROZIN. Yes! . . . Will someone come with me? (*Silence.*) Well . . . if
there's no other way . . .

LEV. Go on, Rozin. Bring Adam here. (*The voice in the distance is
heard again, this time in Yiddish. Old Nadya whispers the text with the
voice.*)

OLD NADYA. (*With the voice from the distance.*) *Yidn fun di haizer, yidn
fun di maliness, hert zu! Helft oifzuchn Rolenickn. Ratevet di ghetto!
Rolenick bahalt zich ois in bgodim fun a froy, in a shvartz kleid, in a hel
fryenhitl. Kukt arum in di haizer, in di maliness: efsher iz or zvishn zich?
Yidn, Ratevet zich! . . .*

Scene 13

*Adam and Young Nadya. Old Nadya starts the dialogue with Adam. She
fades out and Young Nadya fades in. A door perpendicular to the audience.
Adam is in Nadya's room. Nadya stands guard outside the door.*

ADAM. Nadya? Are you there?

OLD NADYA. Yes, Adam, I'm still here.

ADAM. What are you doing?

OLD NADYA. I'm standing on the stairs.

ADAM. Did you hear that voice?

OLD NADYA. Don't be afraid. I've got my gun ready. I'll shoot anybody who comes to take you.

ADAM. You must be awfully tired . . .

OLD NADYA. Don't worry. I won't fall asleep. I'm wide awake. (*There is the noise of someone stumbling on tins and empty cans. It's Rozin. Only his voice is heard, cursing.*)

ROZIN'S VOICE. Damn the dark . . .

YOUNG NADYA. (*Pulling out her gun.*) Who's there?

ROZIN. Me . . . it's me . . .

YOUNG NADYA. (*Ready to shoot.*) Who's "me"?

ROZIN. Me . . . Rozin . . . . (*Once more, the infernal noise of tins.*)

YOUNG NADYA. What are you doing?

ROZIN. Looking for my glasses . . . oh . . . Thank God. (*He appears from the darkness examining his glasses, which are covered with mud.*) Lucky for me, they're not broken because without my glasses, you know. . . . (*Takes a handkerchief and starts polishing his glasses meticulously.*) Excuse my indiscretion, but I was told that Adam's at your place, no? You see, I'm coming from the HQ . . .

YOUNG NADYA. He's asleep. What d'you want?

ROZIN. Asleep? . . . Well . . . (*Scratches his head.*) Well . . . eh . . . look. . . . I don't want to . . . someone who's asleep . . . especially on a night like this. . . . After all he's been through . . . but there's no other way . . . "find the words" . . . easy to say . . . you won't believe it, but there's a chance. I mean, there's a promise . . . a kind of promise from Gens, via Mira, ha-ha. . . . (*Laughs awkwardly.*) You know how everything goes here . . . ha-ha-ha. . . . "Channels" . . . ha-ha . . . in short, there's a possibility that everything will turn out all right, against the odds . . .

YOUNG NADYA. They gave up?!

ROZIN. One could say. . . . Gave up? Not exactly gave up, . . . as I said. . . . There is a chance he could come back.

YOUNG NADYA. Come back? Where from? Where to?

ROZIN. To the ghetto . . . from the Gestapo you . . .

YOUNG NADYA. What are you talking about?!

ROZIN. About Adam . . . errr . . . what else could I be talking about? . . .

YOUNG NADYA. But you said they've given up?

ROZIN. Who's given up?

YOUNG NADYA. The Gestapo!

ROZIN. The Gestapo? . . . No. . . . You don't understand . . .

YOUNG NADYA. So who the hell gave up?!"

ROZIN. "Gave up" . . . that's not exactly the right word . . . on the contrary . . . after they were given the assurance that he might come back, they voted . . . they decided by a simple majority. . . . Could I just talk to him? I've come straight from the HQ. (*Calls out.*) Adam? . . .

YOUNG NADYA. I'm the only link between Adam and the HQ.

ROZIN. But he has to come with me.

YOUNG NADYA. Where to?

ROZIN. First to the HQ.

YOUNG NADYA. No way.

ROZIN. But he has to go to the confrontation . . .

YOUNG NADYA. What confrontation? What the hell are you talking about?

ROZIN. Let me talk to him. Adam?

YOUNG NADYA. No!

ROZIN. (*Calling over her shoulder.*) Adam, can you hear me!

YOUNG NADYA. Don't go near that door.

ROZIN. What's the matter with you? I represent the HQ!

YOUNG NADYA. I don't like your manner.

ROZIN. Maybe we should have committed suicide, all of us.

YOUNG NADYA. What is this?

ROZIN. Go out to the streets, face the crowd, and say: "We'll never give our friend to the enemy." Then take our guns and blow our brains out, sky high, all of us! That's what we should have done . . .

YOUNG NADYA. Will you tell me what this is all about?

ROZIN. The HQ has decided that Adam should give himself up.

YOUNG NADYA. That's impossible. The HQ was against . . .

ROZIN. They've changed their minds.

YOUNG NADYA. How come? . . . Why? . . .

ROZIN. Decisions from the Ze-Ka. . . . Promises made by Kittel. . . . Threats by Gens. . . . Those channels, other channels. . . . The masses not being on our side, the masses. . . . To tell you the truth, I don't understand myself. I guess I'm no good at a mission like this. Whenever one of those situations comes up, when something's got to be done, and everybody looks at everybody else, waiting for someone to volunteer, someone always says "Rozin," and I say yes before I know what's happening . . .

YOUNG NADYA. Rozin . . .

ROZIN. Yes?

YOUNG NADYA. Go back to the HQ and say: Nadya won't let Adam go. He was put into my care, and I'm not handing him over.

ROZIN. Oh, I understand. Believe me, I do. What should I say? . . . If we don't transcend our limitations tonight, we're lost. (*He goes away. Young Nadya runs to one end of the stage, then to the other.*)

Scene 14

OLD NADYA. Where are you running to?

YOUNG NADYA. To an exit?

OLD NADYA. What exit?

YOUNG NADYA. Mrs. Marinovsky, help me . . . give me the key to the attic. I started to wash my laundry and . . .

OLD NADYA. (*Playing Mrs. Marinovsky, answers her in Yiddish.*) Voss far a maisses derzeilst du? (What kind of nonsense is this?)

YOUNG NADYA. All the attics are locked . . .

OLD NADYA. Of course they're locked, by order of our police.

YOUNG NADYA. I don't know where to hang up my wash . . .

OLD NADYA. *Maidelle,* are you *meshuggee?* Even if I had the best will in the world, I wouldn't give you the key. All our lives are at stake. (*She abandons the role of Mrs. Marinovsky and continues to tell the story, while young Nadya performs what she describes.*) Mrs. Marinovsky slammed the door in my face, so I said "pardon me" in the door, and started running wildly from doorway to doorway. It was a huge yard. As I ran across the upper landing, I discovered a hole in the ceiling that led to some unknown attic. I ran down immediately, opened the door to my room, grabbed Adam and said:

OLD AND YOUNG NADYA. Come! Follow me.

Scene 15

ADAM. (*Dressed as a woman.*) Where to?

YOUNG NADYA. I found an open attic.

ADAM. They decided I should turn myself in.

YOUNG NADYA. They'll be here in a minute. Come on!

ADAM. They think that'll win the people's sympathy . . .

YOUNG NADYA. Come on! Let's run away.

ADAM. From whom? Where to? What for? What's the point?

YOUNG NADYA. Now you ask?

ADAM. What do you mean?

YOUNG NADYA. Rozin called to you. You could have answered. You could have opened the door and come out while he was still there.

ADAM. I don't believe this . . .

YOUNG NADYA. You could have gone with Rozin.

ADAM. You too? . . .

YOUNG NADYA. Me too? . . .

ADAM. Tarnished your hero, didn't I?

YOUNG NADYA. What are you babbling about? . . .

ADAM. No wonder my best friends betrayed me . . .

YOUNG NADYA. You mean I'm worse? . . .

ADAM. Don't feel guilty.

YOUNG NADYA. Now you're telling me what to feel?

ADAM. I should have gone at the start.

YOUNG NADYA. Maybe.

ADAM. "I am not Adam Rolenick." . . . "No, I'm not Adam." . . . It all happened there in Gens's office. They all stood up and deserted me. They didn't know what they were doing, and they hadn't yet cooked up all their ideological mumbo-jumbo, but that was the moment of truth. That was the moment of betrayal. The end was in the very beginning. And you. . . . Why did I let you make me so soft?

YOUNG NADYA. I made you soft? Come on. Any other complaints?

ADAM. (*Self mockingly.*) My fault. The man wanted love. . . . . Oh, Nadya . . . (*He tries to embrace her, but she does not let him.*)

YOUNG NADYA. Not now. Your friends will be here any minute.

ADAM. My "friends." . . . I wouldn't want to be in their shoes. (*Holds her.*) Nadya . . .

YOUNG NADYA. Oh come on, Adam, will you!

ADAM. You can't bear to look at me.

YOUNG NADYA. Don't be silly . . .

ADAM. Look at me.

YOUNG NADYA. What do you want?

ADAM. Your eyes have gone cold.

YOUNG NADYA. No.

ADAM. Cold and hard as steel. You don't love me anymore.

YOUNG NADYA. What a time to . . .

ADAM. Am I such a pitiful sight? I see . . .

YOUNG NADYA. I want to save you, you fool. Isn't that enough? (*They embrace.*)

ADAM. I hear voices.

YOUNG NADYA. Come. Let's go.

VOICE. (*From the distance.*) Jews in the houses, Jews in the hide-outs, listen, listen: Help us find Adam Rolenick! Save the ghetto. (*Young Nadya leads Adam. Old Nadya stands up and faces them. They stop. Old Nadya speaks to the Adam she left forty years ago.*)

OLD NADYA. Adam. . . . You're so passive. You let me lead you like a child. Your face is white. Like a sheet of paper. Only your eyes sparkle. Your long nose, with the little hump in the middle, seems longer than usual. So long and stretched out that the bump disappears. . . . You're wearing my mother's robe . . . and your hands, always white, seem whiter than ever. Look. The black tips of your men's shoes under the robe. Let me look at you . . . (*Young Nadya leads him away into the darkness. Old Nadya follows the couple murmuring.*) Adam . . . my love . . .

Scene 16

Outside Nadya's room. 7:00 A.M. The members of the HQ and UPO emerge.

LEV. Where's Adam?

YOUNG NADYA. (*Returns from the darkness.*) I don't know. Here's the key to my room. I went out for a minute, and when I got back he wasn't there. I found the key on the floor, near the door. (*The HQ members go into the dark, and their voices are heard calling out in all directions.*)

VOICES. Adam! . . . Adam! . . . Where are you, Adam . . . (*A shot is heard. Rozin comes running. Niussia comes in from the opposite corner.*)

ROZIN. What happened?

NIUSSIA. He must have shot himself. (*All the other members of the HQ come in. Rozin announces.*)

ROZIN. He killed himself. What happens now? What should we do?

LEV. Get the body. (*Adam appears. He holds his pistol. He throws away the woman's clothes. He confronts his friends.*)

ADAM. You on one side. The Jewish police on the other . . .

LEV. You shot a policeman?

ADAM. Over his head. He ran away. Nothing happened to him. (*He turns and starts walking away.*)

LEV. Adam . . .

ADAM. Yes?

LEV. Where are you going?

ADAM. To Gens. (*Looks at his friends.*) You decided, didn't you? (*He walks into the darkness. Gens and Mira appear from the darkness in another corner. Adam emerges from the darkness and joins them in Gens's office.*)

Scene 17

Gens and Mira. Later also Adam.

GENS. First we attack the German headquarters. We've got to kill as many officers as possible in the first minute. I'll tell Kittel something to get him to my office, and I'll take care of him. At the same time, you'll penetrate Gestapo headquarters. You know how. Carry the grenade on your body. You'll have to get as many of them around you as you can.

MIRA. And what if Adam didn't commit suicide? What if that shot was only . . .

GENS. What's the matter with you, Mira? Are you afraid to die? Be absolute with death and nothing will stop you. It's a matter of decision. (*Adam appears from the dark. Mira is the first to see him.*)

MIRA. Adam? . . .

ADAM. Good morning.

GENS. Good morning. (*To Mira.*) Stay here. The plans have changed. (*To Adam.*) I can't say I'm glad to see you.

ADAM. The feeling is mutual, but never mind. It's the last time.

GENS. You're wrong. Believe me. If you get through this confrontation with Kaslaskas, you'll be free to return to the ghetto. I'll do all I can. You have my word. I'm sorry I can't offer you a more definite guarantee.

ADAM. I have my guarantee. I know too much about your connections to the UPO. You'll want me released before they discover everything I know.

GENS. Ha. That's the spirit. What'll you have to drink?

ADAM. I don't think I finished my vodka last night.

GENS. Mira! Please, bring us some vodka.

MIRA. Sure. (*Exits.*)

GENS. Now, I can tell you the truth? I didn't think your comrades would hand you over to the Germans.

ADAM. What did you expect them to do?

GENS. To say no. You don't surrender your commander. But you had a share in their decision. You did something a commander should never do. You gave up control and total command of the organization.

ADAM. We're a collective. I'm not a dictator.

GENS. That's garbage. (*Mira enters with the vodka.*)

MIRA. Adam . . .

ADAM. Mira . . . Mira . . .

GENS. Do you know that the young boys and girls in your organization, your fighters, were stunned by the HQ decision? They can't believe it. You think they give a shit about Velvele Sharashevsky? Who the hell is Sharashevsky to them? For them, you were and still are the commander.

ADAM. What would you have done in my place? Taken over the organization by force?

GENS. As commander, I would have given the order for a full-scale revolt within seconds of having been freed by my fighters from the Gestapo.

ADAM. And your first act would have been to open fire on your own people?

GENS. If there were no other choice. My friend, when you're the commander and you have a mission, nothing can stand between you and your mission. Whatever stands in the way must go.

ADAM. Very nice. If I had made that choice, what would you have done?

GENS. What could I have done? I would have accepted the new situation. I would have called the entire population of the ghetto to join your revolt and led the last battle at your side ahead of the Jewish Police. We would have gone up in a glorious bonfire, but we'd have made the Germans pay for it. And we'd have all died happy. (*Laughs.*) "on the altar of Jewish honor."

ADAM. I don't believe you.

MIRA. He started the preparations. The plan was similar to yours. Including liquidation of the German officers.

ADAM. Let's do it.

GENS. I envy you. You remained clean.

ADAM. This is your chance. Let's start the revolt. The underground and the Jewish Police together.

GENS. Now? After you've given yourself up and everybody knows the decision of your comrades? Who would follow you? No, Adam. Facts must be respected.

ADAM. Why the hell didn't you give a sign when it was all still possible.

GENS. Because that's not my philosophy. I always said that would be my last resort, when all other doors were closed to us. My philosophy was . . . and remains . . . the theory of numbers. If you can save two people by sacrificing one, offer one and save two.

ADAM. What gives you the right to sacrifice me, to be my hangman?

GENS. I'm not your hangman. It's the Germans.

ADAM. But you collaborate with them.

GENS. When your comrades were confronted with the kind of dilemma that I face every day, they chose my philosophy and turned you in.

MIRA. Instead of committing suicide themselves. (*They turn to her.*) I'll do all I can to get you out. I swear it.

ADAM. It's too late. Our vodka's getting warm. To your philosophy of numbers.

GENS. To your speedy return. (*They drink.*) Do you have any special requests?

ADAM. Some strychnine . . . one never knows.

GENS. (*Produces a small box.*) Here . . . take this. Rub it under your nails. If worst comes to worst, just (*makes a motion of biting nails.*)

ADAM. I want you to see the Red Army parade into our town.

GENS. I want it for both of us. If we can just hold on for another four or five months . . . (*They shake hands. Adam goes into the dark.*)

GENS. (*To Mira, holding a pill.*) You don't know how many times a day I'm tempted to take one of these. But I know I'd be taking twenty thousand people with me to the grave. People who believe in me as they do their God. I can't do it. Damn.

Scene 18

Adam leaves Gens's office and encounters his friends, who emerge from the dark.

ADAM. You're all here.

LEV. Be brave, Adam. Be strong . . .

ADAM. Yes . . . sure. . . . You think that sacrificing me will win you the support of the masses. You're wrong. There will be no revolt. Everyone's looking after his own skin. "As long as I'm all right and it's only somebody else who's dying, what do I care?" That's the beautiful philosophy of the ghetto. We've failed, my friends. We've failed. When the last day comes, people will walk calmly and orderly to the trains without offering the slightest resistance. The fight for freedom is now. The revolt is now . . . or never. Are you ready now to take up your arms and fight? (*He watches them. They all lower their eyes to the ground.*) No. All right. (*He takes out his pistol and hands it to Lev. Lev comes to him.*) Here. Take it. You're the commander now. (*Silence. Adam turns to go. Kittel appears from the darkness accompanied by two Gestapos with machine guns. Adam stops. He confronts Kittel and looks at him. They examine one another. Young Nadya breaks away from the group and runs to Adam.*)

YOUNG NADYA. Adam!

OLD NADYA. (*Echoes.*) Adam . . .

YOUNG NADYA. (*Grabs him.*) Don't go!

OLD NADYA. Adam . . .

YOUNG NADYA. Murderers. You're all murderers.

OLD NADYA. Murderers . . .

ADAM. (*To his friends.*) Do something, for God's sake! . . . (*The members of the HQ grab Young Nadya. They tear her away from Adam and drag her off.*)

KITTEL. I don't understand you people. With such lovely girls, don't you have better things to do at night than run for arms and play this pathetic comedy of resistance? Wouldn't it have been nicer in your warm beds with your warm females. I really don't understand you. (*To his Gestapos.*) Take him away. (*The Gestapos take Adam and vanish into the darkness. The members of the HQ drag Young Nadya away in the opposite direction. She is shouting.*)

YOUNG NADYA. Adam! . . .

OLD NADYA. Adam! . . .

SEP. (*Shakes her.*) Nadya . . .

OLD NADYA. (*Grabs him.*) Adam . . . Adam . . .

SEP. Not Adam. Sep. It's me, Sep.

> Za / za ra za
> za ra za za za za zam
> Hop! (*Plays a magic trick.*) Hop!

(*A small explosion. A puff of smoke. Darkness.*)

THE END

Selected Bibliography

International Holocaust Drama

Anthologies

Fuchs, Elinor, ed. *Plays of the Holocaust*. New York: TCG, 1987.
Skloot, Robert, ed. *The Theatre of the Holocaust*. Madison: Univ. of Wisconsin Press, 1982.
    There are of course many other Holocaust plays not included in these two volumes, two of which continue to stand out: Weiss, Peter, *Die Ermittlung* (The Investigation). Frankfurt: Suhrkamp Verlag, 1965; Hochhuth, Rolf, *Der Stellvertreter* (The Deputy). Reinbeck bei Hamburg: Rowohlt Verlag, 1963.

Criticism

Abramson, Glenda. *Modern Hebrew Drama*. New York: St. Martin's, 1979.
Berger, Alan, *Crisis and Covenant: The Holocaust in American Literature*. Albany: SUNY Press, 1985.
Ezrahi, Sidra DeKoven. *By Words Alone*. Chicago: Univ. of Chicago Press, 1980.
Langer, Lawrence. *The Holocaust and the Literary Imagination*. New Haven: Yale Univ. Press, 1975.
———. *Versions of Survival*. Albany: SUNY Press, 1982.
Mintz, Alan. *Hurban: Responses to Catastrophe in Hebrew Literature*. New York: Columbia Univ. Press, 1984.
Roskies, David. *Against the Apocalypse: Jewish Responses to Catastrophe*. Cambridge, Mass.: Harvard Univ. Press, 1984.
Rosenfeld, Alvin. *A Double Dying*. Bloomington: Indiana Univ. Press, 1980.
Schiff, Ellen. *From Stereotype to Metaphor: The Jew in Contemporary Drama*. Albany: SUNY Press, 1982.
Skloot, Robert. *The Darkness We Carry*. Madison: Univ. of Wisconsin Press, 1988.

Young, James. *Writing and Rewriting the Holocaust.* Bloomington: Indiana Univ. Press, 1988.

Israeli Holocaust Drama

Criticism

Feingold, Ben-Ami. *Hashoa Badrama Haisraelit* (The Holocaust in Israeli drama). Tel Aviv: Hakibutz Hameuhad, 1989.
Ofrat, Gidon. *Hadrama Haisraelit* (Israeli drama). Jerusalem: Tcherikover, 1975.